# The Ceremonial Musicians of Late Medieval Florence

# The Ceremonial Musicians of Late Medieval Florence

## Timothy J. McGee

**Indiana University Press**

*Bloomington & Indianapolis*

This book is a publication of

Indiana University Press
601 North Morton Street
Bloomington, IN 47404-3797 USA

http://iupress.indiana.edu

*Telephone orders*   800-842-6796
*Fax orders*   812-855-7931
*Orders by e-mail*   iuporder@indiana.edu

© 2009 by Indiana University Press
All rights reserved

The paper used in this publication meets the minimum requirements of American National Standard for Information Sciences—Permanence of Paper for Printed Library Materials, ANSI Z39.48-1984.

Manufactured in the United States of America

Library of Congress Cataloging-in-Publication Data

McGee, Timothy J. (Timothy James), date
    The ceremonial musicians of late medieval Florence / Timothy J. McGee.
       p. cm.
    Includes bibliographical references and index.
    ISBN 978-0-253-35304-7 (cloth : alk. paper) 1. Music—Social aspects—Italy—Florence—History—To 1500. 2. Municipal ceremonial—Italy—Florence—History. 3. Florence (Italy)—Social life and customs. I. Title.
    ML3917.I8M35 2009
    780.945'510902—dc22

                                                                    2008031501

1 2 3 4 5  14 13 12 11 10 09

*To Florence with love*

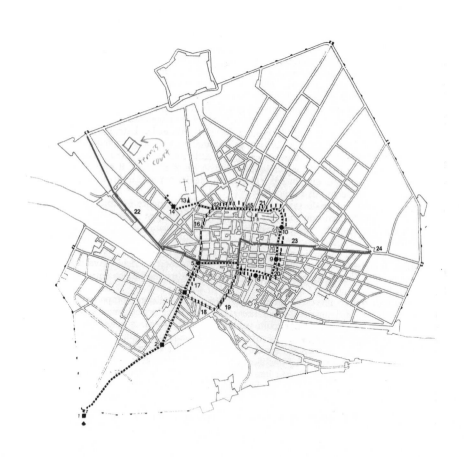

# Contents

# Music Examples and Tables

# Preface

Over one hundred years ago Giuseppe Zippel published the first study of the civic musicians of Florence, a small book of thirty-five pages based on documents he found in the Archivio di Stato in Florence.[1] Zippel's work is an excellent overview of the musicians of the commune from the earliest-known document dated 8 February 1291 [1292][2] up to the mid-fifteenth century. Thirty-five years later Luigia Cellesi published a pair of articles using similar archival documents and covering approximately the same period of time.[3] Over the decades of the twentieth century many more documents were added to the catalogs of the Archivio di Stato, allowing Keith Polk in 1986 to bring that outline forward to the dissolution of the Florentine Republic in 1532.[4] Along with these studies of the ensembles themselves, a wealth of tightly focused historical studies of Italian music and social history also have been published in the last fifty years, allowing a more complete understanding of the civic musicians and their place in the commune. What I have undertaken here, therefore, is to gather together all of these sources of information in order to fill in the outline and bring that picture up to date in terms of currently available material. Building on the work of Zippel, Cellesi, and Polk, as well as that of many other scholars, I have attempted to write a history of the ceremonial musicians employed by the city of Florence over the 250-year period from the beginning of the Priorate in 1282 until the proclamation of a new constitution in 1532, which replaced the Republic with a Principate and led to further changes in the organization of the musical ensembles and their duties. I have chosen to take a wide view of my subject in order to more clearly position the civic musicians in Florentine daily life.

Perhaps the least expected inclusion in this study of civic musicians is the civic herald, a position mentioned only in passing in the earlier studies. During the early centuries the position of herald was known by a variety of titles, and the tradition itself has been misunderstood and greatly underestimated. The post, which can be traced back to the early decades of the fourteenth century, was that of a singer-poet who performed daily for the executives of government and at all official functions, exercising one of the most interesting of Italian medieval musical practices: that of improvising melody for poetry. From shortly after the first appointment to the position in 1333, the herald assumed a number of duties that resembled those of a master of ceremonies, in that he was responsible for overseeing the various elements of civic ceremonies, both private and public, and in exercising that duty he himself often took a major performing role.

When I first undertook this study in 1975 I had hoped to be able to comment extensively on the music performed by the civic musicians. It did not take long before I realized that this was not possible for the years before the mid-fifteenth century, and that my narrow definitions of "musician" and "musical repertory" had to be greatly enlarged if I were to accomplish my goal of tracing the history of these musicians and their role in the social life of Florence. There is little evidence to help us understand what sounds were actually made by these people; the first factual statement of repertory performed by any of the civic musicians does not come until 1459. And there is no written musical repertory known securely to have been performed by civic musicians during the entire time encompassed by this study, although we do have some of the texts set to music by the heralds. Prior to the mid-fifteenth century most of the instrumental musicians probably could not read music. During the early centuries, in their most basic form the civic instrumentalists were often little more than glorified signalmen, serving the commune in important but not necessarily artistic ways. As the decades progressed the needs of the commune changed and along with them the duties of the musicians evolved; additional ensembles were created and the responsibilities of the civic musicians expanded to include more "musical" events, although not until the fifteenth century can one actually discuss any of the musicians in terms of their performance of composed music.

At first I found the lack of information about repertory to be somewhat discouraging—the awareness that for the most part I was studying not noble artists with great repertory but instead lowly civil servants and functional sounds. In fact, there is no way to determine exactly which of their duties were "musical" functions and which were not. At first glance one could dismiss the earliest ensemble, the trombadori (also called the tubatores), as merely noise-making trumpet players. But at the same time the ensemble also included players of the *cennamella* (shawm) and bagpipe, who played music for dancing. We know that by the year 1390 both of these musicians—as members of the new pifferi ensemble—were supplying a rich variety of music that was far from noise making. Rather than trying to sort out exactly which sounds and functions were "musical" and which were not, I have included everything: all of the civic ensembles with musical instruments, the civic herald, and all of their duties.

One of the more sobering aspects of this study has been the revelation that even when the musicians were involved with the highest level of music, their function and social status changed only superficially; for the most part the musicians and their music usually served as background—a type of aural scenery, or perhaps the sound equivalent of wallpaper. I do not think I am being too harsh in drawing this conclusion. To their employers during the late Middle Ages and Renaissance, the civic musicians were valued principally as symbols and tools of the commune and those who ruled it. Certainly, artistic excellence was valued by the civic leaders, although not altruistically, since the quality of the performance of these musicians reflected their employers' taste and standards as well as their wealth and ability to attract the finest artists. But to the rich and powerful of Europe, even the most talented musicians and the most musical of the ensembles often were merely pawns in a much larger game. Exceptions can be found, of course, in individuals such as Isabella d'Este and Lorenzo de' Medici, whose love for music was genuine. But even in those notable cases the motivation for patronizing music and musicians was not completely selfless: the art and artists definitely played a prominent role in the entire picture, but their patrons were not oblivious to the fact that their presence and stature had clear social and political repercussions. This is to say that even in the best of circumstances (speaking from the position of the musicians), their presence in aristocratic circles was only partially due to an appreciation of their artistry.

This realization does not decrease their talent or their art, which obviously flourished in spite of (or perhaps even because of) their place in the larger scheme of daily life, nor does it minimize their importance in the larger picture of history. There is no doubt that certain of the Florentine rulers took great enjoyment from music, but that was not the principal purpose for their support. And if we look at the role of music and musicians in the West during the centuries following those described here, we can see that much of this social situation has remained more or less constant up to the present day. (Nor is music unique among the arts in playing such a role.) Politicians continue to this day to use art and artists in a number of ways to further their political goals; whether or not they have any real personal interest in the art is irrelevant.

Reflecting on the long-standing social reality of music and musicians has, I hope, aided me in keeping my story in perspective—remembering that in the larger social picture music is background rather than foreground. However important music is to those of us who are immersed in the art, when surrounded by wealth and power (as it usually is), it plays only a supporting role. And exactly how that part fit into the public landscape of Florentine life from the thirteenth through the early sixteenth centuries is the subject of the following narrative.

What is attempted here, therefore, is a social history of Florence insofar as civic music, musicians, and musical instruments are involved. It is an unusual way to study social history, since the subject is not usually approached from this point of view, but one that is of value if for no other reason than that it affirms the social role played by one particular group of minor civic employees in the society of the late Middle Ages and Renaissance. In fact, even in the context of the usual studies in music history, the approach taken here is uncommon, since most music histories about this period customarily focus on the sophisticated composed repertory and its courtly setting, mentioning the civic musicians and improvised music only in passing—a treatment not unlike that accorded all of music by social historians.[5]

In a way, my approach can be seen as an attempt to fill a long-standing void. One searches in vain through most general histories for any information about the role played by musicians or, indeed, by any of the performing artists. Artists and their products usually have been ignored or dismissed as completely unnecessary for an understanding of social or political history, and their study has been left to specialists whose work is rarely consulted by that group of scholars who call themselves historians.[6] In studies of the various groups of citizens who played important roles in the history of Florence—including studies of the music—the civic musicians have often fallen between the cracks. There is no place for them in a study of the aristocrats who ruled the city and directed its businesses; they are only briefly considered in studies of the laboring classes, the *popolo minuto*; and they do not fit comfortably in a study of major artists. Yet they had a visible—and audible—daily presence in Florentine life, acting on behalf of the government and assisting in the projection of the self-image of the city. It would not have been possible for anyone to have been in Florence for even a few days during those centuries without becoming aware of their presence. It is true that the civic musicians made no decisions that would affect the course of history, nor did they make apparent lasting contributions to society or art, but they lent a great deal to what might be called the daily flavor of Florence, and their actual importance to the city, although poorly recorded in print, was more substantial than has been believed. To people of all classes, the civic musicians represented the pomp of their city; it would not have been possible to envision any official task or ceremony without the sonorous presence of one or more of the civic musical ensembles, or a civic welcome without a celebratory work by the herald. All of these men were skillful craftsmen, many were quite versatile, and some were even gifted artists. They were called upon for a variety of services to the community and added a unique color to daily life. To describe this study of the civic musicians in present-day jargon, I am attempting to add a "sound track" to two and a half centuries of daily life in Florence.

As I hope to demonstrate here, by ignoring the arts—in particular one area of the art of music—political and social historians have missed the opportunity to add important dimensions as well as vivid color to the telling of their story. The central political characters and their ambitions and accomplishments that completely occupy the standard broad historical studies provide only one dimension to a complex story. As all artists and art lovers understand, the nuances provided by background detail lend a clarity and dimension to those in the foreground that enables a complete understanding of any scene. Music, in fact, was such an integral part of daily life in Florence that a study of the civic music and musicians provides a reflection of the social values and their changes throughout these early centuries to an extent not otherwise available.

What is described here are only those occasions that involved the civic musicians, which means public ceremony for the most part but not exclusively, since musicians on the civic payroll often performed at private functions. These were not the only musicians in Florence, of course. Hundreds of singers, including both unpaid amateurs and paid professionals, sang at the major churches. As well, lay confraternities and laudesi companies employed singers and instrumentalists; instrumentalists were employed by the various guilds; many of the wealthy citizens included professional musicians as a part of their households; and a complete picture of music in Florence would include itinerant professionals, amateurs of all kinds, and the musicians accompanying the constant stream of important visitors to the city. All of these musicians fall outside the scope of the present study, and although I will allude to them from time to time in order to complete a particular discussion, my main focus is on only those musicians who worked for the civic government and their contributions to the culture of Florence.

While working on this book over the years I have published a number of individual studies of the various aspects of musical practices in Italy during the late Middle Ages and Renaissance, many of which have been incorporated into this study. Working on this composite picture has caused me to reinterpret some of the facts and to change or revise some of the conclusions presented in those earlier studies. Thus, a reader wishing to augment the information in a particular section by reference to one of my earlier publications may find discrepancies. In every case the information included in the present book should be considered to be my most recent thoughts on a matter.

# Acknowledgments

Unless otherwise indicated, Latin translations are by Randall Rosenfeld, and the Italian translations are mine with help from Guido Olivieri, Olga Pugliesi, and Enrico Vicentini. The music examples were set by Mark Laver.

As has been noted by numerous scholars in various fields, the Archivio di Stato in Florence is a gold mine of historical documents. Most of the primary material for this study was found there by me and by others, recorded in a variety of different types of documents: statutes, pay records, minutes, letters, diaries, etc., that yield their treasures more or less willingly once discovered. The biggest problem confronting a historian in the Florentine archives is simply finding where to look; the quantity of material is so vast that without help from knowledgeable scholars and archivists one could spend years in fruitless search. Over the 30 years I have worked in the Archivio many improvements have been made there in order to assist the researcher. The archivists have continued to bring the inventories of material up-to-date, and the move to the new building in 1987 brought with it better facilities and a more friendly and helpful staff; I have benefited greatly from all of these and acknowledge the Archivio di Stato and its staff with gratitude. Still, finding one's way through the enormous quantity of historical records in the Archivio is a daunting task, and I wonder how far I would have gotten were it not for the immensely helpful assistance given to me in 1979 by Gene Brucker. There is no doubt that his friendly and informative advice, based on an intimate acquaintance with the Archivio and its holdings, shortened my search by many months and helped me feel more at ease in working with the records. My debt to him is enormous.

I also wish to thank the following for assistance of various kinds over the years: Alessio Assonitis, Elena Brizio, Stewart Carter, Giovanni Ciappelli, Samuel Cohn, Gino Corti, Sabine Eiche, Paul Gehl, Richard Goldthwaite, Rab Hatfield, F. W. Kent, Alexandra Korey, Lynn Laufenberg, Honey Meconi, Anthony Mulho, Herbert Myers, Luisa Nardini, Jennifer Nevile, Robert Nosow, Domenico Pietropaolo, Keith Polk, William Prizer, William Robins, Manuela Scarci, Gary Walters, and Susan Forscher Weiss. My work was also aided by the Connaught Committee of the University of Toronto who granted a six-month Research Fellowship, the Social Sciences and Humanities Research Council of Canada, the University of Toronto who provided sabbatical-year support in 1979–80, 1986–87, 1993–94, and 2001–2002, and by a subvention from the Martin Picker Publication Endowment Fund of the American Musicological Society. I am especially grateful to Harvard University for a memorable year as Visiting Professor at The Villa I Tatti, and for the friendly and helpful assistance of the staff and research associates of the Villa, and in particular, music librarian Kathryn Bosi.

I am grateful to the team at Indiana University Press for the enormous help and support they have provided; to Music Editor Jane Behnken and her assistant Katherine Baber, and especially to Maureen Epp who copyedited the text.

Last but hardly least, I wish to thank the numerous performers who have assisted me in understanding the music and its culture through performance. Thanks are due to the original members of the Toronto Consort who worked along with me as I experimented with numerous practical performance problems. Over the period of twenty-nine years that I taught at the University of Toronto I profited from the dozens of students whom I coached and led through various experiments in early music performance. In addition there have been many conversations with other teachers, scholars, and performers of early music that have led to a greater understanding of my subject. To all of these people, far too many to name, I extend my heartfelt gratitude.

TJM

# The Ceremonial Musicians of Late Medieval Florence

# I

# Ceremonial Florence

Florentines loved a good public display and took advantage of every possible occasion to indulge themselves. From the earliest recorded history of Florence it is clear that the citizens and the government went to great lengths to turn every possible occasion, both sacred and secular, into a ceremony of some type: name days of local saints, visits of foreign dignitaries, elections of local politicians, guild celebrations, the coming of spring, the days before Lent, a military victory. The most formal of the ceremonies were presided over by the executive branch of the civic government and frequently involved an official ceremony on the *ringhiera*, the special platform built in front of the Palazzo della Signoria. Many ceremonies included a procession of some sort, and on the more festive occasions there were games and spectacles that took place in piazzas around the city, races through the city streets on horse or by foot, mock naval battles on the Arno River, wild animal shows, and athletic contests of several kinds. The entire city was involved: the citizens, the streets, the houses, the piazzas, the river, and the churches. As the following chapters will reveal, occasions both public and private, religious and secular, great and small were celebrated with a zest and flair that reflected the enormous emphasis placed on ceremony by the citizens and their government.

Similarly, ceremony without music was inconceivable in Europe during the late Middle Ages, and this was especially true in Florence. No matter what the occasion, formal or informal, music had a constant presence, making a major contribution to whatever atmosphere suited the affair: excitement, solemnity, or frivolity. The city literally rang with musical sounds, including bells in the church towers and government buildings, the daily sacred music provided by church choirs and lay confraternities, and secular music sung and played in the streets, piazzas, and private homes by amateurs and traveling musicians. But the largest single share of celebratory music was contributed by the official musicians of the city, who were commissioned and supervised to ensure the type and quality of music that both suited the occasion and maintained the image of the city: the civic musicians of Florence.

There were two distinct offices filled by civic musicians. One was that of the herald, whose duties were almost exclusively related to civic ceremonies, where he oversaw the proceedings themselves and sang appropriate poetry at the more formal events. The other was that of the civic instrumentalists, who were involved with both sacred and secular ceremonies: leading processions, working with the military, announcing the official presence of the executives of government, and providing music for numerous large and small occasions. The varied types and social levels of events resulted in many different kinds of ceremonies, from extremely formal to casual, and the participation of the civic musicians was adjusted to match the occasion. As the decades evolved and the ceremonial needs of the city increased, the assignments of the musicians changed: the civic herald was relieved of some of his supervisory duties in order to concentrate more fully on the performance aspect of his office. By the end of the fourteenth century the original civic instrumental group, the trombadori, had been divided into three different ensembles—the trombadori, the trombetti, and the pifferi—and at the beginning of the sixteenth century a fourth group—the tamburini—was added, as the city strove to serve its changing ceremonial needs. Although over the 250 years of the Republic the duties and makeup of the civic musicians increased and changed and the type and style of music they performed evolved, their basic purpose remained the same: they were the audible symbols of official Florence, representing the glory of the city state at home and abroad.

Music and ceremony, ceremony and music—the two were inseparable in late-medieval Florence. We begin with a description of the major festive occasions in Florence that were both the setting and the purpose for the participation of the civic musicians.

# Celebrations & Festas

In order to obtain an overall picture of the subject—the celebrations and the ways in which music and the civic musicians contributed—we can begin with a review of the ceremonies, celebrations, and festas—both scheduled and unscheduled—that took place in any one year. A very large number of celebrations were annual events, a part of the regular yearly celebratory calendar of the city. To these were added a great many ad hoc celebrations occasioned by visits from foreign dignitaries, celebrations of military victories, and other unplanned events. When combined, the two sets of occasions added up to an astonishing number; there would seem to have been very few days in the year without a celebration of some type. Not everyone took part on every occasion; the celebration of the patron saint of one of the churches, for example, would have involved mostly the parishioners of that church. But a significant number of festivities were city wide, resulting in a yearly calendar of events that is difficult for a modern reader to comprehend.

Financial support came from every possible source: the citizens themselves, the confraternities that were associated with the churches, the various religious bodies, the guilds, and the civic government—in short, from virtually every person and every organization in the city. The amount of money that was expended on this type of event yearly is, as Richard Trexler states, "nothing short of astounding."[1]

# Annual Celebrations

The basis for the organization of the annual celebrations was a mixture of events that reflected the yearly cycle of seasons (e.g., harvest), the church calendar (e.g., Easter), and civic customs (e.g., election of Priors), as well as the regular activities of smaller organizations such as confraternities, and the social, religious, and political occasions of the individual subdivisions of the city (the *sesti*).

From early in the Middle Ages there were numerous organizations in various parts of the city that planned festivities and competed with one another to mount ever more lavish and splendid events. Davidsohn refers to them as *società di feste*, although they were not actually called that.[2] What he was referring to was the existence in nearly every sacred and secular organization, including confraternities, guilds, parishes, monasteries, and so on, of a "committee" that had as its major duty to plan the yearly celebrations sponsored by that organization. As might be expected, many of these events were centered around local parish churches which functioned as the focal point for the social as well as religious life of the citizens. As a result, a large share of the celebrations had to do with the veneration of local saints, especially the saint for whom each church was named. Within the city walls of Florence there were over fifty such parishes,[3] and when their celebrations were coupled with the many civic celebrations, the result was approximately two regularly scheduled festas per week.

Processions in honor of various saints' days were a normal part of the church calendar. The most important of these involved the participation of clerics, the lay confraternities, civic representatives, representatives from other cities, and representatives of various Florentine civic organizations such as of members of the Signoria and Collegi, the guilds, and the Captains of the Parte Guelfa.[4] Even the minor processions began at the Piazza della Signoria and wandered through the city streets, ending at the particular church for the occasion.[5] All of these would involve singing—chant, hymns, and laude—depending on the particular occasion, and those on the feast days of major saints would also involve the civic musicians who led the procession from one church destination to another. A fixed set of rules controlled those who were to participate as well as any relics that were to be carried under a *baldacchino*, the particular route of the procession, and even the order in which the participants joined the procession.[6]

Of the myriad yearly events, four were considered to be the most important: the feast of Saint John the Baptist (San Giovanni Battista), the patron saint of Florence; the first of May (Calendimaggio), the celebration of the arrival of spring; Carnevale, which precedes Ash Wednesday, the beginning of the austere time of Lent; and Easter, the celebration of Christ's resurrection. These major celebrations occupied nearly all of the five months from the beginning of February to the end of June, during which time many other, smaller celebrations also took place. All four are still celebrated, although not to the extent that they were in the earlier centuries.

## Saint John (San Giovanni)

The celebration of the feast day of Saint John the Baptist, patron saint of the city, takes place on June 24. The early-fifteenth-century chronicler Gregorio Dati described it as the culmination of a series of major church feasts spread out over a period of approximately two months, with preparations beginning with the arrival of spring.

When spring arrives all the world rejoices, and every Florentine begins to think of participating in the beautiful feast of San Giovanni which takes place in mid-summer. From the beginning everyone prepares clothing, accessories, and jewelry. Whoever has wedding banquets or other celebrations to plan waits until that time in order to honor the feast. Two months before [the festa], preparations are begun for the *palio* [horse race]: the costumes of the attendants; the flags and the trumpets; the banners that the subject cities give as gifts, or tribute, to the commune; the candles and other things that one must offer; the people to invite and things to purchase for the wedding celebrations; and the horses that come from everywhere to run in the *palio*; and all the city and the spirited young boys and girls are seen to be making preparations for the festa. At the same time, however, they do not ignore all those activities that show happiness and a spirit full of joy on the feast days preceding [San Giovanni], such as San Zanobi [May 24], the Ascension [forty days after Easter] the Feast of the Holy Spirit [Pentecost/Whitsunday], the Blessed Trinity [first Sunday after Pentecost], and for the feast of Corpus Christi [Thursday following Trinity Sunday]. They dance, play and sing, take part in banquets and jousts and other traditional games, so that it appears that no one has anything else to do prior to the vigil of San Giovanni.[7]

Dati's comments are made in the spirit of a criticism of the manner in which frivolous celebrations become the main occupation of the citizens for long periods of time in place of more deserving projects, which suggests that he was a bit of a curmudgeon. But his diatribe does give an idea of the quantity and types of activities that took place in and around this feast and, as we shall see below, his criticisms are closer to the mark than one might imagine on first reading.

As patron saint, San Giovanni was considered to represent the city, and therefore the celebration of his feast day was as much a celebration of the power and splendor of Florence as it was an opportunity to honor the saint.[8] Nothing was spared and everyone took part; clearly, it was the focal point of the year's public ceremonies. The festa itself is thought to have originated in ancient times at the point when the city dedicated itself to San Giovanni, although specifics, such as the date of origin, are difficult to pin down. In any case, the celebration grew over the centuries, with the various events of each year's celebration evolving through to the present day. It was financed and supervised by the commune, which made sure the streets were cleaned and encouraged the citizens to hang banners from the windows along the procession route. Over the piazza in front of the cathedral of Santa Maria del Fiore (the Duomo), blue cloth known as *rovesci* was hung as a shield from the sun or rain in order to cover the observers as well as displays of merchandise placed in front of the shops.[9] We can obtain some idea of the grandeur of this celebration during the period under discussion by noting the ceremonies as they are recorded in the fourteenth century. There was both a sacred and a secular focus: the former centered around religious ceremonies at the Baptistry of San Giovanni, and the latter around a horse race, a *palio*, and surrounding both of these were numerous accompanying festivities, as Dati pointed out (above).

During the fourteenth century the public part of the celebration began three days prior to the feast day, when all males over the age of fifteen were ordered by the Podestà[10] to carry their candles to the Baptistry and to begin erecting the *rovesci* at the height of twelve meters over the piazza in front of the Baptistry and over the piazza in front of the church of San Piero Maggiore (the terminal point of the *palio*; see number 24 in figure 2). This was supervised by the Arte della Lana (wool merchants' guild).

On the morning of the vigil (June 23), there was a procession that began at the Duomo (the cathedral of Santa Maria del Fiore), wandered through the major streets and returned, followed by a ceremony of candles in the Baptistry.[11] Gregorio Dati describes the morning procession in this way:

> All the clerks and priests, monks and friars, who are from a great number of orders, with so many relics of saints that it is a thing of infinite and grandest devotion, in addition to the marvelous richness of their adornments, with the richest display of gold and silk vestments and of embroidered figures and with many confraternities of secular men following behind the order of whatever church the confraternity is connected to, with vestments of angels and with sounds and instruments of every kind and marvelous songs, making beautiful *rappresentazioni* for those saints and of the solemn occasions that they honor, going two by two, singing the most devout laude. They leave from Santa Maria del Fiore, go through the city, and then return.[12]

Dati's description tells only a small part of the story; the procession was far more elaborate than his account would lead us to believe. It began with the clergy from all of the churches, dressed in their richest vestments, each church displaying its most treasured relics under a *baldacchino*. The clerics were accompanied by the lay confraternities and members of the guilds, led by their officers and assembled behind banners that identified their affiliation. The entire assembly was led by the civic musicians, who played their instruments as everyone processed two by two, lighted candle in hand, through the streets while all of the church bells resounded. (A later custom had some of the groups represented by actors in fantastic costumes, walking on stilts.) As was common of all processions, the participants would sing as they processed. The confraternities, whose custom was to sing and process as a part of their regular weekly activities, would have had a large repertory of sacred songs, known as laude, at their command, and thus the streets would have been full of musical sounds: singing, instruments, church bells, and the joyful noises of a city celebrating itself.

The route of the procession took in a good share of the city, passing by most of the important churches and civic buildings (figures 1 and 2). It began at the Baptistry, went west on the present Via de' Cerretani, moved along the old wall of the city south on the Via de' Tornabuoni to the Ponte Santa Trinita. At that point it crossed the Arno, went east along Borgo San Jacopo to the church of Santa Felicita and then crossed back into the central part of the city over the Ponte Vecchio, moving up the Via Por Santa Maria and into the Piazza della Signoria for a ceremony involving the Priors on the *ringhiera*. Next it moved down the Via de' Gondi to the Piazza San Firenze, turned north on the present Via Proconsolo, and followed the old city walls to the Duomo, picking up additional groups along the way. At the church of San Felice di Oltrarno, representatives from each of the city churches joined in, and following the ceremony in front of the Signoria, the Priors, civic magistrates, and foreign dignitaries became a part of the procession. They in turn were followed by costumed actors who added humor and political satire to the event. Next came the Captains of the Parte Guelfa, who were preceded by their flag (an eagle holding a serpent in its talons) and led by a maiden on an horse decked out in silk, followed by knights, a number of distinguished citizens who accompanied foreign ambassadors, and finally hunting dogs, bird dogs, and hawks as offerings from mountain regions such as Arezzo, Pistoia, and Volterra.[13]

Nearly everyone in the procession carried a candle, some of which were very large and heavy, and most of which were ornately decorated; the size, weight, and embellishment of the candle represented the devotion as well as the wealth and importance of the bearer. Once the procession reached the Baptistry, the candles were presented as an offering, which in many cases was as much an act of homage to the commune as it was an expression of religious faith.[14]

### *Edifici*

The vigil procession was not the only event of its type during the celebration of San Giovanni. One of the more elaborate projects was the construction and procession of the *edifici*: carts (*carri*) elaborately decorated with sacred themes that served as the sets for dramatic enactments. Two days before the feast, the *carri* were gathered in the Piazza della Signoria, where a skit was presented on each of the *edifici* in turn before it moved in procession through the streets, stopping at each of the piazzas to reenact the presentations and ending at the Baptistry of San Giovanni. A contemporary account of the 1454 celebration by Matteo Palmieri demonstrates how lavish such a procession of *edifici* could be.

> On the morning of the 22nd [of June 1454] the procession of all the *edifici* [took place], and I will tell you below what they were that year:
>
> 1. At the front was the Croce of Santa Maria del Fiore with all the choirboys and children, and behind them were six singers.
> 2. The companies of Jacopo, shearer, and Nofri, shoemaker, with approximately thirty children dressed as angels in white.
> 3. The *edificio* of San Michele Agnolo, over which was placed [a picture of] God the Father in a cloud, and in the piazza in front of the Signori they made a play of the angelic battle when Lucifer and his bad angels were expelled from heaven.
> 4. The companies of Ser Antonio and Piero di Mariano, with approximately thirty children dressed as angels in white.
> 5. The *edificio* of Adam, on which a play was made in the piazza representing when God created Adam and then Eve, gave them the commandment, and their final disobedience which expelled them from the garden of Eden following the earlier temptation by the serpent and other scenes.
> 6. Moses on horseback, with a number of horsemen from the people of Israel and other places.
> 7. The *edificio* of Moses, on which a play was performed in the piazza about when God gave him the Ten Commandments.
> 8. Several prophets and sibyls with Hermes Trismegistus and other prophets of the incarnation of Christ.
> 9. The *edificio* of the Annunciation, that performed a play [of the Annunciation].
> 10. Emperor Ottaviano with many horsemen and with Sibyl, who performed the play of Sybil predicting the birth of Christ, and with an exhibit of the Virgin on high with Christ in her arms.
> 11. The Temple of Peace with the *edificio* of the nativity represented in a play.
> 12. A magnificent triumphal temple for the *edificio* of the Magi, in which was another octagonal temple all decorated in silk from the Orient, and a play was made around those temples of the Virgin with the infant Christ and Herod.
> 13. Three Magi with horsemen and more than two hundred horses decorated magnificently, and they came to make their offerings at the birth of Christ.

Interrupting the Passion and the interment because it did not appear to be a part of the festa was the following:

14. A group of Pilate's horsemen ordered to guard the Sepulchre.
15. The *edificio* of the Sepulchre where Christ had risen.
16. The *edificio* of Limbo that carried the Holy Fathers.
17. The *edificio* of Paradise where the Holy Fathers were placed.
18. The Apostles and the Marys who were present at the Ascension.
19. The *edificio* of the Ascension of Christ, that is, when he rose to heaven.
20. Kings and queens on horseback and young girls and nymphs with dogs and other symbols of the living and the dead.
21. The *edificio* of the living and the dead.
22. The *edificio* and its plays of the Last Judgment, with scenes of the Sepulchre, Paradise and Hell, about how faith makes us believe how things will be at the end of the world.

All these *edifici* and their plays were presented in the piazza in front of the Signori and lasted up to the sixteenth hour.[15]

## The *Palio*

The day following the vigil procession, the actual feast of San Giovanni began with an elaborate liturgical service at Santa Maria del Fiore that included all of the church singers of the city, followed in the afternoon by the most popular part of the festa, the *corsa dei bàrberi*, a *palio*. Throughout both days the merchants of the city placed their wares outside of their shops, holding what would be referred to in modern terms as a street sale. In the evenings and on through much of the two nights, the covered piazzas in front of the Baptistry and San Piero Maggiore became the focus of large street parties where hundreds of citizens danced through the evening and into the night. Throughout the city, the streets and piazzas resounded with singing, music, and dancing, as the citizens moved freely between private and public celebrations, while from the turrets of the churches fireworks lighted the sky.

The horse *palio*, the major secular event of the San Giovanni celebration, coursed through the streets of the city on the afternoon of the 24th while the citizens cheered their favorite horse and rider. The event, which became a part of the celebration of San Giovanni in 1288, included up to a dozen horses ridden bareback by brightly dressed jockeys, who urged their charges forward at breakneck speed through the narrow city streets at great risk to themselves, the horses, and the spectators. Before the race began, the *palio* itself—the banner to be presented to the winner—was carried through the route on a decorated cart drawn by two horses dressed in silk in the white-and-red colors of the commune, driven by two pages dressed in the same colors and led by the civic musicians.

At the sound of the bell mounted at the top of the Palazzo della Signoria the race began, starting at the bridge of Mugnone (later called the Ponte alle Mosse in honor of the *palio*), proceeding through Borgo Ognisanti, the Via della Vigna Nuova, Mercato Vecchio, Via del Corso, Borgo degli Albizzi, and ending at the church of San Piero Maggiore (near San Ambrosio; see figure 2). There, with an elaborate ceremony presided over by the Priors and magistrates, and including ornately dressed citizens with their women, the winner of the race was given the *palio* to the accompaniment of fanfares and other festive sounds from the civic musicians and the cheers of the citizens.[16]

The individual families often looked upon the time of San Giovanni as an opportunity to indulge themselves lavishly. Villani relates one such extravagance in 1283 in the contrada of Santa Felicita in Oltrarno. The Rossi family, along with their neighbors and involving more than a thousand men all dressed in white, formed a "court" under a lord named "Amore" that amused itself for over two months with a variety of entertainments that included games, banquets, and costumed parades through the streets. Villani describes them as "joyfully and happily going through the streets with trumpets and other musical instruments and gathering together at banquets, dinners, and suppers" ("andando per la terra con trombe e diversi stormenti in gioia e allegrezza e stando in conviti insieme, in desinari e in cene").[17] The "court" attracted a number of nobles and minstrels from elsewhere, who were welcomed and entertained.[18]

## Carnevale and Easter

The most important celebration in the Christian church calendar was, and is, Easter, which marks the resurrection of Christ in fulfillment of the Old Testament prophecy of redemption for the faithful. Unlike many other feasts whose dates are fixed, that of Easter changes each year according to the lunar calendar and the spring solstice. Depending on the timing of the full moon, the date on which Easter falls can vary between March 22nd and April 25th, although it is always on a Sunday. The joyful celebration of Easter is preceded by Lent, a period of mourning beginning on Ash Wednesday and lasting for forty days. From its inception some time after the eighth century, Carnevale has been the traditional series of revels leading up to Ash Wednesday.[19] Although the date of Ash Wednesday also is variable, depending on the date of Easter, in some cities during the late Middle Ages the commencement of Carnevale was often fixed: in Venice, for example, it began on December 26, whereas in Florence the set date was February 7.[20]

The contrast between Carnevale and Lent could not be more extreme. Because the Lenten period was to be a time of fasting, penance, and spiritual contemplation as a reflection of Christ's forty days of fasting in the desert and eventual death on the cross, Carnevale was given over to excess and overindulgence. Eating meat, for example, which was forbidden during Lent, became an important part of each person's private pre-Lenten activity; the day before Ash Wednesday was known as "Fat Tuesday" (*martedì grasso*, also called *Berlingaccio* in Florence), a reference to the great quantity of meat consumed on that day. The public activities were even more flamboyant.

The carnival season included a great number of public and private activities and events, most of which also took place at other times of the year, including parades through the streets with floats, people in masks, wagons with elaborate tableaux (called either *edifici* or *trionfi*, depending on the theme), and groups of singers performing carnival songs (*canti carnascialeschi*). Francesco Grazzini, writing in 1559, describes the processional wagons as having elaborate costumes, props, sets, and masked singers, all of which moved through the streets of the city, stopping at the various piazzas to perform for the citizens.[21] William Prizer has aptly described the tradition of the wagon *trionfi* presentation as "a miniature music drama moving through the streets of the city, mingling the arts of music, poetry, drama, choreography and costuming."[22] In other words, they were a secular version of the *edifici*, described above.

Jousts, tournaments, and various competitive games, in addition to being a part of the carnival season, were staged throughout the year when a festive occasion arose. In terms of most of the activities listed here, therefore, carnival time can be seen as a concentration of festive events that also were seen at other times of the year. Carnevale was a time to engage in every possible diversion in anticipation of the somber days of Lent. It included all of the events described in the following sections.

## Knightly Games

This type of entertainment refers to the tales of early medieval courtly behavior found in the literature of the fourteenth and fifteenth centuries. Some of these events—jousts, *armeggerie*, and tournaments especially—were favorite events that were also staged at other times of the year in order to celebrate the visit of special guests to the city.

ARMEGGERIE

These began in the fourteenth century as equestrian events staged by an official *compagnia di armeggiatori* to welcome distinguished visitors.[23] They grew to become an elaborately stylized production of war games and contests involving a group of "knights" on horseback and a "Signore" who presided over the event (figure 3).

One of the best documented of such events is that instigated by Bartolomeo Benci on Fat Tuesday of 1464 for the purpose of impressing the young (sixteen-year-old) Marietta di Lorenzo di Palla Strozzi. In order to mount his elaborate *armeggeria*, Benci first sought and received permission from the commune, which allowed him to proceed and also forbade any other citizens to be out on horseback that evening. He was accompanied by eight other young men from highly respected Florentine families,[24] all richly dressed, mounted, and carrying torches, each assisted by thirty pages and eight valets, all dressed in the colors of the house they represented. The festivities began at the home of Benci, where he was presented with the baton signifying that he was the "Signore" for the evening. Following a lavish banquet, the entourage traveled to the home of Marietta to perform the *armeggeria*, which ended with the *Trionfo d'amore*. The *trionfo* itself was a large set mounted on a wagon, which displayed the Benci crest as well as that of the Strozzi, along with various standard representations of love, including Cupid with arrows, on the top of which was a bloody heart in flames. Alongside the wagon were two great horses covered in green silk and decorated in silver, led by pages in the same type of costume, which was intended to be a symbol of hope. As Marietta watched from a window, Benci removed the wings that had been a part of his costume and threw them on the *trionfo*, where they erupted in flames. At that point the brigade moved to the homes of the young women who were the objects of affection of the other eight young men in the party and repeated the performance, returning to the Strozzi home at dawn to perform a morning concert (*mattinata*). The entire event was accompanied by cheers and songs by a large crowd of observers, and instrumental music performed by the civic pifferi.[25]

JOUSTS AND TOURNAMENTS

Fat Tuesday was also the favorite day for the staging of jousts and tournaments. This type of activity, sponsored by the Parte Guelfa, usually took place in the Piazza Santa Croce, although on rare occasions it took place in the Piazza della Signoria (1395); at the Porta San Gallo (1399); and in front of the church of Santa Maria Novella (1406). The actual equestrian contest was only a small part of this kind of festivity (figures 4a and 4b). There were preliminary ceremonies, including a procession through the streets of the combatants and their followers with banners waving and crowds cheering; enormous pomp at the site of the joust as each combatant displayed his colors; and the award ceremony following the contest, where the winner was acclaimed and presented with a "knightly" trophy such as a helmet, lance, or shield.[26] When Lorenzo de' Medici won the joust in 1469 he was presented with a helmet decorated in silver with an embossed image of Mars on the crest.[27] Participants in the joust were young men from the most prominent Florentine families, and on some occasions foreign nobles took part. The violence of the game, the lavish costumes of participants, their entourage, and the many observers, as well as the general sense of festivity, is well illustrated in paintings that memorialize several such events. (For a more elaborate and detailed description of a joust see chapter 5.)

## Battaglie di giovani

These were rather violent games engaged in by groups of young men that included rock throwing and fights with clubs or fists, often resulting in serious harm, even death, to some of the participants. The tradition of this type of game is descended from ancient battle games first recorded in Ravenna in the seventh century. Such games were also described in conjunction with Carnevale in Orvieto in 1199, in a context where they were forbidden. In Florence, the 1278–84 statutes of the confraternity La Compagnia di San Gilio forbade its members to take part in the *battaglia di pugne*, although it is clear that the games continued to take place. The favored day was Fat Tuesday, and a frequent venue was the Arno River, where two groups formed on opposite sides in order to battle one another across one of the bridges.[28]

## Stili

The use of *stili* was a favorite and quite harmless way for the young men to harass the young married women of the city. They would block passage along a street and threaten the passers-by with long sticks (*stili*) in order to exact a small toll from those (especially the young women) who wished to walk past.[29]

## Balli

Dancing was a part of nearly every festival, so there is no surprise in finding that it had a prominent place in a number of carnival celebrations. Dances were organized in private homes and in the palaces of the elite, out of doors within the various neighborhoods and parishes, on a larger scale in the major piazzas, and more spontaneously as young and old danced in lines through the city streets. On some occasions private parties were able to receive permission to cordon off a public piazza, where they would set up a canopy, platforms, and tables, and some rather elaborate decorations. The number of people taking part would vary according to time and place; the evening before Fat Tuesday was a usual time for the organization of a large public dance.[30] Bartolommeo del Corazza records a particularly large dance that took place in 1415 in the Mercato Nuovo, involving (according to his estimate) six hundred women and a "great quantity of men,"[31] and another in the Piazza della Signoria in 1420, in which only fourteen dancers took part (although there were most likely a very large number of observers) and which included a dance contest with judges and awards. As was the usual practice at many of these entertainments, one prominent person called the "Signore" was selected to preside over the event.

> On the 2nd of February [1420] a brigade of young citizens made a rich and beautiful dance festa; around the Piazza della Signori a large fence was erected; and there were two prizes, a garland of crimson within a clasp on top of a large baton, and that was given to the young man who danced best; and a garland in the style of a small crown or necklace, decorated in gilded silver, and that was given to the young girl who danced best. They elected four women who were to judge the honor of the women, and they remained seated on high like judges; and in the same way they elected those who would judge the prize of the young men. The [prize] of the women was given to the daughter of Filippo [blank] d'Amerigo del Bene, and that of the young men to the son of Bernardo Gherardi. The brigade was made up of fourteen, and they were dressed in crimson lined with colored leather on the back, and turned around the outside more than a half *braccio* [approximately 30 cm], with a great bunch of pearls on the left arm, with grand scalloped hoods of white, red, and green, and dress stockings with new designs of red and green, embroidered with pearls. The Signore was [blank] of Agnolo di Filippo di Ser Giovanni; and he came with a dress garment of Spanish crimson and was seated behind the *Mercanzia* in a lordly manner with many tapestries and carpets. And twice during the many dances they were given drinks with *confetti* [sugared candy]: there came twenty-two young men with twenty-two plates of *confetti* full of *treggea* [very small *confetti*] and *pinocchiati* [candy made of pine nuts and caramelized sugar], and with noble wines, and then for the final time, that is the third time, [the serving men entered] with *zuccherini*. Then, because of the occasion, they made a joust in the piazza with long lances without shields, with helmets, and mili-

tary armor. The first time the *pinocchiati* were covered in silver and the second time in gold. The following Monday, [February 3], they all went together on horseback through Florence on large horses. It is said that this was the most beautiful and rich festa that has ever been made in Florence, and [the same is said] about the dance.[32]

As is typical in accounts of dancing and other festas, the narrator dwells on the costumes of the participants and the decorations of the setting, ignoring any mention of the musicians who supplied the music for dancing. In many cases the organization of such affairs was supervised by the civic government, and therefore would have involved the civic musicians. In fact, since there had been a law from the early fifteenth century that only the civic musicians could be employed for official entertainments, either public or private, they would have had a very high profile during all celebrations.[33] This law, of course, did not pertain to musicians hired privately and not involved in official city business, which allowed for numerous instrumentalists other than the civic employees to maintain a full career as performers and teachers.

## Masquerades

Today the idea of a masquerade is synonymous with carnival time, especially so with reference to Venice. It is an ancient idea, often associated with New Year's as well as other times of the year, but in Florence, it was not directly associated with Carnevale until the late fifteenth century, when it was encouraged by Lorenzo the Magnificent and became a regular event during carnival time as well as during Calendimaggio.[34] By the end of the fifteenth century there was an entire repertory of carnival songs (*canti carnascialeschi*), which were sung by groups of masked singers who roamed through the streets on foot or on elaborately decorated wagons (*carri*). Many of the texts of the songs single out various guilds, trades, prominent people, or institutions for mockery, often including thinly veiled sexual double meanings.[35] By the end of the fifteenth century these performances had become part of major productions sponsored by some of the guilds and private citizens that included decorated carts and skits. One of the more unusual of these, because of its serious content, was presented in 1507 on the evening of Fat Tuesday. The *Carro della Morte*, sponsored by Lorenzo and Filippo Strozzi, included the commissioning of a composer to set the text of the carnival song "Trionfo della morte," and an artist to construct and decorate a special cart on which the Strozzi and their associates, costumed as skeletons, sang and acted out the grim text that speaks of penance and the punishment for sin:

Anguish, tears and penance
Torment us constantly;
This, our company of dead
Processes, crying "penance!"[36]

# Lenten Celebrations

It would be a mistake to think that the period between Ash Wednesday and Holy Thursday was completely devoid of celebration. What took place during those weeks was definitely subdued in comparison to the festivities of Carnevale, but although these events took on the guise of the more somber Lenten attitude, processions in honor of various saints continued to take place, and instead of secular entertainments, *sacre rappresentazioni* (sacred plays) were enacted.

## Processions

The processions during Lent followed the usual practice for processions during the year. They were made up of clerics, laymen, members of confraternities, members of the Signoria and Collegi, the Consuls of the Mercanzia and the guilds, and the Captains of the Parte Guelfa, all of whom processed through the city streets with civic musicians leading, and all of the participants chanting and singing hymns. On Palm Sunday, the Sunday before Easter, a procession involving a large number of clerics, lay people, and visitors began at Santa Reparata and ended at the church of San Lorenzo. Six days later, on Holy Saturday, there was a procession in order to transport the newly lighted Holy Fire from the church of San Biagio (presently Santa Maria fuori Porta) to the baptismal font in the Baptistry for distribution to the citizens. Although originally that ceremony involved only the transport of a candle by a member of the clergy followed by the cathedral choir, sometime in the late Middle Ages this was changed to include the Pazzi family, who carried the flame on an ox-driven carriage to the front of their own palace, where the flame was then distributed.[37] Following the events of 1478 it was decreed that this ceremony would no longer involve the Pazzi but instead would be taken care of by the Consuls of the Calimala guild.[38]

## Sacre rappresentazioni

As a Lenten replacement for more secular theatrical activities such as the *giochi delle maschere* (masked games) that were popular during carnival time, *sacre rappresentazioni*, dramatic presentations of sacred stories, became a part of the activities during Lent, especially on Holy Thursday and Good Friday (although they also occurred on other days;[39] see Epiphany, below). The date of origin for these expanded dramas that carry the designation *sacre rappresentazioni* is unclear; there is positive evidence of their presence in Florence from early in the fifteenth century.[40] Nerida Newbigen has found evidence of productions of *sacre rappresentazioni* by laudesi companies from as early as the 1430s,[41] and Cyrilla Barr notes that an Ascension play was performed perhaps as early as the fourteenth century by the laudesi company Sant'Agnese of Santa Maria del Carmine. A performance of the Ascension play in that church is described in 1422, and there was a payment to both the pifferi of the Parte Guelfa and to the civic pifferi in conjunction with a 1425 performance.[42]

The tradition of dramatic reenactment of sacred scenes extends back to the Latin liturgical drama originating at the court of Charlemagne in the ninth century, an idea that spread quickly throughout Europe, with examples found in Italian manuscripts as early as the eleventh century.[43] The earliest of these, the so-called *Quem quaeritis* play, began as a three-line sung dramatization of the visit of the three Marys to Christ's tomb on Easter morning.[44] Over the centuries a number of other biblical stories were chosen for dramatic presentation and added to the repertory, some of them expanded into musical plays of substantial length.[45] Similar to liturgical dramas although presented in Italian rather than Latin, *sacre rappresentazioni* were enactments of stories from the life of Christ, as for example the three presentations that from the 1430s were traditionally mounted after Easter: *The Annunciation of Mary*, in the church of San Felice in Piazza; *The Ascension of Christ*, in Santa Maria del Carmine; and *The Descent of the Holy Ghost*, in Santo Spirito. All three were sung by the laudesi companies of the respective churches and involved stage machinery, lighting, fireworks, and special effects.[46]

As an integral part of the civic observation of Lent, these events had a direct connection to the office of the civic herald (see chapter 3);[47] several of the fifteenth- and sixteenth-century heralds are known to have authored *sacre rappresentazioni*.[48] Other text authors include Feo Belcare and Lorenzo de' Medici, which suggests both their popularity and quality.[49] The performances usually took place in a church and, depending on the subject matter, included processions, acting in costumes, some staging, and the singing of chant, hymns, and laude. Participants were members of the various confraternities that sponsored the events, often including choruses of children such as the members of the *scuola dei chierici del Duomo* (founded in 1436), and sometimes including the civic instrumental musicians. During the late fifteenth century there was a tendency to introduce comic characters and situations into the *rappresentazioni*, "contaminating the sacred with the profane," in the view of one scholar.[50] While far more sedate than their secular counterparts, these presentations provided one more opportunity for the citizens of Florence to gather together and celebrate during the Lenten season.[51]

# Calendimaggio

Calendimaggio is a celebration of the arrival of spring, the ancient symbol of rebirth and renewal. Thought to be of pagan Nordic origin, Calendimaggio is known to have been celebrated in Bologna from the end of the 1200s and was adopted by Florence around the year 1290.[52] The celebration consists of a series of events that occupy more or less the entire month of May, and although the greater part of this festival remained secular, there was some attempt by the church to bring attention to the celebration of Philip the Apostle.[53] From its inception the celebration began on April 30, the vigil of the first of May. As Villani states concerning the celebration during its earliest years, there were dances, games, and banquets—activities quite similar to those described in the accounts of Carnevale.

> [Following the military victories of 1292:] With happiness and well being, every year on the first day of May, the *brigate* and the companies of young men, dressed in silken clothes, and using wooden [barriers] to close off various sections of the city, constructed courts covered with silks and cloths. And similarly [well-dressed] women, young girls, and noble couples walked through the streets dancing in a line with [musical] instruments and wearing garlands of flowers on their heads, taking part in games and celebrations and dining.[54]

Not all events were without problems. Villani notes that on the vigil of Calendimaggio in 1300, during the dance held in the Piazza Santa Trinita, young men on horseback from rival political factions engaged in a sword fight, during which the nose of Ricoverino di Messer Ricovero de' Cerchi was cut from his face.[55]

One of the favorite events during Calendimaggio was a naval battle or other dramatic show that involved boats on the Arno. On such an occasion in 1304 this resulted in a serious tragedy in which two thousand citizens fell into the river and more than a hundred drowned.[56] Villani's account is quite dramatic and allows him an opportunity to moralize:

> For Calendimaggio of 1304, as in the good times of the past in the tranquil and good state of Florence, the groups and brigades of amusement made use of the city to make happiness and feasts. They renewed it [this tradition] and in many

parts of the city, pitting one *contrada* against another, each one doing the best they knew and could. Among the others, since those of the Borgo San Frediano had as an ancient custom to make the most novel and diverse games, they sent an announcement that whoever wanted to know news of the other world had to be, on the day of Calendimaggio, on the Ponte alla Carraia and near the Arno. And they organized [a theatrical event] on the Arno on boats and floating rafts, and made the likeness and figure of hell with fire and other sufferings and torments, and men impersonating demons, horrible to see, and others who took the shape of naked spirits that appeared to be alive, and they were subjected to a variety of torments with loud cries and shrieks and a tempest which appeared hateful and dreadful to hear and to see. And many citizens went there to see the new play, and the Ponte alla Carraia, which was at that time made of wood on pillars, was so full of people that it broke into many parts and fell with the people on it. And many people were killed and drowned and many were wounded, as if the fictitious story had come true, and as it was claimed in the announcement, many went to their death to know the news of the other world. There were great tears and sadness through all of the city, because each [family] is believed to have lost a son or a brother, and this was the sign of future suffering that in a short time would come to our city because of the excess of the sins of the citizens, as we will mention later.[57]

On the whole, however, the Calendimaggio celebrations were full of happy events (see below). When coupled with the private banquets, marriage feasts, parties, and similar kinds of celebration on the other five great spring feast days mentioned by Dati (San Zanobi, Ascension, Pentecost, Blessed Trinity, and Corpus Christi) in addition to Easter, it is not difficult to see more than a grain of truth in Dati's statement about there being little time during the months of spring for anything but celebrations and their preparations.

## The Christmas Season

The birth of Christ, *Natale*, has always been an important event in the church calendar, but in Italy it has never had the position of importance given to it in North America; that place was reserved for Easter. Christmas was observed with a full week of the types of celebrations mentioned above in conjunction with most other feasts: dancing, dining, and dressing in the most elaborate costumes allowed for one's social station. Much of the tradition was private: on the vigil (i.e., Christmas Eve), in each home a large olive branch was placed on the hearth, which was decorated with flowers. When the branch was in flames, the head of the family would sprinkle it with wine while the family prayed and sang. One game that originated among the small merchants was a group called "the good rogues" (*dei buoni briganti*), who in a parody of knightly activity consecrated their members by immersing them in the Arno on New Year's Eve and declaring them "wet knights" (*cavalieri bagnati*). The event ended with a banquet around a large fire.[58]

# Epiphany

The twelve days from the day after Christmas until the celebration of the arrival of the Magi at the manger on January 6—the first exposure of the Christ Child to the people at large—was a general time of celebration, including some rather wild parties. The sacred event of the final day was the taking of newly blessed holy water from the Baptistry to each home.[59] The feast time occasionally included dramatic reenactments of the biblical story, a very special event produced by a lay confraternity devoted to this event, known as the Compagnia de' Magi, which began its activities sometime in the late fourteenth century and lasted until the expulsion of the Medici in 1494.[60] The first recorded enactment is from January 6, 1390:

> On the 6th of January [1390] there was in Florence a solemn and great festa of the holy Magi and the star, [performed] at the church of the friars of San Marco. The Magi, with many companions and innovations, went all around the city on horseback honorably dressed. King Herod was placed at San Giovanni on a well-decorated platform with his people. When the Magi reached San Giovanni they mounted the platform where Herod was and argued with him about the child, and then they left to adore him and promised to return to Herod. And the Magi made offerings to the child but did not return, and Herod persecuted and killed many other children in the arms of their mothers and nurses, and with this the festa ended in the 23rd hour.[61]

During the fifteenth century the ceremony and its presentation by the Compagnia de' Magi became closely identified with the Medici, for whom representations of the Magi were particularly important. Richard Trexler and Rab Hatfield have noted the use of the Magi theme in the Botticelli portrait of the Medici family commissioned for the Lami chapel in Santa Maria Novella (now in the Uffizi Gallery; figure 16) as well as the Benozzo Gozzoli fresco in the chapel of the Palazzo Medici (figure 17).[62]

# Retirement from Political Office

There was also a celebration at the end of term for the supreme executives of Florentine government, the eight Priors and the Standard Bearer of Justice

(Gonfaloniere di giustizia), who were elected for two months of service, during which time they were sequestered in the Palazzo della Signoria. The usual ceremony was a rather plain affair, but on at least one occasion the Captains of the Parte Guelfa felt the need to make a special celebration in honor of the retiring Gonfaloniere:

> On the first day of July 1387, the Lord Priors of the Palazzo [della Signoria] left [i.e., finished their term of office], and the Captains of the Parte [Guelfa] sent many Guelfa citizens for Bardo Mancini, who had been Gonfaloniere of Justice during the previous two months. And there, in the palace of the Parte, many citizens came together to make beautiful speeches, thanking Bardo for magnifying and exalting the Parte during his time in office, and for having exiled the aforementioned citizens and deprived them of their offices. And there, to remunerate him for those things, the Captains of the Parte gave him a horse the value of eighty gold florins clothed in the emblem of the Parte, a lance with a pennant and a shield with the emblem of the Parte, a helmet completely decorated in silver, and a silver cup with the golden emblem of the Parte. And with all of these things preceding him, he was accompanied by a great crowd of honorable citizens all the way to his house.[63]

Although not mentioned in the narration, this type of ceremony certainly would have involved trumpets; either those of the Parte Guelfa or the civic musicians, or both.

## Other Celebrations

The full picture of the Florentine penchant for creative entertainment involves a number of games that were mounted in conjunction with the many other festas, most of them elaborate by any standard of measure, although none quite the equal of some of those already described in terms of the number of people involved or the lavishness and extent of the surrounding activities. Some of these events were standard, having to do with the traditional celebration of an annual feast day, as for example the celebration of Christmas and New Year's, which always included banquets and dancing. Other events were occasional and more spontaneous, brought into being in order to celebrate a military victory or the arrival of a very special visitor. They are described here briefly in order to complete the picture of festive ceremonial Florence. All of the events involved the civic musicians, and many of them included one or more processions through the city streets.

## Other *Palii*

Races through the city streets were a part of many festive occasions. The most elaborate were the horse races that took place during the major feasts such as those of San Giovanni and Carnevale, but there were foot races on some of the occasions that also rewarded the winner with a *palio*. For the winner of the horse race, the *palio* was a richly decorated banner on a standard, which the various families treasured as a sign of power and distinction. It was made of dark red velvet, approximately five meters long, and decorated with *giglio* (the Florentine fleur-de-lis) and a red cross on a field of white (symbol of the *popolo*, or common citizens). For the foot racers, the reward was a piece of red cloth that was to be displayed with pride as a panel on the clothing of the winner. Both kinds of events had a variety of courses, although all of them were routed through the city. The citizens lined the streets and filled the windows and balconies all along the route to cheer their favorite runner or horse, and the buildings were decorated with large colorful banners.

One of the traditional foot races took place on the feast day of Santa Reparata, October 8, in memory of the victory of Stilico over the Gothic king Radagasius, which saved Florence from destruction in the year 405.[64] For that *palio* young boys raced from the fountain of San Gaggio near the Porta Romana to the Mercato Vecchio. Another was held on June 11, dedicated to the apostle San Barnaba and commemorating the defeat of the Ghibellini of Arezzo near Campaldino in 1289 as a result of his intercession.[65] This race course, similar to the horse *palio* on the feast of San Giovanni, began at the bridge of Mugnone and traveled through Borgo Ognisanti, the Via del Parione, Via Porta Rossa, and ended at the Piazza Sant'Apollinare near the Bargello. Although the prize was not as elaborate as that for the horse race, its presentation to the winner was accompanied by a similar ceremony involving the civic magistrates and musicians. As with all other such events, this was merely the focal point for a full day of celebrations and festivities that took place all over the city, involving singing and dancing in the piazzas as well as church ceremonies to commemorate the appropriate saint.[66]

## Hunt (*Caccia*)

A hunt consisting of a party of hunters who go off into the bush to find wild boar, birds, deer, and so on is only one meaning of the word *caccia*. While Florentines did engage in this form of hunting, the *caccia* as a part of a city celebration was another matter and usually referred to the pitting of wild animals against one another in an arena while the spectators looked on, a practice that would be quite repulsive to a modern audience. These "hunts" could take on a number of different guises, as for example the *caccia* that took place in the courtyard of the Bargello in June of 1387, which turned out to be a bit of a disappointment:

> On Sunday, the 15th of June, the Priors sponsored a *caccia* in the courtyard of the Capitano del Popolo [i.e., the Bargello], where some lions were set free against an invincible bull. Finally, after they had fought, the bull was not killed even though he had several wounds from [the lions] and he had been knocked down several times. The bull gored the lions with his horns and kicked them many times, and although there were three lions in the fight, they were so kind that they fought only one at a time.[67]

This event followed by a week a joust that had taken place in the piazza in front of Santa Croce. The winner on this occasion was one Messer Iacot, an Englishman, who won a beautiful shield decorated with a prancing golden lion on a background of white, a lance, and a nicely decorated helmet of fine steel.[68] Both events, the *caccia* and the joust, were sponsored by the civic government. What is not included in the diary accounts that relate these events are details of the usual ceremonies: processions of the participants through the city streets prior to the joust and of the animals before the *caccia*; another procession of the winner following the joust; the formal ceremonies that accompanied both events, including speeches by civic dignitaries and presentation of the prizes; and especially the public celebrations and dances in the piazzas by all of the citizens throughout the day and into the wee hours of the morning. The civic musicians would have been involved in the processions and in sounding fanfares throughout both events, as well as in the music making during the banquets and dances that followed. When we note that these two events transpired just two weeks before the annual feast of San Giovanni and immediately following the elaborate celebrations of Calendimaggio, and that there would also have been several other festas during that time, an image of the enormous quantity and frequency of festivities in Florence becomes clearer.

## Ad Hoc Events

In addition to the busy yearly schedule of celebrations, the city was always ready to celebrate special events. Some of these were political in nature, such as the visit of a monarch from another city; some were religious, such as the visit of a member of the church hierarchy; others were brought on by various crises such as a plague, earthquake, or drought, for which the city would import the *tavola* (painting) of Santa Maria del Impruneta for processions and devotions.[69]

The *tavola* of Santa Maria del Impruneta was considered to have miraculous powers. It was executed sometime in the late thirteenth or early fourteenth century and was housed in the village of Impruneta, just south of Florence, where it remained veiled until it was transported to Florence in time of need.[70] The events surrounding the presentation of the *tavola* were rather elaborate; not surprising, given the severity of the occasion that would prompt such an event. There was always a procession with singing through the city streets, and a Mass during which divine intercession was implored. The *tavola* was always brought in procession from Impruneta during the night, scheduled to arrive at the city gate of San Piero Gattolino at dawn where it would be met by a large procession of Florentine clergy and citizens bearing their most important relics. The combined procession would wend its way through the city streets to the Piazza San Felice, and then to the Piazza della Signoria for an elaborate ceremony. The *tavola* stayed in Florence only during the day and was returned to Impruneta by nightfall. On August 7, 1414, for example, following an earthquake that destroyed some walls, roofs, and two hundred chimneys, there were solemn processions for three successive days. On the third day the *tavola* was brought to Florence, escorted through the city streets and ending at the Duomo for Mass.[71]

A contemporary account describes the ceremony in 1390 which ended with Mass in the Piazza della Signoria.

> Sunday the 16th [October, 1390] there was a general procession through the city of Florence with the bishop, clergy, and parish priests all wearing surplices, and with the head of San Zanobi, the arm of San Filippo, and many other relics, and all the members of religious orders with their crucifixes and relics, and the friars of the Certosa with their great quantity of relics. And on this day the *tavola* of Santa Maria del Impruneta came to Florence and was placed in the piazza of the Signori, and there on the *ringhiera* was made a great platform where the clergy, Priors and Collegi stood, and a higher platform on which the bishop stood to sing Mass, and there were higher platforms highly decorated where the relics were placed so everyone in the piazza was able to see them, and there was another platform for the organs and the singers. And the Bishop preached during the Mass.[72]

The citizens' faith in the power of the *tavola* was often seen to be justified; in the fall of 1444, after five months of drought, rain fell immediately after the *tavola* was brought to Florence.[73]

Visits from political or religious leaders would always result in festivities, the lavishness depending on the importance of the visitor. In addition to a procession and reception by the civic executives, the distinguished guest was always treated to a special banquet, such as the one held on April 30, 1308, in honor of Pope Clement V. The banquet took place at the residence of Cardinal Arnaldo da Pelagrua and included numerous courses of food followed by an entertainment:

> Then came the ninth course, and through the partition was heard but not seen the singing of clergymen with all types of voices—large, less large, medium, small, and childlike—with a sweet gentleness that caused silence in all the room because the attentive ears of everyone caused speech to stop because of the sweetness of the gentle melody. When the song ended and the final food course was cleared, fruit of all kinds was brought, and two trees were placed on the table of the Pope ... When the fruit was placed on the table the master cook of the Cardinal entered with a group of his companions carrying instruments. And there were more than thirty of them holding falcons with bells, which is a Roman game. And they entered dancing very happily through the room, and in this way they circled the table three or four times and then left.[74]

It should be understood that most of the events involving the welcoming of distinguished visitors included as pro forma events processions, fireworks, formal presentations, speeches by civic magistrates, officers of a guild, or religious leaders, and all were accompanied by dances and banquets throughout the day and on into the night. The streets would be decorated with entrance arches, the buildings with banners and flags, and the citizens would be out in their best dress lining the route of the procession. The civic musicians played an active role in all of them; the trombadori, bannitori (town criers), trombetti, and pifferi sounding through the streets in processions, playing for the dances, and enhancing the formal presentations. It would be difficult to exaggerate the presence of music and ceremony in the daily life of Florence during these centuries.

Given the crowded yearly calendar, many of these ad hoc events coincided with already scheduled celebrations, providing a reason for making them even more elaborate. But if nothing else was scheduled, Florence was only too happy to add one more event to the busy calendar. In most cases there was a regular format of standard procedures that could be implemented and applied to the situation, or adjusted to the nature of the visit and the importance of the visitor.

An idea of how this type of ceremony was assembled can best be illustrated by detailed descriptions of three of the more elaborate ceremonies that took place in the fifteenth century, one having to do with a state visit from a foreign dignitary, the other two being "in-house" events: the appointment of a new commander-general of the Florentine army, and the knighting of a military hero. The descriptions will also provide an opportunity to examine the extent to which the civic musicians participated in such events.

## The Visit of Galeazzo Maria Sforza

In 1471 Florence was host to Galeazzo Maria Sforza (1444–76), who in 1466 had succeeded his father, Francesco I, as Duke of Milan. The stated purpose of Galeazzo's journey was a pilgrimage to the Franciscan church of Santissima Annunziata, a church that had held special meaning for his father, although it was more likely that this was simply an excuse the restless young Duke used for taking a trip.[75] The Sforza party left Milan on March 4, traveling by way of Pisa and Lucca, and eleven days later made its grand entry into Florence. The Duke did not travel lightly. According to official documents, the entourage that accompanied Galeazzo and his wife, Bona of Savoy, numbered over a thousand people: both the Duke and Duchess had brought attendants of every rank from nobles to servants, which included approximately 1,500 horses and mules.[76] An existing list of those accompanying the party classifies the people according to official rank, beginning with the Duke and his fourteen noble advisors, followed by military leaders, physicians and priest, seneschals, courtiers, *camerieri* and other officials of the chamber, officials outside the chamber, and officials of the household. The list for the Duchess is similarly grand and arranged in the same manner.[77] A contemporary Florentine account describes the Duke's party as it entered the city, which gives an idea of the costumed extravagance of the entry itself:

> There was a livery for his greater *Camerieri*, all dressed in crimson, and each one well mounted on horseback, with a greyhound on a leash. There were also sixty pages, all dressed in green velvet, on huge coursers, all with fittings of gold and silver, and saddles covered with brocade of various colors and crimson. In similar fashion they led from 65 to 70 mules with coffers and carriages, all with covers of embroidered silk. Of the order and decoration of the Duchess's damsels, and their wagons, I will say nothing; and the same for the great preparations here, which are things almost incomprehensible, and Your Lordships can imagine better than I can describe.[78]

As was the custom on such occasions, the Duke brought with him from his court four singers who sang at the daily Mass he attended, three additional

musicians who both sang and played string instruments, all twenty court trumpeters to announce his presence in public, and a group of six pifferi for other
occasions that would be important to embellish with music.[79]

The Florentines reciprocated with similar grandeur. The Duke's entourage
was welcomed by a large group of "the most eminent citizens and many youths,
all in their most ornate dress, as well as all of the civic musical ensembles," who
had "spontaneously" traveled eight miles from the city in order to escort them.[80]
Entrance to the city was at the Porta al Prato, one of the two passages through
the city walls to the west, and the combined tumult of visitors and welcomers
paraded through the city, receiving the cheers of the crowds of ordinary Florentine citizens who lined the streets. They processed from the city gate to the
Piazza della Signoria, where the Duke and Duchess dismounted and ascended
the steps of the *ringhiera*.[81] Next, the visitors moved in procession to the church
of Santissima Annunziata, the expressed purpose of the visit,[82] and then to
the Palazzo de' Medici on Via Larga, home of Florence's most eminent and
powerful family, which had been lavishly decorated for the occasion and where
the Duke and Duchess were to stay for the eight days of their visit. During the
following days the itinerary included an official visit by the Duke to the Palazzo
della Signoria, the seat of government, where he addressed the civic magistrates
in the Sala del Consiglio, followed by a visit to the church of Santa Maria del
Fiore. Because the event took place during Lent, the secular spectacles that usually accompanied such welcomes, such as jousts, *pallii*, and wild animal shows
in the various piazzas, did not take place.[83] Instead, three *sacre rappresentazioni*
were performed: on March 17 *The Annunciation of Mary* was performed at the
church of San Felice in Piazza;[84] on March 19 another *rappresentazione* (probably *The Ascension of Christ*) was presented at Santa Maria del Carmine;[85] and
on March 21 *The Descent of the Holy Ghost* was performed at the church of
Santo Spirito, during which the church caught fire, burning the roof and all
the interior and leaving only the walls. This was the only performance the royal
party did not attend.[86]

## A New Commander-General

A somewhat different procedure was followed for traditional ceremonies that
involved only the city itself. One such event took place during the summer of
1485, when Florence was forced to appoint a new commander-general of the
army to replace Count Rinuccio, who had been killed during the recent military
campaign to capture Sarzanello, the castle of the city of Sarzana. Because the

castle was situated in an important position on the Italian coast approximately halfway between Pisa and Genoa, it had been fought over by Florence and Genoa for several decades. In 1484, as a part of the Peace of Lombardy negotiated by Pope Sixtus, the castle was awarded to the family of Agosto Fregoso rather than to either of the two cities. But when neither city relinquished its claim on the castle, Fregoso, realizing that he could not defend it, gave it to the Bank of San Giorgio, a holding company made up mostly of Genoese. The Florentines, predictably, were not pleased with this solution. As explained by Machiavelli, their legal position was that the Pope did not have jurisdiction over the castle, and therefore could not rightly give it to Fregoso,[87] and they therefore resumed their efforts to capture it. While the Florentine army was preparing to renew its attack on Sarzanello, an opportunity presented itself for an attack on Pietrasanta, another important coastal city. The Florentines were successful in taking Pietrasanta, defeating the Genoese army that had arrived to assist in its defense, but in the process they lost their captain-general, Count Rinuccio. A few weeks later the Florentine army, minus its captain-general, attempted to take Sarzanello but was stopped by the reinforced Genoese troops, leaving the Florentines with an unfulfilled mission.

It was imperative that the Florentine government immediately select a new commander-general in order to continue the pursuit of Sarzanello. After a short deliberation the choice of the Signori was Niccolò Orsini, Count of Pitigliano,[88] and plans were immediately begun for the ceremony of public investiture which would take place on July 17. It was important for the stability of leadership, however, that the newly chosen military leader be invested as quickly as possible, and therefore, on the advice of an astrologer concerning the most auspicious time for such an appointment, Orsini was summoned to Florence from the encampment near Pisa on June 24, the feast of San Giovanni, to receive the baton of generalship. A letter from Guidone Aldobrandino to Ercole d'Este reports the event:

> Signor [Niccolò Orsini], the Count of Pitigliano, has come here incognito. This morning, which is the day of San Giovanni, at the hour of 18 and a quarter, he appeared at the palace of the Signori and all of the Signoria gathered at table for the solemnity of the day, and the Gonfaloniere raised himself from the table and went with the Chancellor [Bartolomeo Scala] and a few others into a room and gave the baton to the Count at the time chosen by the astrologer. It was said that after a few days there would be a [public] ceremony, and the Count returned to Pisa.[89]

For an account of the public ceremony that took place on July 17, we have the testimony of the Florentine herald, Francesco Filerete, who recorded the event in the *Libro cerimoniale*:

Niccolò Orsini, Count of Pitigliano, took the baton on the 24th of June, as the astrologer had appointed, at the hour of 18:30, in the year 1485. Later, at the convenience of the other Signori, the public ceremony was held as will be described below, observing the [precedent of] other ceremonies, as they are known from the ceremony for Gostanzo, etc.[90] Such was the ceremony: He arrived from the direction of Pisa. He was met by the Podestà and all the public instruments. He came from the Ponte Vecchio to the piazza [della Signoria] by way of Borgo San Jacopo. He dismounted at the middle of the loggia [dei Lanzi], and our Signoria awaited him on the *ringhiera*. Then they went to be seated, and all the speakers sat down according to the usual order and custom. The platform was full of a large number of citizens in addition to the Ten of Balia.[91] Bartolomeo Scala delivered the oration.[92] [Orsini] was first given the lilied banner and then the lilied helmet and the shield, which the captain ordered to be taken by his squadron leaders. Finally they gave him that which they had given him before [the baton of generalship]. Following the address by the Gonfaloniere, the captain took his leave. He was accompanied a third of the way across the *ringhiera* by the Signoria, who then returned to their seats. The return procession went from the Prestanze to the Badia, from Fondamenti, turning at the Carnesecchi, up over the bridge of Santa Trinita, through the Via Maggio to Santa Felice in Piazza, and down by Santa Felicita and across the [Via] Bardi to the Ponte Rubaconte, from Santa Croce to the corner of the Rondini; and came to rest at the Alessandri house.[93]

## Knighthood

One of the enduring traditions carried over from feudal times was that of knighting, another occasion that called for an elaborate ceremony.[94] An account of one such presentation at the beginning of the fifteenth century is contained in the autobiographical notes of Jacopo Salviati, which provide unusually vivid details of the ceremonies that surrounded the bestowal of gifts on these kinds of occasions, details that are absent from the accounts quoted above but which undoubtedly characterized all such ceremonies.

Salviati was being rewarded for his military accomplishments during the war against the Milanese troops of Gian Galeazzo Visconti. In the closing years of the fourteenth century Visconti had set himself the goal of conquering most of northern Italy. By 1400 he had isolated Florence by subduing Perugia, Siena, and Pisa, and then in 1402 his troops closed the ring by capturing Bologna. Fortunately for Florence, the unexpected death of Visconti from the plague as he was preparing to attack threw his forces into confusion and saved the city.[95] In May of 1404 Jacopo Salviati was sent to take charge of the Florentine troops in order to extinguish the last gasp of the Milanese forces and the Florentine rebels who supported them, a task he accomplished in a few months. The grateful Priors and the Ten of Balia immediately decided to reward him with six hundred gold florins and contacted him in the field, inviting him to the city to be knighted. In Salviati's words,

> I replied to them that I was happy to accept the honor which they had offered me, and therefore I departed immediately from Bibbiena and came to [the abbey of] San Salvi outside the gate of La Croce on Saturday, October 11, 1404, accompanied by many military men who had come with me for this event. The next morning, Sunday, October 12, I was met by the three Rectors of the city, that is, the Podestà and the Captain and the Executor, and by all of the knights who were then in the city along with many more citizens. I left the abbey of San Salvi on horseback and in military dress in the midst of the Rectors and accompanied by all of the knights, citizens, and the military.
>
> I entered Florence and went to the Piazza della Signoria, and because this was an unusual and noble event and the weather was good, a great multitude of people came to watch. Having arrived in the Piazza, we found our Signori seated on the *ringhiera* in their usual place, and the Ten of Balia seated at their feet. There was a great wooden scaffolding on the side of the golden lion, and on this scaffold, seated because of his gout, was the Gonfaloniere, Messer Lotto di Vanni Castellani, who also had been made the Syndic for the commune by the legislative councils mentioned above at the same time they decided that I would be made a knight. Also on the scaffolding was Messer Cristofano Spini and Messer Tommaso Sacchetti, and Ser Viviano dei Neri the legislative notary, and me, and no one else. And the aforesaid Ser Viviano, having said some words in my honor on behalf of the commune and of the Signori that were present, and having myself answered with elegant words, I took off a jacket of red velvet with scarlet, and I donned another one of white velvet with a vermilion cross that is the coat of arms of this *popolo*. And the aforesaid Messer Cristofano helped me to put on the right spur, and Messer Tommaso the left one, and after I put on my helmet the aforesaid Messer Lotto made me a knight in the name of the People of Florence, placing his sword on the said helmet.
>
> Having done this, on behalf of the commune the aforesaid Ser Viviano presented me with a rich and beautiful gilded helmet of silver, and on this helmet there was a big and beautiful gilded silver lily, and [they gave me] a big pennant with the coat of arms of the *popolo*, with a horse all covered with a silk cloth [which bore] the coat of arms of the *popolo*, and similarly [they gave me] a shield with the same coat of arms. And having received them, I thanked the Signori with what I considered to be sincere words, and I departed accompanied by all those who had accompanied me on entering Florence, and with that gift presented earlier, which was the six hundred florins that were allocated to me.
>
> Then I went to the house of the Parte Guelfa, where I found the Captains seated in their usual place, and they asked me to sit next to them while one of

them spoke of me with great praise. And on their behalf and from that blessed house and all of the Guelfs, they gave me a rich and noble silver helmet adorned with gold, and on it a head of an eagle in the style found on similar gifts made by the Parte Guelfa, made of silver adorned with gold, and then [they gave me] a grand pennant with the arms of the Parte and with a horse covered with silk having the same arms, and with a shield with the aforesaid arms. Accepting these gifts, I answered to the words they had said with words that I believed appropriate to theirs and their gift, and I left from there.

And accompanied by the aforesaid and with those gifts [received] earlier, I went to [the Baptistry of] San Giovanni where I gave an offering of two new gold florins, and with the same people accompanying me I returned home, and there each person took leave of me. And the same morning our magnificent Signori invited me to eat with them, and in my company were all the knights of this city as well as many other valiant men, and it was a beautiful and honorable assembly.[96]

Certainly the selection of gifts on this occasion was particular to the military honor, but their lavishness, as well as the ceremonial way in which they were bestowed, must have been similar on the two other occasions narrated above. The additional, almost duplicate, ceremony at the headquarters of the Parte Guelfa was a reflection of the military nature of the Parte itself as well as of the knighthood, and dramatically illustrates the still-imposing position of the Parte at the beginning of the fifteenth century.

Because most civic award ceremonies involved many standard ingredients, the accounts, including that of the civic herald in the *Libro cerimoniale*, tended to include for the most part only the variations from normal procedures or the unusual. Since music was a standard part of all such occasions, it is rarely included in the official narrative, even though it played a major role. It was to be assumed that the regular format was followed, and therefore in spite of the absence of detail for any one occasion, it is possible for us to fill in the blanks by assembling the details mentioned in a variety of other sources. The resulting composite picture reveals that the ceremonies themselves as well as the role played by the civic musical ensembles were far more extensive than the individual accounts, such as those quoted above, would lead one to believe.

As the accounts state, the very beginning of this type of ceremony was the welcoming procession which, although not always mentioned, would have included the Florentine civic musicians. In the fifteenth century this would have consisted of the trombadori ensemble of six players of large trumpets, a woodwind instrument player, and a drummer; the six (or eight) trombetti who played small trumpets; the pifferi, made up of three shawm players and a trombone; and the six bannitori (town criers) with their trumpets. The musicians would have moved through the city as a part of all of the processions: those preceding and following the welcoming ceremony, and including the final exit from the city. They would have played continuously along the route, making festive sounds to add to the pomp and excitement of the occasion. In the case of the Sforza visit, there would also have been the sounds of the Milanese musicians— an additional twenty trumpets and six more pifferi—on each occasion, which includes each time the Duke traveled to and from the Medici residence during the eight days of his visit. At appropriate times throughout the welcoming ceremony on the *ringhiera*, the trombetti and pifferi (playing separately) would have been heard, highlighting and underlining the ceremony by sounding fanfares to punctuate the individual events, including the greeting, the speeches, the presentation of gifts, and the close of ceremonies.[97] Similar musical participation would also have been included in the ceremonies at the home of the Parte Guelfa, which had its own corps of trumpets and pifferi.

In addition to performances by the instrumental musicians, as a part of many such civic ceremonies that took place on the *ringhiera* in front of the Palazzo della Signoria, the Florentine herald would sing a poem of praise, often of his own authorship, composed in honor of the distinguished guest. This would be in addition to orations delivered by the Chancellor,[98] the Gonfaloniere, or other prominent citizens. On the occasion of Orsini's investiture, the guest of honor was also celebrated with an additional poem, "Alla battaglia," possibly written by Gentile Becchi, Bishop of Arezzo,[99] and probably sung *all'improvviso* rather than read. There is no mention of this poem in any of the documents, but the text itself exists, which exhorts the captain-general to return to the field and capture Sarzanello, thus clearly identifying the occasion for which it was written.[100]

> To the battle, quickly to the battle. Everyone must arm himself with armor and chain mail. To help the excellent captain, everyone must quickly be armed and go forth. Forward, valiant men, one by one: Signor Julio, Organtino, and Paulo Orsino. Sarzanello must be cleaned away. . . . Come on, good leader, quickly advance with Captain Marchese Gabriello. Place yourselves in battle array. Clear them away from around Sarzanello. Who are the Genovese? They do not appear to be prepared, the cursed people.[101]

Poems were a standard part of the celebrations in honor of military events, and singing poetry *all'improvviso* was the standard method of performance (see chapter 3).[102]

During Sforza's visit, when the Duke made his official visit to the Palazzo della Signoria to address the government on the day following the welcoming ceremony, he would have been invited to dine with the Florentine Priors at their special Mensa, an event that regularly included music performed by the civic trombetti, the pifferi, the herald, and on special occasions such as this, with singers borrowed from the church of San Lorenzo as well as jugglers, actors, and other lavish entertainment. While staying at the Medici palace, the Duke and Duchess would have been entertained daily following dinner with performances by a variety of musicians, including members of the Medici family and household, some of the civic pifferi, and various other instrumentalists and singers from the city. In the case of the new captain-general, it is probable that musical entertainment also would have been a part of Orsini's stay at the home of the Alessandri. Although nothing is known of the domestic social practices of the Alessandri family, most of the culturally elite families employed musicians at least on special occasions if not on a permanent basis, and the ability to perform music was one of the many social attributes of the cultured class. A good example of a similar occasion is related by Pietro Gori concerning the reception for the sons of the King of Naples (Ferrante I) at the home of Benedetto Salutati in 1476:

> The guests were summoned to table by the sounds of the trumpets and the shawms . . . Each food course came to the table promptly at the sound of the trumpets. And in the midst of the banquet there was a masked mummery performed by eight young men who were the musicians of the King's chapel, dressed as hunters with horns and dogs, and as birds of prey. And having arrived in the room in front of the tables, they sang the most beautiful songs in a new manner, and then they departed.[103]

Although not specifically mentioned, it is probable that the pifferi also performed for the several hours of dancing that typically followed all banquets. Performance at a banquet by an ensemble such as the costumed singers from the Neapolitan royal chapel would have been something associated only with the most unusual of occasions (which is undoubtedly why it was described in the document), but the presence of trumpets, pifferi, and singers, as well as actors, jugglers, and other entertainers would have been fairly common for a banquet. In short, music would have played a significant part in all of the ceremonies, public and private, surrounding these celebrations, and the musicians of the commune would have been involved in most of it.

It is important to note the extent to which tradition was observed in the three official ceremonies related above, and the number of elements that were a standard part of ceremonial practices. The particulars of each ceremony included a basic set of events that were adjusted and modified for each occasion, but in the main, they remained constant over the time period under discussion here. The result was a carefully orchestrated procedure involving a number of symbolic traditions, assembled and executed as much to celebrate the city itself as to honor its distinguished guests and citizens. As the above accounts make clear, the Florentine ceremonial welcoming routine included the following elements and their possible variations:

- Greeting at the city gate. Usually the guests were greeted at one of the city gates, but on some occasions, such as the Sforza visit, citizens and musicians traveled outside the city to accompany the guest, with the distance traveled by the citizens proportional to the prestige of the guest and the importance of the visit.[104]

- Entrance procession through the city streets lined with citizens, some of the more important of them seated on grandstands. The procession itself was often an elaborate affair involving hundreds or sometimes thousands of citizens on foot and on horseback, some wearing their finest clothing, others wearing the symbolic costumes or colors of their guilds, carrying flags and banners representing the guilds, and a *baldacchino* mounted over the heads of the distinguished guests. As the procession wended its way through the streets accompanied by the ringing of the bells in all of the city churches, fireworks from the church towers added to the excitement and bonfires glowed in the many piazzas along the route. Banners hung from many of the buildings, and for special guests, temporary arches decorated with garlands were erected along the way. There were standard procession routes specified for each of the many types of occasions, and even the order of those who walked in procession was standardized according to the nature of the event.[105]

- Dismounting of the visitor in the Piazza della Signoria. As the visitor approached the members of the Signoria seated on the *ringhiera*, the distance traveled across the front of the Loggia dei Lanzi before dismounting was considered to be a sign of respect on the part of the visitor. It was noted above that in approaching the civic officials, Galeazzo Sforza dismounted in the middle of the Loggia, which was a political statement on his part. Even more respectful would have been for him to dismount at the beginning of the Loggia, something a lesser guest would be expected to do. But if he would have traveled all the way along the Loggia to the beginning of the *ringhiera* before dismounting, it would have been considered an insult to his hosts.[106]

- Welcome on the *ringhiera* in front of the Palazzo della Signoria. There was a particular order in which the Priors and Gonfaloniere sat on the platform, and when other guests were invited to join them, their seating was also clearly planned in order to demonstrate their relative social and political position. It should be noted that the executives of government would be wearing their elaborate ceremonial robes of office, and that the guests as well would be wearing ceremonial dress indicative of their place in society. The place on the platform where the government officials met the guests was carefully calculated; the most important were greeted at the steps of the *ringhiera*; for others the officials would travel partway across the platform; and for lesser guests they remained in place, requiring the guests to travel to them.[107]

· Orations. The number of orations and the importance of the orators reflected the importance of the guests, the most distinguished of whom were addressed by the Chancellor. Other speakers included the Gonfaloniere, various local clergy, and Florentine dignitaries. By the late fifteenth century this element had become so ritualized that there was a standard format for the orations, depending on the occasion.[108]

· Presentation of gifts. The nature of the gifts depended on the purpose of the ceremony and the importance of the guest. In the case of military ceremonies the gifts were the symbols of office (the baton of generalship) and traditional battle wear (helmet, shield, sword). On other occasions they could be welcoming presents as diverse as a horse, jewelry, a ceremonial flag, or even items of clothing richly decorated.

· Exit from the *ringhiera*. Again, the importance of the guest determined the distance that the Signori accompanied their guest back across the platform.

· Recession. Following the ceremony the guests were paraded through the streets, ending at the palace of the Florentine elite where they would be accommodated during their stay, or to the home of the Parte Guelfa. The procession usually did not take a direct path but wound through the streets of Florence and crossed the bridges, its length depending on the importance of the occasion and the guest.

· Dinner at the Mensa of the Signoria. From at least as early as 1387, important guests were invited to dine with the Priors in their private dining room in the Palazzo della Signoria. This would usually occur on the day following the official welcome. As described in chapter 3, the Mensa ceremony was elaborate and included music performed by the herald, the pifferi, and other city musicians.

· Final exit from the city. This usually took place several days after the welcoming ceremony, marking the guest's departure from Florence.

Mirroring the entrance procession, it included the civic musicians and citizens and normally followed a set path leading to whichever city gate would exit in the direction the guest intended to travel.

· Selection of date and time. As was noted in the decisions concerning the installation of the captain-general, an astrologer was consulted to choose these elements for maximum good fortune. When circumstances allowed, important civic dates were chosen for such occasions, such as the feast of San Giovanni. But with so many important sacred and secular dates in the Florentine calendar, it was rarely difficult to make a particular ceremony coincide with a feast day of some type.

## Distinguished Visitors

An excellent example of the coupling of an ad hoc visit with the annual celebrations is the 1459 visit of the fifteen-year-old Count Galeazzo Maria Sforza during Calendimaggio, twelve years prior to his 1471 visit discussed above. Young Galeazzo was sent to Florence by his father, Francesco I, Duke of Milan, for the purpose of giving him an opportunity to meet Cosimo de' Medici and strengthen the relationship between Florence and Milan, as well as to meet Pope Pius II (Aeneas Silvius Piccolomini, from Siena, pope 1458–64), who was making his way from Rome to Mantua to attend a church council.[109] The two visitors were in the city from April 17 to May 5, a period of time that included the beginning of the annual May celebrations. The visit of these two distinguished people is the best documented series of events of the period, with detailed descriptions found in the official *Libro cerimoniale* of Florence, Benedetto Dei's *Cronica*, the journal of Paolo di Matteo Pietrobuoni, Giusto d'Anghiari's "Cronica," Giovanni Cambi's "Istorie," and two anonymous and lengthy poems in *terza rima*.[110] The composite picture provides an unusual amount of detail, which allows us to see how a number of the above-mentioned events and practices fit together. Over the term of their visit the distinguished visitors were treated to entertainments that included banquets, a joust, a *caccia*, an *armeggeria* with a *trionfo*, a performance a *sacra rappresentazione*, *The Ascension of Christ*, at Santa Maria del Carmine,[111] and a grand ball in the Mercato Nuovo. One of the narrators tells us that the days all included morning and evening musical performances—*mattinate* and *serenate*—performed by the civic musicians.[112]

The event began with the arrival of young Galeazzo at the gates of Florence on April 17, along with an entourage of five hundred that included the Archbishop of Milan, the captain-general of the Milanese forces, various barons, knights, counts, and a number of other nobles.[113] The party was met by a mounted delegation of more than three hundred of the most distinguished Florentine citizens, the Priors, the Podestà, and the Capitano del Popolo, along with all of the civic musicians and the herald, as well as other ministers of the government. The elegance of the entrance ceremony is described in an anonymous contemporary poem:

> *La strada in giù e 'n su di gente piove,*
> *chè gli andò incontro ciascun cittadino,*
> *ch'a onorarlo ognun volentier move.*
> *Per tutta la città in ciascun confino*
> *si serrar le botteghe pe' precetti*
> *che fecero i signor del mio domino.*
> *Andògli incontro pifferi e trombetti*
> *I rettori e con vestir d'argento*
> *e pien di perle cento giovinetti,*
> *con questo solenne ordinamento*
> *entrò in Firenze il sir di gran lignaggio*
> *reverito fu da chi v'è dentro.*
> *Era dinanzi il suo bel carriaggio,*
> *cinquanta mul coperti a sua divisa,*
> *fu di gran magnificenza saggio.*[114]

[People came pouring out into the streets to meet him, and each citizen was happily moved to honor him. Through all the city in each section the stores were closed by order of the Signori of my city. The pifferi, trombetti, and the rectors went to meet him, and dressed in silver and covered with pearls were a hundred young boys, and in this solemn order the man of grand lineage entered into Florence and received reverence from all the inhabitants. In front of his beautiful carriage were fifty mules covered in the colors of his crest, which made a grand and magnificent display.]

The order of procession through the city streets was as follows: Florentine *famiglia* (staff); *famiglia* of Galeazzo; trombetti; Florentine youths and Milanese foot soldiers; civic pifferi with the herald; Galeazzo with the Priors of Florence; knights from both parties; all the other Florentine citizens. When the procession arrived at the Piazza della Signoria it was welcomed with a great sound of trumpets and bells. Then the usual welcome ceremony on the *ringhiera* took place, after which Galeazzo proceeded to the Medici Palace where he would stay for the duration of his visit.

Pope Pius II arrived a week later (April 25), accompanied by a number of nobles from various cities as well as ten cardinals, sixty bishops, and a large number of priests.[115] He was met in the suburban monastery of San Gaggio by the Captains of the Parte Guelfa, who escorted him under the banner of the Parte Guelfa to the gates of Florence, where he was met by the civic leaders. The Pope was seated on a throne covered in gold brocade and was carried through the city streets on a litter by nobles and princes from Romagna who were in his party.[116] (His request that the Florentine Priors carry the litter was rejected.)[117] The procession, now led by the banner of Florence, was conducted in the solemn manner of a religious procession with relics, torches, and sacred songs, and in addition to the distinguished members of the Pope's party mentioned above were included the Florentine Priors and clergy, the Florentine *famiglia*, the Roman court along with all the Florentine youths, a large number of citizens and knights, and the minor magistrates. Galeazzo Maria Sforza followed behind the Pope on horseback, leading the cardinals and other clergy. Before reaching its destination of Santa Maria Novella, where the Pope was to reside in the papal apartment, the procession stopped at the Piazza della Signoria for the usual welcoming ceremony and then proceeded to Santa Maria del Fiore, where the Pope prayed. The civic herald noted that although both of the welcoming processions took place during rainstorms, all the participants comported themselves with the utmost dignity and solemnity.[118]

The anonymous poem describes the Pope's procession in these terms:

> *In prima incominciarono a passare*
> *a due e tre e quattro insieme stretti*
> *più di mille cavagli, a non errare,*
> *e doppo loro e' pifferi e' trombetti*
> *che suon leggiadri, dolzi e peregrini*
> *givan sonando con ordin perfetti;*
> *e poi seguieno i degni cittadini*
> *che alla santa apostolica fede*
> *incontro s'eran fatti il dì festini.*[119]

[At the beginning more than a thousand horses (I do not err) began to pass in lines of twos, threes, and fours, and after them the pifferi and the trombetti who made lovely sounds, sweet and uncommon and sounding with perfect order; and then followed the important citizens who were appointed *festini* for the day by the holy apostolic faith.]

This was not the only sacred procession to take place during the visit. The morning following his entrance into the city (April 26), the Pope traveled from Santa Maria Novella to the Duomo in a procession that included a large number of citizens as well as the civic magistrates. His words were received with honor and he was thanked on behalf of the Signori with "marvelous and copious gifts."[120] On another of the days (unspecified in the accounts), there was a solemn and grand procession in honor of the Pope that included *sacre rappresentazioni* and *edifici* on a total of forty-six carts. The only account of the event is that by Benedetto Dei, who records the names of participating groups, which included a number of churches and confraternities.[121]

Both departures (Galeazzo Sforza on May 3, Pope Pius II two days later) are also recorded as being accompanied with the usual ceremony, meaning extended processions through the city streets. The day preceding his exit, Galeazzo was presented with gifts that included two silver basins decorated with the emblem of Florence, two tankards, two large boxes of candy (confections), and twelve engraved cups, all of which weighed 125 pounds and was valued at two thousand florins.[122] The banquets, which took place each evening, were lavish. Cosimo de' Medici took the trouble of ordering the finest food, wine, and decorations from all over northern Italy and across the Alps, and at his banquets there were musicians playing "every sort of gentle respectable instrument."[123] The entertainment following one banquet that took place in the Medici suburban villa at Careggi impressed Galeazzo to the point that he wrote back to his father, telling him of the performance of Antonio di Guido, the most famous Florentine performer of the time, who sang improvised verse while playing the *lira da braccio* (see discussion in chapter 3).[124]

On April 29 a joust took place in the Piazza Santa Croce. The piazza was cordoned off, platforms erected for the audience, tapestries hung from the windows of the surrounding buildings, and the various pieces of equipment needed for the joust were erected in the center of the piazza. Seven young Florentines participated in the event,[125] which was presided over by a team of six judges.[126] Each participant entered to the sound of trumpets, preceded by pages carrying standards with the colors and heraldic emblem of the participant, and followed by twenty lancers, with everyone mounted on decorated horses. First honors went to Antonio Boscoli and second to Braccio Guicciardini, both of whom were presented with decorated helmets, after which "the fine cavaliers left the field to the sound of the pifferi and other instruments, returning to their homes with their neighbors."[127]

Both distinguished visitors were invited to meet with the Signori during their stay. The visit of the Pope on May 2 is noted in the *Libro cerimoniale* without additional remarks, although it is probable that he was invited to dine at the Mensa with the Signori. Galeazzo had visited the Signori on the previous morning, May Day, where he was treated to a lavish banquet at the Mensa that included "every kind of splendid food and elegant wine,"[128] which was just the beginning of the round of events mounted to celebrate the arrival of spring.

Following the banquet the young prince was treated to a *caccia* in the afternoon, and in the evening an *armeggeria*, traditional events for the celebration of May 1, although in honor of the distinguished guests, these were especially elaborate.

For the *caccia*, the Piazza della Signoria was cordoned off with a high fence to contain the animals and protect the citizens, and some platforms were erected around the periphery to accommodate the viewers. The balconies and windows overlooking the piazza were full of people, as were the rooftops.[129] Inside the enclosure were cows, bulls, horses, wolves, wild boar, wild dogs, a giraffe, and a large number of lions—the number of lions depends on who was writing the account: either twelve (Paolo di Matteo Pietrobuoni and Giusto d'Anghiari), sixteen (*Libro cerimoniale*), or twenty-six (Benedetto Dei). But added to this *caccia* was an unusual event which Benedetto Dei explains in detail:

> And they placed in there twenty-six live lions and lionesses, and among them they placed wild boars and wolves and bulls and strong wild horses, and other wild animals, and they made a *caccia* in the piazza which was surrounded by many platforms. And also at the *caccia* there was placed in the Piazza della Signoria a large round ball the height of approximately four *braccia* [approx. two and a half meters],[130] in which there was a live man placed and situated in a way that caused the ball to move wherever he wished it, and he raced after the lions and wounded them through certain holes and openings in the ball in a way that did not allow him to be hurt by those animals. It was a beautiful, grand, and ingenious thing, never before done in Italy. And this idea came from a Florentine who had seen it done in the countries of the Sultan and in Syria.[131]

The accounts, especially that in the manuscript Florence, Biblioteca Nazionale Centrale, Magl. 1121, go into some rather gory detail about the animals trembling with fear while the ferocious lions attacked them, and describing how at one point a lion approached the place where Galeazzo Sforza was watching and seemingly bowed to the Count.[132]

That evening Galeazzo watched from an upper-storey window as an *armeggeria* took place in Via Larga in front of the Medici Palace (similar to figure 3). As with the other entertainments, everyone was in extraordinary dress, the horses were decorated, and the streets were brightly lit with torches.[133] The twelve participants were all Florentines,[134] each assisted by twenty pages and the same number of servants carrying large torches. Everyone passed in procession through the streets, starting in the Piazza San Marco and led by thirty musicians, including the civic trumpeters and pifferi. First came the warriors and all of their assistants, the last of them being young Lorenzo de' Medici, age ten, who was the "Signore" for the event, dressed in a golden jacket and cape exactly as depicted by Benozzo Gozzoli in the Medici Chapel fresco (figure 17). Immediately behind Lorenzo, on a wagon drawn by two horses and led by fifty costumed youths, was a *trionfo*, the *Triumph of Love*, which was a four-sided tower approximately three meters tall, ornamented in silver and gold that was polished to reflect the lights. Large gold balls with falcons were mounted on the four corners, with three diamonds between them. Fire spewed from openings on all sides. On the very top was a nude youth with wings and a bow and arrow, impersonating Cupid. The sources do not say much about the actual *armeggeria* other than making general remarks about the shining helmets and flashing lances and the gallantry of all participants.

The ball, which took place on April 30, was held in the Mercato Nuovo and was perhaps the most splendid of all the events. As usual, the narrators dwell on the grand costumes of all the participants, the lavish decorations of the setting, and the enjoyment of all of the dancers. The richest of the narrations is in one of the poems which paints a vivid picture of the way in which this type of festa would take place, including the decorations of the market area, the arrangements of seats, the placement of the musicians, the social order of the dancing, and even the names of some of the dances that were performed (the dances are discussed in chapter 6):[135]

> And as the new day dawned everyone was very happy on arising because on this day in the New Market a ball is to take place: and they have already begun the arrangements. And as I told you already, now I can confirm that there is a fence around, and many seats, and above, one also finds a covering.... The wise organizers had a beautiful dais made as a worthy place for the great Count and the Pope, and the inside of the market matched the exterior in appearance. It was prepared with a great splendor of fabrics, tapestries, pillows, and wall hangings. Above, there was a sky canopy of rich cloth and more of it behind [the dais] and on all the sides. The floor of the dais was covered with carpets and all the high royal chairs that were around, shining and bright, adorned with backs and cushions as I know you can guess so well, laid out in such a way that was never [before] seen. There were three ranks of seats all around, each one higher than the other so that both those sitting in the front and in the back could see. And there seemed to be a provision that the first row near the fence would be for the important and worthy citizens and the next, a bit lower to the side, for women who could not dance because of age or pregnancy or widowhood. Only the front rank had been decorated so that women and girls who would spread the festive mood all around should occupy it. Opposite the coat of arms of the Signoria, above the fence, a raised place was prepared for the pifferi and trombone.... So big was the crowd that I cannot estimate ... but it was believed that there were more than 20,000. And there would have been many more if the circumference

[of the enclosure] had been larger. . . . Thus the young brigade were waiting for the ladies who had to come, beautifully and magnificently adorned. It was at this time that I saw the pifferi and trombone arrive and go to their place. There was an escort of twenty trumpets next to the fence at the beautiful entranceway who made a grand and beautiful flourish [*stormeggiata*] whenever women came to the entrance. . . .

Later, toward the end, the noble Count came to the fence with his great lords and champions. Each trumpeter took his trumpet and played an extemporaneous flourish until the count entered and joined the others. . . . At that time the pifferi and trombone began to play a *salterello* artistically designed in all its proportions. Then each noble and nimble squire took a married lady or a young girl, first one then the other, and began to dance. Some promenade around and some jump, some change hands and some take leave from a lady while others invite one. Some in parties of two or three make a beautiful dance. Two young girls, united in their courteous purpose and with a smiling face and with radiant and polished cheeks went to invite the noble Count, making a bow down to the ground with a most ornate and ready *reverance*.[136] The military captain stood up and bowed to them and then entered into the middle [of the floor] and danced, not making any mistakes.

The pifferi who performed the dance music were undoubtedly the civic musicians of Florence, but the poem also mentions the presence of twenty trumpeters who played ensemble flourishes whenever women arrived as well as solo flourishes upon the arrival of Galeazzo. The poem goes on to describe refreshments served at the dance, in which pages preceded by trumpeters carried trays of confections, water, and wine through the throngs. These trumpeters may well have been a combination of both the Florentine trumpeters and those in Galeazzo's entourage. At that time the Sforza household trumpeters numbered eighteen,[137] and it is certain that Francesco's son would have brought some of them with him.

None of the accounts make any other mention of musicians from Milan, but we do know that the Milanese court had an ensemble of three or four pifferi as well as singers, lute players, and string players.[138] Galeazzo certainly would have brought some of these performers with him, both for his own enjoyment and to impress his hosts during his sixteen-day residence at the Medici Palace. Cosimo de' Medici had at his command the civic trombetti and pifferi, his own household musicians, and his selection of singers from the church choirs, and as we have seen, one of the most famous Florentine poet-singers, Antonio di Guido. We can imagine, therefore, that the music accompanying the evening banquets—a combination of the Medici and Sforza groups—would have been quite extraordinary.

There is no doubt that the visits of young Galeazzo and Pope Pius II inspired Florence to do its utmost in terms of ceremonies.[139] But the events that took place during the visits—the processions, *edifici*, banquets, *sacre rappresentazioni*, jousts, *caccie*, *armeggerie*, *trionfi*, and balls—were not unusual happenings in the city. In fact, not even the concentration of so many events in the space of two and a half weeks (April 17–May 5) was unusual for Florence. What was unusual was that the visit of two distinguished guests probably resulted in events that were a bit more lavishly presented—which is why they are so well documented. For the most part, however, the accounts present a good idea of the quantity and variety of ceremony that took place in Florence on a regular basis. On reflection, we might be inclined to adopt the opinion expressed by Gregorio Dati: "They dance, play and sing, take part in banquets and jousts and other traditional games, so that it appears that no one has anything else to do."[140] Dati was referring only to the preparations before the feast of San Giovanni, but his comment would seem to apply to a very large part of the year.

# 2

# The Trombadori

A large portion of the music that accompanied the ceremonies and festas described in chapter 1 was provided by the trombadori, the first of the civic instrumental ensembles formed by the commune in the thirteenth century to add ceremonial pomp to civic occasions. The ensemble originally was made up of six trumpeters (*tubatores* or *trombadori*), one cymbals player (*cimbalellario*), and one woodwind player (*cennamellario*). All wore costumes that identified them with Florence and had banners suspended from their instruments showing the image of *giglio* (the red lily, symbol of Florence) on a white background (trumpets and banners are shown in figure 6a). Over the decades of the late Middle Ages their numbers and types of instruments changed slightly, but the basic ceremonial purpose of the trombadori remained the same. We have continuous record of their employment only from the year 1292, when they were reappointed for a period of three years, but it is clear that the traditions represented by these civic employees did not originate at the time of the surviving documents. What we are dealing with is a long-standing tradition that would seem to be pan-European in its basic concept, with local variations according to particular geographical areas. The ceremonial traditions in the cities of northern Italy are all quite similar throughout the period under investigation here, attesting to a continuing and similar association of musicians with civic ceremonies throughout the late Middle Ages. Fortunately, documents do exist for several of the north Italian locations and thus, by looking closely at the sparse but similar records from a number of cities, it is possible to assemble a composite view of what probably took place in Florence in the century prior to the time recorded in the surviving documents.

Trumpets and drums have been associated both with ceremonial events and the military since ancient times. They were among the traditional symbols of civic authority in ancient Rome, announcing the presence of nobles as they moved through the streets. They lent pomp to tournaments, parades, processions, and various civic activities in cities throughout Europe, and they accompanied the military in the field, where they served to frighten the enemy and functioned as signalmen to relay directions to the soldiers in battle. They are depicted in all of these capacities in the literature and iconography of numerous societies of Europe and Asia, including iconographical sources from early Greek and Roman times. In late medieval Europe, wind musicians—especially trumpeters—are found in all communities of any size, where, in addition to the duties mentioned above, they also served as watchmen from the city towers, standing on guard for fire or approaching military threats, and watching for local citizens who ignored the nighttime curfew. In this capacity they were referred to in Germany as a *wachtman* or *turhutter*,[1] in England as waits,[2] *wachters up de halle* in Bruges,[3] and in France as *gaychiatores*.[4] In the late thirteenth century the Parisian music theorist Johannes de Grocheio still associated trumpets and drums with the military: "Some instruments by their sound may move the souls of men more than others, for example the drum and trumpet in war games and tournaments."[5]

The constant mention in the literature throughout the Middle Ages of trumpets as the accepted symbol of authority, as well as their presence in the iconography, gives strong evidence of a steady and unbroken tradition that was observed all over Europe, varying only in minor local details.[6] The tradition of civic instrumental ensembles and their function was common to communities in France, Germany, England, and Spain, as well as in Italy. It is not surprising to note, therefore, that the involvement of trumpet ensembles in the ceremonial traditions observed by all of the larger cities in northern Italy were quite similar to one another regardless of political organization. Although the governing body in Florence experienced major changes in organization from the thirteenth to the sixteenth centuries, there was little direct effect on the kinds of civic ceremonies or the way they were observed. The ceremonies grew in number and size over the decades in reaction to the fluctuating economic and political fortunes of the city, but with little change in substance until the dramatic revisions to the ceremonial traditions enacted in the late fourteenth century (see chapter 4).

# Background of the Instrument Ensemble

By the late twelfth century Florence had evolved from a feudal, agrarian community into a mercantile city-state. Its political organization resembled that of many other north Italian cities in which the government was in the hands of consuls of *boni homines*, a group of leading citizens usually numbering twelve. At the end of the century, following similar trends in other Italian municipalities, the Florentine consuls enacted a constitutional change that transferred the executive authority from the consulate to the office of the Podestà, itself a remnant of an earlier system imposed on the province in 1162 by Emperor Frederick I Barbarossa. Originally the *potestates* were simply agents of the emperor, entrusted to collect taxes and maintain peace. When reintroduced as a supplement to the consuls around the year 1200, the Podestà of Florence served as an agent of the consuls, able to act only with their approval. He was always a foreigner, often a nobleman from Lombardy, was usually appointed for one year, and was required to take an oath to uphold the constitution and adhere to the orders of the executive council. He was the chief magistrate of the city and the head of the judiciary and the police force, both of which he brought with him.[7] It is to this office, that of the Podestà, that we can look as the most probable location for the more-or-less permanent organization of a set of ceremonial musicians, and in fact, this is the office that presents the earliest records of occasions on which ceremonial musicians would traditionally play a part: visits to the city by heads of state, church officials, and military leaders, all of whom would have been welcomed by the Podestà in a ceremonial manner.

Records of just such a musical organization can be found in the nearby city-state of Siena, where occasional payments were made to ensembles of trumpet players from as early as 1230. The Sienese ensemble and its duties are described in the first city statutes of 1262, where it had become the responsibility of the Podestà to hire three pairs of trumpeters for ceremonial purposes.[8] The civic statutes of Bologna of 1250 provide for a similar group of trumpeters which also was associated with the office of the Podestà and the Capitano del Popolo.[9] Additional evidence that connects trumpet ensembles with the identification of political authority in Italy can be traced back to at least as early as 1240, when Frederick II, the Holy Roman Emperor residing in Arezzo, had four silver *tubae* and one *tubecta* (large and small trumpets) made to order.[10] Since details are lacking in the Florentine records, it is important to note that there were close parallels between the organization of the governments in Siena and Bologna and that of Florence, as well as in the relationship of all of these communities to the German emperor, suggesting that traditions and procedures recorded in one location were likely to have been common to them all. In viewing the accounts of the Florentine Podestà, therefore, it would be reasonable to assume that although no musicians are mentioned, he too would have employed an ensemble of ceremonial musicians for occasions such as the 1283 visit of King Charles of Naples, who led an army to Sicily that according to the chronicle of Paolino Pieri included a number of Florentine soldiers:

> And going with him for the Commune of Florence were three hundred knights, of whom fifty were Knights of the Golden Spur, and fifty young nobles, and each one had at least two companions, but there were some who brought six, and some four, but some had not even enough money for two companions. And foot soldiers numbered five hundred, all with white overgarments[11] with a lily of vermilion inside.[12]

Following his victory at Messina, the king returned north, passing through Florence, where he knighted eight of the soldiers:

> King Charles left Prince Charles, his son, to guard the kingdom . . . and passed through Florence on the 14th day of March 1283, and was received by the Florentines with great honor, and in Florence he made eight knights among the Florentines, Lucchese, and Pistoiese.[13]

According to the traditions observed in neighboring cities as well as those that are recorded later in Florence, it is likely that the army had in its employ a number of trumpets for both ceremonial and practical purposes. We can also assume that on their arrival in Florence, as with the visit of Galeazzo Maria Sforza nearly two hundred years later (see chapter 1), a group of local trumpet players, wearing clothing that identified them with the commune and with pennants bearing the symbol of Florence hanging from their instruments, would have met the visitors at one of the city gates in order to lead a procession through the streets with great pomp and ceremony while the citizens cheered their passing. The visitors would have been escorted to the palace of the Podestà, where a welcoming ceremony for the king would have been presided over by the Podestà, probably including orations and poetic presentations by local luminaries such as the Chancellor and other literary figures, following which they would have continued their procession through the city streets, again led by the civic musicians, as they exited through one of the city gates. The knighting ceremony, presided over by King Charles, would have included the same kinds of details described in the knighting ceremony in chapter 1.

Given the long tradition of ceremonial musical ensembles and the similarities in the various ceremonial practices of north Italian cities,[14] it is also possible to speculate that sometime in the early thirteenth century Florence would have followed patterns similar to those documented in Siena and Bologna, in which the established symbol of governmental authority, the office of the Podestà, would be represented by sets of trumpeters hired for particular ceremonial occasions.[15] In addition to functioning within the welcoming processions and ceremonies, the trumpeters would have preceded the Podestà when he ventured out in public as a way of announcing his official presence, and their fanfares would have added pomp to all ceremonies within his palace. At some point an increase of such occasions would have made it economically advantageous to appoint such a group to salaried positions, probably sometime around 1250. The chronicle of Paolino Pieri, which is a year-by-year account of events in Florence between 1080 and 1305,[16] hints at the growth in the number of such ceremonies as Florence continued to loosen its connection with foreign imperial control while its importance as a mercantile center increased. The parallel growth in the power and stature of the guilds eventually led to the bulk of executive power being shifted from the office of the Podestà to an assembly of representatives of the major guilds, a group referred to as Signori or Priori. As we shall see below, once the Priorate was firmly established, control of the ceremonial musicians also shifted to the new executive council, and it is at that point that the first actual records exist confirming the appointment of the civic musical ensemble in Florence.

The change of governance from imperial to local control moved in spurts, beginning in the late twelfth century. Although Florence had received a charter in 1187 from Henry VI, Frederick Barbarossa's son and imperial successor, the connection to the German emperor remained strong until 1197, when Florence took advantage of Henry's premature death as an opportunity to join together with other Tuscan towns to resist foreign rule and establish local authority. But it was not until a vacuum created by the death of Frederick II in 1250 and the departure from Florence of his illegitimate son Frederick of Antioch, Podestà since 1246, that imperial control ended. At that point the power began to shift more fully from the office of the Podestà to the guilds under the new regime of the *popolo*, which involved a reorganization of the commune into twenty neighborhoods, each with a distinct standard (*gonfalone*) and standard bearer, as well as rectors and a militia.

The new ruling council, known as the elders (*anziani*), comprised twelve good men—two guildsmen from each of the six districts (*sesti*)—and was headed by the Capitano del Popolo, the representative of the militia of the guilds,[17] who replaced the Podestà as the chief military and judicial officer. All of these institutions were abolished during the period 1267–82, the time when Charles of Anjou was Podestà, although the guilds themselves remained. Charles chose to exercise his office from afar and rarely appeared in the city, which resulted in a degree of local freedom during which time a number of new Florentine merchant families grew in wealth and power. The last step in the creation of the Priorate, an executive committee made up of six Priors of the Guilds, came in 1282 when the defeat of the Angevin military forces by the Sicilians weakened Charles's military—and therefore political—power, which in turn provided the Florentines with the opportunity to expel his representatives and shift much of the remaining civil authority to a council of guildsmen.[18] Although the Priors did not immediately become the supreme executive—that authority remained for a short time in the hands of the Fourteen, a ruling group established in 1280—by early in 1283 the power had passed to the Priors and they alone had the ability to initiate legislation and make policy decisions.[19] The office of the Podestà remained in place, as did his two traditional councils (the General Council of three hundred and the Special Council of ninety), and the holder of the office continued to be a foreigner whose major responsibilities were to act as chief judge and to lead the army in times war, although the new structure placed him under the supervision of the Priorate.[20]

The period of several decades following the initiation of the Priorate was a time of enormous growth in terms of attention to external manifestations of civic pride and the ceremonial aspect of life in Florence. This was demonstrated most spectacularly by the building of civic monuments and the enlargement of the city outline. Beginning almost immediately, the walls of the city were moved to their final profile (figure 1), one that lasted until the mid-nineteenth century and still is visible in remnants of both walls and towers and marked by the large *viali* that were paved following the destruction of most of the walls. The Piazza of Santa Maria Novella (1289) and that of Santa Croce (1294) were enlarged in order to accommodate ceremonial events; building of the Badia was begun (1285); the Duomo, or Cathedral of Santa Maria del Fiore, was begun in 1296 on the site of the smaller Santa Reparata; and the home of the new executive wing of the government, the Palazzo della Signoria (originally the Palazzo dei Priori, now the Palazzo Vecchio), first proposed in 1285, was finally begun in 1299 and occupied as the seat of government in 1302.[21] In the process of all of this revision, renovation, and building, the attention of the executives was also drawn to the musical component of ceremonial Florence, and it is at this point that we have the first documentary evidence for the civic musicians: executive records of their appointment (in the *Provvisioni registri*), pay records, and eventually, statutes.

The earliest record of a civic musical ensemble in Florence is found in the *Provvisioni registri* from February 8, 1292.[22] This coincides with the time that the Priors were assuming more of the authority previously held by the Podestà, including the establishment in 1293 of a new post among the Signori, that of the Standard Bearer of Justice (Gonfaloniere), whose responsibility was to administer the sentences of the court.[23] The document records the appointment of the trombadori: six trumpets, one reed instrument, and one pair of cymbals, and the term of appointment on this occasion was for three years, although in later years it changed to one year at a time. The number of trumpet players in the document—six—is the same as that in the Siena ensemble from the mid-thirteenth century, suggesting that it was the standard number, and therefore we can probably assume that this had been the number in the civic ensemble for several decades under the authority of the office of the Podestà, until control of their appointment was transferred to the Priors.[24] How long the other two musicians, the *cennamellario* and *cimbalellario*, had been a part of the ensemble is not possible to determine. Sienese documents list two percussion players, drum (*tamburo*) and cymbals (*cembalis*), as early as 1230, which establishes the fact that the civic musical ensembles in the early thirteenth century sometimes included instruments other than trumpets. The first mention of a reed instrument in this company in Siena is from 1251, when a *cialamella* (another word for *cennamella*) along with a trumpet accompanied the Podestà and the army on a trip.[25] But the inclusion of a reed player as a regular appointment in the ceremonial ensemble of Siena did not begin until 1310.[26] There is no suggestion in the wording of the 1292 Florentine document, however, that anything new or out of the ordinary tradition is being proposed. The only probable change, therefore, would have been the transfer of supervisory responsibility of the musicians to the Priorate from the office of the Podestà. Nor is there anything in the nature of the change of government that would suggest an immediate revision of the substance or format of whatever had been the long-standing ceremonial traditions involving the civic musicians.

Once the trombadori were moved from the control of the office of the Podestà to that of the Priors, there is no mention in any documents as to the ceremonial representation of the office of the Podestà. Since the holder of that office continued to have political power and status, it is reasonable to believe that he would also be served by trumpet players whenever acting in his official status. Whether he continued to call upon the civic musicians on these occasions or whether he appointed his own ensemble is not known.

Although only six of the eight members of the ensemble played trumpets, the civic documents always refer to the entire ensemble as the trombadori

or tubatores, both words meaning trumpets. As part of the visible authority of the government they were present on all occasions when Florence was
acting officially. This meant that they accompanied the civic officials in all of
their public appearances, as for example when they moved about the city. They
were present to represent Florence on all ceremonial occasions, such as the
welcoming of foreign guests to the city; they led the ceremonial processions
through the streets; and they frequently visited foreign cities accompanying
the executives or their ambassadors. The trombadori also were present at all
the regular civic and religious celebrations described in chapter 1; they accompanied the Florentine military in the field; and frequently were sent on their
own to appear at the celebrations of other cities as the official representatives
of Florence.[27] The actual wording of their appointment presents a summary
of the governing body and illustrates the formal method adopted for making
such appointments:

> In the name of God, amen. In the year of the Lord 1291 [1292], fifth indiction,
> commencing the eighth day of the month of February. The nobleman, Lord
> Scellio, a man of Lord Bartholecto of Spoleto, Podestà of the City and Com-
> mune of Florence for the second time, when the convocation was proclaimed
> by the sounding of the bell, with the banner of the said Commune, he had
> assembled in the customary manner the General Council of Three Hundred
> Men, and the Special Council of Ninety Men and the Consuls of all the Twelve
> Greater Arts and the Commune of Florence. In which council, indeed, recorded
> by me, B. the notary, all matters and every single matter were expounded and
> read successively on the 18th day of January last, in the Council of the Hundred
> Men, and following immediately after on the 28th of the same month of Janu-
> ary last, in the Special and General Councils of the Lord Defender, and the
> Captain and the Consuls of the Twelve Greater Arts of the City of Florence
> successively. These were proclaimed and made in due order, and authorized
> according to the form of the legal regulations and the statutes of the said Com-
> mune, proposed, prepared, and confirmed upon the provision and choice of the
> Lord Priors of the Arts, in the period and for the period of three years, begun in
> the previous month of January. This was enacted concerning the below-written
> six large trumpets [*tubatores*], and one shawm [*cennamellarius*], and one cymbals
> [*cimbalellarius*], according as and according to the acts of the aforementioned
> said Councils, fully and expressly written by public authority in my hand, that
> of B. the subscribed notary.
>
> The names of these *tubatores* and *cennamellario* and *cimbalellario* are as fol-
> lows: Guglielmo di Nero, Catena di Dietaiuti, Pacino d'Ubertino, Guglielmo di
> Giacomo, Balduccio di Buono, Matteo di Niccolo, six *tubatores* of the Commune
> of Florence; Gianuccio di Niccolo, of the parish of St Laurenzo, *cennamellario*;
> Lore, called "Anghara," of the parish of St. Felice in Piazza, *cimbalellario*.[28]

The government took great pride in this ensemble and insisted that they not only play well, but also, since they officially represented the government of Florence, that they be appropriately dressed "for the honor of the commune."[29] To ensure both of these standards, representatives of the government auditioned the performers, and the city provided them with costumes that they were obliged to wear when performing. The uniforms, which were replaced twice a year, on Christmas and the feast of San Giovanni (24 June), included a cape emblazoned inside and out with *giglio*, the symbol of Florence. At some point there may have been an attempt by some of the civic musicians to exchange their uniform for ready cash, because the statutes of 1325 make it clear that they could not ask for the cash value in place of a new cloak, nor could they pawn or sell their cloak under pain of immediate dismissal from the ensemble with no possibility of reinstatement. They were also provided four times a year with new *pennone*, heraldic pennants emblazoned with *giglio*, which were to be suspended from their instruments.

In addition to their duties within the city walls, the trombadori also were required to have horses in order to serve outside of the city, both with the military and separately as representatives of Florence in other cities on special occasions. The earliest description of these duties is found in the statutes of 1325:[30]

> [A]nd when they go either into the army or on cavalcade for the commune, the financial officers are obligated to pay—to each of them—fifteen soldi per day beyond the salary previously mentioned; and they may neither take nor receive [payment] over and above that until they have gone and remained, and been present and returned from the army or the cavalcade. And they are to have and maintain horses in the cavalcade and army—that is, every one of them without exception. And when for any reason they should go beyond the city of Florence by order of the Podestà and Defender, and the Captain on account of that army practicing, and drilling, and returning to the city on the same day they leave, as often happens, the financial officers should pay them four soldi and no more for each day, for the transport services of their horses, notwithstanding any other chapter of the constitution of the commune.[31]

What is being described is several different types of service. The first was to accompany the military for extended periods, for which the trombadori received fifteen soldi per day in addition to their regular monthly salaries of four lire each (five for the *cennamellario*), undoubtedly to pay for the living expenses of the musicians and their horses. They could also be sent outside the city on day trips to represent the government, which was a common event, and on those occasions their fee was four extra soldi each to pay for the care of the horses. The civic documents record many such assignments, as for example, a request in 1295 for extra pay to be given to Catena di Dietaiuti and Matteo di Niccolo, two of the trombadori, for having accompanied the military in the company of the Podestà, the Capitano del Popolo, and some ambassadors of the commune on a journey to Pistoia for seventeen days.[32] The civic trombadori were also sent to accompany foreign mercenary troops when they fought under the flag of Florence.[33]

At the time of the Priors' second renewal of the civic musicians in 1295, this time for only a single year, the *Provvisioni* include the additional detail that the trumpet players must perform on instruments made of silver, which the musicians themselves were expected to provide:

> And it will be judged that these men are expert in those offices, minstrelsy, and positions, and are very reliable. And that by law they are to present themselves to the said commune with silver trumpets, which they have had obtained at their own expense for the honor of the said commune.[34]

There is no statement concerning the other two instruments, the *cennamella*, and *cimbalella*, perhaps because there was only one of each of them and therefore no need for legislated uniformity, but more likely because it was only the silver trumpets that were a part of a long tradition that included the material from which the instruments were made (see below).

In 1361 the government decreed that the trombadori were all to live in the same quarter of the city, a parish later known as San Michele delle trombe (the church is no longer in existence).[35] If this regulation was actually enforced it did not endure for long; occasional identification of the parish of residence in the pay records over the following decades as well as the *catasto* (tax records) of 1427 indicate that the civic musicians lived in a variety of quarters, although as late as the mid-fifteenth century many of them still did live in close proximity to one another.[36]

## *Bannitori*

One additional group of ceremonial trumpet players should be mentioned here: the bannitori, or town criers, a separate group whose duty it was to announce the various civic proclamations in eight places in each of the city's quarters. This again was a widespread tradition in which a set of men were appointed to announce the official decisions to the public, including notices and banishments made by the principal civic officials such as the Priors, the Standard Bearer of Justice, the Capitano del Popolo, and the Podestà. Similar posts are recorded from as early as the mid-twelfth century in other cities such as Siena, Perugia, and Milan.[37] The six Florentine bannitori, one for each *sesto*, wore a uniform of a single color, either green or scarlet, which was replaced twice a year by the commune,[38] and around their necks hung a silver ornament called a *maspillos* that identified them as bannitori of the city. They were required to be able to read and write, and were to equip themselves with a good horse (the particular value of the horse is stated in some of the records), and to carry a small silver trumpet from which they hung a pennant with the insignia of the Capitano del Popolo, a vermilion cross on a white field. The earliest reference to them is in a *Provvisione* of 1307.

> On the commune having six bannitori.
>
> Further, in order that the commune of Florence maintain its customary decent and adequate [ensemble of] bannitori who have high and clear voices, it has been decided and decreed that there are to be only six bannitori of the commune of Florence who are capable of performing the office of heralding the proclamations of the Podestà, the Captain, and other officials of the commune of Florence. They are to be local citizens who identify their families. They are to know how to read and write. Each of them is to have two robes annually and to have a small trumpet [*trombettam*] made of silver. Each of them also is to have and possess one horse which is not registered in the cavalry, and it must be worth at least twenty florins of gold. So that these things may be done efficiently the Lord Priors of the Guilds and the Standard Bearer of Justice are bound to and ought to elect two good, respectable citizens of the city of Florence who can put this into effect, and in regard to this they are to have full power to do everything which will be appropriate.[39]

The bannitori often performed from horseback; the reason for the horse was not only to move quickly around the city, but especially to travel to the suburbs and nearby countryside to make their announcements. The procedure was that a bannitore would arrive at a piazza or street intersection in his appointed *sesto* and sound a call on his trumpet three times in order to summon the citizens from their homes or places of work. Once they were gathered, he would read out the official proclamation and then move on to the next location to repeat the process.[40] That the most notable member of this ensemble was the poet Antonio Pucci (died 1388), who was a bannitore for seventeen years,[41] suggests that the position was a quite respectable post, far in excess of what the casual statement of requirements would suggest. It would seem to have required well-educated men of considerable talent.[42]

The bannitori are mentioned here because of the trumpets and because they played a part in civic ceremonies. There is no suggestion that the sounds they made with their trumpets were much more that attention-getting fanfares, which of course was the principal function of the trombadori at this time as well. The difference is that for the bannitori, the trumpet call was solely a way to assemble the citizens for another purpose. For the trombadori, the fanfares and ceremonial sounds were the total reason for their existence, and as we will see below, the trombadori did spawn a distinct musical ensemble at a later date. There are occasional records of someone moving from the bannitori to the trombetti (the ensemble of small trumpets established in 1387), but otherwise that ensemble did not contribute to the artistic musical life of the commune nor did it evolve into anything more artistic. Throughout the period discussed here, the bannitori and their role in civic ceremony remained unchanged. It is probable that they too were involved in ceremonial processions; there are numerous statements in the documents about important visitors to the city who "were met by all the trumpets of the city," and the implication is that this refers to the bannitori as well as the trombadori (otherwise the document would state that they were "met by the trombadori"). The only documentary evidence to support this conclusion is an entry in the *Provvisioni* of 1466, in which the bannitori were directed along with the trombadori and pifferi to perform in the procession of the *tavola* of Santa Maria del Impruneta through the city.[43]

# *The Instruments*

## Trumpets

The principal instrument of the trombadori throughout their existence was a long, straight trumpet. There are a number of different lengths and shapes of trumpets found in the iconography of the late Middle Ages, but those used by the trombadori were undoubtedly the large, straight, ceremonial instruments approximately four and a half to five feet in length, mostly cylindrical, ending in a small flared bell.[44] This is probably the model for the two large instruments depicted by Luca della Robbia in 1431 on one of the panels of the Cantoria in Santa Maria del Fiore (figure 5). A sixteenth-century document describes them according to their weight: "Six trombadori with long silver trumpets of six pounds, six ounces."[45] Although cumbersome and awkward to maneuver, especially on horseback, the trumpets produced a strikingly dramatic image in public with the colorful banner of the commune suspended from them. These instruments, which were the principal ceremonial trumpets of the Gothic pe-

**Example 2.1.** Overtone Series.

riod, are frequently referred to as *buisine* and can be found in iconographical representations from all areas of Europe.[46] In the Florentine records, when there is any possibility of ambiguity, the performers are referred to as trombadori in order to distinguish them from the players of the smaller *trombetta*, the bannitori, and later from the ensemble known as the trombetti, who played shorter instruments. It is believed that the large instruments were capable of sounding only a few notes, perhaps the first four partials of the harmonic series: the fundamental note, its octave, the next octave, and a fourth below the highest pitch (see example 2.1).[47] Beginning late in the fourteenth century, instrument makers developed a method of bending the tubing, which allowed them to produce a number of different shapes, such as an S shape or "folded" forms, shortening the overall length of the instrument for practical purposes while retaining the same quantity of pipe or even extending its length (see figures 5, 6a and 6b, 7, 8, and 9).[48] The bent and folded instruments also were more conical, and it is thought that they were capable of several additional pitches.[49] There is no evidence, however, that the trombadori of Florence adopted any of the new shapes, the reason probably having to do with a reverence for tradition.

By 1316, the *Provvisioni* note the addition to the civic ensemble of a player of the *trombetta*,[50] a smaller straight instrument, undoubtedly the same instrument played by the bannitori. These instruments are described as having half the weight of the larger instruments played by the trombadori: "eight trombetti with long trumpets of three pounds, three ounces [each],"[51] which suggests that trumpets of the trombetti were half the size of the instruments played by the trombadori. The smaller trumpet also was more conical throughout its length and ended in a bell with a flare wider than that of the larger instrument played by the trombadori. It is this instrument, the *trombetta*, that also can be found by the late fourteenth century in a new S shape. From that point forward, trumpets can be found in all three shapes: straight, S, and folded. A late fifteenth-century sculpture by Benedetto da Maiano depicts the instruments of the Florentine trombetti ensemble (not the trombadori) in the S shape, although it is not clear at what point the ensemble adopted instruments with that shape.[52]

It is common in modern discussion to refer to trumpets generically as "brass instruments," and in fact, the modern academic society devoted to their study is called The Historic Brass Society. But brass was not one of the materials used to make trumpets during the late Middle Ages; they were made of horn, wood, silver, copper, and other metal alloys,[53] but not out of brass until the mid-fifteenth century, when a process was developed for processing brass in sheets.[54] Until that time brass could only be cast, which eliminated it as a viable material for making trumpets.[55] As attested by numerous Florentine documents, the trumpets used by the trombadori, trombetti, and bannitori are always specified as being made of silver. Silver was also recorded as the metal of choice for the civic musicians of Venice and Siena, as well as for those in a number of other Italian cities,[56] which establishes the fact that in some areas the material from which a trumpet was made, as evidenced by its color, was considered to have been symbolic (copper or latten, the other possible materials,[57] would have been a dull gold color). Requirement of silver trumpets was not consistent throughout Europe, especially after the mid-fifteenth century development that allowed the use of the much less expensive brass. From that time on, both silver and brass are mentioned with regard to instruments in Germany and the Low Countries, France, and England.[58] In Italy, however, during the period under discussion here, the tradition appears to have been that ceremonial instruments were always made of silver. The tradition may well have had its basis in an Old Testament passage from the Book of Numbers ("Make for yourselves two trumpets out of malleable silver," Numbers 10:2), in which silver is considered to be the sign of divine eloquence.[59]

The earliest-known document to record an order for trumpets is from Arezzo, where silver instruments were commissioned in 1240 for the Holy Roman Emperor Frederick II.[60] As evidence that this tradition continued for several centuries in some north Italian cities, we have not only the specifications for Florentine musicians but also the records of Siena from the early fifteenth century, where the manufacturers are also identified. There were at least two Sienese companies of silversmiths who were entrusted to make instruments for the city. In 1412 the government ordered two silver trumpets for the palace trumpeters from silversmiths Jacomo d'Andreuccio del Mosca and companions, for which the exact weight of the silver was specified. Two years later two additional silver trumpets were ordered to match the earlier pair, this time from Mariano d'Anbruogio and Goro di ser Neroccio. In 1470 the palace silver trombone was sent for repair to Francesco di Antonio and company, goldsmiths, who used silver from an older instrument to repair the new one.[61] Although there are no similar records for Florence, we can speculate that the instruments purchased there also were crafted by local silversmiths,[62] although it is known that in 1469 Lorenzo de' Medici ordered two trumpets and a trombone (presumably for the use of the civic musicians) from Giovanni Bentivoglio in Bologna.[63]

The developments that allowed for the use of brass for trumpets originated near Nuremburg in the early fifteenth century and resulted in that city becoming an important center for the manufacture of trumpets and trombones, supplying instruments for a large number of European courts.[64] By the end of the sixteenth century the standard material for the manufacture of trumpets in Europe, including Italy, was brass sheet,[65] although silver was still used for ceremonial instruments closely attached to monarchs.

## Cennamella

The instrument that was called the *cennamella* (from Latin *calamus*; reed) is a double-reed instrument that is commonly referred to today as a shawm. (In Italy it was also referred to as *ciramella, ciaramella, cemmamella,* and *piffaro,* among other names.) The instrument is thought to have come to Europe from the Middle East; one of its earliest artistic images in Europe appears among the Arabic-style representations in the Spanish manuscripts of the Cantigas of Santa Maria, originating at the court of Alfonso X, "el Sabio," King of Castile in the mid-thirteenth century.[66] As with all instruments, the shawm evolved over the centuries, although the basic, unchanging features were the use of a double reed, the construction from wood, and the use of finger holes (as seen in figures 6b, 8, 10, and 14).[67] A folk version of this instrument, called *cialambella, cialamedda,* or *cialamella,* is still in use in the Italian countryside, especially in Sardegna and Corsica.[68] The iconography from the fourteenth century shows an instrument in the treble range (low note approximately d') with seven finger holes, with a range of approximately two octaves, capable of playing all of the notes of the diatonic scale as well as several of the chromatic pitches. By the end of the century there was also a larger version in the alto range a fifth lower, known as a *bombarda* because the fontanelle and metal rings resembled a canon (figure 10).[69]

It was a common practice throughout Europe to include a shawm among the civic ceremonial musicians; the Florentine trombadori from its earliest documented record always included a player of the *cennamella* (with minor, short-term exceptions), but the actual use of such an instrument among a set of trumpets, drums, and cymbals is far from clear. Iconographical representations of the ensembles rarely depict a lone shawm player in such a scene.[70] In the literary passages that mention the entire ensemble of civic musicians, the reference always appears in a large ceremonial context, such as the following passage from *L'Intelligenza* by an anonymous thirteenth-century Florentine poet:

*Quiv'era una donzella ch'organava*
*ismisurate dolzi melodie,*
*colle squillanti boci che sonava,*
*angelicali e dilettose e pie.*
*Audi'sonar d'un'arpa, e smisurava,*
*cantando un lai come Tristan morìe;*
*d'una dolze viuola udi' sonante,*
*sonando una donzella lo 'ndormante;*
*audivi suon di gighe e ciunfonie.*
*Audivi suon di molto dolzi danze*
*in chitarre, e 'n caribi smisuranti,*
*e trombe, e cennamelle in concordanze,*
*e cembali alamanni assai trianti,*
*cannon mezzi cannoni a smisuranze,*
*sufoli con tambur bene accordanti;*
*audivi d'un leuto ben sonare*
*ribebe, et otricelli, e ceterare,*
*salter e altri stormenti ben sonanti.*[71]

[Here there was a young girl who played on the organ long sweet melodies with the pious, angelic, delightful, and ringing voices. One hears the sound of a harp, [and someone] freely singing a lai about the death of Tristan; and a sweet viola is heard sounding, a young girl playing without rest; and one hears the sound of a violin and an *organistrum*.[72] One hears the sound of many sweet dances on the guitar and enormous *caribi*,[73] and trumpets and shawms playing together, and rather pleasant German cymbals; large and small psalteries in abundance, flutes well coordinated with drums; one hears a well-played lute, rebec, bagpipe[?] and *cetera* [small lute], psaltery, and other instruments well played.]

The scene depicted here is one of a mass of sounding instruments, similar to the sounds of a procession or of a large ceremony, where all of the civic musicians would have gathered together to add excitement to an occasion. But other than this kind of assembly, there is little evidence that all of the civic instrumental musicians performed together on a regular basis. The few notations that cite extra pay for members of the trombadori when they are sent to accompany the military usually list only the trumpet players and occasionally the percussionist; the shawm player is never mentioned in this regard.

Since the shawm has never been considered to be a heraldic instrument, its inclusion among the civic musicians must have had other purposes, although there is very little on which to base speculation as to the duties of the *cennamella* player. The only hint comes from a reference to him as *della sveglia*, a phrase that means "sounding the alarm." The first such mention is in the *Provvisioni registri* of 1296, where the performer is listed as "Gianuccio di Niccolò ... player of the *cennamella*, that is, of the alarm" (*cennamellarius sive de svellia*).[74] In the records of April 4, 1300, his duties are stated as "to hold the office for the benefit of the office or *ministerium* of sounding the *cennamella*, or the alarm, for the commune."[75] A similar reference can be found in the civic statutes of 1325, where again Gianuccio di Niccolò della Svellia is named *cennamellario*.[76] This kind of reference continues in the records of 1347, where the *cennamella* player is listed as "Matteus Johns della svelglia," and in 1376 the position is given to "Grullo Donati, svegliaraino."[77] The case is further complicated by a record at the monastery of Santa Trinita that for a special occasion in 1362, in addition to the usual trio of two trumpet players and a nakers player from the civic *trombadori*, two French musicians were hired: one who played a bagpipe (*cornamusa*), and the other *lo sveglione* and other instruments.[78] There is no indication of the function of any of these instrumentalists, nor why the monastery hired French musicians when the civic ensemble at that time had players of both instruments.

Unfortunately, no further information is given to augment these cryptic references, but as late as the early sixteenth century there is reference to an individual in one of the carnival songs (*canti carnascialeschi*) as a *sveglione*—sounder of the alarm. The instrument he played is called a *ronzolone*, or "buzzer," probably referring to the sound made by the shawm, all of which suggests that whatever the alarm duty was, it continued throughout the period under investigation here:

[Q]*ueste lunghe ronzolone*
*non star punte sonar grette*
*ed ancor queste sveglione*
*far un suon tutte perfette.*[79]

[This long buzzing instrument by no means plays softly, and also this sounder of the alarm makes a most perfect sound.]

The first thing that comes to mind about a sounder of the alarm is the position of tower watchman in medieval Germany and fifteenth-century England, which had to do with watching for danger such as fire or military attack, or sounding the curfew.[80] In Florence, however, this kind of alarm was sounded by the bell-ringers,[81] which means that the duty of the *svegliaraino* must have had to do with some other function—perhaps something akin to the sounding of reveille.

The preceding discussion gives rise to the speculation that the eight members of the early civic musical group probably did not usually serve as a single unit. When the occasion called for *tutti strumenti civici*, as for example in a triumphal procession or *mattinata*, undoubtedly all of the civic instrumentalists, including the *cennamella*, would gather together to add to the festive sound. But it is unlikely that the usual daily assignments required the *cennamella* player to join the trumpeters and percussion players for their heraldic functions. It is more probable that the listing of the *cennamella* player with the trombadori meant only that he was one of the musicians employed by the Commune of Florence; an accounting and bookkeeping practice that was not intended to convey any performance implications. During the fourteenth century the player of the *cennamella* is usually paid more than the other members of the ensemble, although the reason for this is never stated.

To add yet another confusing aspect to the question of the *cennamella* and its function, following the significant changes to the civic musical establishment in the 1380s (see below, chapter 4), the list of trombadori continued to include a player of the *cennamella*, always referring to him as a *cennamellario* (or *svegliaraino*), while at the same time a separate group of players was instituted, the pifferi, which included two different sizes of shawms that were referred to in the pay records variously as *ciramelle*, *cornette sive ciramelle*, and *bombarde*, as well as *cennamelle*. At the same time, the reed instrument in the trombadori was never called by any of the other names used for the instruments of the pifferi—it is only referred to as a "*cennamella*."[82] This is true also in a sixteenth-century document that describes the officials in procession: the shawm player with the trombadori and *naccherario* is "a musician who plays the bronze [-colored] *ciambanelle*, with a long red and white tassel and with a silver sword at his side."[83] But a few lines later in the same document the shawms of the pifferi are referred to only as "pifferi," without further description: "Four pifferi and two trombones of silver."[84]

Two possible answers come to mind as an explanation for the differences in the names given to what usually has been assumed to be the same instrument in the two ensembles. One possibility is that just as with the several different names for trumpets, the variety of names for the shawm referred not to different instruments but to different functions: *cennamella* would normally refer to a shawm that was played by a member of the trombadori, who had "sounding the alarm" (i.e., signaling) as his most characteristic duty. The names referring to the instruments played by the pifferi, on the other hand, would have referred to their function as part of an ensemble that played a different repertory, including music for dancing and other more artistic occasions, described in detail in the following chapters.

At the same time, we should also consider the possibility that the two instruments may not have been physically identical. In one of his poems on the seasons, the fourteenth-century Sienese poet Folgore da San Gimignano describes a scene in which the nobles "sing and dance in the style of Provence while listening to the music of new instruments from Germany ("danzare e cantare a la provenzalescha / udi nuovi stormenti di la mangnia").[85] At least one of the new dance instruments brought by the *oltramontani* was a double-reed instrument that looked a bit different from that used by Italians. From iconography we know that the details of shape of the fifteenth-century shawm are not the same as those of the present-day folk *cialamella*, and these differences could well have existed in the late fourteenth century. Although the instruments in question were both double reeds with similar ranges, the difference in their appearances may well have been sufficient to warrant different names:[86] the Italian instrument would continue to be known as a *cennamella*, whereas the new instrument from Germany was called a "piffaro," after the name given to those who played it. Evidence in favor of this speculation can be found in the reference to a trio of German *pifferi* playing shawms and bagpipe who were visiting Florence in 1384 and were noted in the *Provvisioni registri* to have played a *cornamusa* and other instruments.[87] Apparently the scribe did not recognize the "other instruments" as being the same as the *cennamella* played by the musician in the civic trombadori.

To add to the complexity and uncertainty about this issue, in present-day rural Italy where the instrument is still played, the word *cialambella* is also one of the names for a bagpipe.[88] It is not likely that the word *cennamella* (and its related forms) was used to refer to the bagpipe in late-medieval Florence, but the later tradition reminds us that instruments are named as often for their function or mode of sound production as for their specific sound properties or physical appearances. Since both shawm and bagpipe use a reed, on that level they would be the same. (See below for additional speculation as to the function of the *cennamella* player.)

## Cornamusa

In 1356 a player of the *cornamusa* was added to the trombadori, a position that lasted until the 1380s, when the *cornamusa* was removed from the trombadori to become part of the newly formed pifferi ensemble. The instrument referred to as a *cornamusa* is undoubtedly a bagpipe. In images throughout Europe from the mid-fourteenth through to the sixteenth century, a duo of shawm and bag-pipe was commonly depicted, often in the company of dancers (figure 10).[89] It would seem that not only were these two instruments often paired together, but also that at least one Florentine musician could play both: the person first appointed to play *cornamusa* in the trombadori was Luca di Silvestro, who began in 1357[90] and continued for forty-four years as a member of that ensemble until replaced by Silvestro di Luca in 1401,[91] undoubtedly his son. In 1386, however, when the *cornamusa* was removed from the trombadori, Luca remained in the ensemble but as player of the *cennamella*. The *cennamella* player he replaced at that point was Grullo di Donati, who is later listed as a member of the pifferi, where he played with the two other pifferi.[92] (Although we know that the ensemble at that time was made up of two shawms and a *cornamusa* and we know the names of the musicians, the records do not specify which of the instruments each musician played.)

Nothing is ever stated in the Florentine documents to suggest what was the function of the bagpipe in the civic ensemble, but given the popularity of the bagpipe as a melodic instrument for dancing, both alone and in duet with a shawm, it is probable that providing dance music for a number of civic social occasions may well have been part of the duties of the civic *cornamusa* player—perhaps the major part, given the large number of festive occasions that included dancing. Again, as in the case of the *cennamella* player, although the *cornamusa* was always listed with the trombadori in the fourteenth century, there is little evidence that reed instruments usually played with trumpets. Noting that the *cornamusa* was a member of the pifferi at the end of the century—also in the company of shawms—brings up the possibility that from the initial appointment of the *cornamusa* in the mid-fourteenth century, the two instruments, bagpipe and shawm, may have performed as a musical duet. (This function is also implied in the hiring of the two French musicians at Santa Trinita in 1362, see above.) Noting that a large number of the regularly scheduled civic festas involved dancing, and that initially the only civic musicians whose instruments lent themselves to dance music were the percussionist and the *cennamella* player, one can easily imagine that by the 1350s there was a strong need for another dance instrument, the bagpipe, to be added to the ensemble.

To continue with this line of speculation, given the similarity of playing technique on both bagpipe and shawm, it may well have been the case that from the beginning the reed instrument player appointed to the civic ensemble could play both instruments, the choice depending on the particular occasion (bagpipe being preferred for dances, shawm for the *sveglia* duties). In that case, the appointment of an additional reed player in 1356 may have been another acknowledgment of the increasing number of festive occasions for which dance music was needed. The more detailed information available about the musical activities of the *cennamella* and *cornamusa* once they are a part of the pifferi in the 1380s raises the suspicion that they may well have had a far more extensive musical repertory and function much earlier than has been believed, performing on a number of more social—as opposed to ceremonial—civic occasions. As Davidsohn concluded, from the middle of the fourteenth century, the Mensa of the Signoria (the noontime and evening meals of the Priors and Gonfaloniere) became increasingly more elaborate, including regular performances by the civic herald.[93] As will be seen in the following chapters, by the end of the fourteenth century the civic pifferi were also daily participants at the Mensa, and so it is not difficult to imagine that the mid-century addition of the *cornamusa* to the civic music ensemble may well have had several purposes, including performance duties at the private Mensa of the executives of the government as well as dances on public festive occasions.

## Percussion Instruments

The earliest records of the trombadori include a single percussionist, a player of the cymbals (*cimbalellario*).[94] In 1304 a nakers player (*naccherario*)—a player of a pair of small "kettle" drums hung from his belt or over the neck of a horse—was added to the ensemble. A description of the nakers player in procession mentions that he wore a cloth draped over him and his instrument: "One *naccherino* who sounded nakers, [adorned] with a cloth drape with two *gigli* and a cross in the middle, and which covered the nakers."[95] (Figure 7 shows what is described.) The nakers player remained in the ensemble throughout the period, but the position of cymbals player was discontinued in 1350. The purpose of the percussion was undoubtedly to enhance the ceremonial effect of the trumpet fanfares. We should be aware, however, that the instrument named in the pay records—cymbals or nakers—was not necessarily the only percussion instrument played by that performer. The named instrument probably was the principal assignment, but anyone skilled at either instrument undoubtedly was capable of playing other percussion instruments as well should the need call for it, as for example a large tabor for a military assignment, or a tambourine for dancing. The *Provvisioni registri* for June 19, 1298, which appoints Matteo as cymbals player, states that "Matteus knows very well how to play the *cemballellas* . . . and other instruments as well."[96] Confirmation of this versatility is found in 1305 when a new member, Cascio, is appointed as player of the cymbals and Matteo moves to the new position of *naccherario*.[97]

# Changes to the Ensemble during the Fourteenth Century

The 1317 appointment of a player of the small trumpet to the trombadori, noted earlier, may also be considered to have marked a change of some type to the ceremonial practices, or more likely, additions to the duties. From the first mention of a *trombetta* in 1317 until the establishment of a separate ensemble of small trumpets (the trombetti) in the 1380s, there was always at least one *trombetta* in the trombadori (during the years 1347–51 there were two). The purpose of this addition is never stated, but it is more than likely that the single *trombetta* did not usually serve with the six large trumpets—neither written records nor iconographical representations attest to the mixture of small and large trumpets as a regular functioning group (although for major ceremonial processions all the civic instrumentalists would have performed). Only a single piece of documentary evidence discusses a particular use of the *trombetta*, and that is in conjunction with the military: a petition of 1371 from Francesco di Lapo, player of the *trombetta*, complains about his pay for the seventy-three days he spent the previous fall in Lombardy serving under Captain Manno de Donatis.[98] The document does not mention any other member of the ensemble sent with the military on this occasion, and so we may conclude that he served as a lone signalman. Since later in the century the purpose of appointing a separate ensemble of *trombette* was to represent the Priors (see chapter 4), it is also possible that this was a part of the intention in 1317—that at least one of the duties of the new *trombetta* player was specifically to represent the Priors as part of their symbol of authority. The pay records always name the *trombetta* player separately from the players of large trumpets, and the notices of appointment after 1356 often separate both the *trombetta* and *cornamusa* from the other members, placing their names in a separate column or on a separate part of the page, which may be an indication that their duties were not the same as the players of large trumpets.

The shorter *trombette* and the new shapes that were developed later in the century brought with them the potential of a more varied selection of notes and much higher sounds than their longer, more cylindrical counterparts. Although the longer instruments played by the trombadori probably played only a few notes, it is thought that the shorter instruments were capable of playing many more notes, perhaps as high as the eighth partial in the harmonic series (see example 2.1), although there is no secure knowledge of exactly what were

Table 2.1. Makeup of the Civic Trombadori Ensemble, 1292–1530

| Year | Large Trumpets | Small Trumpets | Cennamella | Percussion | Bagpipe |
|------|------|------|------|------|------|
| 1292 | 6 | | 1 | cymbals | |
| 1295 | 6 | | 1 | cymbals | |
| 1298 | 6 | | 1 | cymbals | |
| 1300 | 6 | | 1 | | |
| 1304 | 6 | | 1 | cymbals, nakers | |
| 1317 | 6 | 1 | 1 | cymbals, nakers | |
| 1320 | 6 | 1 | 1 | cymbals, nakers | |
| 1324 | 6 | 1 | 1 | cymbals, nakers | |
| 1331 | 6 | 1 | 1 | cymbals, nakers | |
| 1346 | 6 | 1 | 1 | nakers | |
| 1347 | 6 | 2 | 1 | cymbals, nakers | |
| 1350 | 6 | 2 | 1 | cymbals, nakers | |
| 1353 | 6 | 1 | 1 | nakers | |
| 1355 | 6 | | 1 | nakers | |
| 1357 | 6 | 1 | 1 | nakers | 1 |
| 1358 | 6 | | 1 | nakers | 1 |
| 1375 | 6 | 1 | 1 | nakers | 1 |
| 1386 | 6 | 1 | 1 | nakers | |
| 1390 | 6 | | 1 | nakers | |
| 1450 | 6 | | 1 | nakers | |
| 1475 | 6 | | 1 | nakers | |
| 1500 | 6 | | 1 | nakers | |
| 1530 | 6 | | 1 | nakers | |

the ranges of these earlier instruments.[99] In any case, even if the *trombette* could play only the first several partials, the smaller size of the instruments means that the sounds would have been higher than those of the trombadori. Whereas the function of the long straight trumpets performing alone could be assumed to be entirely heraldic and limited to four relatively low pitches, when coupled with the higher pitches of the shorter *trombette* during major ceremonies and processions, the combination of low and high sounds would have been quite stirring.

By the early fifteenth century the sound potential of trumpets was further extended with the addition of a slide mechanism that eventually led to the instrument we know as a trombone. During the last third of the fourteenth century a telescoping pipe was attached to some instruments at the mouthpiece which enabled the new instrument, a slide trumpet, to perform the entire chromatic scale, a clear indication that this new instrument was intended to function in a repertory more extensive than fanfares and heraldic sounds.[100]

# The Members of the Instrumental Ensembles

The documents suggest that throughout the existence of the trombadori, all of its members were Italians, and probably local. This is certainly true of the bannitori, who, according to the statute cited above, were to be Florentines. The practice in the pay records for the trombadori was to identify by city of origin any foreigners (meaning anyone from outside of Florence), whereas the locals are usually identified according to the *sesto* or the parish of their residence. In the earliest records five members of the trombadori are identified as living in San Lorenzo, and one each in San Paulo, San Piero Maggiore, and San Felice in Piazza.[101] In other cases the musicians are simply identified as Florentines, as for example in the 1367 appointments of the small trumpet and bagpipe: Francesco Lapo de Florentia, *trombectino*, and Luca di Silvestro de Florentia, *cornamuse*.[102] Many of the members remained in the ensemble for a number of years. The most notable of the earliest recorded members are Gianucio di Niccolò, who played the *cennamella* for over forty years, appearing in the earliest record of 1292 and retiring in 1332, and as noted above, the bagpipe player Luca di Silvestro, who played for forty-four years, beginning in1357 and remaining in the ensemble until replaced by his son, Silvestro di Luca, in 1401.

In summary, we can note that throughout the first one hundred years of the Republic, Florence was represented ceremonially by an ensemble of eight or nine instrumentalists, mostly trumpet players, who were employed to establish by sight and sound the majesty of the city and its government. They also lent ceremonial pomp and excitement to all festive occasions: processions, presentations, jousts, games, as well as some sacred feasts; they accompanied the military and represented the city of Florence at celebrations in other cities. The trumpet-playing bannitori, whose main duty was more functional than celebratory, could also be called upon to add to the general sound mass on the most festive occasions. As well, the presence of a shawm in the trombadori from the very beginning and a bagpipe from the mid-fourteenth century suggests that the responsibility of the civic instrumentalists may also have increasingly involved providing music for dancing. These functions, which undoubtedly began before the establishment of the Republic, continued on throughout the period and beyond as the civic musical ensembles continued to grow in number, variety, and repertory in response to the evolving needs of the city.

# 3

# The Civic Herald

The civic herald was one of the most visible figures in ceremonial Florence. He was present at all official ceremonies, featured prominently in a role that could best be described as master of ceremonies.[1] His obligations included writing and singing poetry on the most formal of these occasions, and until the end of the fourteenth century he was the only musician on the civic payroll other than the trombadori. The post of herald, which undoubtedly existed at least unofficially throughout the thirteenth century, lasted well into the period of the grand dukes. While the position underwent a number of changes in title and combinations of duties over the fourteenth and fifteenth centuries, it always contained the principal duty of the ceremonial poet-singer.[2] In the earliest official documents that record such a post, the civic statutes of 1322–25, it is referred to as *istrio* (actor), but it is clear from the stated duties that this is the post that 130 years later would be called herald. The actual title *araldo* is not found officially until the appointment of Francesco Filarete in 1456, although a decade earlier Anselmo di Giovacchino Calderoni (herald 1442–46) referred to himself unofficially as the civic herald in one of his verses: "Io son Araldo al popol fiorentino,"[3] and one of the poems he performed at the Certame Coronario in 1441 includes the line, "sarà 'l mio frutto; ma pur come araldo," referring to the post he held at that time in Urbino.[4]

In the mid-fourteenth century the duties associated with the office of the herald were combined with supervisory tasks, which were gradually lessened as the ceremonial aspects of the position grew. From the beginning, however, the responsibility of the herald was supervision of the practical arrangements necessary to assure the proper decorum at official ceremonies, into which the holder of the position entered as a full participant, that is, as the master of ceremonies. Given the importance of ceremony in Florence, the position was always one of enormous responsibility, and was recognized as such. The civic herald was chosen by the Priors. Initially he was attached to the office of the Podestà, although eventually the appointment was transferred to the staff (*famiglia*) of the Signoria. But it is clear that from its beginning, the position of herald was understood to be different from the other members of the staff, who were recruited from the lower levels of society. As we shall see below, the appointee was always a highly educated and multi-talented person, and the earliest official documents referred to the herald/*istrio* as *cavaliere*, meaning that he was knighted, an honor not bestowed on other members of the *famiglia*.[5]

The herald played a major role in the planning and execution of civic ceremonies, animating them (thus the original title of *istrio*),[6] and both composing and singing appropriate verse in honor of the occasion. Soon after the establishment of the Priorate, a major portion of the herald's singing duties took place at the daily Mensa of the Signoria, where he performed while the executives of government took their meals in their private dining room in the Palazzo della Signoria. The position occasionally involved serving as a member of the entourage of a Florentine ambassador, or on some occasions even acting as an ambassador to other communities, where the herald, often in the company of members of the civic musical ensembles, represented Florence.[7] In addition, most of the heralds were also involved to some extent in dramatic productions, including *sacre rappresentazioni*.[8]

The earliest recorded appointment to the position appears in the *Provvisioni registri* of 1333:

> Likewise, the above-mentioned Priors of the Guilds and the Standard Bearer of Justice, noticing that in any (as it were) noble city, as much in the province of Lombardy as in Tuscany, there are skillful singers for their recreation and delight, to whom vestments are given by their Rectors in honor of the cities and those Rectors, and among other eminent and skillful singers Lord Percival, son of the late Gianni, is said to number, who is living in the city of Florence, and is so valued in the daily exercise of his craft here. In honor of the said city, and for the recreation and delight of her citizens, it is thought fitting for such men to be provided with vestments, as in other noble cities. After first careful consulta-

tion was held about these things among the Twelve Good Men, and not until, according to the form of the statute, when the action was set forth, and the division was held, and the secret examination according to the black and white beans was carried through by the authority of the office and the matter and in all ways, and of the right by which they more beneficially hold their power, did they foresee, arrange, and determine that the honorable Podestà, and the Captain and Defender of the people and Commune of Florence are to be held and obligated to give to the said Sir Percival and to deliver within three months present and future after entry to their office one honorable robe of that Podestà or Captain for his use. And that in the letters which should be sent to such a Podestà, or to a Captain and Defender, of the notification of election of such a Podestà, or of such a Captain and Defender, let the above be inserted. But if the said Lord Podestà, or the said Captain and Defender will not observe the above, and do not quickly deliver or give the promised robe to the Lord Percival (on behalf of either of them) as it is promised, the treasurers in the treasury of the Commune of Florence legally, freely, and with impunity ought to, and will withhold from the salaries owed by the Commune to the same Podestà, and the Captain and Defender (no matter which of them offends) ten gold florins, which will be released, delivered, and given freely to the Lord Percival himself, for the permitted reasons.[9]

Although the wording makes it clear that this is the initiation of the official position of *istrio*, it is certainly not the beginning of the tradition. It is probable that this is neither the first appearance nor even the first appointment of an *istrio* in Florence. A statement from approximately ten years earlier in the civic statutes of 1322–25 forbids the Podestà or any one in his office from allowing others to make such an appointment.

> That the Podestà may not ask anyone to give vestments.
>
> It is decreed and ordained that neither the Podestà of Florence, nor anyone from his household, can neither request, nor is permitted to ask of any citizen or inhabitant of the *contado* of Florence that they give their vestments or robe to any *istrio*; and if they should do the contrary, they [i.e., the Podestà or any member of his household] are to lose two hundred lire from their wages. And this is understood to apply likewise to the Captain of the Commune of Florence, and to any foreign official of the above said Commune.[10]

Looking at both statements, it is possible to see that the issue here is not the establishment of a civic herald, but an attempt to limit the association of the herald to the household of the Podestà by insisting that the vestments he is to wear be from that office. From the tone of the prohibition in the statute it would seem that the Podestà must have been farming out the position to various elite families, allowing them to dress the herald in their family colors, whereas the

Priors were insisting that he remain exclusively associated with the office of the Podestà by wearing only the vestments of that household.[11] Why the Podestà would have wanted to do this is not stated, but the first motive that comes to mind is financial—that the person whose colors were worn by the herald also paid his wages. Whatever the reason, the statute insists that the *istrio* can only wear the robe of the Podestà, thus establishing the presence of an *istrio* at least as early as 1325.

It is highly probable that there had been a function such as that performed by the *istrio* associated with the office of the Podestà from before the institution of the Priorate, as a part of the ceremonial trappings of the office of the ruler of Florence, although as the statute suggests, the way in which it was administered had been quite loose. The 1325 statutes of the Podestà were drawn up shortly after full control of the city had been returned to the Florentines following nine years of Neapolitan dominance (1313–22). On the departure from the city of the representatives of King Robert of Naples, the Florentines made a number of moves to reclaim their authority over the city and to reassert the power of the Priorate as the supreme executive, as for example by reinstituting the office of Capitano del Popolo, an office that had been suspended during the Neapolitan presence.[12] The insistence that the civic herald should only be associated with the office of the Podestà can be seen as one more step in the strengthening of the powers of the Priorate and the tightening of its controls over the office of the Podestà.

The post of herald as part of the ceremonial practices in courts and cities throughout Europe was a tradition of long standing. In the north it was closely tied to tournaments and to the servants who touted—heralded—the deeds of their knights.[13] There was always a close link between the herald and the singing minstrel inasmuch as the praises usually took the form of sung poetry, although the two functions usually were not performed by the same person.[14] This clearly was the background of the Italian tradition, and although it always involved some connection with tournaments, the details were somewhat different from the northern practice in that it involved a single performer and a much stronger emphasis on sung poetry. In that respect a close relationship can be seen with the tradition of the troubadours, who practiced their art in the cities and courts of southern France and in northern Italy, although the subject matter of troubadour poetry mostly concerned aspects of courtly love. The Italian tradition was that of the *cantastoria* (singer of history/stories), whose performances included a much broader range of subject matter. This tradition was more closely allied to that of the ancient village bard, the poet-singer who tells tales of the past, relates the news of the day, and comments on all types of subjects. In the late Middle Ages the practice of the *cantastoria* was uniquely Italian and extremely popular, and thus it is reasonable to think that officially or unofficially, someone would have carried on the tradition via the position of herald in Florence from at least as early as the mid-thirteenth century, and perhaps much earlier.[15]

It would not have been essential that an officially appointed poet be employed by the city to act only in that capacity, or in fact that he be employed at all, in order to carry out those duties. It could just as easily have been done on an ad hoc basis whenever the need arose (in a manner similar to the early employment of instrumental musicians as discussed in chapter 2). Given the popularity of poetry in Tuscany and the presence of so many fine poets in Florence, possible unofficial candidates for the performance of such a role during the thirteenth century are numerous. One such candidate would be Brunetto Latini (ca. 1220–94), poet, orator, political activist, and the first permanent Chancellor of Florence, who perhaps not incidentally wrote the following lines in his *Il Tesoretto:*

> *Hacci gente di corte*
> *che sono use ed acorte*
> *a sollazzar la gente,*
> *ma domandan sovente*
> *danari e vestimenti.*
> *certo, se tu ti senti*
> *lo poder di donare,*
> *ben déi corteseggiare.*[16]

> [There are men of the court who are capable of entertaining the people although they demand money and clothing for this. Certainly if you feel yourself capable of giving you should shower them with kindness.]

Because of his renown as a poet as well as his presence in the government, Latini would have been an obvious choice to compose and perform poetry on celebratory occasions. But there were many other Florentine poets who wrote in the vernacular and who aimed their works at the general population, as distinguished from those whose poetry was more suited for courtly circles; a distinction made by Dante in his description of the Tuscan vernacular poets in his *De vulgari eloquentia.*

> After this we come to the Tuscans, who, rendered senseless by some aberration of their own, seem to lay claim to the honor of possessing the illustrious vernacular. And it is not only the common people who lose their heads in this fashion, for we find that a number of famous men have believed as much: like

Guittone d'Arezzo, who never even aimed at a vernacular worthy of the court, or Bonagiuta da Lucca, or Gallo of Pisa, or Mino Mocato of Siena, or Brunetto [Latini] the Florentine, all of whose poetry, if there were space to study it closely here, we would find to be fitted not for a court but at best for a civic function [*municipalia*].[17]

The distinction of the work of certain Tuscans as "civic'"(*municipalia*) has been interpreted by literary scholars as Dante's way of grouping these men stylistically with other, older Tuscan poets in order to differentiate that group from those who wrote in the "new style."[18] As the present discussion suggests, however, the label probably was far more specific, intended to single out those poets whose works functioned on a public, civic level, in the tradition of the public poet-singers known as *cantastoria* and *cantimpanca* described below.[19]

Giovanni Villani, writing some fifty years after Latini's death, noted that one of Latini's contributions to Florence was to make the citizens aware of the importance of good speech, again associating him with public performance:

> In Florence in the year 1294 an illustrious citizen named Sir Brunetto Latini died, and he was a great philosopher and a consummate master of rhetoric, mastering the art of eloquence [*dittatore*]. And he was of those who taught Cicero's *Rhetoric*, and he wrote a good and useful book ... and was a chancellor of our commune. He was an earthly man, but we mentioned him because he was the instigator and master in refining the Florentines, and making them aware of speaking well and in leading and governing our republic according to Politics.[20]

Villani's word *dittatore* can be understood as a reference not just to the oration of prose, but also to poetry presented in song, as discussed below in relation to other poets. Later documents indicate that civic chancellors usually played an active part in ceremonial functions,[21] a tradition that could have begun with the first person to hold the post. But Latini would not have been the only available poet in civic office at the end of the thirteenth century. Another notable poet was Guido Cavalcanti (ca. 1250–1300), who was elected to public office in 1284 and again in 1290.[22] In fact, during the first several decades of the Republic, writers whose work would answer to Dante's classification of "civic poets" numbered significantly among those chosen for the offices of Prior and Gonfaloniere, enlarging the possible selection of capable dignitaries who would have been part of the government executive and thus well placed to serve in the capacity of herald or civic poet on any significant occasion. Possible early candidates include the poets Pacino di Ser Filippi Angiolieri (Gonfaloniere 1294–95); Lapo Saltarelli

(Prior 1292); Dino Compagni (Prior three times and Gonfaloniere once between 1289 and 1301); and Dante himself (Prior in 1300).[23]

Rather than marking the first appearance of a herald in Florence, therefore, the 1333 document appointing Sir Percival might better be understood as the first time that it was the Signori who officially appointed an *istrio*, another step toward control of civic functions similar to that taken in 1292 with reference to the other public ceremonial symbol, the trombadori. Another possibility is that the 1333 appointment may also have signaled the time when the need was felt for a permanent, as opposed to an ad hoc, appointment to these ceremonial duties, reflecting an increase in the quantity of ceremonial occasions. What is not probable is that prior to this document the ceremonial tradition of the city of Florence had lacked a poet-musician—whatever his status or title. The long-standing tradition of such a custom in northern Italy and the Florentine respect for such ceremonial traditions argue for a long and continuous history of a civic herald.

The 1333 document indicates that even though the Signoria is making the appointment, the *istrio* is still to be attached to the office of the Podestà. Further, the document notes that the newly appointed *istrio* was a knight (as was Latini),[24] indicated in the *Provvisione* by the honorific *domino*, and that he was to be given an official robe, similar to other prominent members of that office, the Podestà and Captain, who also were knights. (The cause of the extended discussion in the *Provvisione* as to what would result if the Podestà refused or neglected to bestow the official robe is unclear, but it seems to suggest that the Priors were not confident that the Podestà would immediately agree that the Priors should be appointing someone to this office. Is it possible that at this late date, fifty-one years after the establishment of the Priorate as the supreme ruling body, that the Podestà was still resisting certain aspects of the realignment of power and authority? I cannot think of another motive for the discussion.)

A glimpse of the larger picture of the poet-singers, as well as the position and activities of the civic herald, is provided by several of the statements in the 1333 *Provvisione* appointment of Percival. The recognition that there were similar posts in other cities in Lombardy and Tuscany hints at the breadth of the tradition. In fact, the popularity of the art of *cantare all'improvviso* in Florence was such that throughout the era the city continued to produce a large number of poet-singers; it was a training ground for numerous gifted performers who found work in other civic centers such as Siena, Perugia, and Urbino.[25] It is surprising, therefore, that in their 1333 appointment, instead of choosing one of the many local poets, the Priors chose Percival, apparently a visitor who had been performing in the city. Given the probable level of competition for the position, Percival must have been exceptionally talented, as the appointment suggests. There is a hint in the wording of the appointment that he had probably already been the de facto *istrio*, performing on an informal basis, and therefore the purpose of the document was threefold: 1) to make the position official and full-time, in imitation of other communities, by creating a permanent position within the civic government; 2) to institute such a post at the level of a knight; 3) and possibly, to assert the right of the Priors to make such an appointment to the office of the Podestà.

The name of the new herald, Percival, is probably a stage name rather than a true given name. It is likely a reference to the Grail knight Percival, found in several of the European literary traditions. In Italian literature the name Percival is often associated with people from Genoa, which is a possible clue to Percival's place of origin (he is not otherwise identified, and nothing more is known of him). [26] Villani's *Nuova cronica* includes references to a "Percival" in the context of a Genoese involved in Florence in the year 1286, [27] and in Franco Sacchetti's novella 144, "Messer Prinzivalle" is one of two Genoese described as "very amusing men, lesser courtiers who often made entertainments to amuse their masters," [28] an apt description of a person to be chosen as the herald of Florence. In taking the name Percival, therefore, the newly appointed herald may well have been intentionally linking the position to the long-lasting practices of the ancient village bard and the medieval minstrel. [29] Ezio Levi makes a case for Italy receiving influence in this matter from the jongleurs of France, many of whom practiced their art in northern Italy during the late Middle Ages. [30] In the early thirteenth century the noted troubadour Raimbaut de Vaqueiras composed verses about courtly life in Monferrato, [31] and other troubadours are known to have worked at the Malaspina court of Lunigiana, as well as at other places in the Veneto and Lombardy regions. [32] The tradition is portrayed in the twelfth-century *Roman de la rose* by Jean Renart, where the many talents of a jongleur named Juglet are described:

> *Il ert sages et de grant pris*
> *et s'avoit oï et apris*
> *mainte chançon et maint biau conte.*
>
> [He was intelligent and of great renown, having heard and learned many songs and many a fine story.] [33]

The same poem describes other jongleurs—sometimes called minstrels—who played and sang while recounting stories, and significantly, mentions the tale of Percival:

*lors vindrent li menesterel.*
*Li uns note un, li autres el,*
*cil conte ci de Perceval,*
*cil raconte de Rainceval,*
*par les rens devant les barons.*

[Then entered the minstrels. This one played one piece, that one another, one performed the story of Percival, another that of Roncevaux, circulating through the rows of barons.][34]

Recently, the activities of the fictitious jongleurs described in the poem have been related directly to those of actual jongleurs and minstrels in both secular and sacred settings during the twelfth and thirteenth centuries, indicating how widespread this tradition was and how central a role it played in society.[35] There is reason to believe that the custom of a singing poet originated even earlier, having a heritage in Italy that can be traced to both the practices of peasant Tuscany and those of classical antiquity.[36] Civic records from the thirteenth century make it clear that many Italian cities had a strong tradition of employing minstrels on a number of public and private occasions. San Gimignano documents from as early as 1231 record payment to several *joculatori* in the service of the Podestà,[37] and in 1276 both *istrionibus* and *giullari* are recorded in his service.[38] A *buffone di corte* is recorded at the court of Carlo II in Naples in 1299,[39] and in Siena the employment of this kind of entertainer for private feasts had become so popular by the late thirteenth century that a law was issued to regulate their number.[40] Italian references to a singer in the style described here as that of the herald often employ the words *cantastoria* (singer of tales), *canterino* (singer), and *cantimpanca* (*panca* refers to a raised platform on which the performer often stood as he sang; see figure 11).[41]

The earliest known *canterino* named as such is one Jacopino in Verona in 1227, although *joculatures* are recorded in that city from as early as 1168. A *cantimpanca* functioned in Bologna in 1289, and similar references can be found throughout the fourteenth century in Siena, Pisa, and Lucca, to name only a few of the north Italian cities where such activity flourished.[42] Davidsohn notes that in Florence during the mid-thirteenth century, minstrels and actors were closely associated with the festivals of the Ghibellini, which then resulted in their lack of popularity among the Guelfa once the latter came to power.[43] This did not totally discourage performances—minstrels were present in Florence at the feast of San Giovanni in 1290.[44] And in fact, the political issue itself appears to have affected only the more popular types of celebrations. As the evidence below will strongly suggest, it is highly unlikely that the Guelfa aversion to the inclusion of minstrels on Ghibelline social occasions would have affected the ceremonial tradition of the city and the function of the civic herald.

There has been considerable disagreement among scholars of social history and Italian literature as to whether the performers of late medieval poetry, including improvisers such as the herald, sang or spoke. Evidence that the tradition of presenting poetry in improvised song was practiced even in conjunction with the most elevated literature can be seen in many of the texts themselves, as for example in the *Aeneid*, written in the century before Christ by the Mantuan poet Virgil, which begins with the line "Arma virumque cano" ("I sing of arms and men"). Internal proof that in thirteenth- and fourteenth-century Italy even the most sophisticated poetry was still intended to be sung in this manner can be found in the works of Dante and Petrarch, where there are clear references to singing the poetry.[45] Franco Sacchetti's novella 114, for example, concerns an incident in which Dante encounters a blacksmith who is singing his verses in the free style in which one would sing a song. Dante scolds him, not for singing the poetry, but for not singing it in the way this type of poetry was intended.[46] In Dante's *Vita nuova*, Amore instructs the poet that his *ballate* should "be accompanied by gentle harmony" ("falle adornare di soave armonia").[47] Relevant to this subject is the statement by Alberico da Rosciate from Bergamo, written between 1343 and 1349, explaining in a prologue to the first canto of Dante's *Inferno* the origin and nature of the word *commedia*, which, he points out, according to ancient tracts was delivered to the sound of a flute (*fistula*):

> Then comic actors appeared, that is, colleagues who together recited comedies, that is, [stories] of the great things that occurred, the first actor singing, the second answering and responding to the first. And these actors are in our tradition and appear mostly in parts of Lombardy where there are [also] some singers who sing of the deeds of great lords in rhyme, the first declaring and the second answering.[48]

According to Alberico, therefore, there was a style of presenting a *commedia* that involved two actors alternately singing the text, a practice he tells us was mostly found in Lombardy. I conclude that the novelty of the practice has to do with the presence of two singers, whereas the norm would have been for only one presenter to sing the lines. But in both practices, the lines were sung. (It is interesting that the writer singles out Lombardy for the two-singer tradition since in their appointment of Percival, the Florentine Signori also mention Lombardy as having a strong *cantare* tradition.)[49] There is no evidence that during the period in question poetry was commonly spoken rather than sung; it would seem that that concept is from a much later time.[50]

Much of the confusion concerning the performance of the herald and other singer-reciters centers around the meaning of the word *recitare*, which is found in some of the archival and narrative records describing the activity, and is compounded by the duties of the office, which included the presentation of both prose and poetry. All of the appointees were both orators and poets (and many of them were playwrights as well). The confusion as to how they presented their material originates with modern scholars who equate *recitare* with the modern English "recite," coupled with the assumption that the common practice of later centuries—of presenting poetry in a spoken format—was also the custom in the late Middle Ages.[51] *Recitare*, however, has a far wider set of meanings, including that of *recitativo* in opera, where it refers not to spoken delivery but to a type of singing that employs a relatively simple and perfunctory melodic setting of text, as distinguished from the more flamboyant melodic types known as *aria*, *arioso*, and so on. (There is also some evidence that even when orating prose the presentation would have been sung; see below.)

There are ample citations in the documents of the period that make it clear that the herald actually did sing his verse—as did the *cantastoria*—but it would seem that then, as now, writers have difficulty finding terms that distinguish between full-blown melody and the more modest melodic form such as that employed in a simple psalm-tone setting. It is this latter style that is the probable basic mode of performance for the herald, in which the melodic content is more or less subservient to that of the text.[52] An example of the ambiguity of reference can be seen in one of the documents that records payment to the early fifteenth-century Florentine herald Antonio di Matteo di Meglio (herald 1417–42), which refers to him on one page as "singer [*cantatore*] of moral verses at the Mensa of the Signori" and on the next as "chanter [*recitatore*] of canzonas and moral verses and other similar things."[53] Earlier, Jacopo Salimbene (herald 1352–75), is referred to in a 1354 document as "Jacopo delle Parole,"[54] while his last appointment in 1375 mentions his ability to "adorn appropriate words with delightful sounds"; clearly a reference to his ability to improvise a melodious vocal line for the poetry as well as praise for his ability as an orator.[55] A year later he is described as "chanting [*recitando*] moral songs and sonnets, and many other useful, beautiful, worthy and most pleasing compositions."[56]

Even clearer is the statement appointing Antonio di Piero di Friano to the position of civic herald in 1393, on the death of Giovanni di Giorgio da Trebbio.[57] The deceased is referred to as "chanter [*recitator*] of moral subjects and similar things in the vernacular in the presence of the Priors," and Antonio is elected to "chant [*recitandum*] moral songs [*canti morali*] and similar things at the Mensa in the presence of the Priors and the Standard Bearer [of Justice], as is customary."[58] A similar equation of verbs for "speak" and "sing" can be found in Boccaccio's *Decameron*, where each evening following dinner one of the members of the *brigata* is asked to sing. On the first day "Emilia sang [*cantando*] lovingly the following canzona"; but at the end of the third day Lauretta is commanded "to begin a dance and recite [*dicesse*] a canzona," to which she responded "with a voice so gentle."[59] It is clear, therefore, that when describing the activities of the herald or any other poet, the words *cantare* and *recitare*, *dicitore* and *cantore* are interchangeable; the difference having to do with the individual writer's perception of the chant-like singing of poetry as being closer to speaking or to full-blown singing.[60] The word selected in the archival documents to describe this activity of the herald depended on whether the person recording the event regarded it primarily as poetry incidentally accompanied by melody, or as a unified entity of words set to music. But in either case, the activity itself required the herald to deliver his poetry in music, regardless of how it was classified or identified. And one might easily imagine that the extent of the melodic content on any particular occasion would have varied depending on several factors, including the nature of the text, the occasion, and especially on the artistic talents of the performer.[61] To understand the musical aspect of the herald's presentation it is helpful to examine the process and tradition of improvised singing in Italy.

## *The Cantare all'Improvviso Tradition*

It would be difficult to over-emphasize the importance of *cantare all'improvviso* performance in the culture of Italy during the late Middle Ages and Renaissance.[62] Because of its spontaneous nature, little of the poetry is preserved and nothing at all of the music, which unfortunately has misled most cultural historians (and many musicologists) to virtually ignore it and to concentrate instead on those musical traditions for which there is surviving notated evidence.[63] In spite of the paucity of extant material, however, there is considerable secondary evidence that the practice was both widespread and an essential ingredient of Italian culture. Throughout the late Middle Ages and Renaissance the ability to improvise melodies for poetry was considered to be one of the attributes of a cultured person, a point made clearly in the *Decameron*. On each of the occasions when Boccaccio's ten young people present poetry it is clear that it is to be sung, although no music survives for most of the canzonas included in the stories, nor is there any existing melody mentioned which might be borrowed for the text.[64] The canzonas are identified only as poetic texts, and yet each member of the party is expected to present them as song when asked. It is highly probable, therefore, that what was being described by Boccaccio belonged to the same tradition of improvisation as that of the herald.[65] The clearest and most direct description occurs in one of the stories. In the seventh story on day ten, Minuccio d'Arezzo, a singer and player (*cantatore e sonatore*), is called upon to help console a lovesick young girl by playing a *stampita* (a dance)[66] on his *vivuola* and sweetly singing a few canzonas. Later in the story Minuccio accompanies a verse sung by the *dicitore in rima*, Mico da Siena (one of the poets listed in Dante's *De vulgari eloquentia*, see above), and then he sings a few songs with his *vivuola* while the king is eating. There is little doubt that the instrument referred to as the *vivuola* is the five-string fiddle, and that the poetry is performed in the *cantare all'improvviso* tradition.

## The Five-String Fiddle

Typically in the *cantare all'improvviso* tradition the improvising singer accompanied himself instrumentally, and the instrument most often depicted in the iconography of the period is a five-string fiddle (*vivuola, viola, viella, vielle*; see figures 11, 12, and 13). Images of this instrument are found in stained glass, manuscript illuminations, paintings, and sculptures from as early as the twelfth century. Most are from Italy, but there are also examples from Saxony, Austria, France, and England, suggesting that although it was most popular in Italy, the instrument was pan-European during the late Middle Ages.[67] The fiddle is singled out by two music theorists writing in Paris around 1300: Johannes de Grocheio identifies it as the most versatile of all instruments, capable of performing every type of song and musical form,[68] and Jerome of Moravia provides three possible tunings for it.[69] The popularity of the instrument grew in Italy during the fourteenth through the sixteenth centuries and into the seventeenth, when it finally disappears from the literature and iconography. Over that period of time it existed in several different sizes and shapes. In the late fifteenth century it acquired two additional strings and was known as the *lira da braccio*.[70] Five strings is the norm in the earlier depictions, but by the early sixteenth century most of the iconography shows seven, a number that may well have been chosen by the humanists to more closely align the instrument symbolically with the seven strings on the ancient *kithara* or lyre.[71] It is clear, however, that regardless of the number of strings or the actual name assigned to the instrument, the performance repertory was that belonging to the *cantare all'improvviso* tradition.

The instrument in question is unique in that it combines both plucked and bowed strings; on the five-string instrument four of the strings cross the fingerboard and can be stopped by the fingers of the left hand, changing their pitches. These are to be sounded by the bow, which is held in the right hand. An additional string is placed off-board, that is, it does not pass across the fingerboard and therefore its pitch cannot be changed. The off-board string can be sounded as a drone by the bow or, more commonly, plucked by the thumb of the left hand (figure 12).[72] The performer, therefore, could play sustained notes with the bow and at the same time provide his own rhythm by plucking the off-board string, and all this took place as he sang poetry, improvising both his melody and its accompaniment. It is significant that in a large number of depictions the bridge of the instrument is flat, meaning that the bow can not easily single out one string (with the exception of the highest string on the side away from the plucked string). This feature makes it easy for the instrument to play several strings at once, sounding either multiple drones or chords, and separates this instrument from those bowed instruments with a curved bridge, which are intended to be played melodically by allowing the performer to single out one string at a time for a continuous melodic line. In other words, the very construction of the instrument was intended to facilitate its use in accompanying a sung melody rather than as a melodic instrument.[73]

The instrument was sometimes referred to as a *viola da braccio*, which is more accurate than *lira*; the word *viola* was one of the Italian words used to designate a bowed string instrument, whereas *lira* (lyre) generally implies an instrument that is plucked. The *lira da braccio*, of course, combines both types of performance, but the word *lira* was carefully chosen to describe not the instrument itself, but its function and repertory; it was considered to be the late-medieval replacement for the lyre of David, thus linking the *cantare all'improvviso* tradition with that of the singing poets of biblical times and especially those of ancient Greece.[74] During the Renaissance the *lira da braccio* represented not only the *kithara* from ancient Greece, but Orpheus' Classical lyre, the lyre of Apollo the sun god, and the lyre (or sometimes harp) of King David, and was often used as the symbol of poetry.[75] Although from a physical aspect the ancient *kithara* and lyre would have been more accurately represented by a medieval or Renaissance harp than by a *lira da braccio*, since it was plucked rather than bowed, the two instruments—*kithara* and five-string fiddle/*lira da braccio*—were directly related on the level of function: their association with accompanied serious poetry. Jacopo Passavanti, Prior of Santa Maria Novella, describes in his *Specchio della vera penitenza* of 1354 the typical scene of a *canterino* who makes "great even strokes of the viola bow in order to cover the sound of the turbulent and agitated crowd" ("I gran colpi pure con l'archetto della viola' per coprire il brusio della folla turbolenta e agitta").[76]

There are also many references to the use of a lute or a harp as an accompanying instrument for this repertory, but the *lira da braccio* came to be symbolic of this kind of presentation and was represented as such in the iconography.[77] One of the most celebrated improvisers of the fifteenth century, Pietrobono di Burzellis from the court of Ferrara, who accompanied himself on his lute while singing, was frequently referred to as Pietrobono del Chitarino, symbolically referring to his lute as a *kithara*. In 1459, Antonio Cornazano, a poet, statesman, and dancing master at the Sforza court in Milan, praised Pietrobono by comparing him to Apollo and Orpheus and claiming that "his music rivals the heavenly harmonies, can revive the dead, turn rivers and stones, and even change people into statues."[78] References to performers who sang *all'improvviso* to their own accompaniment are found throughout the documents and literature of the time and are represented in the iconography.

*Cantare all'improvviso* can be thought of as a particularly Italianate performance practice. Although improvised musical performances, both vocal and instrumental, could be found in all areas of Europe during this period and after, the tradition of *cantare all'improvviso* was especially cultivated on all levels of Italian society long after it was replaced by composed polyphony in the cultured circles of the rest of Europe. Lorenzo the Magnificent, for example, is known to have played the *lira da braccio* (as did Isabella d'Este in Mantua);[79] Marsilio Ficino mentions Il Magnifico's singing *all'improvviso*; and Angelo Poliziano wrote to Lorenzo with praise for his son Piero's ability to sing in this manner.[80]

In Florence and in many other cities in northern Italy, the frequent public performances of the poet-singer, or *cantimpanca*, were an important part of daily life, providing entertainment as well as political and social commentary for the passing citizens (figure 11).[81] Many of these artists had a favorite weekly time and performance venue, and developed a loyal following. In the last half of the fifteen century, for example, the most popular Florentine entertainer was Cristoforo, called "L'Altissimo," who often sang in the piazza in front of the church of San Martino al Vescovo.[82] This piazza was a popular one and was the preferred location of a number of the popular poet-singers, including Antonio di Guido, the favorite *cantimpanca* of Lorenzo de' Medici.[83] The popularity of this kind of entertainment is demonstrated by the fact that performances in just this one location took place on three or four days each week.[84]

One indication of the very high profile this tradition retained in the fifteenth century is the Certame Coronario, the famous contest that took place in the Duomo of Florence in October of 1441, during which a number of literary figures sang their poetry over a period of several days in front of a distinguished audience. The event was organized by two exceptionally prominent citizens, Leon Batista Alberti and Piero di Cosimo de' Medici, and among those taking part were the Florentine herald Antonio di Matteo di Meglio, who sang his own verses as well as some written by Mariotto d'Arrigo Davanzati. Also present and participating was Anselmo Calderoni, appointed civic herald the following year, who sang his own *canzone morale*.[85] The audience included the secretaries of Pope Eugenius IV, the archbishop of Florence, the Venetian ambassador, the Priors, numerous prelates, and a large segment of the elite citizens of the city.[86]

The tradition of improvised singing retained its prominence throughout the fifteenth and sixteenth centuries, although, as will be discussed in chapters 4 and 6, it came to be threatened by the encroaching popularity of the French tradition of composed polyphony. Improvised singing was employed in the performance of sacred dramatic productions (*sacre rappresentazioni*) from at least as early as *Dì del Giudicio*, a collaboration between the herald Antonio di Matteo di Meglio and Feo Belcare in the mid 1440s.[87] (The association of the Florentine herald, dramatic productions, and improvised singing can be traced back to at least the preceding century to productions by the herald Jacopo Salimbene.)[88] Its continuing prominence is attested to by the *all'improvviso* performance of the title role in Angelo Poliziano's *Orfeo* some time in the 1470s (or perhaps the 1480s)[89] by the poet Baccio Ugolini, one of the most famous improvisers of his day.[90] Ugolini's performance on that occasion was praised by Lorenzo de' Medici, who referred to it as singing *ad lyram* (meaning with a *lira da braccio*),[91] again making the connection with the ancient tradition of singing poetry to the accompaniment of a lyre.

Pietro Bembo wrote that the early fifteenth-century Venetian poet Leonardo Giustiniani "was held in greater esteem for the manner of song with which he sent forth his poems than for his mode of writing."[92] And in his 1473 *Dialogus de neapolitana profectione*, Ludovico Carboni begins his description of his trip from Ferrara to Naples with the following lines: "Your Francesco should be called with his lyra, for verses should not be presented without singing, and my voice is hoarse from extreme fatigue." And later on he states, "Indeed I perform my verses as I usually do, with my Apollonian cithera [probably a *lira da braccio*, but possibly a lute] in my hands."[93] Carboni, too, was celebrated for his improvisational abilities, being compared to Amphion by Raffaele Zovenzoni, one of his Ferrarese colleagues.[94]

An excellent description of this type of performance which also relates the singing style to oratorical techniques is included in a 1489 letter from Angelo Poliziano to Pico della Mirandola, describing a performance by Fabio Orsini at his father's palace in Rome:

> He [Orsini] filled our ears, or rather our hearts, with a voice so sweet that . . . I was almost transported out of my senses. . . . His voice was not entirely that of someone reading, nor entirely that of someone singing: both could be heard, and yet neither separated one from the other; it was, in any case, even or modulated, and changed as required by the passage. Now it was varied, now sustained, now exalted and now restrained, now calm and now vehement, now slowing down and now quickening its pace, but always it was precise, always clear and always pleasant; and his gestures were not indifferent or sluggish, but not posturing or affected either.[95]

The art of improvisation was a subject taken up by the Italian humanist Paolo Cortese in his early sixteenth-century *De cardinalatu*, in which he discusses the three different types and relates them to French, Spanish, and north Italian styles of singing:

> The manner of singing can be perceived in a description of three parts. The first part concerns the Phrygian, the second the Lydian, and the third the Dorian, so named. In the Phyrgian the souls of the listeners are usually spared the more violent exertions of voices. Included in this type is the singing, according to religious usage, of the French musicians in the Palatine chapel on saints' days and weekdays. The Lydian type can appear in two guises. The first is called "combined," the second is called "simple." In the "combined" the souls of the listeners are brought in an affecting mode to sorrow, tears, and pity, as can be seen where the papal *novendilia* [nine days of mourning for the death of a pope] and the senatorial *parentalia* [annual memorial services for dead cardinals] are customarily celebrated. This type of plaintive singing has always been used by the Spanish people. The "simple" is measured more sluggishly, as we experienced through those affecting verses of Virgil, which were sung customarily to Ferdinand II by the poet Cariteo. On the other hand the Dorian manner is in a much more temporally uniform mean, as in that type which they wish to be perceived as established by the holy Gregory in *aberruncato*; a calm manner of singing is established as if in a sacred brook. From this stems the whole practice of our singing in litatorial and precentorial pieces and songs, and when comparing these songs they are grouped together. Litatorial pieces are those in which are all types of *pythongi*, proses, and analogical meters, and praise is given to musicians who can arrange these well. . . . Now these modes of songs are usually considered to correspond to the *ottava rima* and *terza rima*, which are said to have been first established among us by Francesco Petrarch, who sang the pub-

lished songs *ad lembum*.[96] Currently Seraphino d'Aquilano is the foremost of those reviving this type of song, from which stems that entwined and measured uniting of words and music, that nothing can be sweeter in the use of the modes. So great and growing is the number of those imitating the accompanied singers [i.e., *cantastorie*] that all Italy seems to be singing in this style.[97]

It is interesting to see that Cortese makes a connection between the tradition of singing employed by his contemporary, Seraphino d'Aquilano, and that of Petrarch, which lends additional strength to the idea of the continuity of this style. And although Cortese specifically identifies *ottava rima* and *terza rima* as the poetic forms most popularly used for improvised performance, there is considerable evidence that nearly all poetic forms lent themselves to this mode of presentation. It is true that most of the surviving poems from the *cantimpanca* repertory are indeed in *ottava rima*, but this is a somewhat unreliable picture of the earlier practice due to the fact that what has been preserved is mostly from no earlier than the late fifteenth century, a time when *ottava rima* and *terza rima* were enormously popular forms. Yet we can see that these forms were not always the most preferred ones: all of the poems to be sung in the *Decameron* are *ballate*; the Florentine civic herald is officially recorded as having performed *canti morali*, a general category that includes *capitoli, sonetti,* and *sirventesi*, as well as other forms; the improviser Giovanni Cieco di Parma wrote and sang *capitoli* and *sonetti petrarcheggianti*; and in Naples the favorite form for improvisation was the *strambotta*.[98] It would seem, therefore, that the improvising singers were not restricted to any particular poetic forms but could choose whatever was popular and appropriate to the occasion, with the selection evolving along with popular taste in various locations throughout the decades.

Identification of the *cantare all'improvviso* style as an Italian national trait is emphasized in the work of Alfonso de' Pazzi, a popular Florentine poet of the mid-sixteenth century who was often praised in prose and poetry for his improvisatory skill. De' Pazzi wrote several sonnets attacking the noted Florentine chronicler Benedetto Varchi, in which he contrasts his own ability as improviser with that of musicians who sing "by note," that is, those who sing music that is composed and written down. De' Pazzi's sonnets, a canzona by "Il Lasca,"[99] and a prose diatribe by Pasquino Patritio Romano make it clear that even as late as the mid-sixteenth century in certain intellectual circles in Florence and in Rome, improvisation was still considered to be the true Italian style, as opposed to the written musical repertory which was associated with the foreign composers from northern Europe.[100] The importance of this tradition is still in evidence as late as 1623, when a dispute in Rome over the merits of two famous sopranos was resolved by having each of the singers improvise a melody and accompaniment to an *ottava rima* they had not previously seen.[101]

In addition to their public performances, the *all'improvviso* singers also were often invited to entertain privately at the homes of the elite families, where they would perform after dinner for the enjoyment of distinguished guests. On first hearing Antonio di Guido while visiting Florence in 1459 (see discussion in chapter 1), the young Galeazzo Maria Sforza was sufficiently impressed that he sent the following letter to his father in Milan, singling out this one performance from all of those presented during his stay:

> After dinner, we retired to a room with all of the guests. We heard a maestro Antonio sing, with the *citara* [probably a lute],[102] and if your Excellency does not know him at least you must have heard of him. He sang with such dignity and style that the greatest poet or orator in the world, presented with such a task, would perhaps not have earned such praise for performing it. From now on I will be singing his praises, for indeed, his performance was such that everyone showed their wonder and admiration, and especially those who were most learned. I don't know if Lucan or Dante ever did anything more beautiful, combining so many ancient stories, the names of innumerable ancient Romans, fables, poets, and the names of all the muses. I was greatly impressed by him.[103]

The wording of Galeazzo's praise is revealing in that he compares Antonio not to other musicians, but to two famous poet-orators: one from the time of Nero, the other the most revered Italian from the previous century. On this occasion Antonio's performance was in the style of an epic poem; from the poetry that survives from that time it is possible to conclude that the work he performed was most likely a tale of several hundred lines in which the singer weaves together stories and fables from the past, suggesting that they have something to do with the present honored guest. The lines are sung to the accompaniment of an instrument and most likely improvised to some extent in order to fit the occasion.[104] This kind of mixture was not an unusual subject matter for those who sang *all'improvviso*. Although we have no record of what Antonio sang on the occasion when Galeazzo heard him, we do have a number of examples of his poetry, including the following sonnet in which he indulges in the type of historical and literary amalgam mentioned in Galeazzo's account:

> *In concave caverne aspri leoni,*
> *famelici, crudeli, a preda istretta,*
> *grandine, pioggia e balenar con fretta,*
> *pel mondo tempestar folgore e tuoni,*
> *aspidi, tigri, bavalischi e dragoni,*
> *e Mungibel quando più fiamme getta,*

*la prima furiosa aspra vendetta,*
*e presi a mezze l'onde e faraoni,*
*e 'n fiamme e 'n sangue e 'n cener Tebe e Troia,*
*e Silla e Mario, Mezenzio e Nerone,*
*Tideo sopra 'l teschio, Erode e Giuda,*
*e corra Acan, Amano e Chirone*
*e tutti accolti insieme in canto e 'n gioia,*
*respetto alla mie pena acerva e cruda.*[105]

[In hollow caverns lions breathe, hungry, ruthless, ready to prey; hail and rain flashing quickly, storming through the world with lightning and thunder, asps, tigers, basilisks and dragons, and Mungibel [a dragon] when it throws more flames, the first furious taste of vengeance, and taken in the middle of the wave and pharaohs, and in the flames and in the blood and in the ashes of Thebes and Troy, and Sulla and Marius, Mezentius and Nero, Tideus over the skull, Herod and Judas, and Achan, Amano and Chiron run, and all are gathered together in song and in happiness, by the means of my bitter and coarse pen.]

A rather idealized picture of both the occasions and the repertory for this kind of artistic invention is set out in a lengthy poem from the end of the fourteenth century known as the *cantare dei cantari*, consisting of fifty-nine stanzas in *ottava rima*. The poet makes it clear that his repertory consists of the most famous tales and legends, stories from the Bible, and notable local occasions. It is relevant that the birth of Sir Percival is included among the subjects mentioned.

[F]orse per me si gitterebe u motto,
Perché, lasciando questi, i' non venisse
Alla tavola nuova in Camelotto,
De re Artù parlar ciò che si scrisse,
E di Ginevre e messer Lanciolotto,
D'Isotta, di Tristan, di Lionisse,
Di Breobis, e messer Agravano,
E l'Amoratto, cavalier sovrano.
La nascita di messer Princivallo,
E del Verzeppe ogni torniamento,
Brunoro e Gariette a cotal ballo.
. . .
Inteso avete oma' come cantare
vi posso della Bibbia e de' Troiani,
d'Alba, di Roma e d'ogni loro affare,
d'Alesandro, de' Greci, e de' Tebani,
e ogni storia qual bella vi pare,
de' paladin l'ottavo e de' pagani,

*ogni ventura in rima o novelletta:*
*chiedete omai la qual più vvi diletta.*[106]

[Perhaps for me it would possible to coin a saying, because without these I
would not be able to come to the new table in Camelot, to speak that which
was written of King Arthur and of Guinevere and Sir Lancelot, of Tristan and
Isolda, of Lionisse, of Breobis and of Messr Agravano, and of Amoratto the
sovereign knight, the birth of Sir Percival, and of Verzeppe[107] that Brunoro
and Gariette dance in every tournament. . . . You have by now understood that
I am able to sing to you of the Bible and of the Trojans, of Alba, of Rome and
of all their things, of Alexander, of the Greeks and of the Thebans, and every
story that appears beautiful to you, of the eighth champion and of the pagans,
all offered in rhyme or in short stories [i.e., prose]; you [may] request, however,
that which delights you most.]

It is also interesting to see that the poet, here in the guise of a *canterino*,
tells us that he sings prose as well as poetry, which is evidence that this kind
of *all'improvviso* performance was not restricted to poetry. Singing prose is
also implied in Angelo Poliziano's letter describing the performance of Fabio
Orsini, quoted above, and both of these statements help us make more sense
of the fifteenth- and sixteenth-century theoretical treatises that draw parallels
between the *cantare all'improvviso* performance tradition and rhetorical delivery. Johannes Tinctoris, in his *Liber de arte contrapuncti* of 1477, goes back to
the early Roman model of the *kithara* player as well as rhetoric as he instructs
composers to incorporate melodic and harmonic variety in their works:

> This is the eighth and, consequently, the last rule, that variety must be most ac-
> curately sought for in all counterpoint, for, as Horace says in his Poetics: "One
> who sings to the kithara is laughed at if he always wanders over the same string."
> Wherefore, according to the opinion of Tullius [Cicero], as a variety in the art
> of speaking most delights the hearer, so also in music a diversity of harmonies
> vehemently provokes the souls of listeners into delight; hence the philosopher
> [Aristotle], in his Ethics, does not hesitate to state that variety is a most pleasant
> thing and human nature in need of it.[108]

Later, both Nicola Vicentino (1555) and Gioseffo Zarlino (1588) exhort the *canterino* to adopt rhetorical practices such as varying volume and speed as a way
of making their performances more effective.[109] Given the nature of poetry, it
would be difficult to include very much of the rhetorical performance devices
used in singing without losing the sense of meter and rhyme. If, however, the
references are also to the performance of prose, a greater margin exists for the
insertion of such devices. Now we can look back at some of the other rather
curious statements about reciting and singing quoted above (for example, Poliz-

iano's description of Fabio Orsini's voice), and see that the references often were to the presentation of prose.[110]

It is clear, therefore, that those who sang *all'improvviso* needed to be exceptionally talented, well-rounded, and well-educated individuals. In addition to being capable poets, they were required to have an extensive acquaintance with history and literature, a practical ability in the art of oratory, skill at playing a musical instrument, and the ability to improvise both melody and accompaniment—and to execute all of this more or less spontaneously.[111] Spontaneity, however, while lending a sense of excitement to a performance, brings with it the risk of technical error when the singer is improvising poetry, a subject addressed in an *ottava rima* by L'Altissimo, where he asks his audience to recognize that improvisation includes this possibility:

> *S'ognun che m'ode con l'orecchio attento*
> *stassi a comprender questo mio lavoro,*
> *m'iscuserà se talhor con l'accento*
> *or pur col verso io uscissi del decoro.*[112]

> [If everyone who listens to me with attentive ear understood this work of mine, he will pardon me if now and then, with the accent or even with a line, I depart from propriety.]

Paolo Cortese underlines these perils in his comment on the improvisatory performances of Bernardo Accolti, where he makes the somewhat unkind observation that "[a]lthough he recites improvised verses, and although one should be prepared to make allowances for [faults deriving from] the rapidity [of the exploit], most of what he does is commendable, and very little needs to be forgiven; [yet his is] the merit of a prolific but unreflexive talent."[113]

The performance practice of the herald of the Signoria, therefore, made him neither unique nor unusual; he was simply one of many poet-musicians engaged in an age-old practice. He was exceptional only in that his official position gave him the singular privilege of chanting his verse at all official civic functions, and especially at the private Mensa of the government executives.

## The Herald as Knight

Florentine society did not include titled nobles. Instead, its powerful families—those who owned property and were eligible for election to political office—were known as the "elite" (*grandi*), although no specific titles were used.[114] The

Florentines did, however, follow the European tradition of creating knights, a title that was originally linked to military valor but which by the fourteenth century had become an honorary distinction that no longer carried only that connotation.[115] As noted above, the earliest appointment to the position of herald carried with it the title of *cavaliere*, or knight. That practice continued for the remainder of the Republic, and the induction ceremony on such an occasion was quite colorful. A document exists from October 31, 1446, recording the ceremony for bestowing knighthood on the newly appointed herald, Gregorio di Antonio di Matteo di Meglio, which demonstrates the level of esteem accorded the position.

> Andrea [di Silvestro Nandi], the above-mentioned Standard Bearer of Justice, immediately . . . received and promoted the same Messer Gregorio to the dignity of knighthood and he honored him [Messer Gregorio] with the belt of knighthood, and in token of the said knighthood he girded him [Messer Gregorio] with the sword and the servants of the above-mentioned lordship placed on him the golden spurs; and he also placed garlands of silver olive [leaves] on his head and gave him an accolade with his right hand, and he did, said, and complied with all other things in the above-mentioned [rites] and also the appurtenances, dues, and requisites. When these things were completed a great noise was made of trumpets and shawms and reed instruments by the trumpeters and pifferi and musicians of the above-said lordship, according to the ritual and customs observed in like matters at other times.[116]

Although no specific place is mentioned, this is the kind of public ceremony that was conducted on the *ringhiera* outside the Palazzo della Signoria. The herald is proclaimed a knight, an olive wreath is placed on his head, and he is given a sword and spurs that symbolize knighthood. And as the document states, as with all public ceremonies, the event was accompanied by all of the civic musicians. We can assume from the accounts of other, similar public ceremonies, that the honored herald would have entered and exited the Piazza della Signoria in a procession.

As elaborate as this ceremony may seem, the herald was considered to be a "lesser" knight. In comparison, the ceremony and events surrounding the knighthood of someone from the ruling elite was far more elaborate, as for example, that performed for Jacopo Salviati after his successful military victory in 1404, discussed in chapter 1, or the knighting that took place two years later, on October 26, 1406 for Francesco Casali of Cortona and Piero di M. Benedetto Gaetani di Pisa. On that occasion the men to be honored were met on horseback at the church of Santa Maria Novella by "all the knights of Florence and Pisa," as well as by all of the elite citizens, who accompanied them to the Piazza della

Signoria, where they dismounted and joined the Priors and other dignitaries on the *ringhiera*. The Gonfaloniere presided over the ceremony in which the honored men were presented with some of the usual symbols of knighthood—a golden cincture with a dagger, golden spurs, and a sword—and had their silver olive wreaths exchanged for wreaths of gold. Finally, in addition to the usual set of gifts, they each were given a horse, which brought to a close the first part of this ceremony presided over by the Signoria.

When, as in this case, the knighting involved the ruling elite there was an additional ceremony at the office of the Parte Guelfa, at which the honored men were presented with a pennant and shield decorated with the arms of the party. (The symbolism of this gift was related to the very origin of the Parte Guelfa in the early thirteenth century as a military society of the elite. Throughout the fourteenth century the Parte considered itself virtually identical to the government, a view affirmed in the statutes of 1325. Although their political power had dimmed considerably by the early fifteenth century, they maintained a presence in official ceremonies such as this.)[117] Then, following the ceremony at the home of the Parte Guelfa, the honored knights remounted their horses and, accompanied by twenty members of the military dressed in green and white, and blue and white, they went to the church of San Giovanni where they dismounted, made an offering at the alter, remounted, and returned to Santa Maria Novella. Three days later a joust was held in their honor in the Piazza Santa Maria Novella.[118] Although not included in the accounts, there is little doubt that the knighting ceremony on the *ringhiera* at the Palazzo della Signoria included a speech by the Chancellor and a poem sung by the civic herald (in this case it would have been Antonio di Piero di Friano) in praise of the two new knights. The civic musicians would have taken part in the processions and provided fanfares and other musical sounds at both of the ceremonies.

It can be seen that although the basic knighting ceremony remained the same on all occasions, that for the elite citizens involved many more gifts as well as special recognition by the Parte Guelfa. In comparison, the heralds were clearly on a lower level, but they were indeed knights and as such stood above all other civic employees.

## The Herald & the Mensa

From the earliest document appointing Jacopo Salimbene as herald in 1352, it is evident that among the most important of the heraldic responsibilities were those in conjunction with the ritual of the Mensa, the twice-daily communal meals held in the privacy of the Palazzo della Signoria. It is not certain which of the rooms originally served this purpose; the earliest record comes from the late fifteenth century, when the Mensa was held in the Sala dei Gigli, a spacious room on the second floor, located conveniently at the foot of the stairs descending from the third-floor kitchen. The inventory of 1532 records the room as containing a *credenza*, three large trestle tables, and a round table for musicians (*desco tondo per li sonatori*).[119] Those who were entitled to eat at the Mensa were the members of the supreme executive of government, the Priors (originally six, but augmented to eight following the constitutional reforms in the mid-fourteenth century), and the Standard Bearer of Justice, or Gonfaloniere. Also present were a few senior members of the *famiglia* (the Signoria staff), and occasional distinguished visitors and guests of the city. To both entertain and inspire them, the civic herald sang moral songs (*canti morali*) while they dined. (The scene would be similar to that depicted in *Herod's Feast*, figure 13.)

The *famiglia* of the Signoria consisted of those employees who worked in the Palazzo Vecchio, whose total number continued to change over the decades, as did the requirements for which of the members were to live in the building and eat at the Mensa.[120] In the mid-fourteenth century the *famiglia* consisted of nine *donzelli*, the personal orderlies of the Priors; seven members of the *fanti*, who guarded the palace and the Signori; twelve *mazieri* (messengers); the nine *trombadori*; and the notary. Exactly which of these were entitled to eat at the Mensa of the Signori is not stated; originally all of them may have been involved, and there seems to have been more than one dining hall. Those civic servants who were required to live in the Palazzo had rooms, including eating facilities, in the third-floor attic.[121] An inventory of 1367 lists separately items for the *sala de' priori* and the *tavole da magiare dove mangia la famigla*, which seems to suggest that the *famiglia*, or at least some of them, must have eaten apart from the Signori.[122] In 1451, long after the Mensa had become a grand celebration, there was a complaint from the Priors about the amount of noise made during meals by the *famiglia*, suggesting that some of them may have dined at the Prior's Mensa.[123] The statutes of the fourteenth century state that all of the *fanti* and *donzelli* were to live in the Signoria, but by the time of the statutes of 1415, the *fanti* were merely required to eat and drink there, and the number of *donzelli* required to sleep in the palace was reduced to two.[124] As Nicolai Rubinstein points out, the government of Florence grew to such an extent during the early fifteenth century that the building itself, which had more than enough space when constructed in 1300, had become overcrowded.[125] In fact, by the end of the fifteenth century, even the civic herald was no longer required to live or dine at the Palazzo.[126]

The "moral songs" that were the specific assignment of the herald during the Mensa refers to a category of poetry in a number of different poetic forms that included not only moralizing texts, as the term suggests, but also sacred themes, historical subjects, and stories of love and virtue. The important element was that the themes were to be ennobling; they were to uplift the spirits of the listeners. The duty of the herald, therefore, was to supply the executives of government with daily tales of virtuous behavior as a way of encouraging them to carry out their own responsibilities in accordance with high moral values. In selecting his themes for presentation, the herald was in a position to choose examples from literature that were analogous to current problems. Similar to the court jester, the herald was privileged to comment on the issues currently before the rulers, and he provided daily instructions on virtuous conduct in the form of rhymed poetry chosen from whatever literary sources would seem to be appropriate. And like the other *cantastorie* discussed above, the herald needed to be an extremely literate person, well acquainted with history, the Bible, and a great deal of literature.

As can be seen from the above descriptions of the position, the duties of the herald also required someone with both organizational skill and artistic talent. In the mid-fourteenth century, the herald had to be capable of tending to the daily disposition of the commune's property, overseeing the public and private civic ceremonies, writing intelligent and clever verse, improvising a vocal line with accompaniment, and have some ability with writing drama. There is very little detail available about how much the early heralds were involved in drama, but the earliest records use the word *istrio* to describe him, and the appointment of Jacopo Salimbene in 1352 states clearly that he wrote comedies: "Quod probus vir dominus Jacobus Salimbenis civis Florentinis, suis oblectas auditores eius conmediis."[127] We do know that later heralds were involved in writing dramatic works, as for example the *sacra rappresentazione* collaboration involving herald Antonio di Matteo di Meglio and Feo Belcare in the mid-1440s, mentioned above. Most of the heralds of the fifteenth century are known to have been involved in dramatic productions, up to and including Giovan Battista di Cristofano dell'Ottonaio (herald 1517–27).[128]

Of all the requirements, the ability to compose poetry was probably the most demanding, since the herald would have been called upon to supply verse in honor of all important occasions—an ever-growing number—in addition to his obligations at the Mensa of the Priors, which happened twice each day.

Although we have documentation concerning the position of herald and all of the men who held the post after the mid-fourteenth century, actual examples of the poetry have survived for only a few of them. The obvious reason for this lack is that a part of the tradition included improvisation. Undoubtedly some of their verse would have been written down, especially those poems that were of broad interest and which the poet thought to be his best work. But much of the herald's subject matter, especially that intended for the Mensa, would likely have been on current topics and therefore of ephemeral interest; this material would be less likely to have been recorded. The surviving material, which extends from pedantic doggerel to fairly decent verse, indicates that not all incumbents were equally artistically gifted,[129] although some of them, notably Anselmo Calderoni and Antonio di Meglio, were capable of quite respectable artistic creations.[130]

It is important to understand at this point exactly what is meant by the word "improvised" in the present context. Both here and in reference to performance by the instrumental musicians, it does not necessarily mean completely spontaneous and unrehearsed. As with poetic and musical improvisation in the present day, it often included various degrees of preparation. Often certain key elements of the product are thought out in advance, and a good improviser always has a large repertory of stock elements that can be inserted when something original does not immediately come to mind. Improvisation, therefore, is a combination of prepared and unprepared elements in varying degrees that are assembled only in performance, as distinguished from a script that is completely prepared in advance. The amount to which any particular performance would be spontaneous would vary depending on a number of elements, including the skill of the individual performer.

The earliest surviving examples of poetry written by the civic heralds date from the end of the fourteenth and the early fifteenth century, and although they provide a glimpse of the tradition, it is not possible to securely identify the purpose or the occasion for which many of the poems were written. The extant material does, however, give us some idea of the style of this kind of poetry and a sample of what kinds of subjects the heralds addressed and the ways in which they addressed them; the "rerum moralium in vulgari et similium," as the document of 1392 described them.[131]

Both the moralizing and political nature of the herald's poetry can be seen in the scolding tone of the opening lines of a canzona that probably refers to the Ciompi revolt, written by Giovanni da Trebbio (herald 1377–92; his official title was "Chavaliere di Chorte e Sindacho e Referendario."):[132]

*La division che 'n te, Fiorenza, è nata*
*fra' cittadini odiosi e malcontenti,*
*di tutto il senno spenti,*
*all'animo m'induce pena dura.*

[The division that is within you, Florence, is born amongst the hateful and unhappy citizens, deprived of all wisdom. It brings me hard pain.][133]

The spirit of these words suggests that this may have been one of the poems presented at the Mensa in 1380 to remind the Priors of their duty to resolve the conflict that would soon change the makeup of the governing bodies.

At the same time, it was also the duty of the herald to sing the praises of local heroes, as in the following excerpt from a sonnet by Antonio di Meglio (herald 1417–42),[134] written in honor of Niccolò da Tolentino, Captain General of the Florentine army, on the occasion of his victory over Siena in 1433.

*O trionfal Fiorenza, fatten bella*
*gauldi in eterno, popol glorioso,*
*po' che 'l franco potente e valoroso*
*Marte novello a' per tua fida stella;*
*cioè il tuo Tolentin, che 'l mond'apella*
*più ch' altri per virtù d'arme famoso,*
*ch' egli è colui che vien vittorioso,*
*tal che tua gloria esalta e rinovella.*

[O triumphal Florence, you are given beauty, eternal bliss, and proud citizens, now that you have a brave, powerful, and valorous Mars for your faithful star; that is, your Tolentino, whom the world praises as famous for valor in arms. It is he who has become victorious in such a way that your glory is exalted and renewed].[135]

This type of elaborate laudatory verse (one of three written to celebrate this particular occasion) typically would have been performed by the herald during a public ceremony in front of the Palazzo della Signoria following the usual procession, where Tolentino would have been honored by the Priors and presented with some gifts as a show of the city's official gratitude for his success.

Antonio di Meglio was also the author of a poem labeled *canto dell'araldo* that praises Pope Eugenius IV (pope 1431–47) on the signing of a peace treaty with King Sigismund in 1433, which ended the long conflict of Florence and Venice against Milan. The Pope, Gabriel Condulmer, was from Venice and had close ties to the Medici, and in fact was instrumental in mediating the return of Cosimo de' Medici from exile in 1434. The verse would probably have been presented and performed at a ceremony at the Signoria in 1434, while the Pope was in exile in Florence and living at Santa Maria Novella.

*Viva viva oramai, viva l'onore,*
*viva la gloria della santa fede,*
*po' che Dio tal concede*
*franco duca e campione a suo' difesa,*
*Viva viva la santa madre Chiesa!*
*Viva Ugenio quarto, el pastor santo,*
*più ch'altro del gran manto*
*del glorioso apostol Pietro degno!*[136]

[Hurray, hurray now, long live the honor and the glory of the holy faith, for God sends a bold leader and champion to its defense. Long live the Holy Mother Church. Long live Eugenius IV, the holy pastor, worthy above all others of the great mantle of the glorious apostle Peter.]

# The Heralds of the Republic

From the assorted bits of evidence that remain today, it appears that the men who served as heralds were quite talented people.[137] The position required administrative and diplomatic skills as well as substantial ability in the arts: poetry, *cantare all'improvviso,* and theater. As might be expected, not all of the heralds possessed these talents in equal measure, but the archival documents attest to people of outstanding ability. In the earliest known appointment, that of Sir Percival in 1333, the government acknowledges the need for a full-time herald whose talents will bring honor to the city, and they pass over all of the local talent—which would have been considerable—to select a foreigner. Documents of appointment over the following two hundred years of the Republic continue to reinforce this image of serious effort on the part of the government to select a herald whose administrative talents and public performance ability adequately reflect and represent the grandeur of Florence.

Following Percival, the next name associated with the position of herald is that of Gello, a name found in a document of 1352 that notes his death and announces the appointment of his successor.[138] Beyond that, however, nothing further is known for certain about this herald, although it is tempting to identify him with Gello dal Borgo San Friano, an associate of Buffalmacco in the early years of the century.[139] Gello dal Borgo's description matches the talents

**Table 3.1. Individuals Known to Have Held the Position of Herald during the Republic**

| | |
|---|---|
| Percival | 1333–13?? |
| Gello | 13?? –1352 |
| Jacopo Salimbene | 1352–1375 |
| Geronimo di Meglio | 1376–1377 |
| Giovanni di Giorgio da Trebbio | 1377–1392 |
| Antonio di Piero di Friano | 1393, 1396–1416 |
| Francesco di Gherardo | 1394–1396 |
| Antonio di Matteo di Meglio | 1417–1442 |
| Anselmo di Giovacchino Calderoni | 1442–1446 |
| Gregorio di Antonio di Matteo di Meglio | 1446–1448 |
| Simone di Giovanni d'Ambrogio da Chianciano | 1448–1450 |
| Bartolomeo d'Antonio di Bartolomeo | 1450–1455 |
| Francesco di Lorenzo di Iacopo (Filarete) | 1456–1505 |
| Angelo Manfidi da Poppi | 1500–1527 |
| Giovan Battista di Cristofano dell'Ottonaio | 1517–1527 |
| Jacopo di Niccolò del Polta (Il Bientina) | 1527–1539 |

of later heralds: he was a *canterino* with dramatic ability, and is known to have taken part in a performance of the *Rappresentazione dell'Inferno*.[140]

Gello's successor was Jacopo Salimbene, who first appears in civic documents from 1350, replacing one Ser Giovanni Calvi Affricani in the position of *sindico proveditore e referendario*, that is, supervisor of supplies for the Signoria and supervisor of the office concerned with announcements, reports, and representations.[141] In 1352, on the death of Gello, the position of herald (*istrio*) was added to Salimbene's portfolio along with the other two offices.[142] Thus, beginning at least with this herald, it became the tradition for a single person to serve as majordomo of the Signoria as well as master of civic ceremonies and herald; a not-incompatible coupling of responsibilities.[143] Over the next sixty years, however, as the public and private ceremonial duties took up increasing amounts of the herald's time, he was gradually relieved of this kind of supervisory responsibility.

Salimbene remained herald from 1352 to 1375, and his activities shed a bit more light on the breadth of duties attached to the post, which included ambassadorial missions, a service he undertook even before his appointment as herald and which continued afterward.[144] As reported above, the document appointing him as herald also praises him for his theatrical talents, thus making clear that the position of *istrio* from the very beginning did indeed require ability in theater as well as poetry. Over the years he was referred to in official documents as "Jacopo delle Parole" and praised for his public *all'improvviso* performance as rendering "words combined with delightful sound."[145]

Salimbene was replaced briefly by Geronimo di Meglio (1376–77), about whom little is known. Geronimo is documented a few year later as serving in the *famigilia* as a *donzello* following his short term as *sindico e referendario*. He is referred to in 1379 as *buffone*, but he is called "Messer," meaning that he was not knighted, and it is therefore probable that he served only as a temporary appointment. He was most likely the uncle of Antonio di Matteo di Meglio, herald from 1417–42, and great-uncle of Gregorio di Antonio di Matteo di Meglio, herald from 1446–48.[146]

Giovanni di Giorgio da Trebbio served as herald from 1377 to 1392. He had been a member of the *famiglia*, first as a *donzello*, and later transferred to the post of *sindico e referendario* by exchanging positions with Geronimo di Meglio.[147] A document five years after his first appointment refers to Giovanni as *dominus*, and the pay records frequently refer to him as *Cavaliere di corte*, signifying that he had been knighted.[148] His term of office included the dramatic upheaval of governing procedures triggered by the Ciompi Revolt, an event referred to in one of the few surviving verses known to have been written by a fourteenth-century herald (quoted above). On his appointment, the duties of *sindico proveditore* were passed over to the *donzelli*, undoubtedly a reflection of the increasing number of ceremonial events in the yearly calendar requiring the attention of the herald.

The last person to hold the office of herald during the fourteenth century was Antonio di Piero di Friano, who served briefly in 1393, and then from 1396 to 1416. During the two-year period from 1394 to 1396, the position was filled by Francesco di Gherardo, a *canterino* who was appointed in spite of a criminal record for assaulting a local tailor with a sword two years earlier.[149] Little else is known of Francesco, but there are a few documents referring to Antonio di Friano, including his mission as ambassador to Rome in 1408.[150] It was during the time of Antonio di Friano that the position of *sindico e referendario* and that of singer of moral songs at the Mensa were separated, freeing the herald of the obligation to perform at the daily meals (see discussion in chapter 4).

Quite a bit more information has survived concerning some of those who served as herald in the fifteenth century, including a representative amount of poetry for some of them. Several extant collections of poems from the early fifteenth century contain works by both Antonio di Meglio and Anselmo Calderoni. The literary company that they kept, both literally and in terms of their appearance in collections of poetry, was quite distinguished. It includes the other competitors in the Certame Coronario: Michele di Nofri del Gigante, Benedetto di Michele Accolti d'Arezzo, Mariotto d'Arrigo Davanzati, Francesco d'Altobianco degli Alberti, Antonio degli Agli, M. Leonardo Dati,[151] as well as Niccolo Cieco, Coluccio Salutati, Bernardo di Ser Jacopo Dalla Casa, Jacopo di Dante Alighieri, Paolo dell' Abbaco, Burchiello, Giovanni di Maffeo da Barberino, and Ciriaco d'Ancona.[152]

It can be seen that Antonio di Meglio's politics were adjustable to the situation. Sometime before 1434 he wrote poetry in praise of the Albizi; in one *sirventese* he calls them "true friends of the republic," but on the return of their arch-rivals, the Medici, he changed his allegiance and celebrated the triumph of Cosimo in a canzona (see chapter 5), and in 1440 he wrote three *capitoli* on the death of Cosimo's brother Lorenzo.[153] Among his surviving works are two sonnets written for Pope Eugenius IV at the time of the 1439 Council in Florence (see above). And on the occasion of the visit of Francesco Sforza in 1445, although sick with gout at the time and unable to leave his bed, Antonio wrote two sonnets to honor the occasion and sent his son Giovan Matteo to perform them for the Count.[154] In collaboration with Feo Belcari sometime between 1444 and 1448, Antonio wrote the earliest datable *sacra rappresentazione: Dì del Giudicio.*[155] Antonio Lanza considers Antonio di Meglio's political poetry to be of primary historical importance.[156]

Anselmo Calderoni (1393–1446), who was born in Florence and whose father was an *approvatore* of the commune (a supervisory position), first served as herald in Urbino under Guidantonio da Montefeltro beginning in 1422. Throughout his career he was a regular visitor at the bottega of Burchiello, with whom he exchanged poetry known as *tenzioni*.[157] Although Antonio di Meglio continued to hold the post of herald of Florence for most of the first half of the century, Calderoni was also a literary presence in the city throughout those decades, applying for and receiving the position of herald in 1442 when di Meglio fell ill.[158] By then he had been campaigning for the position for some time, complaining in one of his verses that his talents were not recognized in his own country (i.e., Florence).[159] One of his verses, written sometime between 1434 and 1440, is an undisguised effort to ingratiate himself with the Medici:

> *O lume de' terrestri cittadini,*
> *O chiaro ispecchio d'ongni merchatante,*
> *O vero amicho a tutt'opere sante,*
> *O onor degl'illustri cittadini;*
> *O speranza dei grandi e dei piccini,*
> *O socchorso d'ongnun ch'è bisogniante,*

*O di popilli e vedove aiutante,*
*O forte scudo de'toschan chonfini.*

. . .

*Dobbian fino alla morte*
*per Chosimo e Lorenzo tutti noi*
*poveri, preghar sempre Iddio per voi.*[160]

[O light of earthly citizens; O clear mirror of every merchant; O true friend of all holy works; O honor of the illustrious citizens; O hope of the great and small; O refuge of everyone in need; O helper of orphans and widows; O strong shield of the Tuscan borders. . . . Until we end in death, all of us poor people must always pray to God for you, Cosimo and Lorenzo.]

The three short-term heralds following Calderoni—Antonio di Meglio's son Gregorio, Simone da Chianciano, and Bartolomeo di Bartolomeo—have left little of note to mark their terms in the office.[161] The next herald, however, Francesco di Lorenzo, later known as Francesco Filarete, the longest-serving herald (herald 1456–1505),[162] is better documented. In turn, he has provided us with a substantial amount of information concerning the official ceremonies of Florence by way of a ceremonial log, the *Libro cerimoniale*.

Filarete (1419–ca. 1505) is first recorded as a member of the household staff of Matteo Ceffini and Jacopo Guicciardini in 1452, where he learned some of the skills that served him well throughout his career. He must have been quite talented in diplomacy, serving through the period of the Medici expulsion in the 1490s and continuing in the position into the time of the new anti-Medici regime. Even though he had praised the Medici family in verse form over the preceding decades,[163] on the occasion of their expulsion in 1494 he was perfectly capable of identifying himself immediately with the new powers in the city, writing "Della rinnovazione della libertà," a *capitolo ternario* extolling the virtues of the group who had driven the Medici from the city.[164] We know, however, of one incident that would have resulted in his permanent dismissal except for the intercession of young Lorenzo de' Medici. In 1464 Filarete's close friend Cristoforo Landino, a noted Florentine philosopher and Medici intimate, wrote to his student Lorenzo de' Medici—at that time age fifteen—to ask him to use his influence to restore Filarete to his position. It seems that the herald had been found keeping a woman in his room at the Palazzo della Signoria, which was strictly forbidden. Landino's reasons for requesting Lorenzo's intercession were that this was an unusual breach in Filarete's normally upstanding behavior, and that he was the only support for his family, which consisted of his mother, pregnant wife, and three children. Landino uses the opportunity to praise Filarete as Lorenzo's faithful and useful follower, and mentions that Filarete was a fellow member of the Accademia Platonica, a humanist academy established by Lorenzo's grandfather Cosimo.[165]

On his appointment as herald in 1456, Filarete was referred to as "a singer with a *lira da braccio*" (*canterinus cum violamore*), and in 1469 as "a guitarist, that is to say a violinist" (*quitarrista seu violinista*), a rather awkward way to describe someone who plays an instrument that is both plucked and bowed, as was the *lira da braccio*.[166] In addition to the usual set of talents possessed by heralds, Filarete also was an architect: at the invitation of the Duke of Mantua he was involved in the construction of the Gonzaga rotunda in the church of Santissima Annunziata dei Servi in 1470; and in 1490 he entered a design into the competition for the facade of the Florentine Duomo.[167] While serving as herald in 1504, he was named to the committee that decided on the placement of Michelangelo's *David*, where (assisted by his son-in-law and assistant herald, Angelo Manfidi, *il sichondo Araldo*) he apparently led the discussion and defended the placement of the famous statue in front of the Palazzo della Signoria. The jury on that occasion consisted of five artists including Andrea della Robbia, three goldsmiths, an embroiderer, the civic herald, and Giovanni Cellini, the head of the civic *pifferi* (see chapter 5).[168]

During the reforms of the *famiglia* enacted in 1475–76,[169] Filerete was directed to compile the *Libro cerimoniale*, an account that begins in the year of his first appointment (1456) and continues on to 1527 (completed by Manfidi.)[170] The book is extremely helpful in providing ceremonial details, although it is far from encyclopedic: it concentrates on the most important of the ad hoc affairs, citing only a few of the hundred or so yearly events. The account of any particular event is limited to commentary on those things that were unusual, such as a variation from the standard processional route, the varying distance the Priors traveled across the *ringhiera* to welcome the guest, or other special events that were outside of the standard format. Nevertheless, the account is rich in details that help us understand how the herald and the civic musicians were involved in the ceremonies. One such example is the revealing commentary in the account of the 1459 visit of Galeazzo Maria Sforza, son of the Duke of Milan, where Filarete tells us that the Signori, the Podestà, and the Capitano del Popolo were among the three hundred or so people, all richly clothed, who went out to greet the distinguished visitor (see details in chapter 1): "We sent all of the musicians of the republic and the herald [Filarete] to supervise the order of the ceremony and the pomp of the entrance."[171] When the Pope returned to Florence the following January, Filarete tells us, "And thus we sent to meet him our magistrates and all the musicians, that is the trumpets and pifferi, and me again to supervise, in as much as it is my duty to observe the order of such events."[172]

As another provision in the 1475–76 reforms, Filarete was given the liberty to no longer eat at the Mensa. This is significant because from the earliest records of the office one of the principal duties of the office had been in conjunction with the ceremony at the Mensa. But beginning early in the century, as a result of the increasing number of ceremonial responsibilities, additional *canterini* had been hired regularly to perform at the Mensa (see discussion in chapter 4). Although the custom of singing *canti morali* along with other entertainment continued at the Mensa, the 1475 revision suggests that by that date the herald was no longer needed to oversee these events; his time was more and more taken up with supervision of the larger public celebrations. There is no suggestion, however, that he did not continue to write poetry and sing *all'improvviso* on all important ceremonial occasions. A few of Filarete's poems survive in collections, including an ode in praise of Federigo da Montefeltro, duke of Urbino, on the occasion of his installation as Captain-General of the Florentine army in June of 1472.[173]

Filarete's successor, Angelo Manfidi da Poppi (herald 1500–27), who married Filarete's daughter Teodora in 1497, had first been a member of the Medici household serving Lorenzo's son Giuliano. He was a friend of Michelangelo Buonarroti, and in 1507 acted on his behalf by approaching the Standard Bearer of Justice, Piero Soderini, about various concerns of the sculptor.[174] First appointed as assistant herald in 1500, on the death of Filarete in 1505 Manfidi took over as principal herald and author of the *Libro cerimoniale*. He included at the very end of the *Libro* three of his own poems: two for Il Magnifico's grandson, Lorenzo di Piero di Lorenzo, the Duke of Urbino and ruler of Florence, when he was presented with the baton of the Captain-General of Florence in 1515 and on the occasion of his marriage in 1518. The third poem probably was written on receipt of the news that Il Magnifico's son Giovanni had just been elected Pope Leo X.[175] Manfidi's son, Francesco (Francesco di Messer Angniolo araldo) also was a *canterino* and is recorded as having sung at the Mensa in 1508 on the feast of San Giovanni.[176] There is no other record of Francesco, who did not succeed his father in the position.

In spite of the lavish praise from Angelo Manfidi in the poems written in his honor, Lorenzo di Piero (Lorenzo the Younger) was not completely satisfied with Manfidi's activities as herald and appointed Giovan Battista dell'Ottonaio as co-herald (1517–27) during the last ten years of Manfidi's term in office, undoubtedly in the hope that the prolific playwright and popular poet would add some excitement to the office. Ottonaio wrote a number of *sacre rappresentazioni*,[177] but he is best remembered for his *canti carnascialeschi*, the humorous and sometimes lascivious secular songs intended to be sung at carnival time. Significantly, Ottonaio was paid considerably more than was Manfidi: twenty-one lire, six soldi, eight denari, as compared to Manfidi's sixteen lire per month.[178] When we see that the last herald of the Republic, Jacopo di Niccolò del Polta, known as Il Bientina (herald 1527–39), was also a noted writer of *canti carnascialeschi*, it is evident that on the return of the Medici to power, there was far more emphasis on the herald becoming involved in drama and in the more secular public events, as opposed to the more serious ceremonial functions of the previous centuries, a preference highlighted by the difference in salary between Giovan Battista dell'Ottonaio and the more traditional Angelo Manfidi. Although the emphasis clearly had shifted, we should note that the men appointed to achieve the new goals were quite gifted; the last heralds of the Republic, similar to those first appointed, were highly respected as talented artists, a trend that continued into the period of the dukes with the appointment of the actor Domenico Barlacchi as herald in 1539.[179]

**Figure 1.** Map of Florence, 1462. Piero del Massaio, Manuscript illumination, Paris, Bibliothèque Nationale, Ms Lat 4802, fol. 132v.

**Figure 2.** Map of Florence. After AnnaMaria Testaverde Matteini, "La decorazione festiva e l'itinerario di 'rifondazione' della città negli ingressi trionfali a Firenze tra XV e XVI secoli." *Mitteilungen des Kunsthistorischen Institutes in Florenz* 32 (1988), page 340.

Procession of Pope Leo X. dotted line:
1. Arch at Porta Romana
2. Arch in Piazza San Felice
3. Arch at Ponte Santa Trinita
4. Oblisk
5. Arch in Piazza Santa Trinita
6. Trajan's Column in Mercato Nuovo
7. Hercules in Piazza della Signoria
8. Arch in Piazza della Signoria
9. Arch at the Palazzo della Podestà
10. Arch at Canto de' Bischeri
11. Facade resembling the Castel Sant' Angelo
12. Arch at Canto de' Carnesechi
13. Equestrian statue in Piazza Santa Maria Novella
14. Arch at the Entrance to the Sala del Papa in Santa Maria Novella

Procession on the feast of San Giovanni (counterclockwise). picket line:
15. Baptistry
16. Via Tournabuoni
17. Ponte S. Trinita
18. San Felicità
19. Ponte Vecchio
8. Piazza della Signoria
20. Via Proconsolo
21. Duomo

Palio. solid line:
22. Borgo Ognisanti
6. Mercato Nuovo
23. Via Corso, Borgo degli Albizzi
24. San Piero Maggiore

**Figure 3.** Giorgio Vasari, Giostra del Saracino in Via Largo. Florence, Sala Gualdrada, Palazzo Vecchio. Photo credit: Scala/Art Resource, N.Y.

Figure 4a. (above) Apollonio di Giovanni di Tommaso, *Tournament in the square of Santa Croce, Florence.* Yale University Art Gallery. University Purchase from James Jackson Jarves.

Figure 4b. (below) Italian, Florentine, *Wedding Cassone with a tournament scene.* London National Gallery, NG4906.

**Figure 5.** Luca Della Robbia, Cantoria in Santa Maria del Fiore. Florence Museo dell' Opera del Duomo. Photo credit: Scala/Art Resource, N.Y.

**Figure 6a.** Trumpets of Florence, 1465. Ulrich von Richenthal, Prague, Státní Knihovna, Ms XVI. A. 17, fol. 128.

**Figure 6b.** Musicians of the Emperor, 1465. Ulrich von Richenthal, Constance, Rosengartenmuseum, Ms K, fol. 39.

AMPLISSIMO HOC APPARATV ET PVLCHRO ORDINE POMPA FVNEBRIS BRVXELLIS À PALATIO AD DIVÆ GVDVLÆ TEMPLVM PROCESSIT CVM REX HISPANIARVM PHILIPPVS CAROLO V. ROM. IMP. PARĒTI MŒSTISSIMVS IVSTA SOLVERET

Joannes a duetecum. Lucas duetecum. Fecit

**Figure 7.** Van Doetecum, "Funeral Ceremony of Charles V at Brussels." Engraving. Brussels, Bibliothèque Royale de Belgique, no. II 8052 C.

**Figures 8 and 9.** Hans Memling, triptych panels, left and right wings of Najera triptych. Antwerp, Musée des Beaux-Arts, #779, 780. Photo credit: Scala/Art Resource, N.Y.

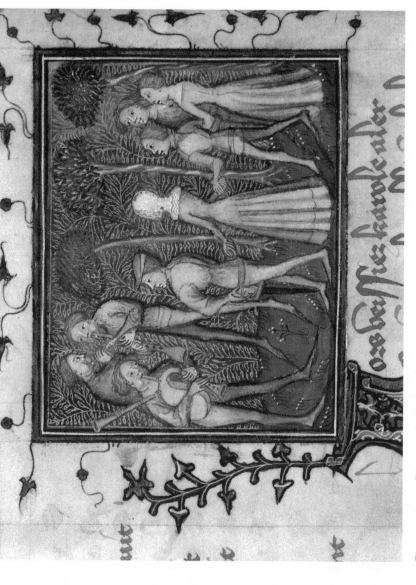

Figure 10. Anon., "Dance in the Garden of Mirth." Guillaume de Lorris and Jean de Meun, Le Roman de la Rose (ca. 1380), Oxford, Bodleian Library, Ms E. Mus. 65, fol. 3v.

**Figure 11.** Cantimpanca. Anon. woodcut. Frontispiece from *Historia d' Appollonio di Tiro* (Florence, after 1550), Florence, Biblioteca Riccardiana, Ed.r.675.2.

**Figure 12.** Andrea di Bonaiuto, Allegory of the Dominican Order, detail. Florence, Spanish Chapel, Santa Maria Novella. Photo credit: Scala/Art Resource, N.Y.

**Figure 13.** Giotto, Herod's Feast. Florence, Santa Croce, Cappella Peruzzi. Photo credit: Erich Lessing/Art Resource, N.Y.

**Figure 14.** Anonymous, Adimari Wedding Cassone, detail. Florence, Galleria dell' Academia. Photo credit: Nicolo Orsi Battaglini/Art Resource, N.Y.

Figure 15. Pieter Bruegel the Elder, "The Three Soldiers." 1568. © New York, The Frick Collection, 1965.1.163.

**Figure 16.** Alessandro Botticelli. Adoration of the Magi. Florence, Galleria degli Uffizi. Photo credit: Scala/Art Resource, N.Y.

**Figure 17.** Benozzo Gozzoli, Procession of the Magi, detail. Florence, Medici Chapel, Palazzo Medici-Riccardi. Photo credit: Scala/Art Resource, N.Y.

**Figure 18.** Raphael, Pope Leo X (with Cardinals Giulio di Giuliano de' Medici and Luigi de Rossi). Florence, Galleria degli Uffizi. Photo credit: Scala/Art Resource, N.Y.

**Figure 19.** Giorgio Vasari, Pope Leo X, Entrance to Florence in 1515. Florence, Palazzo Vecchio, Sala di Leone X. Photo credit: Scala/Art Resource, N.Y.

# 4

## Revising the Ceremonial Traditions

The last two decades of the fourteenth century witnessed changes in the essential nature of the organization of the government of Florence, which in turn affected the ceremonial practices that involved music and the civic musicians. As noted in the preceding chapters, membership in the civic musical ensemble and the duties of the civic musicians continued to evolve throughout the fourteenth century, mirroring the gradual changes in civic ceremony. But the changes of the 1380s were particularly drastic, reflecting an entirely new self-image of the Florentine government which set the Priors along a new path. Although the alteration of the composition of the Florentine political scene following the Ciompi Revolt is well known, by noting the revisions in the civic ceremonial practices that resulted and searching through the causes of these changes, it is possible to see rather clearly how the Ciompi upheaval succeeded in causing modifications well beyond any intention on the part of the lowly workers who took part in the uprising.

During the one hundred years following the 1282 establishment of the Priorate, all changes made with regard to the civic musicians were relatively minor as the government adjusted its ceremonial procedures in response to the evolving society. Throughout most of the fourteenth century the original group of trombadori, consisting of six large trumpets, a percussion instrument, and a reed instrument, continued to be the basis of the instrumental ensemble. The 1317 addition of a small trumpet and the 1356 addition of a bagpipe reflected the continual expansion in the quantity and type of ceremonial functions that involved music, but by and large, throughout most of the century the duties of the civic musicians remained close to those of the past. The same can be said of the office of the civic herald, whose duties grew in quantity as a result of the increase in civic ceremonies but remained basically unchanged.

The revisions of the 1380s, however, were on a different scale, caused by a conceptual change involving the way in which the Priors viewed their position, which in turn caused basic changes to the office of the civic herald, the civic musicians, and some fundamental innovations to the ceremony of the Mensa. In the larger picture, these changes encouraged and hastened the incursion of northern cultural tastes among the citizens of Florence, reflecting an alteration in cultural focus that, instead of evolving slowly as it had over the preceding centuries, was rather abrupt. The government's initiation and implementation of change reflected the influence of northern courts on Florence and the felt need of the Priors to mimic northern practices, as we shall see below. The result was a reorientation of ceremonial Florence away from its medieval model toward that of the new Renaissance. Elsewhere in Europe, especially in the areas to the north of Italy, new ceremonial and social customs had been evolving since mid-century as a result of new thinking and revised values. Throughout most of this time Florence had remained somewhat aloof, continuing to honor its traditional values and customs until pressures from a number of sources, prodded by political unrest, succeeded in wrenching the city out of its introspective medieval habits.

## The Winds of Political Change

In the 1340s Florence experienced severe domestic problems that would define its history for the next several decades. An economic recession was exacerbated by a series of epidemics and social turmoil. The treasury had been seriously stretched by an unsuccessful campaign against Lucca in the 1330s; the two largest Florentine banks, those of the Bardi and the Peruzzi, went into bankruptcy; a serious epidemic in 1340 that killed several thousand of the approximately ninety thousand inhabitants was followed eight years later by the Black Death, which reduced the population by an additional forty thousand; and finally, there was the disastrous reign of Podestà Walter of Brienne, Duke of Athens, which ended with his expulsion from the city in 1343. These events resulted in a realignment of the political power structure that had a disruptive effect on the city for the next several decades. During the 1350s and '60s, Florentine military forces twice fought against Milan (1351–53, 1369–70), and the city was twice threatened by the troops of Emperor Charles IV (1354–55, 1368). All of this made a serious drain on the city finances, resulting inevitably in higher taxes for everyone, especially the peasants in the surrounding countryside and those who were members of those trades that were without guild representation in the government.

The political reforms that took place later in the century were long in preparation, dating back at least as early as the 1360s, when a strong new rivalry surfaced within the ranks of the upper classes led by two large, opposing families. On one side was the Albizzi family under the leadership of Piero degli Albizzi, with close ties to the older ideals of the Parte Guelfa: dominance by the aristocracy, and support for alliances with both the papacy and Naples. The other position was that of the Ghibellines, represented by the family of Uguccione de' Ricci, who feared the dominance of the Parte. This faction favored a substantial representation by artisans and held far more flexible and pragmatic views of foreign relations. The factional rivalry continued to weaken the Florentine government throughout the 1360s and '70s, producing increasing tension on the level of foreign relations, including those with the papacy in Avignon. In 1375, under the belief that the Papal States posed a threat to Florentine independence, Florence initiated a war against the papacy. In retaliation, Pope Gregory XI placed the city under interdict in 1376, further destabilizing the harried government and intensifying the unrest of the citizens to a point that culminated in a sequence of political demonstrations that are generally referred to as the Ciompi Revolt.[1]

In 1378 the cloth workers of Florence, the Ciompi, organized a revolt that historians, beginning with Leonardo Bruni, once considered to have been one of the most significant events in the late Middle Ages. Although more recent assessments have modified that position, it is still acknowledged that the Ciompi Revolt played a critical role in the changes that followed, initiating a process that led to cultural as well as political revision.[2] Initially, the uprising involved only two opposing factions in the cloth-making industry: one side was composed of those having minor social and economic status—the subcontractors, brokers, and factors; the other side included the lowly laborers who were without property or any social position and had little to lose by pressing for change. The principle that was at stake was the laborers' desire to be given a voice in the governance of the guilds and in the civic government as a whole alongside the merchants and artisans; a direct assault on one of the most basic tenets of the Parte Guelfa, which did not have any interest in sharing power with the lower classes. The issues were those of interest to all lower-class workers, and the insurrection quickly gained popularity and spread to involve laborers from a number of other trades. Their demands included tax reform, the abolition of financial privileges enjoyed only by the rich, a two-year moratorium on small debts, and judicial restraints. The event was marked by bursts of local violence that included the setting on fire of the palaces of many aristocratic families, the destruction of guild and communal records, and the lynching of a police official. At one point in the uprising, the reformers succeeded in creating three new guilds for those workers who performed the least skilled assignments, and achieved electoral changes that would have them represented by two seats on the Priorate, three in the college of the Twelve, and four in the college of the Sixteen.[3]

The workers, however, were neither unified nor organized, and predictably were subdued within two months. The immediate result was that the laborers lost the battle and their guilds were dissolved, although in larger terms the revolt did have an impact: their voices had been heard and the government of Florence changed, even though many of the changes were short-lived. The revolt succeeded in upsetting the government to the extent that for the next three years (1378–81), a much greater amount of power was entrusted to the guilds, with the members of the ancient families for the most part excluded from government.[4] Although much of what the Ciompi had fought for had been reversed, the lower-class workers still held seats in the government during these years and were able to make their voices heard, at least for a short period of time.

In a society where both wealth and economic power were concentrated in the hands of the upper classes, a government dominated by the lower classes proved to be unstable, and beginning in 1382 the Parte Guelfa began to reassert its power through a series of moves that would eventually return control of the government to the conservative patricians; what John Najemy calls "a consciously articulated response to, and repudiation of, the corporate approach to electoral politics."[5] Left over from the revolt, however, was the principle of expansion of the class of citizens eligible for office, and the lower guilds held their two seats in each Signoria. But the sharing of power was eventually restricted to those who had paid taxes continuously for thirty years; in other words, people of substance. For fifty-two years—until the Medici gained power in 1434—this conservative patrician government continued its gradual tendency toward government that favored the rich and powerful and oppressed the poor.

The resumption of power by the aristocrats that began slowly in 1382, however, did not necessarily mean that all of the old traditions returned as well. The change in the balance of power during the preceding three years proved to be an opportunity to make some basic changes in procedure, and as a part of the government's shift in focus, the members of the Signoria decided to revise the ceremonial representation in order to reflect the changing self-image of Florence.

It is not that these new ideas and practices were unknown in Florence during the last decades of the fourteenth century; in some ways Florence was a leader among north Italian cities, especially in the intellectual field. But there existed some strong contradictions. Whereas the intellectual and literary part of the city had embraced the advancing humanist movement, the artistic and musical world held on to older images, and the official, ceremonial aspects of the government had been slow to react to the changes adopted elsewhere. By the last half of the fourteenth century, some of the aspects of ceremonial Florence were an over-extended version of earlier medieval traditions that had been pushed beyond their capacity and needed to be changed. At some point it was decided that what was needed was not more extension or enlargement of the traditional medieval models, but a complete revision, aligning the civic rituals of Florentine society with changes that had taken place in other areas. As Hans Baron observes, for northern Italy the transition from the fourteenth to the fifteenth century was marked by an enormous break with the past in terms of the arts and in the intellectual field. The work of artists such as Brunelleschi, Donatello, and Masaccio, for example, differed from that of their predecessors far more abruptly than between any other two generations of the Renaissance, while a similar break with the humanism of Petrarch transpired at the hands of writers such as Niccoli, Bruni, and Poggio.[6] The same can be said for the changes in ceremonial traditions, and as a result, there was a serious revision in the makeup and role of the civic musicians.

The pressures for ceremonial change that can be seen most easily are those in the political arena, as summarized above, but once begun these had far broader implications for the society of Florence, jolting certain traditional practices of the city-state out of the Middle Ages and into the Renaissance; a conversion of orientation from the sacred sphere to that of the secular, following the lead of countries to the north.

# From Istrio to Knight of the Curia

As noted in chapter 3, the ceremonial duties of the herald had grown to such a degree over the decades that by the time of the appointment of Giovanni di Giorgio da Trebbio in 1377, the description of the office no longer included the position of *proveditore*, supervisor of supplies. The earlier coupling of the *referendario* position with that of *sindico proveditore* was dropped in 1375 when those household duties were transferred to the *donzelli*,[7] leaving a more logical pairing of the duties of singer at the Mensa with the ceremonial responsibilities of the *referendario*, a position that was now described in terms of its ritualistic dimensions, an acknowledgment of the increasing pressures of the ceremonial aspect of the position. Shortly afterward, on the occasion of Giovanni di Giorgio's reappointment in 1383, the title of *istrio* was changed to a new and far more elevated title: *Miles curialis*—Knight of the Curia.

> The magnificent Lord Priors of the Guilds and the Standard Bearer of Justice of the People and Commune of Florence: noting to what extent Messer Giovanni Giorgio da Trebbio of Florence, curial knight [*Miles curialis*] of the said Commune, and up to this time frequently chosen and considered for syndic and referendary of the previously mentioned Commune, in the same office or administration has and deports himself laudably and prudently; and, considering this, those Lords wish to honor the same with gratitude and favor, as much for the honor of the said Commune as for his proven merits.[8]

A few years later the phrase *Cavaliere di Corte*, Knight of the Court, is also found as a synonym for the position,[9] an indication that the Signoria was prepared to describe itself in foreign terms, equating the city-state with a court. (The same position in Venice was called *Cavaliere del Doge*.)[10] The statutes of 1415 describe the positions of singer of moral songs and that of *miles curialis*, *sindico*, and *referendario* as two separate positions, another interesting change that attests to the growing duties in each of the posts; until this point the two positions (in addition to that of *proveditore*) had usually been given to the same person.[11] Significantly, the descriptions are found under a single rubric in the statutes:

> And let them have—and they must have—a singer of moral songs at the table [i.e. Mensa] of the previously mentioned Lords, and also at whatever [other occasion] they may wish, with a salary of three gold florins every month, as above. And let them have one curial knight [*militem curialem*], a syndic and referendary of the Commune of Florence, who at their banquets and feasts will pay them honor, in speaking and composing speeches, and in joining him [i.e. the singer

of moral songs], who must go wherever he should be sent by them. Such a one is to have for his salary ten lire every month, as above, and over and above [this], let him have from the Podestà of the city of Florence in each half-year one livery of the value of twenty-five gold florins.[12]

There is no doubt that by the turn of the century the ceremonial duties had, for all intents and purposes, turned the holder of the position into a full-time herald,[13] a point acknowledged by the changes in duties as well as the more exalted titles, and especially in the hiring of additional poet-singers to take over the daily singing obligations at the Mensa. The revision of duties at the Mensa allowed the herald time to deal with the more public ceremonies as well as the additional role of accompanying ambassadors on various missions. As Filarete stated in his *Libro cerimoniale*, it was the herald's duty to "supervise the order" of all public ceremonial events.[14]

It is not clear when the Signoria revised the heraldic duties so that they could be shared, but in 1401, during the period when Antonio di Piero di Friano was the official herald (*cavaliere cortegiano e referendario del comune*),[15] a singer named Cristofano was paid for singing at the Mensa, and in 1404 another singer, Antonio di Matteo di Meglio, who would soon become the civic herald, was paid by the government as a singer of songs (*cantoris cantilenarum*).[16] The two Antonios continued in the service of the commune for the next twelve years: Antonio di Piero, the herald, who apparently presided over all ceremonies including the Mensa, and Antonio di Matteo, who served as the singer of moral songs at the Mensa, exactly as described in the 1415 statute. Both men were knights, and both were well respected as poet-singers. On the death of Antonio di Friano in 1416, Antonio di Matteo was appointed in his place as herald, a post he held for the next twenty-six years until poor health forced him to retire in 1442.

But these records do not tell the entire story of singers at the Mensa during this period. In 1409, while both Antonios were still present and listed on the pay records, an additional singer, Bernardo (also called Barnaba) di Cristofano, was also employed to sing at the Mensa.[17] These arrangements continue for a number of years until 1416, when the financial documents record pensions to Bernardo as well as to another singer, Piero di Bartolo di Giusto, both of whom are identified as having sung at the Mensa.[18] What is notable about this is that pensions were awarded only to those people who had served the city for a number of years,[19] meaning that the number of singers who performed more or less regularly at the Mensa during the first decades of the fifteenth century was higher than the regular pay records reflect: possibly as many as four altogether. Until this notice of a pension for Piero di Bartolo di Giusto in 1416, he is not found on the payroll, although the fact that he was formerly a singer at the Mensa is stated very clearly in the record of his pension (*cantore di canzoni alla Mensa dei Signori*) and repeated in the records for several additional years. Clearly, by the end of the fourteenth century the need for civic *cantastorie* had grown considerably, resulting first in the reassignment of the position of *proveditore* to relieve the herald of that responsibility. Soon afterward, the government employed additional poet-singers to assist the herald in his regular duties in connection with the progressively elaborate performances at the Mensa (see below). And although the earliest official notices of the additional singers begin only in 1401, there is reason to suspect that the need had begun sometime earlier—perhaps as early the mid-1380s in conjunction with the other changes described below—resulting in the occasional or part-time appointment of additional singers.

## *New Instrumental Ensembles*

The innovations in the organization of the instrumental musicians during this period was even more dramatic than those to the position of herald. In addition to the traditional trombadori ensemble that since the beginning of the Priorate had represented the Commune of Florence as a whole, two new musical ensembles were instituted, the pifferi and the trombetti, whose principal duties were to represent specifically the Signori: the eight Priors and the Standard Bearer of Justice. This symbolically set the nine executives apart from the remainder of the Florentine government by assigning to them their own musical representatives. The statements of purpose that accompanied the formation of the two new groups make it clear that this is no mere "housekeeping" adjustment; it represented an entirely new self-image for the Signoria. A document of October 1386 states that the Signoria, wishing "not only to preserve but to augment the honor of the Mensa of the commune," appoints three pifferi to serve the Priors and the Standard Bearer of Justice.[20]

A year later the player of the *trombetta*, the small trumpet, was removed from the trombadori and a separate ensemble called the trombetti was established, consisting of two small trumpets (expanded to four by 1393 and five by 1396), "for the honor of the Lord Priors of the Guilds, the Standard Bearer of Justice, and the people of the Commune of Florence," meaning, however, that they too were connected directly to the Priors and Gonfaloniere.[21]

The intention of these moves was to change dramatically the status of the chief executives, setting them apart from the rest of the commune by having them represented ceremonially in public by their own musical groups. What the executives of the city-state had done, therefore, was to present themselves as "princes" by taking on ceremonial trappings similar to those found in many of the most elaborate royal courts throughout the remainder of Europe.

Members of these new musical groups were given costumes similar to those of the trombadori, but to set them apart they also received an insignia that marked them as the musicians of the Signoria: a *smaltum* that they were to wear on their chests, consisting of a small round ceramic emblem with a red lily (*giglio*) set against a silver background. The pifferi were required to ornament their instruments with silver, and the trombetti were to have trumpets of silver,[22] thus continuing the symbolism of silver musical instruments as the proper representation of political authority. As with the trombadori, there was concern about the uniform quality of the instruments that the pifferi and trombetti were to provide for themselves. A 1396 document directed that the combined value of the *smaltum* and trumpet was to be no less than forty-five florins (a value nearly equal to a trumpet player's entire yearly wages).[23] The salaries paid to the new groups were nearly twice that paid to the trombadori—two florins per month for each of the pifferi and trombetti (raised to three florins by 1390 and four in 1396), versus five lire (one and one-quarter florins) for the trombadori. (See the discussion of comparative salaries in chapter 5.)

The instrument played by the members of the trombetti was, as the name implies, a small trumpet. What the instruments played by the pifferi were, however, is not stated quite so clearly. In the initial appointment of 1386, the musicians and their instruments are identified as follows: "Franceschino d'Alessandro, *sonatore di bombarde*, Felice di Simone da Firenze, *sonatore di cornete*, et Nanni di Maso Massay da Sesto, *sonatore di cornamuse*."[24] The *bombarda* was the alto shawm, and although the word *cornamusa* usually referred specifically to the bagpipe, occasionally it was used in a more general sense to refer to any reed instrument.[25] As discussed in chapter 2, the duet of shawm and bagpipe was a popular combination in the last half of the fourteenth century,[26] a bagpipe having been added to the trombadori in 1356,[27] and thus bagpipe probably is the meaning of *cornamusa* here. The *cornete* is more of a problem. In the accounts of 1393 it is referred to with the spelling *cornetto*,[28] giving rise to the possibility that it could be the wooden cup–mouthpiece instrument known from the late-fifteenth and sixteenth centuries as a *cornetto*.[29] In later records, however, including one from 1387, it is referred to as a *cornete sive ciramella*, a "horn, that is to say, a reed,"[30] which suggests that the word probably refers to the soprano member of the shawm family.[31] Iconography from the period depicting an ensemble made up of two shawms with a bagpipe confirms the suspicion (see figure 10).

The two new ensembles, the trombetti and pifferi, had mostly domestic duties related directly to the Signori. The trombetti were to accompany the members of the Signoria when they moved through the streets, announcing their presence and gathering the citizens by sounding their instruments, a responsibility formerly entrusted to the trombadori. The trombadori, on the other hand, found themselves more frequently assigned to accompany the military and to represent the commune at celebrations in other cities, as well as fulfilling their more traditional function in conjunction with large Florentine ceremonies. The trombetti and pifferi were sometimes called upon to participate with the other musical ensembles in celebrations of the commune as a whole, as for example in welcoming a distinguished figure to the city, when both of the new ensembles plus the bannitori were required to augment the sound made by the trombadori in procession.[32] Even on those occasions, however, the ensembles performed separately. The *Libro cerimoniale* account of the procession leading Count Galeazzo Maria Sforza into Florence, for example, makes it clear that the musical ensembles were spaced throughout the procession rather than grouped together (see chapter 1, "Distinguished Visitors"). An additional obligation for the pifferi and trombetti was a requirement as a part of their regular duties to play at the church of Orsanmichele on Sundays as well as for various special church celebrations: the vigil of the feast of the Blessed Virgin, Easter, and whenever the image of the Mother of God was exhibited, as for example when the *tavola* of Santa Maria del Impruneta was paraded through the streets in times of crisis. On these occasions they were directed to make a *mattinata* (*mattinatam facere*), that is, to play music, although what they were to play is never stated.[33] The principal responsibilities of the two new ensembles, however, were with specific reference to the Signori, especially the daily performances at the Mensa during the noon and evening meals.[34] This also meant that the trombetti and pifferi were to eat at the Mensa, a privilege never granted to the trombadori.

## The Ceremony of the Mensa

With the institution of the new musical ensembles and their assignment to the Mensa of the Signoria, that ceremony took on an entirely new appearance.

The original idea of the private Mensa grew from the necessity of feeding the sequestered executives. Originally these occasions bore a close resemblance to the mealtimes of monks inasmuch as they were usually closed affairs (i.e., no visitors), and the diners were presented with uplifting thoughts in the form of moral songs sung by the herald, a practice that closely resembles the monastic custom of readings from scripture during mealtimes.[35] With the changes made to the ceremony at the end of the fourteenth century, however, that image no longer prevailed. Although the singer of moral songs continued to be a part of the Mensa, the occasion itself was changed both in purpose and content: more and more distinguished visitors were invited to dine with the executives, and a substantial amount of entertainment of various types was added.

Beginning in the late 1380s the formal beginning of each meal was marked by fanfares played by the new ensemble of trombetti, who summoned the diners to the Mensa. The trombetti would also intersperse fanfares throughout dinner, announcing each new course as the meal proceeded and introducing the various entertainers and performers. The three members of the pifferi were also present as regular members of the Mensa and performed throughout the mealtime, and we have noted above that singers in addition to the civic herald also appeared regularly at the Mensa. It is also apparent that when the occasion warranted it, numerous other performers and entertainers were added to this basic format. We can only speculate at how and when the changes began, but by the early decades of the fifteenth century the Mensa had taken on a complexion that was in stark contrast to its original monastic form. The extent of the change can be seen in Gregorio Dati's description:

> It is said that it [the Mensa] is as well appointed and richly decorated and as well served as any Mensa of any other Signoria in the world; and by decree, pifferi, musicians [sonatori], actors, jugglers, and all things of amusement and magnificence are performed, because every two months six hundred gold florins are assigned to their Mensa. But they [the Signori] spend little time there, for they are soon called to sit to attend to the needs of the commune, which always gives them a lot of business to take care of and there is never a lack of things to do.[36]

Although the evidence is somewhat sketchy with regard to the quantity and frequency of entertainment in the revised celebration of the Mensa, the facts reported below do seem to support Dati's picture. Payment records for the Signoria as well as documents of various other organizations hint at a rather large number of entertainers who performed at the Mensa on both a permanent and occasional basis. It also appears that there were a number of performers "borrowed" from elsewhere who do not appear on the payroll. The extent to which these extra entertainers were present at the Mensa is difficult to ascertain, but the few details that have surfaced suggest that there may well have been a large number of performers on a fairly substantial number of occasions.

In the *catasto* of 1427, Pagolo di Ser Ambruogio (called "Vinci") stated that his profession was "piffero,"[37] a fact confirmed in the civic pay records of 1404 which include his name among the civic pifferi, although he is recorded as such only that one year.[38] Pagolo was a versatile musician, capable of playing bowed and plucked strings in addition to the shawm. Although not found on the civic payroll after 1404, through the years 1405–37 he was employed by the Oratorio of Orsanmichele, where he performed on viola, rebec, lute, and "other instruments," and was hired on special feast days by the laudesi company of San Zanobi.[39] It is of interest to note that his appointment to Orsanmichele states that he is also required to perform at the Mensa of the Signoria on viola and other instruments "whenever he is requested, without further payment."[40]

During the years 1425 through 1430, the civic pay records include Corrado di Federigo della Magna (i.e., from Germany), player of the viola, and Guglielmo di Currado de Alamania (also from Germany), player of the lute, among the list of salaried employees of the commune, although where and when they performed is not stated.[41] It is likely that like Pagolo, they too were expected to perform at the Mensa at the pleasure of the Signori, and probably at churches such as Orsanmichele, where their talents would have been in demand in conjunction with the laudese societies.[42]

The pension records of 1416–17 also mention one Cernobi di Landino, who according to one account had been a "juggler and cast member" (*gioculatore et acompagnatore*) at the Signoria, and according to another statement an "actor and member of the *famiglia* of the Palazzo della Signoria" (*buffone e famiglio del palagio del popolo di Firenze*);[43] undoubtedly one of the actors and jugglers referred to by Dati. In 1422 Cernobi was replaced by Bernardo di Cristofano, who had been on the payroll as a singer at the Mensa since 1409, and now was called "singer and entertainer at the table of the Signori" (*chantatore e giucholatore a la tavola dei Signori*).[44] As with some of the singers, the fact that both Cernobi and Bernardo received a civic pension is evidence that their employment was on a permanent basis over a period of at least ten years.

Additional information about Mensa entertainers comes in the form of a letter that was sent in January of 1406 from the Signoria to Cardinal Baldassare Cossa (later antipope John XXIII, 1410–18) in Rome. The purpose of the note is to alert Cardinal Cossa to the plight of the northerner Giovanni di Daniele di Fiandra "an honest man well educated in music," who was the teacher of two boys who sang at the church of San Lorenzo and at the Mensa of the Signoria.[45] The message asks for help in returning the boys, who had run away. It is unlikely that the boys would have sung alone; they were part of the choir of San Lorenzo, and therefore the reference is probably to performances that included the adult members of the San Lorenzo choir as well as the two boys.[46] We do not know how frequently the San Lorenzo choir members performed at the Mensa, although the letter does state that the boys entertained "often."

When taken as a whole, these bits and pieces of evidence allow us to interpret the narrow and inconsistent information found in the pay records and to round out the description of the entertainment at the Mensa. It is clear that the civic pay records do not reflect the number of entertainers who performed there. Numerous performers—"musicians, actors, jugglers, and all things of amusement and magnificence" in Dati's words—did indeed entertain the Signori and their distinguished guests, although most did not appear in the standard payroll accounts. Many of them must have been paid out of petty cash or from other, non-specific accounts, since Dati mentions six hundred gold florins spent on the Mensa in each two-month period. That amount would probably have been directed to finance entertainers hired on an ad hoc basis, as distinguished from the herald and the two instrumental groups that were full-time salaried appointments and accounted for separately. But it is also probable that some of the other entertainers were paid through a different kind of arrangement. Pagolo di Ser Ambruogio's appointment required him to play at the Mensa without further compensation as a part of his contract with the Oratorio of Orsanmichele. As implied in the letter about the two choirboys, vocal music was often supplied to the Mensa by members of the choir of San Lorenzo; and thus it is probable that singing at the Mensa was one of the duties of the members of the San Lorenzo choir. In that case, money transferred from the civic treasury to the church would not carry a detailed account of the purpose. Conversely, the singers could have been paid from the current account. Or their contract with the choir may have required them to perform at the Mensa without further compensation, similar to Pagolo di Ser Ambruogio's arrangement at Orsanmichele. As will be seen in chapter 5 in conjunction with the musicians who performed privately for the Medici family, there would seem to have been a Florentine tradition of musicians receiving their wages as members of a church staff while also having other obligations that are not recorded. It is abundantly clear, however, that the civic payroll does not accurately reflect the number of entertainers who performed at the daily Mensa of the Signoria.

Undoubtedly, the lavish events mentioned by Dati were reserved for special occasions and guests, and probably did not take place at each meal. But even the standard daily entertainment—trumpet fanfares and dinner music by the pifferi—was a far cry from the original concept in which only the herald sang his *canti morali*. The number of distinguished visitors as well as ceremonial occasions continued to grow over these decades, and so we can speculate that by the beginning of the fifteenth century a fairly elaborate mealtime would have taken place several times in any week.

## *Symbolism & Change: Influence from the North*

By the end of the fourteenth century the image of the Signoria, in public and in private, with or without distinguished guests, was clearly that of a princely court represented publicly by its own ensemble of trumpets, and with splendid entertainment at mealtimes; a rather drastic change from earlier practices. The addition of the two musical groups to the ceremonial staff of the civic government during the 1380s was a serious revision of the Florentine tradition, and one that stretched the concept of a Republic. Because the instrumental ensembles themselves were traditional and carried symbolic significance, by creating these new ensembles for the purpose of representing the executive wing, the government of Florence was announcing a significant shift of the image of the Signoria. From the earliest records of civic musicians in Europe, trumpets had been a symbol of power and authority, and all cities employed an ensemble similar to the Florentine trombadori. But in addition to their role of representing the governing body or the monarch, by the fourteenth century trumpets were also a sign of nobility. It was a longstanding tradition for kings, princes, and even lesser nobles to employ trumpet players, usually in pairs, to precede them in public, displaying the coat of arms of their patron emblazoned on pennants that hung from the instruments. Following the institution of the trombetti in 1387, on all ceremonial occasions in Florence the traditional trombadori represented the authority of the city and its government as they had always done, while the senior executives were accompanied exclusively by the newly instituted ensemble of trombetti, symbolically setting the Priors and Gonfaloniere apart and raising their status to that of nobility. The significance of this representation is that it flies in the face of the origin, intention, and symbolism of the century-old Priorate. The Priors were Priors of the Guilds, that is, representatives of the merchants and entrepreneurs (major guilds), as well as of the skilled artisans (minor guilds). Thus to adorn themselves with the trappings of nobility was to change significantly the symbolic relationship between the executives of government and the governed.

The association of trumpets with nobility and with dining was one of long standing and quite familiar to citizens of Florence. Francesco da Barberino, Florentine notary and poet, made direct reference to this association in his *Reggimento e costumi di donna*, written in the early fourteenth century, where a description of a banquet during the festivities surrounding the marriage of a queen includes the following lines:

> *Or si conviene oggimai di mangiare.*
> *Suonan le trombe e li stormenti tutti*
> . . .
> *Dà la trombetta, e lo sposo co' suoi*
> *piglia sua parte di gente com' vuole.*
> *Donne amorose gioiose e piacenti*
> *dotte e gentili e di comune etate*
> *piglian la sposa e menolla com' decie;*
> *dànnole luogo a sedere alla Mensa.*[47]

[Now one gathers together for dinner at the sound of the trumpets and the other instruments. . . . Announced by the trumpet, and with the betrothed taking his part among the people, the amorous, joyous, and pleasant women of the same age take the bride as they were told, bringing her to sit at the table.]

This contrasts directly with a contemporary description of the marriage ceremony of a woman from a lower class, which therefore takes place without the trumpets:

> *Fassi il mogliazzo* . . .
> *La dota è il saccone e la predella* [= *cassapanca*]
> *va senza tromba la donna novella.*[48]

[The dowry is the mattress and the chest; the new bride goes without [being heralded by] the trumpet.][49]

Da Barberino continues on in his description of the royal dinner to include singing as a part of the grand setting, confirming the constant presence of both instrumental and vocal music as a part of this kind of grand ceremony:

[C]*anti soavi e sollazzi d'attorno.*
*Frondi con fiori, tapeti e sendali*
*sparti per terra*
*e gran drappi di seta alle mura,*
*argento ed oro, e le mense fornite.*[50]

[Gentle and amusing songs surrounded them. The dining room was furnished with branches with flowers, carpets and silks distributed over the ground, and large gold and silver drapes of silk on the walls.]

The image of vocal music along with heraldic trumpets in a noble setting was therefore well known to Florence. What was new was that it had not previously been associated directly with the Priors. In fact, official Florence was quite direct about who in society could take on airs and who could not. The civic statutes included sumptuary laws that limited the lavishness of costumes and other public displays of wealth.[51] In 1362, for example, the family of Matteo Bonacosi was censured and fined by the judiciary for violating the statute that limited the extent of a marriage feast, including the type and quantity of food, the presence of musicians and entertainers, and the costumes that could be worn.[52] In a society where every aspect of public life was subject to sumptuary laws, all citizens would have been quite aware of the implications of public behavior, and therefore these changes in the way in which the government officials represented themselves would have been noted and their symbolism clearly understood.

The institution of the pifferi represented a different aspect of this transformed image; no particular symbolism was associated with an ensemble of pifferi, but their adoption by the Florentine executive was a part of the reorientation of that image. The Florentine ensemble is only the second such group known south of the Alps,[53] although ensembles of reed players were established elsewhere in Europe earlier in the fourteenth century.[54] The earliest Florentine ensemble was made up of three instruments: soprano and alto shawms and a bagpipe (*cennamella, bombarda,* and *cornamusa*). Europeans had adopted the shawm from the bands of the Arab world in the thirteenth century, and Florence itself had employed a shawm player (*cennamellario*) as a member of the trombadori from its earliest permanent employment in the late thirteenth century.[55] As we have seen in chapter 2, a bagpipe was added to the trombadori in 1356, and is often recorded as performing in public with the shawm. Woodwind instruments as a separate musical entity, however, were not commonly found in Italy until the end of the century.[56] That tradition was more common in Germany, Switzerland, France, and the Low Countries, where the presence of two or three shawm players (also including a bagpipe) as a distinct musical group grew in popularity during the last third of the fourteenth century.[57]

A few years before the pifferi were established at the Signoria, the citizens of Florence had been exposed to just such an ensemble from the north. In 1384, three foreign musicians, Henrici Johannis, Angeli Johannis, and Petri Hermanni, all of them recorded as pipers from Germany (*de Alamannia pifforum*) and players of the *cornamusa* and other (unspecified) instruments, had come to Florence and were performing in public.[58] This was in direct contravention of the civic law that forbade anyone but the civic musicians to play in public,[59] and the foreigners were summarily arrested, fined, and sentenced to jail.[60] The specific offense for which they were penalized was for playing *mattinate*, a very general term meaning that they played music in the morning, an obligation that was added to the duties of the Florentine pifferi four years later.[61] It is important to note that the foreign ensemble was referred to as pifferi, and that it most likely consisted of the same instrumentation adopted two years later by the Signoria: two shawms and a bagpipe.[62]

Florence was undoubtedly influenced to adopt the pifferi ensemble in imitation of the northern ceremonies in which these reed ensembles were employed by courts to supply music at banquets, and by municipalities to perform for dancing on sacred and secular feast days and to augment the festive sounds made by the ensembles of trumpets at important ceremonies.[63] It was also the northern court tradition to add vocal ensembles to banquets on special occasions. A typical grand courtly banquet, therefore, would have included the trumpets sounding fanfares, while the reed ensembles provided dance music and alternated with vocalists in providing dinner music.[64] Such use of ensembles of trumpets and reed instruments is recorded in conjunction with celebrations at all of the important courts in France, Burgundy, the Low Countries, and at the papal court in Avignon.[65]

Even closer to Florence would have been the nearby and extremely powerful court of Milan, a sometime friend and sometime adversary of Florence, which was heavily influenced by the culture of France and Burgundy from as early as the reign of Luchino Visconti (ruler 1339–48). A madrigal text written for Luchino by Jacopo da Bologna, for example, contains the name of the important French music theorist Philippe de Vitry, suggesting that French music was well known in Milan from as early as the first half of the fourteenth century.[66] The French influence in Milan continued through the ascendancy in 1378 of Giangaleazzo Visconti, whose wife Isabelle was the daughter of King John II of France.[67]

# The Court of Burgundy

There is no doubt that the model adopted by Florence was present in all of these northern centers (France, Burgundy, the Low Countries, Avignon, and Milan), and Florence had direct contact with all of them in the last decades of the four-teenth century. One court stands out, however, as a possible major influence: the court of Burgundy, where, not incidentally, some of the pifferi were im-ported from Germany.[68] Under the reign of Duke Philip the Bold (1364–1404), the Burgundian court increasingly became the most lavish and influential in Europe, setting a pattern of grand ceremony and elegant style that was widely imitated. As Richard Trexler observes, the ceremonial ritual developed in Bur-gundy literally created that state's identity.[69] Once he inherited the county of Flanders in 1384, Philip had the resources necessary to indulge himself and his court with the best of everything, and he seized the opportunity to turn every public and private event into a grand spectacle. He equated ostentatious display of wealth and art with political and social power, exerting enormous influence on courtly practices throughout the remainder of Europe as other monarchs attempted to imitate him.[70] Among his court employees were a num-ber of musicians—in 1367, twenty-eight musicians were regular members of his household—including minstrels, instrumentalists both local and imported, and a separate chapel choir.[71] To these permanent members of his court he frequently added hired musicians from elsewhere, adding to the splendor of a special occasion and impressing important guests.

It was at Philip's court, for example, that the art of courtly dancing became highly stylized, especially in the form of the intricate *basse danse* in which each dance had its own particular sequence of steps. The complexity and individu-ality of the dances required the nobles to spend hours in rehearsal in order to learn the sequences and execute them gracefully, raising this social activity to the level of a minor art form. The Burgundian *basse danse* format was quickly adopted by all of the finest courts in England, Spain, Germany, and northern Italy—especially at the Sforza court in Milan—where it was known as the *bassadanza* and immediately became a popular feature at all noble social events (discussed in chapter 6).[72] It is important to note that in the Burgundian *basse danse* tradition, the music was often supplied by an ensemble of three pifferi. The membership of this ensemble evolved over the century, beginning with the same instrumentation as in the Florentine pifferi, replacing the bagpipe with a slide trumpet in northern ensembles around 1410, and exchanging that instrument for a trombone by the end of the fifteenth century. Italian ensembles were a bit slower to adopt these changes.[73] (See figure 14.)

Florentine merchants and ambassadors would have been well acquainted with the Burgundian court. The business interests of the Florentine merchant class took them to all of the important trade centers of Europe. The banking families especially would have had partners or managers resident for long periods of time in cities such as Paris, Bruges, and Avignon,[74] where they had plentiful opportunities to observe the northern ceremonial traditions. Gregorio Dati, a manufacturer of silk, records in his diary that he made a number of business trips to Brussels in the late 1370s, and to Paris, Orléans, and other northern cities throughout the 1380s and '90s.[75] Florentine merchants and ambassadors were frequent visitors at the court of Philip the Bold, who entertained lavishly in all of his places of residence, including his Parisian residence, the hôtel d'Artois, his palace in Dijon, and his residences in Flanders, and he brought his minstrels with him on his frequent sojourns throughout the areas under his governance.[76]

The institution of the pifferi in Florence in 1386 followed less than two years after the date that Philip assumed the court of Flanders on the death of Louis of Male and at that time added three more minstrels from that court to augment those already in his service.[77] Coincidentally, just one month prior to the establishment of the pifferi in Florence, three Florentines were present at the French court for the purpose of gathering information about new political affiliations. Gherardo Buondelmonti, Vanni Castellani, and Filippo Corsini were sent as ambassadors to the court of Charles VI to help facilitate a marriage between one of his daughters and the son of the Duke of Anjou, as well as to achieve other, unspecified objectives.[78] The three men were distinguished citizens whose opinions would have been highly respected: Buondelmonti and Castellani were among the twenty men knighted in a special ceremony in March of 1382, following the *parlamento* which resulted in electoral reforms referred to above.[79] Although this ambassadorial visit would have been just one of the many occasions when Florentines would have had direct contact with the ceremonial splendor of the northern courts, its timing and the political involvement of the three Florentines suggest that their visit may have had a bearing on the details of what transpired back home with regard to the realignment of Florentine ceremonial practices.

Further circumstantial evidence of the Burgundian influence can be found in the fact that not only were the two new Florentine musical ensembles a copy of those in Philip's court, but so were their costumes: Philip's musicians wore an escutcheon on which his coat of arms was executed in silver.[80] A direct echo of this can be seen in the *smaltum* that the members of the two new Florentine musical ensembles were directed to wear on their chests.

It is not known whether the Florentine ceremonial practices were specifically changed to resemble those at the court of Burgundy. It is clear, however, that the Florentines were looking north for their model, and that the new tradition they adopted was one that was widely popular in all of the socially, politically, and economically influential courts of the north, with that of the Duke of Burgundy being the clearest example.

Whatever its source, the addition of both the trombetti and the pifferi to the Mensa was yet one more indication of the changing image of the Florentine government executive. Whereas previously the center of attention during dinner had been the presentation by the civic herald of topical verse that was to act as the catalyst for sober thoughts and elevating ideas, music at the Mensa was now expanded into a combination of extravagant ceremony and entertainment. The importance of the singer of *canti morali* was therefore correspondingly downgraded, set as it now was against a backdrop that included the trombetti, the pifferi, invited instrumentalists and singers, jugglers, actors, and so on. Although he continued to provide the same type of verse as in the past, the traditional singer at the Mensa was no longer the center of attention; the *cantastoria*'s role had been reduced from central entertainer and *provocateur* to that of cast member in a twice-daily show. There can be little doubt that the basic ideal of the Mensa had been changed to reflect the new courtly self-image of the executive members of the government as well as a new concept of the purpose of their communal meals. With the post-Ciompi restructuring, the Mensa discarded its previous monastic image in favor of the newfound northern model. The orientation changed from that of the humble, serious, and self-effacing monks to that of the ostentatious princes of the secular world, and, not incidentally, to the "Princes of the Church"—the pope and the cardinals and archbishops who had adopted many of the ceremonial trappings of the secular courts.[81] It is interesting, therefore, to consider why the Priors would wish to adopt these new customs and what significance—both socially and musically—these changes represent.

With reference to the type of poetic repertory presented by the herald at the Mensa, Francesco Flamini stated, "In these poems most notable of all seems to be the seriousness of the intention. No *ballate* and madrigals, nor lascivious *canzone a rigoletto* were performed at the Mensa of the Signoria."[82] But whereas Flamini may have been correct with regard to the poetry sung by the heralds or their assistant *cantatori*—the surviving literature is uniformly serious—the same could not be said of the remainder of the entertainment after the changes in the late fourteenth century. In the new setting of lavish enter-tainments, the *canti morali* must have seemed oddly out of place; a reminder of the original intention of the event, but now virtually drowned out by the other entertainments.

The timing of these changes at first suggests that they might have been enacted as a part of the new patrician return to control of the Florentine govern-ment; a dramatic illustration of the Parte Guelfa's resumption of power. The return of the government to aristocratic control, however, was not immediate; throughout the 1380s the majority of elected officials were still artisans, shop-keepers, and professional men. During the time when the two new musical ensembles were instituted, very few members selected for the Signoria were patricians. Only nine of the fifty-four members of the Signoria selected between May 1386 and April 1387 were from the established prominent families, and the March–April term of 1387 did not include a single patrician.[83] The extension of political involvement to include non-elite members of the major guilds—what John Najemy has identified as the beginning of civic humanism[84]—brought with it this change in values. The humanists proposed a state that emphasized the freedom and development of the individual, an idea that appealed to a broad range of the population.[85] It was the newly empowered citizens, therefore, not the patricians, who changed the image of the Signoria from one of servants of the people to that of celebrated nobles, and who wished to display their new-found majesty by employing images identical to those of the most splendid and ostentatious ruler of Europe.

As Gene Brucker concludes, even though it was not instigated by the elite, the new concept of the civic executive coincided neatly with the desires of the aristocrats who came into power at the end of the fourteenth century. Whereas the constitution was still based on the principle of governance by representa-tives of the guilds, in reality, beginning at the end of the fourteenth century it was the members of aristocratic families with administrative and diplomatic skills who were elected to govern. The new crop of more politically minded civic leaders built on this base, adding distinction to their ranks by choosing the noted humanist and rhetorician Leonardo Bruni as Chancellor (1427–44), and with a new burst of civic energy they appointed Filippo Brunelleschi to finish the cathedral. In 1439, thanks to the efforts of Bruni, Florence was host to the church council that discussed the union of the Western and Eastern churches and which culminated in a huge celebration at the Duomo.[86] These new visionaries were well aware of their accomplishments; they saw themselves as the heirs of Rome, and they became the instigators of the Florentine Renais-sance.[87] Their strength was not only intellectual but also financial; the wealthy civic leaders did not hesitate to use their fortunes to pursue their ideals, a point made by Leon Battista Alberti in the 1430s when he identified a strong financial base as essential for men to accomplish "great and noble deeds."[88] Whereas the *Nuova cronica* written in the fourteenth century by Matteo and Filippo Villani centered around literature, art, and the military, later writers such as Cino Rinuccini and Cristoforo Landini concentrate on the wealthy merchants.[89]

It is evident that the image of the Priors as nobility fit in nicely with the newly formed vision of the place of Florence in the world. Gregorio Dati, in the statement quoted earlier, is quite proud of the quality and the grandeur of the Mensa which made that aspect of ceremonial Florence equal to the lavish displays elsewhere. It was, as he states "the equal of those in the finest courts of the land." In 1459 the final step was taken along the path of acknowledging the transformation of the executive image when a special government commission (*balìa*) changed the title of the Signoria from "Priors of the Guilds" to "Priors of Liberty," citing the rationale that the new title was more fitting for the dignity, distinction, and beauty of the leaders of Florence than was the older, more lowly association with the guilds.[90]

## *Importation of a New Musical Repertory*

The 1380s addition of the northern-style musical ensembles—especially the pifferi—brought more than just symbolic changes to Florentine culture. The pifferi ensemble was not simply a new trio of instrumental musicians; this particular combination of instruments brought with it a unique style of performance and, more importantly, a particular repertory. The daily presence of the pifferi at the Mensa of the Signoria, therefore, marks the addition of a northern musical tradition and presumably, the introduction of a new repertory in the place of what had been mostly a local entertainment for the executives of government. Further, and of great importance to the cultural life of Florence, because of its wide local exposure, the ensemble of pifferi and its repertory had a very broad influence on Florentine musical tastes that extended far beyond any single group of Priors and distinguished guests at the Mensa. The members of the executive were chosen from the most prominent citizens in the city, and every two months nine new highly influential people were elected to those positions and exposed daily at the Mensa to the repertory performed by the pifferi. The public at large would have heard the pifferi on the numerous occasions of public celebrations, and the law that only the civic musicians could be hired for private celebrations ensured that whatever repertory was popular with the pifferi was quickly spread to all of the upper-class households. Although undoubtedly instigated by a relatively small number of elite citizens who admired the musical practices in northern courts, the institution of this single musical ensemble had an immediate and long-lasting impact on the musical tastes of the entire community. The adoption of a northern-style musical ensemble resulted in a cultural influence far beyond the probable intention of simply bringing Florence in line with northern ceremonial trends and increasing the entertainment aspect of the daily mealtimes of the executive body.

# The Pifferi & the Repertory at the Mensa

Up to this point in the historical narrative of the civic instrumental musicians it has not been possible to discuss musical repertory. Until the establishment of the pifferi in the mid 1380s, the sounds made by the civic ensembles were severely limited by the instruments played by the trombadori and bannitori. The trumpets, both large and small, could not play all of the notes of a scale, but only those within the acoustical overtone system (see example 2.1), and therefore what they played was restricted mostly to fanfare-type sounds. Since their purpose was to bring a sense of pomp and excitement to official occasions and to announce the presence of the officials of government, this was entirely satisfactory. When the Signoria instituted the pifferi, however, they had a completely different objective: a desire to hear music. The shawm was capable of most of the notes of the chromatic scale, and had sufficient range to play most of the contemporary repertory. In addition, the members of the pifferi were quite versatile in terms of the instruments on which they performed. The word "piffero" refers to a reed instrument—the shawm—and throughout the history of the pifferi it was the custom to refer to members as piffero players. The name is misleading, however, in that it suggests that they played only that instrument. Musicians of the late Middle Ages and Renaissance, including members of the pifferi, routinely performed on a variety of musical instruments, especially other woodwinds.[91] (Ability to sing and play a musical instruments was fairly widespread; it was considered to be an attribute of any educated person and was not uncommon among the lower classes.[92] In 1414, for example, an applicant for a position in the guards of the Florentine

Signoria claimed also to be able to perform on musical instruments and sing.[93])
Documents from Brescia record payment in 1408 to Bartolomeo, piffero of
Count Guido of Urbino, who made four flutes (*flauti*, probably recorders), for
the Brescia pifferi.[94] It was noted above that Pagolo di Ser Ambruogio called
himself a piffero but played viola, rebec, lute, and other (unspecified) instruments in addition to the shawm, both at the Mensa of the Signoria and at the
church of Orsanmichele. And the document appointing Bartolomeo Cecchini
of Urbino to the Florentine pifferi in 1405 (possibly the same Bartolomeo who
made the *flauti* for Brescia) refers to him as a player of the *cennamella*, although
he knew how to play other instruments as well.[95] The search for the repertory
of the pifferi, therefore, need not be restricted to the limitations imposed by
their traditional instruments. There is evidence that members of the pifferi
were well-trained musicians; when making an appointment to the ensemble,
the *Provvisioni registri* frequently comment that the applicant has been judged
to be an expert. Indeed, the strongest evidence that the motive for creating
the pifferi had to do with music is the fact that from its beginning the ensemble was a duplicate of one that served Philip the Bold, the most musically
astute monarch in Europe. Undoubtedly, therefore, at least some of the music
supplied by the pifferi at the Mensa closely resembled that performed by the
minstrels in the northern courts.

There was a considerable difference between Franco-Netherlandish and
Italian music during the first half of the fifteenth century. The evidence presented above concerning the adoption of a northern musical ensemble and the
presence of a northern singing master who was involved with performances at
the Mensa strongly suggests that the importation of northern court practices
included a new emphasis on foreign musical repertory; one of the many signs
that Florence was looking north for its cultural values. Calculating the pace or
intensity of the musical changes and the influence of the pifferi and their performances, however, is not easily done. There is no extant music that has been
definitely associated with the pifferi, nor are there any detailed descriptions of
performances prior to 1459 that mention the repertory they played.

Since this type of instrumentalist did not usually read music before the
late fifteenth century,[96] the music that they performed was a combination of
improvised music or repertory played from memory. Some indications of their
repertory and their influence can be gathered from other sources, including the
musicians themselves, the tradition of the pifferi, and anecdotal accounts.

One possible indication of the type of repertory performed by the pifferi
comes from the actual personnel of the ensemble (based on the assumption
that the presence of only local musicians would imply local repertory, whereas

musicians from elsewhere would suggest a broader repertory). For the first five and a half decades of its existence (1386–1443), the pifferi remained a rather constant ensemble of three musicians and included both locals and foreigners. For the first several years the three founding members of the ensemble, Francesco d'Alessandro, Felice di Simone da Firenze, and Giovanni di Maso da Sexto (= Sesto Fiorentino),[97] apparently all local Italians, continue to appear in most of the pay records, with the occasional substitution for one or more of them with other Italian-looking names such as Grullo di Donato and Puccio di Bartolo. By 1394 Grullo seems to have become more-or-less a regular member, replacing Francesco, until his dismissal in 1398 for unspecified reasons, to be replaced the following year by the first obviously foreign name: Niccolao Niccolai, Teotonico (i.e., from Germany).[98]

The nationality of the performers is not always obvious in the pay records since foreign names are often given in an Italian form (e.g., the northern musician Johannes de Johannes d'Alemagnia is often recorded simply as Giovanni di Giovanni). But occasionally their place of origin is noted, and thus we know that in 1405 none of the three musicians was a Florentine, although two of the three were Italian: Bartolomeo di Cecchino from Urbino, and Cristofano di Taccho from Pesaro, who played respectively soprano and alto shawms (*cennamella* and *bombarda*),[99] and Niccolao from Germany, who also played the shawm and was designated the player of the contratenor part (*sonator ceramelle contra tenorem*), thus adding solid proof to the suspicion that the pifferi performed polyphonic music.[100] A year later Bartolomeo was replaced by another northerner recorded as Angelino di Piero della Magnia.[101] In 1415 two of the three shawm players were northerners: Marco d'Andrea da Alemannia played treble shawm (*ceramelle*), and Georgio Johannis de Alemannea played the alto shawm (*sonator cuiusdam instrumenti nuncipati la "bombarda"*),[102] along with the Italian treble shawm player Filippo di Ceccho da Pesaro (son of Cristofano di Taccho).[103] Throughout the next twenty years the ensemble remained fairly steady with three shawm players, most of whom were foreign (i.e., not from Florence, although some were from elsewhere in Italy). In 1437 a fourth member was added to the group: Bastiano di Marco of Florence (son of Marco d'Andrea da Alemannia), whose instrument is not recorded but who was probably an additional shawm player.[104]

What we can see from the pay records over the first fifty years of the ensemble's existence, therefore, is that Florence began the pifferi as an ensemble identical to that present in the northern courts and to the German model that had been present in the city in 1384: two shawms and a bagpipe. By 1400 they had removed the bagpipe in favor of three shawms, which was more or less in line with changes in the membership of similar ensembles elsewhere in Europe. At the same time, although the musicians were originally all Italian, they were frequently replaced by German performers (or at least German-speaking northerners). The implication of the change from two shawms and a bagpipe to an ensemble of all shawms is that there was a desire for music that was more harmonically complex than that which would have been possible with the constant drone notes of a bagpipe. That the ensemble engaged in polyphonic improvisation is suggested by the presence of two different sizes of shawms—meaning that they played in different ranges—and reinforced by a statement from as early as 1409 that one of the musicians played the contratenor line.[105]

The implication of mixed nationalities among the players, which included Florentines, other Italians, and increasingly more northerners, is that the repertory they performed must have been one that was heavily international and therefore did not require only musicians who had a long acquaintance with the traditional local repertory and musical style. Much of the music performed by the pifferi, both in public and at the Mensa, therefore, must have been international in its style, a point made above concerning the vocal music performed at the Mensa by members of the San Lorenzo choir. International repertory at that time was usually Franco-Netherlandish; Italian repertory circulated almost exclusively in Italy. As will become evident in the following chapters, once this move toward the importation of northern repertory and performers had begun, it continued throughout the remainder of the century.

The basic performance technique of the instrumentalists employed by the city of Florence for performance at the Mensa was based on rote memorization and improvisation (see chapter 6). The members of the pifferi, as well as the other instrumentalists, would have had an extensive repertory of memorized material which they could perform with elaborate extemporaneous ornamentation. The standard Italian instrumental repertory of the period would have included polyphonic elaborations of established dance tenors, such as those found in the various Italian dance treatises of the time (discussed in more detail in chapter 6), and monophonic dances similar to the *saltarelli* and *istanpitte* found in the manuscript London, National Library, Ms Additional 29987, a collection of Italian vocal and instrumental music copied in Pavia (near Milan) around 1400 (see example 4.1a below and discussion in chapter 6).[106] This would have been augmented by the extensive song repertory of the time, which, depending on the particular song and the occasion, would have been performed either as monophonic tunes or elaborated with improvised polyphony. All of the wind and string players who were hired on a temporary basis for performance at the Mensa would have been as capable as the pifferi at performing both from memory and *all'improvviso*.

At the end of the fourteenth century the only musicians who could be expected to read music were choir members, lutenists, and organists, of which there were many available in Florence.[107] This extends the possible repertory at the Mensa to include the written polyphony of the period performed by singers or by the lute and keyboard players, or possibly by a combination of instruments and voices.[108] The visiting choir members from San Lorenzo could have sung as a choir, as soloists, or in small ensembles. It is doubtful that their church repertory of chant would have been a part of the Mensa performances, but the choir members also would have had a selection of devotional songs, including the popular laude, that would have been appropriate on more solemn occasions (e.g., the visit of a prelate), and undoubtedly, the individual choir members would have had extensive solo repertories of both sacred and secular material that could be brought forward as the occasion warranted. Much of the Italian choir repertory during this period would have been monophonic, although there is clear evidence that in Florence at that time polyphonic music was sung at the Duomo and Baptistry.[109] And in the 1406 message to Rome asking for help in returning the two boys who had run away from the San Lorenzo choir (discussed above), we find the statement that the Flemish singing teacher instructed the boys *in harmonias musicas*, that is, to sing written polyphony. The probability is quite strong, therefore, that the San Lorenzo choir also was well trained in northern polyphony, both sacred and secular, enlarging the repertory possibilities to include more or less the entire gamut of local (Italian) and northern (Franco-Netherlandish) music.[110]

A comparison of fourteenth-century music from Italy with the Franco-Netherlandish material shows that the two repertories were stylistically quite different. Italian music tends to be far more "rhapsodic" and melodically loose in its formation, with a relatively simple harmonic construction that shows a close relationship to improvised music, whereas the northern repertory is more studied and precisely sculpted. The melody of a monophonic Italian dance, for example, can go on for hundreds of measures as smooth-flowing decorations around the various notes of a scale. In example 4.1a, the opening of the first of four long sections of the Italian *istanpitta* "Tre Fontane," the first twenty measures are a decoration of the pitch D; the music then moves to a decoration of the pitch A.[111] In contrast, the first section (of seven) from the French *estampie*, example 4.1b, is not only much shorter (eleven measures versus 105), but in place of ornaments built around scalar notes, it has a more clearly defined melodic and rhythmic structure.

**Example 4.1a.** Istanpitta "Tre fontane," opening section, first pars. London, British Library 29987, fol. 575v. Transcription from McGee, *Medieval Instrumental Dances*, p. 84.

**Example 4.1b.** "La quarte estampie reale," first pars. Paris, Bibl. Nat. Fonds français 844, fol. 104v. Transcription from McGee, *Medieval Instrumental Dances*, p. 62.

Polyphonic vocal compositions show similar traits. The upper line in the Italian composition, "Come in sul fonte" by Lorenzo da Firenze (example 4.2a), consists of a number of rapidly moving decorative passages over a relatively simple structural tenor, whereas the top line in the French composition "Dolour me tient" (example 4.2b), has more clearly formed melodic and rhythmic patterns, and the tenor line is more harmonically active.[112]

My examples have been carefully chosen to emphasize the differences between the two musical styles; other examples could be chosen that would not be so radically different from one another—the Florentine composer Francesco Landini, for example, borrowed from the French style in his music.[113] But the vast majority of Italian music until the mid-fifteenth century was much closer in melodic and harmonic style to that shown in example 4.2a. The history of Italian musical style in the fifteenth century is generally that of a transformation from the loose improvisatory style seen in example 4.2a to a gradual absorption of French tastes in melodic shape, harmonic content, and textural complexity.

**Example 4.2a.** Lorenzo da Firenze, "Come in sul fonte," opening section. Florence, Bibl. Medicea Laurenziana, Ms Palatino 87 (Squarcialupi Codex). Transcription from Pirrotta, *The Music of Fourteenth-Century Italy*, vol. 3, p. 2.

**Example 4.2b.** Anonymous, "Dolour me tient," first section. Reina Codex, Paris, Bibl. Nat., 6771, fol. 82v. Transcription from *Polyphonic Music of the Fourteenth Century*, vol. 20, p. 110.

# Other Sources of Northern Musical Influence

In addition to the model of the court of Burgundy, another source of northern influence on musical taste came directly from the papal court at Avignon, where northern singers and instrumentalists were employed.[114] Even before Pope Gregory XI moved to Rome in 1377, bringing with him his musical ensembles, northern musicians traveled with papal envoys who visited various Italian cities, impressing their hosts with their performers and their repertory, which resulted in the importation of northern musicians to a number of Italian courts. Gregory XI brought with him to Rome his northern chapel master Johannes Volcardi (from near Antwerp), who stayed on in the position under the Neapolitan Pope Urban VI.[115] Following Urban VI's election in 1378, the papal residence transferred permanently to Rome from Avignon (where it had been since 1309), but kept its household of northern musicians, repertory, and ceremonial customs. Reinhard Strohm has documented a large number of musicians from Liège who served in Rome as well as in the most important north Italian cities, beginning in the late fourteenth century.[116] As the home of the leader of the Christian church, Rome had enormous influence over the rest of the Christian world by example as well as by edict. When the musical preferences of the papal chapel—especially when resident in Rome—leaned in the direction of northern repertory and performers, it could not but influence choices in other Italian cities.

To reinforce the Italian exposure to foreign musical repertory, the Council of Pisa (1409), and especially the Council of Constance (1414–18, convened to end the Great Schism), aided the cause of interest in a variety of European musical styles by assembling in one place musicians from all parts of Europe. Each of the attending cardinals brought his household musicians along, which allowed an exchange of repertory and musical ideas among the performers and composers.[117] Not all of the exposure on that occasion was to sacred music: when King Sigismund of Hungary (secular overlord of the Council of Constance) received a golden rose from Pope John XXIII, the procession included a composite group of twenty-three trumpeters and forty pifferi chosen from the musical ensembles of a variety of Council participants; and a special celebration by the Florentines on June 24, 1415 (the feast of San Giovanni) was announced by five trumpets and three pifferi.[118]

None of the regional musical styles remained quite so isolated after this convocation. Exposure at the Council of Constance to English repertory no doubt was at least partially responsible for the adoption of certain English harmonic practices soon afterwards in the vocal music of Franco-Netherlandish composers. That the English were captivated by music from the continent is suggested by a number of compositions by Italian and Franco-Netherlandish composers in English sources shortly after the close of the conference.[119] For the Italian representatives and their musical entourage, the Council was one more contact with the repertory and style of the northerners, something that was becoming increasingly more familiar back home. That the northern secular repertory as well as its style was making an impact in northern Italy is attested by the fact that many Italian manuscripts from the late fourteenth century contain French secular repertory.[120] Even more telling is that nearly all of the north Italian secular manuscripts from the early fifteenth century contain almost as much French as Italian repertory, and after 1415, French repertory dominates.[121]

The more broadly international influence on Florence by way of Roman contact continued through the lengthy residencies of Pope Martin V and his successor, Pope Eugenius IV. On his journey from Constance back to Rome, the newly elected Martin V (Oddone Colonna from Rome, pope 1417–31) stopped in Florence for a visit of eighteen months (February 1419 to September 1420), along with his household musicians, many of whom were northerners. This would have given ample time for the citizens of the city to hear the international repertory of the Pope's chapel choir when it performed on many occasions, both at Santa Maria Novella and in the Duomo, and on some occasions out of doors in the piazzas.[122] The same opportunities were present during the residency of Pope Eugenius IV (pope 1431–47), who spent 1433–43 exiled in Florence (a time when he aided in the return of Cosimo de' Medici), dedicated the cathedral Santa Maria del Fiore in 1436, and presided over the church council in 1439 that discussed the uniting of the Eastern and Western churches.[123] All of these papal visits provided opportunities for the Florentine musicians to intermingle with those of the papal chapel and exchange ideas and repertory, strengthening the preference of Florentines for northern-style music of all kinds.[124]

French influence can also be seen in the Italian didactic literature of the time. *Ars cantus mensurabilis*, a music treatise probably written in Florence in the last quarter of the fourteenth century,[125] borrows heavily from the treatise *Libellus cantus mensurabilis* written early in the century by the French theorist Johannes de Muris (active in Paris and Avignon, among other French cities).[126] All of the musical examples in the *Ars cantus* treatise are written in French notation, and a number of them are by French composers.

By late in the fourteenth century, musical tastes in northern Italy had ceased to be exclusively directed toward a local product, and in adopting that attitude Florence fit in with the general trend that was becoming increasingly evident in all major northern Italian cities. By the beginning of the fifteenth century, ensembles of pifferi could be found in the Italian cities of Venice, Milan, Rome, Lucca, Modena, Ferrara, and Siena, to name only a few. The works of northern composers such as Guillaume Dufay, Gilles Binchois, Johannes Ciconia, Hugo de Lantins, and Bertrand Feragut were performed in the courts and major churches of many of the most important Italian cities as far south as Naples. It was the sophisticated and complicated polyphony of the northern composers that was in demand to celebrate the most formal events in Italian society. As the fifteenth century progressed, Italians increasingly patronized Franco-Netherlandish music and musicians, often in preference to Italians and their music, when the occasion called for a celebratory motet or Mass. The frequency with which northerners were the composers selected to write music for special occasions indicates the extent to which their skill in that field was respected, as the following examples indicate: a motet to celebrate the completion of the dome for Santa Maria del Fiore in Florence (Dufay, 1436); a motet for the marriage of Cleofe Malatesta in Rimini (Dufay, 1420); motets in honor of the Venetian Doges Michael Steno (Ciconia, 1406) and Francesco Foscari (Lantins, 1423).[127] For these grandiose occasions Italian-style music was judged to be inadequate; a decision that helped to create a class distinction between native and foreign music, with the local product decidedly in second place.

Comparisons of the quantity of performances of Italian versus foreign repertory are difficult to make owing to the fact that much of the Italian tradition involved extemporization, but several facts make it clear that in courtly circles in northern Italy as well as everywhere else in Europe, French music, as well as French manners and Flemish art, was *au courant* during this period. Singers, composers, and instrumentalists were imported from Burgundy and the Low Countries by all major cities in Italy, and there exists a significantly large number of music manuscripts with northern repertory commissioned by or for Italian courts.[128] A case in point is the earliest known Italian manuscript intended for instrumental performance, the Faenza Codex, probably originating in Ferrara between 1420–40, which includes instrumental elaborations of approximately thirty-four secular compositions, half of which are Italian and the other half French.[129] Evidence that French secular vocal repertory was becoming more and more fashionable in Florence comes from manuscripts known to have been prepared for Florentines at that time, most of which have a very large quantity of French material.[130]

As we have seen, the imitation of northern instrumentation in the pifferi ensemble was undoubtedly motivated by the increasing interest among north Italian aristocrats to adopt Burgundian musical fashion. There is little doubt that in terms of music, the aristocratic community of Italy valued the northerners' art—composed polyphony in a style quite unlike that practiced by most Italians—and that in some places it surpassed the traditional Italian fare as the preferred repertory. Sophisticated and artistic Italians seem to have been torn by the poles of tradition and novelty, represented by their own basically monophonic tradition versus the contrapuntal polyphony of the northerners. On the one hand they seemed to have recognized the value of their own art and its repertory, yet on the other hand they were drawn to the more internationally fashionable French style.

While there is no doubt as to the rising prominence of the northern repertory, Nino Pirrotta presents a clear case for the esteem in which the native art was held during the fifteenth century. According to his carefully reasoned research, Italian accounts of festive occasions invariably single out the Italian performers of the traditional repertory presented in the traditional monophonic practice, sometimes to the complete exclusion of polyphonic music that is known to have been performed on the same occasion.[131] (An interesting example is the letter sent by young Galeazzo Maria Sforza to his father in 1459, following a banquet in his honor presented by Cosimo de' Medici, discussed above in chapter 3.

Although there would undoubtedly have been a large and varied quantity of entertainment on that occasion, including performances of the fashionable French repertory, Galeazzo mentions only the *cantare all'improvviso* performance by Antonio di Guido.)

In spite of the Italian reverence for their own tradition, however, the influence of the newly imported repertory was quite broad throughout the Italian peninsula. Northern repertory, northern singers, and northern singing teachers were incorporated into the sacred music choirs of the larger churches,[132] and so by the third decade of the fifteenth century Italians were inundated by the musical sounds of their northern neighbors.[133] It was the pifferi ensembles who were some of the earliest and the strongest purveyors of this trend, both in Florence and elsewhere. From their earliest appearance in Florence in 1386 through the first half of the fifteenth century, the members of the pifferi entertained the diners at the Mensa with an increasingly impressive and varied repertory that must have included music both in the local Italian style and that in the more fashionable Franco-Netherlandish style.[134] When on the more lavish occasions all of this was coupled with additional singers, instrumentalists, actors, and jugglers, we can see that Gregorio Dati's claim, quoted above, that the Mensa in Florence was as grand as any Mensa anywhere was probably very close to the truth. There is little doubt that the most elaborate of the performances would have been reserved for special guests and special occasions, but even the daily presence of trumpet fanfares, one or more singers of moral songs, and instrumental music provided by the pifferi would have made even the most ordinary dinner at the Mensa a rather splendid event.

With their ubiquitous public presence, their dominance over music at the private entertainments of the culturally elite, as well as the daily exposure of their music to the leaders of the government, the civic pifferi lent enormous strength to the northern cultural invasion. As we will see in chapters 5 and 6, traditional Italian repertory continued to have a very high profile in Florence throughout the remainder of the Republic and beyond, but more and more it shared its place with a foreign repertory that continued to grow in popularity and to have a strong influence on the musical style of Italian composers.

# 5

# Civic Music & the Medici

The history of Florentine civic ceremonies and the musicians who performed for them in the last one hundred years of the Republic is closely connected to the Medici family: to their ambitions for the city; their vision for the growth of civic pride; their personal involvement in the details of civic ceremony; and the amount of attention they paid to the quality of the civic musical ensembles.[1] (Alessandro Botticelli's painting of the Medici family is figure 16.)

The return of Cosimo de' Medici in 1434 from his year of exile in Venice was a political and cultural milestone that marked new directions for the city. The conservative patricians, headed by Rinaldo degli Albizzi, who had controlled Florence since 1382, had been under heavy criticism for their foreign policy. Military involvement in a series of disastrous wars between 1390 and 1433 had emptied the treasury and burdened the citizens with intolerable taxes.[2] Following an unsuccessful campaign to conquer Lucca (1429–33), the conservatives were replaced by a more "popular" faction under Cosimo's leadership.[3] The change was welcomed by many of the citizens and memorialized in numerous poems, including one by the civic herald identified in one manuscript as "A canzona by Sir Antonio di Matteo, knight herald of the magnificent Signoria of Florence, composed in 1434 following the cheering of this crowd and comforting the citizens in the knowledge that they had received so many favors from God."[4] The poem, which begins as follows, would have been performed by the herald on the *ringhiera* in front of the Palazzo della Signoria during a public ceremony welcoming Cosimo and his family back to the city. The implication of the manuscript identification is that the poem was composed spontaneously.

> *Poi che lieta fortuna e 'l ciel favente,*
> *l'etterno iddio benengnio e grazioso*
> *tanto a quest'alma patria esser si vede,*
> *genuflesso le man gli occhi e la mente,*
> *o populi fiorentino figlouolo.*

[Since, with fortune smiling and the heaven's favorable sky, we see the eternal God so benign and gracious toward our bounteous fatherland, I genuflect with hands, eyes, and mind. O Florentine son of the people.]

At the same time, the old regime was the target of highly critical and insulting poetry, such as the poem condemning Rinaldo degli Albizzi, also by Antonio di Matteo, who a few years earlier had sung Albizzi's praises:

> *Crudel Rinaldo, Cavalier superbo,*
> *Privato di mia schiatta e d'ogni onore,*
> *Ingrato alla mia patria e traditore,*
> *Fra costor pendo il più inquo ed acerbo.*
> *Aspido della monte e del colore,*
> *Strambo, travolto, ontuoso, e pien d'inganno*
> *Son di Messer Rinaldo il brutto Ormanno,*
> *Che pendo al lato al padre traditore.*[5]

[I, Cruel Rinaldo, proud knight, deprived of my lineage and of every honor; ungrateful to my country and a traitor, hang among those most unjust and bitter [citizens]. I am Sir Rinaldo's bad son Ormanno, snake of the mountain and of strange color, eccentric, crushed, disgraced, and full of deceit, who hangs at the side of the traitorous father.]

Numerous poems by heralds and others were written in praise of the Medici, including many that expressed extreme and unrestrained admiration similar to that of Antonio. Examples include the sonnet "O lume de' terrestri cittadini," probably written by Anselmo Calderoni prior to his selection as herald (see chapter 3), and an homage by Giovanni di Maffeo da Barberino that is introduced as "A *capitolo* made by Giovanni di Maffeo expressing thanks to Cosimo de' Medici."[6]

Not everyone was quite so happy about Cosimo's return; the barber-poet Burchiello greeted the news with a scathing criticism beginning, "O humble people mine, you do not see how this perfidious tyrant, wicked man, harshly with force of veiled deceit tramples upon our sovereignty."[7] Burchiello fled the city immediately afterward and took refuge in Siena, although by 1441 he had found his way back into the good graces of the Medici.[8] In general, however, Cosimo was admired by a large number of Florentine citizens. His public image was that of a learned and generous man who had the best interests of the city and its inhabitants at heart, and he went to great lengths to create and sustain that image.[9] By means of an extraordinary talent to persuade and conciliate, he was able to work behind the scenes to guide Florence through three relatively stable decades that saw the city grow in international stature.[10] According to Vespasiano da Bisticci, one of Cosimo's skills was that he presented his ideas in such a way that they always appeared to come from someone else.[11] He served as Gonfaloniere on three occasions early in his career (1435, 1439, 1445), and was one of the *Dieci di Balia* (Ten of Balia) six times, but although he was de facto Signore of the city-state, he took pains to appear in public as no more than one of the citizens.

The Medici position in Florence as a distinguished and wealthy family was not one of long standing, but was based almost entirely on the accomplishments of Giovanni di Bicci de' Medici (1360–1429), who during the late fourteenth and early fifteenth centuries built a broad and prosperous network of businesses, including a bank.[12] On Giovanni's retirement in 1420, his sons Cosimo and Lorenzo took control and amassed enormous personal fortunes. Under Cosimo's guidance the Medici bank gained control of the papal accounts of the Alberti Antichi company, a clever political and financial accomplishment.[13] Early in his career, Cosimo expanded his personal interests to include the artistic and intellectual community, setting a pattern that would be carried out by his descendants throughout the remainder of the century. He spent large sums of his considerable private fortune on public projects such as the building of churches, libraries, and monasteries, which strengthened the position of the city in the eyes of the world and the image of Cosimo in the eyes of its citizens.[14] Among his commissions was the Palazzo Medici on Via Largha, which stands out as a marvel of late medieval architecture. Once it was completed in the late 1450s, it became the unofficial diplomatic headquarters from where Cosimo guided the city's foreign relations with brilliance, forming alliances with foreign heads of state that brought both prosperity and security to the city.[15] As an important part of his civic vision he actively patronized numerous architectural and artistic projects, most notably his unprecedented financial support of the reconstruction at the church of San Lorenzo.[16] He commissioned artists such as Filippo Lippi and Fra Angelico, and played an important role in the growth and development of the choirs at the Baptistry and at San Lorenzo.

# The Instrumental Ensembles

The three groups that were composed entirely or mostly of trumpets—the trombadori, the trombetti, and the bannitori—remained more or less unchanged to the end of the Republic, both in their numbers and duties, as can be seen by a comparison of the statutes of 1325 and those of 1415.[17] The salaries of the trombadori had increased from the initial four lire per month (five for the *cennemella* player) to five lire for everyone, although a tax was to be deducted in 1415, whereas it was not in 1325. The only other changes to that ensemble were the removal of the player of the small trumpet to a separate ensemble in 1387 (leaving the ensemble with eight performers) and an increase in the value of the cloaks they were to be given twice a year—from ten lire to twenty lire, ten soldi—which undoubtedly reflected the increase in the cost of clothing.[18] Otherwise, their obligations and benefits remained virtually the same as found in the earliest records at the end of the thirteenth century. During the same period the number of bannitori remained at six and their obligations remained the same although the financial arrangements changed: they received a salary of seven lire, as compared to five lire in 1325, but also they received a fee for services. As discussed in chapter 4, the striking changes in the city's ceremonial observances had to do with the institution of two new musical ensembles, the trombetti and the pifferi. Once they were created as a separate ensemble in 1387, however, the only change in the trombetti for the remainder of the period of the Republic was their number: from the original two performers, the trombetti grew to four in 1390, five in 1394, fluctuated between five and six after 1406, between six and seven after 1410, and remained at seven or eight after 1447. There is little reason to suspect that there was any change to the musical content of their repertory, fanfares and other festive sounds, although given the high profile and obligations of the trombetti vis-à-vis the Mensa, we can imagine that what was played was highly imaginative and skillfully performed.[19]

The major changes were to the ensemble of pifferi, which increased in number, changed its instrumentation, and expanded its duties: the ensemble was changed from the original two shawms and a bagpipe to three shawms by 1400; a fourth shawm player was added to the ensemble in 1437; in 1443 the instrumentation was changed to three shawms and a "trombone." Later in the century their number was occasionally augmented to five or six by the addition of an occasional fourth shawm after 1494, and an occasional second trombone or fifth shawm by 1510, imitating the general European trend in the number and instrumentation of pifferi ensembles.[20] With the return of the Medici in 1512, the pay records indicate as many as five shawms on the payroll along with one trombone for special occasions.[21] (This is the number of pifferi on the list of those who received special tips for performing at the August 1515 ceremony for the presentation of the *bastone* of generalship to Lorenzo the Younger [Lorenzo il Magnifico's grandson; see below].)[22] But soon after that date the ensemble moved in the direction of more trombones, ending in 1531 with two shawms and three trombones. The most important change to this ensemble was the continuing expansion of their function and repertory over the century, which was accompanied by the addition of a variety of musical instruments each of the pifferi played.

The addition of the fourth shawm player to the pifferi in 1437 probably was done in imitation of the wind bands in cities to the north. Similar ensembles in France, Germany, and other north Italian cities had increased their membership from three to four earlier in the century, a reflection of changing musical practices and tastes (see discussion in chapter 4). But in the early 1440s the executives of government (and probably Cosimo de' Medici) were apparently unhappy with some aspect of the pifferi and decided to make changes. Rather abruptly in August of 1443, all four of the incumbent members of the ensemble, Santi di Gherardo of Florence, Bastiano di Marco of Florence, Filippo di Cecchino of Pesaro, and Giorgio di Giovanni from Germany ("Georgius Johannis de Alemannea"), three of whom had served in the ensemble for over twenty years, were summarily dismissed with pension.[23] In their places four northerners were appointed, and just as dramatically, accompanying legislation was passed that henceforth all members of the pifferi were to be foreign (*forenses et alienigeni*; literally, "non-Florentine and born elsewhere").

> Authority residing in the Priors and colleges to hire three non-citizen shawm players and one player of the bent trumpet [*tube torte*].
>
> Fifthly, the provision written above. . . .
>
> That the Priors and colleges, or two-thirds of them, can, and have the power to select and hire for the service of the commune up to three pifferi and players of shawms [*ceramelle*], and one player of the bent trumpet [*tube tortuose*] with the said shawms, who are non-citizens and foreigners [*forenses et alienigeni*], who are such as were neither in, nor were enrolled in the service of the Commune of Florence, for the period and term of one year, commencing as will

be specified in their appointment. They have until the end of October next
to do this. They are to receive with the duties the salary, benefits, and other
things appointed for the pifferi of the same commune, these things to be paid
for from the funds and by those [officials] and in that manner, and which the
aforementioned pifferi and sonatori are customarily paid [i.e., the foreigners
will be paid from the same sources as the indigenous players, and they will be
paid at least as well]. . . .

   With this added to the proclamation: that the salary of the said player of the
bent trumpet [*tube tortuose*] be the same as that of the trumpet players of the
same commune, for every month, individual salaries for individuals reckoned
suitably. . . .

   With these conditions, namely, that such as are to be hired must and ought
continually to wear at the breast an enamel or silver shield with the sign of the
red lily, and beyond the previously mentioned matters they must have a shawm
[*piffero*] or *ceremella*, or silver trumpet, just as the regulations of the said commune set out.[24]

The pay records for that date name the newly appointed musicians, all labeled "Alemanni": Johannes de Johannes de Colonia, Niccholaus Johannes de
Basiler, Johannes Benadeti de Constantia, and Georgius Arigi di Spuga;[25] that
is, from Cologne, Basel, Constance, and Augsburg.[26] At the same time the instrumentation of the ensemble was altered: instead of all shawms, as played by
the departing musicians and which had been the instrumentation since 1400,
the instruments played by the new foreigners are clearly noted in the *Provvisione* as three shawms (*tres pifferos et sonitores pifferorum sive ceramelle*) and an
instrument that is named in the records as a "bent trumpet" (*tube tortuose*) and
"trombone," but which probably was a slide trumpet since there is no record of
the invention of the instrument now called the trombone until the very end of
the fifteenth century.[27]

   No reason is provided in the government documents for the abrupt change
of personnel other than the desire to have all foreign musicians in this ensemble. But since two of the dismissed players were already foreigners (Filippo
di Cecchino of Pesaro and Giorgio di Giovanni from Alemagna), the decision
must have been based on elements other than simply the birthplace of the musicians. Since the new members were added to the civic pifferi all at once rather
that one at a time, as in past practices, it is possible that they came to the city as
an already formed ensemble. A similar event took place two years later in Siena,
which, although it does not provide a motive for the change, can throw some
light on the way in which the Florentine government may have proceeded. In
1445 the city of Siena dismissed their ensemble of Bolognese pifferi, who had
been in place for a number of years, and replaced them with a completely new

band: three pifferi from Avignon and a trombone player from "Alemagna."[28] To do this the Sienese concistory contacted Maestro Garino, a shawm player in Avignon, and asked him to choose two additional shawm players and a trombone player and bring them to Siena as soon as possible, where they would be given lifetime appointments (rather than the usual appointment for one or two years). Frank D'Accone speculates that the recommendation for Maestro Garino would likely have been the result of contacts made by Sienese bankers and merchants, many of whom had a long history of dealings in Avignon.[29] We know that this technique of recruitment was also employed by the Medici, who requested assistance in this regard from agents who were employees of the Medici bank and other enterprises, and from Florentine ambassadors to other cities and courts, who were asked to scout for talented musicians with specific skills. When identified, the musician would be contacted and offered a position at a Florentine church or with the civic instrumental ensembles (see below).

This may well have been the process followed by Florence, perhaps based on the knowledge that the new ensemble members would bring with them a more up-to-date repertory or performance practice. It was a general perception in Italy that the finest pifferi were those from north of the Alps, as evidenced by one of the poems in *Il Saporetto* from around 1415, in which the hero is praised for his piping ability by comparing him to a piper from Flanders: "A lark had never been heard to sing as well as Solazzo on this wind instrument, who was the equal of a piper from Flanders."[30] Another poet, Simone Serdini (ca. 1360–1419, known as "Il Saviozzo"), who worked in Rimini at the court of the Malatesta in the early decades of the fifteenth century, also acknowledges the superiority of "German" pifferi with the following lines:

> Ancora voi, maestri di stormente,
> voi nel cantare non mi siate muti,
> che di farmi morir costei si pente!
> Arpe, sonate, quitarre e liuti
> e piffari e trombetti de la Magna,
> che 'lvostro dolce suon d'amor m'aiuti!

[Again you, masters of instruments, when you sing do not cause me to be mute, because she will be sorry that she makes me die! Harps, sonate,[31] guitars and lutes, shawms and trumpets from Germany, may your sweet sounds of love help me.][32]

By mid-century there was a growing tradition in the north Italian courts to hire pifferi from the other side of the Alps; as early as 1407 at least three of the seven pifferi in Brescia were "Alemanni";[33] and the most prominent piffero in Ferrara was Corrado de Alemania, who was recruited from Monferrato in 1441 and remained in Ferrara for forty years.[34] (The exception to this tendency would seem to be Venice, where from the initial formation of the Doge's ensemble in 1458, all members were Italian from the Veneto.)[35]

The change from all shawms to an ensemble of three shawms and a slide trumpet exactly duplicated the instrument ensemble popular in the northern courts at that time. In this matter Florence and the other Italian cities were considerably behind the northerners. Although in the late fourteenth century the northern court ensembles consisted of various combinations of wind instruments, by 1440 their membership had become more-or-less standardized to the point where this instrumentation was widely known as the "Alta Cappella."[36] The addition of a slide trumpet (*trombone*) to the 1443 civic pifferi, therefore, is yet another sign of the continuing northern influence on the musical tastes of Florence as well as on all of northern Italy. The addition also parallels the growth of the presence of northern polyphonic music and personnel in the chapel choirs that were first established at the Duomo and the Baptistry in 1439, in imitation of northern practices.[37] Given the amount of Cosimo de' Medici's financial involvement in the Florentine church choirs and in their recruitment, we can probably assign to him, either directly or indirectly, responsibility for invigorating the civic pifferi by importing a fresh new group of northern musicians at this time as another of his direct interventions in order to bring to the city the finest and most up-to-date manifestations of art.

The newly appointed foreign pifferi were highly valued and were soon paid higher salaries than the musicians they had replaced. Prior to 1443, the monthly pay for the pifferi had been four and a half florins (a half-florin raise from the salary stated in the 1415 statutes), which, after a deduction of half a lira for housing, resulted in a net pay of seventeen and a half lire (I am using Richard Goldthwaite's data for the year 1450: one florin is the equivalent of four lire or eighty-two soldi).[38] On the grounds that the new foreign musicians were not accustomed to such a low salary, the city executives raised their pay in 1445 by four and a half lire, to provide a gross monthly pay of twenty-two lire, ten soldi, which would result in a net pay of twenty-two lire (five and a half florins) after the housing deduction.

> With all due reverence it is requested of your magnificent and powerful lords, the Lord Priors of the Guilds and the Standard Bearer of Justice of the People and the Commune of Florence on behalf of the players of the shawm and bent trumpet [*tube tortuose*] under your jurisdiction that their salary is four and a

half florins for each month for each of them which, after the deductions have been made for rooms, reverts to the smaller sum of seventeen and a half lire per month.

And because some of them brought their wives and families and others would like to bring them because they intend, the Lord willing, to make them and their descendants permanent residents in this country, but the expenses of those who brought their family were great and so will be the expenses of those wanting to bring their families. For this reason and also because they are not by nature accustomed to live with such great parsimony as those who were raised in these parts, they cannot manage on such a small salary and cannot provide for their families' needs, nor can they go well dressed and adorned as is fitting to your most excellent authority. They have already spent enough on clothes and other things required for their duties. . . .

It is devoutly entreated and sought from you, the above said lords . . . that their salary be increased and . . . established at twenty-two lire and ten soldi for each of them for each month of the coming term.[39]

The most valued of the civic pifferi, in Florence as elsewhere, was the player of the slide trumpet. In 1452, after the executives learned that their slide trumpet player, Johannes de Johannes from Cologne, had been approached by agents from other cities, it was decided that in order to keep him the government would raise his salary by an additional eight lire per month, which resulted in a monthly gross salary of thirty lire, ten soldi (seven florins, two and a half lire). Further, unlike the other civic musicians, there was to be no deduction from his salary for rent, which effectively provided him with a total of nearly one and a half additional florins per month, meaning that his monthly net salary was two florins, ten soldi higher than the other three pifferi.

It has come to the attention of the magnificent and powerful Lord Priors of the Guilds and the Standard Bearer of Justice of the People and the Commune of Florence that the present player of the slide trumpet [*tube tortuose*] who plays with the pifferi of the commune excels in that office, as is known by all, and it is known that he was requested privately on behalf of some princes and rulers to serve them . . . they [the Priors] believe that increasing his salary will discourage him from going elsewhere and encourage him to remain in the service of this commune. . . .

The Priors deliberated . . . and came to a decision on the fourth day of the month of September in the year of the Lord 1452, that the said present player of the slide trumpet be given and paid a greater salary than what is provided for now, namely, an increase of his salary by eight lire for each month in which he serves the commune . . . the aforesaid increase of his salary without any deductions or withholding.[40]

The offer was successful: Johannes de Johannes remained in the service of the commune for another twenty years until replaced in 1472 by Jacobus Johannes de Alamannia (possibly his son).[41]

At mid-century the monthly salaries paid to the various civic musical ensembles, therefore, were clearly unequal, a fact that probably reflected the difference in their relative musical ability as well as the difference in the quantity of time required of each of the ensembles. The trombone player, at seven and a half florins per month (plus rent), was at the top; followed by the other members of the pifferi, who were paid five and a half florins; then the trombetti, who made four florins; and the lowly trombadori, who received only five lire. As a comparison with other members of the *famiglia*, the bellringers received four lire per month, the *donzelli* five lire, and the cook at the Palazzo della Signoria twelve lire.[42] These are not completely accurate comparisons, however, because a number of the positions in the *famiglia* included perquisites such as housing and meals, or supplemental payments from separate funds.[43] But it is clear from the quoted figures that the two new groups, the pifferi and the trombetti, were quite well rewarded for their work, whereas the trombadori were making little more than they had 150 years earlier.

The difference in pay levels for the musical groups continued along this line for the remaining years of the Republic, with the pifferi clearly the favored ensemble; see table 5.1. This inequity persisted even in the assignment of specific tips from the government on special occasions that went directly to the individual ensembles rather than to the pooled sum. In 1515, all *famiglia* members who were involved in the ceremony for the presentation of the baton of the captain-general to Lorenzo the Younger were given tips. The trombadori received eight and a half florins to split among its seven members (eight lire, nine soldi = one florin, one lire, nine soldi each);[44] the eight trombetti divided twelve and a half florins (ten lire, eighteen soldi = one florin, three lire, eighteen soldi each); the six bannitori divided four and a half (five lire, three soldi each), but the six pifferi received twelve florins (two florins each), which was the same reward as the *comandatori, mazieri,* and *donzelli* received. For the other members of the *famiglia* the reward was usually half a florin, although the cook received one and the herald six.[45]

We should also be aware that unlike most of the other civic employees, the musicians were able to add to their income substantially by performing both inside and outside of the city.[46] Their civic salary, therefore, represented only a portion of the wages they gained through performance. They must have taken excessive advantage of this during the 1440s, causing in 1448 a reiteration of the provision already present in the 1415 civic statutes that forbade any of the

Table 5.1. Monthly Pay: Florins, Lire, Soldi

| Year | Bannitori | Trombadori | Cennemella | Trombetti | Pifferi | Trombone(s) |
|------|-----------|------------|------------|-----------|---------|-------------|
| 1294 |           | 0,3,0      | 0,4,0      |           |         |             |
| 1307 | 0,3,0     | 0,3,0      | 0,4,0      |           |         |             |
| 1317 | 0,3,0     | 0,3,0      | 0,4,0      | 0,3,0     |         |             |
| 1325 | 0,3,0     | 0,4,0      | 0,5,0      | 0,4,0     |         |             |
| 1390 | 0,4,0     | 0,5,0      | 0,5,0      | 3,0,0     | 2,0,0   |             |
| 1394 | 0,4,0     | 0,5,0      | 0,5,0      | 3,0,0     | 3,0,0   |             |
| 1400 | 0,7,0     | 0,5,0      | 0,5,0      | 4,0,0     | 4,0,0   |             |
| 1450 | 0,7,0     | 0,5,0      | 0,5,0      | 0,16,0    | 0,22,10 | 0,30,10 (+rent) |
| 1475 | 0,12,0    | 0,5,0      | 0,5,0      | 0,16,0    | 0,22,10 | 0,36,00 (+rent) |
| 1500 | 0,12,0    | 0,5,0      | 0,5,0      | 0,16,0    | 0,22,10 (+rent) | 0,29,10 (+rent) |
| 1525 | 0,13,0    | 0,5,0      | 0,5,0      | 0,16,0    | 0,29,10 (+rent) | 0,29,10 (+rent) |

*Note:* Because the ratio of lire to florins increased from 2½:1 to 7:1 over these 230 years, the actual value of many of the musicians' salaries decreased.

ensembles to perform outside of their regular duties without the express permission of the government. It would seem that a part of the problem was self-inflicted, in that the Priors themselves had agreed to send their civic musicians to foreign festivals at times when they were needed at home:

> The trombadori, pifferi, and other players of the commune are not to go outside the city for any feast nor within the city to perform any *seranata* or *mattinata*.
>
> Considering that many feasts happen outside of the city of Florence and in diverse lands and places, the magnificent and powerful lords, the Lord Priors of the Guilds and the Standard Bearer of Justice of the people and Commune of Florence are often asked by those making the said feasts that they may lend such musicians to them, for which there might be a pressing need to have trombadori and pifferi and other musicians belonging to the lordship [of Florence] for honoring the said feasts. Those requesting the pifferi and trombadori do so without intending harm to the city of Florence. This practice results, however, in the Priors going to some services or feasts without their musicians, or with too few. This results in disgrace to the same Priors, and consequently to the Commune of Florence. Wishing therefore to provide in some way a limit and a stricter method so that the practice may happen less frequently than at present, a solemn deliberation ought to be held concerning these matters, together with

the offices of the Standard Bearers of the Guilds of the people and the Twelve Good Men of the said Commune. . . . No trumpet player or member of the tubatori or any of the pifferi or musicians of the commune or of the palace of the Florentine people can go outside the city of Florence to another city, castle, or location for the purpose of performing, or to any festival or ceremony which is taking place there unless previous express permission is given and the decision of the Lord Priors of the Guilds and the Standard Bearer of Justice and of the Colleges has been determined and voted on by them by at least thirty-four or more black beans. And if it [the vote] is less, it [the request] is understood to be refused by the force of the present provision.

Furthermore, none of the aforesaid musicians of the palace can go within the city of Florence to play a *seranata* or a *mattinata*, or to go to any oratory, [or home of any] ambassadors, lords, captains, generals, or constables, or to any other person of whatever status or position, with the exception of those civic officials for which permission is customarily granted, under the same penalty and the aforesaid prejudices unless previous express permission has been granted and the issue determined by the Lord Priors of the Guilds and the Standard Bearer of Justice.[47]

With the institution of the first part of this law, the problem of Florence not having sufficient musicians to serve its own festas would seem to have become less severe; it is not addressed again in any further legislation, although as can be seen below, the problem occurred again when the musicians themselves did not follow orders vis-à-vis how many of them could be absent from the city. The problem considered in the last part of the *provvisione*, about the musicians playing at other institutions or at the homes of various people within the city without expressed permission from the Signoria, was a continuing problem, and the prohibition was repeated in 1467 with a penalty of a hundred-lira fine and reiterated in 1475.[48] Not every citizen had to request permission, however, since the *provvisione* exempts certain unnamed "civic officials" for whom permission apparently was automatically granted. That list must have included the Medici, since there is ample evidence that the civic musicians performed for them on many occasions (see below), although the *provvisioni*, which record numerous petitions each year, never record a petition from the Medici.

It was in the best diplomatic interests of Florence to honor the special occasions of other cities and rulers by sending official representatives such as the herald and the musical ensembles. For travel to nearby cities that would involve only a day or two, the entire group of musicians could be sent if the occasion did not conflict with a Florentine celebration. For travel to cities more distant that would require many days' absence, the Signoria often sent only a few members of an ensemble, reserving the others for local needs. This is what was attempted with regard to the group sent to Naples in 1477 as ambassadors of the city to honor the wedding of King Ferrante of Aragon. After receiving the request, the Signoria decided to give permission to four of the six trombetti as well as to the Herald and a *donzello* to make the trip. It would seem, however, that the other two trombetti and one of the pifferi decided to go along without permission, leaving the Mensa with no trumpets and only two pifferi (the trombone player had recently died and was not yet replaced), which was clearly unacceptable.

There were two issues here: the musicians acting against orders, and the absence of sufficient musicians to carry on the day-to-day ceremonies at the Mensa. In formalizing their complaint, the Priors noted that the same problem had arisen a month earlier in conjunction with a trip to Pisa to honor the Duke of Calabria, when more musicians made the trip than were given permission, but on that occasion the musicians were not fined as the law would have allowed. In this case, however, the Signori decided to discourage such action by the musicians; they fired and fined the three who made the trip without permission, taking back their salaries for the time they were away. This should have ended the matter, but two months later a new Signoria reversed the decision, voting against both the firing and the fine, reinstating the musicians and returning the pay that had been subtracted from their salaries.[49]

When one or more of the ensembles was given permission to perform for other communities or for private occasions, the money received was to be shared with all of the other civic musicians. According to the civic statutes of 1415, no matter which ensemble performed, the total amount received as a tip was to be divided into three and shared among all of the musicians with equal parts going to the trombadori, the trombetti, and the pifferi, and those shares further divided among the members of the individual ensembles.[50]

> Everything which is received by the performers as a large fee or as a gift or object, or given to them or granted to them or promised in some way, the third part is understood to be and shall be given to the *tubatori, nacharino,* and *cennamellario,* leaving two remaining parts which belong to the trombetti and to the pifferi of the said commune and thus it must be divided among them and not otherwise.[51]

Although this arrangement of pooling the extra income to be shared by all was socially quite advanced for its time, it was not exactly an equal sharing of the tips. The members of the pifferi would individually profit more than the other musicians, since they shared their third of the total amount only four ways, as opposed to the seven or eight members of each of the other ensembles. It is also probable, however, that the pifferi were more often employed in this fashion than were the other two groups, being in constant demand for wedding receptions, banquets, and other officially approved private entertainments at the homes of the elite. Guaranteed in the same statute was a government-enforced monopoly by the civic musicians over all music performed in the city on official occasions. No musicians other than the civic ensembles were permitted to perform, either in public or private, meaning that the pifferi especially, but also the trombetti and to a lesser extent the trombadori, were assured of a constant flow of extra work from which all of the civic musicians would profit.[52]

The use of musicians as official envoys of the city was not new, but the institution of the two new ensembles increased the number and kinds of occasions when musicians could be requested. From as early as we have records, the trombadori were sent as official representatives of the city to perform in processions or for festas in other cities as well as for smaller festivities within the city, including church celebrations and the wedding processions of the more distinguished citizens. A regular source of paid employment within the city was the various lay religious societies, such as that at Orsanmichele, that hired trombadori, trombetti, and pifferi to celebrate their major feast days,[53] but there are numerous records each year of the ensembles being sent to participate in festivities in cities such as Milan, Bologna, Venice, and Naples.[54] After the creation of the trombetti and pifferi, the occasions within the city also included banquets, dances, and other activities that often took place in private homes, and for which the Signori granted requests for the official presence of one of the civic ensembles, "official" meaning presumably that they would be in uniform.[55]

In order to hire the civic musicians, it was necessary to petition the government, and the civic documents record that permissions were granted on a regular basis: in a typical year permission would be granted approximately two to three times a month. In the first six months of 1478, for example, the pifferi were approved for appearances at private events at the homes of eight citizens and three visiting nobles, as well as at the oratorios in Perugia and Peretola; the trombetti were approved to play for a church procession; and the trombadori were sent to take part in the festa of the church of San Jacobi in Pistoia.[56] An example of an official private occasion would have been the visit to Florence in 1476 by Alfonso, son of King Ferrante of Naples, who was entertained at the home of Benedetto Salutati, as described in chapter 1. Although the event took place in a private home, we can be sure that this entertainment was a part of the city's official welcome of Alfonso, and for that reason we can be sure that the trumpets and pifferi who are described as taking part in the entertainment were those of the Florentine civic ensemble.

# *Final Addition to the Musical Ensembles*

There was one more addition to the civic musical groups after the turn of the sixteenth century. In 1509 an ensemble referred to in the pay records as the *tamburini* was appointed, consisting of two performers who played flute and drum (*zufolo et tamburino*).[57] They were assigned to the Signori, as were the trombetti and pifferi, but were paid considerably less (four lire per month, as compared to the pifferi at twenty-nine lire, ten soldi, and the trombetti at sixteen lire. Their pay was even lower than the five lire paid to the trombadori).

> The magnificent and excellent Signori, desiring to increase the number of performers and to have a larger variety of sound for the public honor and magnificence of the Signoria, provide and order that by virtue of the present *provvisione*, Giovanni di Benedetto Fei, called Feo, and Michele de Bastiano, called Talina, players of *zufolo* and *tamburino*, are officially appointed and named to the service of the magnificent and excellent Signori every time that the Signoria will go outside the palace and also whatever other times they will be requested. [They are appointed] with a salary of four lire per month for each of them, without any other benefits.[58]

It is interesting to speculate on the function of this new ensemble, and since this is the only reference to the tamburini I have found (other than records of payment), speculation is all that is possible at this time. The combination of flute and small drum was a common one during the Middle Ages and later, although they were usually played by a single musician and usually referred to as pipe and tabor. The iconography suggests that the usual function of pipe and tabor was for dancing, and the scene is usually rustic.[59] It would seem, however, that the combination being referred to in this document is the two-man version of a transverse flute and a somewhat larger field drum found in late fifteenth-century iconography, which is presently referred to in the scholarly literature as "the Swiss pair." This ensemble is depicted in both military and dance contexts (see figure 15).[60] (It has been one of the puzzles in the study of musical instruments that the transverse flute, which was fairly common in the thirteenth and fourteenth century, all but disappears from the literature and iconography in the fifteenth century only to resurface as a member of the "Swiss pair" at the end of the century, and then is found a bit later as a consort instrument.)[61]

One of the more curious parts of the Florentine appointment is that the tamburini are required to go with the Signori when they journey outside the Palazzo della Signoria. This was the role traditionally played by the trombetti, and there is no reason to believe that the trombetti did not continue to serve in that capacity. One would assume, therefore, that on an official trip the Signori would still be preceded by the civic trombetti, whose presence continued to symbolize political authority. But, we may then ask, what would have been the role of the tamburini? The appointment states that there was a need for a larger variety of sounds, but it is difficult to imagine that this implies that a flute and drum were added to the fanfares made by trumpets. The "Swiss pair" must have performed separately, either to provide military-like marching music for the procession, or dance music in conjunction with the purpose of the Signori's trip, or both.

From around the time of the tamburini's appointment we have a Florentine carnival song that refers to these instruments: the "Canto di lanzi tamburini." This is one of a set of songs known as *canti dei lanzi*, written in Florence around the end of the fifteenth century to poke fun at the German-speaking mercenary soldiers who served in Florence and spent their time in the Piazza della Signoria in the space still known as the Loggia dei Lanzi.[62] The nature of this kind of text is to make fun of the mercenaries' inferior command of the Italian language and their single-minded pursuit of young Florentine women. The songs use a vocabulary that, because of the poor grammar and mistaken pronunciation, lends itself to double entendre. In order to accomplish these objectives the factual material within the poem has to be fairly accurate, which allows us to rely on the details with regard to the instruments themselves and their use. In the absence of any other information about the tamburini, I reproduce a translation of the complete song text:

> Lanzi tamburini we are, come from Germany to play drums and flutes [*tambure e flute*] where there is war and good wine.
>
> In these lands we have seen so many beautiful feasts and celebrations that we don't want to look for other wars but rather, to a man, to stop at these; and should good wine go to our head, we never leave a drop undrunk.
>
> We carry large drums because they give a loud sound; we put large, dry, hard beans in them at all times and bouncing about, they make a sound harmonious and near-divine.
>
> It is quite true that in humid weather it doesn't give a clear sound, but then take from the front and apply at the back with discretion [i.e., tighten the bindings]; those who work the thongs and cinctures are very dextrous.
>
> We have flutes that are large, long, and well bored; beautiful ladies, we can show them to you, they all play sweetly, good in front as well as on the side [i.e., transverse flutes and recorders], at the beginning and at the end.
>
> One should hold one's hand close to both hole and flute and if the tone is flat, keep it clear even if it should drip like a mill-course and not produce a clear sound as our training has taught us.

And if you too, beauteous ladies, should wish to learn how to play, we are quartered in Piazza Padella opposite the hot baths, where the school in customary use affords pleasure to Florentines.

We wish that you as friends not spend money elsewhere; it is enough that you spend at the sign of the Hole and the Stick where we have our rooms, and give often so as to allow for drinking and sipping.[63]

It is probable that it was the northern mercenaries who first introduced the "Swiss pair" to Florence, although the names of the musicians (Giovanni di Benedetto Fei and Michele de Bastiano) suggest that these two were Italians.[64] Other than that, I know nothing more about this ensemble or its function among the civic musical groups. The addition of the tamburini in 1509 increased the number of civic instrumental players to twenty-three: seven trombetti, five shawm players,[65] one trombone, eight trombadori, and two tamburini. The tamburini seem to have remained a part of the civic musical scene in Florence for only three years. They appear on the lists of *famigilia* in 1510 and 1511 but not after that date,[66] and they are not included in the 1515 list of members of the *famiglia* who were given tips for the ceremony awarding Lorenzo the Younger the captain-generalship. It would seem that they were hired during the last years of the period when the city was controlled by Piero Soderini, "Gonfaloniere for life" (1502–12), along with Chancellor Niccolò Machiavelli, but were not continued once the Medici returned in 1512.

## Household Entertainments

Although little is known about domestic music in the households of the Florentine elite families during the time of Cosimo de' Medici, we do know that from the very institution of the chapel choir at the Baptistry (known as the Singers of San Giovanni) in 1439, the singers were also privately employed to perform for the Medici. This fact Cosimo took pains to conceal, since private employment of musicians would have been seen as an imitation of the monarchs elsewhere in Italy; an image contrary to Cosimo's official posture as simply another of the elite citizens of Florence, a "first among equals." Nonetheless, he was personally involved in the recruitment, selection, and financial support of the choir members under the guise of his general interest in maintaining the city's image.[67] Although it would be logical to conclude that most of the choir members' private service at the home of Cosimo would have been in conjunction with ceremonies in his private chapel, there is evidence that they participated in other types of events. In a letter of 1455 to Giovanni di Cosimo, Ginevra, wife of Cosimo's brother Lorenzo, reports having gone to Mont Fiesole for a festa with "Piero, Lucrezia, Angniolo della Stufa, and the Singers of San Giovanni."[68] There is no information as to what the singers performed on this occasion, but the word "festa" suggests that it would have been secular. It is probable that at the Medici palace the members of the choir performed both sacred and secular music, depending on the occasion, much as they did for Lorenzo's entertainments later in the century (discussed below). For the festa mentioned in the letter, it is probable that secular music such as ballatas, canzonas, and dance songs were the repertory. We also know from Galeazzo Maria Sforza's 1459 letter to his father (see ch. 3) that as a part of the entertainment of special guests, Cosimo invited the *cantastoria* Antonio di Guido, who performed *all'improvviso* with his *lira da braccio* in the traditional Italian style. This suggests that the lavish and better-documented private banquets and entertainments mounted by Lorenzo the Magnificent at the Palazzo Medici and the villa at Careggi later in the century, many of which included the civic musicians and *cantastorie*, may have been patterned after those of Cosimo.

## *Piero de' Medici*

The period of Cosimo's son Piero as head of the Medici family was limited to the five short years, from the death of Cosimo in 1464 to his own early death in 1469 at age fifty-three. Piero did not ascend to de facto leadership of the city without serious opposition from a Florentine political faction led by Niccolò Soderini, whose position was strengthened when Galeazzo Maria Sforza succeeded his father Francesco as Duke of Milan in 1466 and sided with Piero's Florentine enemies. Without the Milanese support that had been crucial to Cosimo's control, both Venice and Ferrara aligned with the anti-Piero faction and made a move to take advantage of Piero's weakened position. Piero became aware of the plot and managed to rally his supporters, which resulted in the banishment of Soderini and the strengthening of Piero's position, which lasted until his death. As a result, there was little notable change to the political and cultural life of Florence during the time of Piero.[69]

There is no doubt that Piero de' Medici continued his father's tradition of opening his palace to visiting dignitaries, including the young Ippolita Maria Sforza, daughter of Francesco Sforza, Duke of Milan, who stopped in Florence in June of 1465 on her journey to Naples en route to her marriage with Alfonso,

## Table 5.2. Inventory of Piero de' Medici's Household, 1456

a small book of music

a book of music in parchment

a large book of music in paper

a book of song [*canto*] in paper

a book of song [*canto*] in parchment

a book of song [*canto*] covered in vellum with clasps[1]

a reed organ with two keyboards, bellows and case

a Flemish organ with one keyboard and case

a double rotta with case

a flemish double harp with cover

a local harp with cover

a Flemish lute with cover

a local lute in a case

four Flemish woodwind instruments [*zufoli*]

three local woodwinds [*zufoli*]

three woodwinds [*zufoli*] with silver[2]

*Notes:*

1. The word *canto* could also mean "chant." Unfortunately, it is not possible to determine whether these three books are of sacred or secular music.

2.

Uno libro di musiche piccholo; uno libro di musicae moda in membrane; uno libro di musiche grande in papiro; uno libro di canto in pagino; libro di canto in membrana; libro di canto coperto di velluro con affibbiatoni. Uno orghano di channe a due mani con manichi e cassa; Uno orghano fiamingho a una mano colla cassa; Una rotta doppia colla cassa; Una arpa doppia di Fiandra colla vesta; Una arpa nostrale colla vesta; Una liuto di Fiandra colla vesta; Uno liuto nostrale nella cassa; Quattro zufoli fiaminghi; Tre zufoli nostrali; Tre zufoli forniti d'ariento.

ASF: MAP, CLXII.

There are several different woodwind instruments that were called *zufoli* during the fifteenth century, including transverse flute, recorder, panpipes, and possibly shawm. On this problem see Castellani, "I flauti," pp. 189–91; and McGee with Mittler, "Information on Instruments." It is probable that in most instances the word *zufolo* was simply intended to mean "woodwind instrument" without intending to differentiate. Most confusing is the reference in the poem for Tuesday by Folgore da San Gimignano which includes the line "e sufoli e flauti e ciramelle," which suggests that he had a specific instrument in mind for the *zufolo/sufolo*—possibly the recorder. Quoted in D'Accone, *Civic Muse*, p. 421. Piero de' Medici's high regard for music is noted in a 1467 letter from Antonio Squarcialupi to Guillaume Dufay, ASF: MAP VIII, 131, published in Gaye, *Corteggio inedito di artisti dei secoli* vol. 1, p. 208.

Duke of Calabria. Contemporary letters record that her party was grandly received by the civic trumpets and pifferi and a welcoming party of Florentines that included one thousand horsemen, and that she was treated to the usual reception by the Signori on the *ringhiera*.[70] Ippolita stayed at the Medici palace and went often to dance at the home of Antonio Pucci. The Strozzi letters note that this kind of celebration was not being held at the Palazzo Medici because of the period of mourning for Cosimo, who had died only a few months earlier.[71] Ippolita was known as a magnificent dancer, and on this trip she included her dancing master, Antonio Cornazano (and possibly one or two other dancing masters).[72] No doubt she danced with young Lorenzo, whom she had met a few months earlier when he represented Florence at her engagement party in Pavia.[73]

As did his father Cosimo, Piero continued to support the arts. Music had a fairly high presence in his household, as evidenced by the inventory of his possessions taken in 1456 which lists organs, harps, lutes, and woodwinds [*zufoli*], as well as several books of music (see table 5.2). Most of his family members were actively engaged in music making: Piero's wife, Lucrezia Tornabuoni, was a singer, and it is clear that there was a ready availability of music lessons at the Palazzo Medici for all of the children, suggesting that there may have been several musicians and/or music teachers on the household payroll. Daughters Bianca and Lucrezia (called Nannina) sang and played keyboard instruments, and son Lorenzo learned to play *lira da braccio*, keyboards, and to compose.[74] It is likely that one of the keyboard teachers for the family was Antonio Squarcialupi (1416–80), organist at the cathedral and one of the most respected keyboard players of his era, who in 1445 composed a canzona for Lucrezia Tornabuoni.[75] Squarcialupi had been a familiar of the Medici from early in the time of Cosimo, a connection that continued when Lorenzo came to power and later included Squarcialupi's organist son, Francesco.

Information about Piero's daughters' musical ability comes to us from a contemporary letter. The occasion was the visit to Florence in February of 1460 by Pope Pius II and his entourage, who were returning from the Council in Mantua. (The Pope's visit ten months earlier on the way from Rome to Mantua is described in chapter 1.) The day after the papal party arrived, Bianca de' Medici, fourteen years of age and wife of Guglielmo de' Pazzi, went in the company of several Pazzi women to the lodgings of the Cardinal of Rohan, a member of the Pope's party. There Bianca performed on the organ to great praise, and later the Vice-Chancellor Rodrigo Borgia asked them to visit at his apartment, where:

Bianca tuned the pipes of the organ that King Alfonso [of Naples] had given to maestro Antonio [Squarcialupi], the organist, saying that he was giving him this instrument because he was the best [organist] he had ever, or would ever, hear. Once the organ was tuned, [Bianca's] sister [Nannina], who is about eleven years old, began to pump the bellows of the organ, and not knowing what would please Monsignor [Borgia], I had [Bianca] perform two songs for him; "Fortuna" and "Duogl'angoseus" and then she played another, highly unusual one. . . . When she had finished playing in camera, Monsignore and the ladies went into the hall and danced until about 7:30, first *balletti*, then *saltarelli*, and finally the *ballata*. . . . When the dance was finished, everyone ate something and then Bianca played an angelic song on the organ, then she sang a *canzonetta* with her sister, and then, in addition, another young girl began one that says "Moum cuer chiantes ioussement."[76]

The description tells us quite a bit about the training as well as the ability and repertory choices of these young ladies. Bianca not only played the organ—a small portative instrument—but also knew how to tune it, and the use of an organ belonging to Antonio Squarcialupi again suggests his teacher–student relationship with the Medici children. Bianca's repertory included intabulations of the French polyphonic chansons "Fortuna," and "Dueil angoisseux,"[77] as well as an unnamed canzonetta—probably an Italian piece—that she and her sister sang, again indicating the international nature of the repertory, whether amateur or professional. And although the letter does not state that the canzonetta sung by Bianca and Nannina was polyphonic, it is highly likely that it was; the song performed by the other young girl, "Mon cuer chante joyeusement,"[78] is a three-part chanson by Gilles Binchois, meaning that it probably involved two additional singers on the lower parts.[79] The letter does not mention other musicians, but their presence can be inferred from the statement about the dances, which implies instrumental musicians, perhaps the household musicians of the Medici or Pazzi, or possibly members of the civic pifferi.[80]

## *Lorenzo de' Medici*

(Benozzo Gozzoli's depiction of Lorenzo at age ten is figure 17.)

Much of Lorenzo the Magnificent's political strength was based on his methodical cultivation of a complex system of favors, including patronage appointments, that provided him with enormous influence on all levels of government, a network even more extensive than that developed by his grandfather

Cosimo.[81] Even before Lorenzo inherited leadership of the family and the city at age twenty, on the death of his father Piero in 1469, he had visited the courts of many of the major Italian cities, where he established political bonds that would assist him throughout his career.[82] He was also very much involved in the arts, including a close association with the civic musicians and the civic herald. He was an avid and active supporter of painters and architects, as were his predecessors, but rather than remaining only on the level of patron, Lorenzo actively participated as a performer and creator in the fields of music, drama, dance, and literature.[83] In addition to performing music, he wrote poetry, songs, a *sacra rappresentazione*, and designed dance choreographies.[84] He was a complicated man, as attested by his admirer, historian Francesco Guicciardini:

> Lorenzo was a man of many outstanding virtues. He also had several vices, some of them natural, some the products of necessity. He had so much authority that the city, one might say, was not free in his time; and yet it abounded in all the glories and happiness there can possibly be in a city that is free in name, but in fact is tyrannized by one of its citizens.[85]

Lorenzo's palace was a gathering point for philosophers and humanists, who mixed freely with the creative and performing artists in an atmosphere that encouraged interdisciplinary experimentation and exchange of ideas. Throughout his life Lorenzo encouraged the arts on a public as well as a private level. He purchased and commissioned art and encouraged others to do so, supported the building and restoration of public monuments, and actively encouraged certain of the public festivals and ceremonies as a way of engendering civic pride.[86]

He was actively engaged in a number of the public celebrations, as for example his participation as one of the thirteen contestants in the joust that took place during Carnevale of 1469.[87] At that time Lorenzo was twenty years of age; he would be married in four months (June 4), and the following December, on the death of his father Piero, he would assume the leadership of Florence. A lengthy poetic account of the joust by Luigi Pulci indicates the way in which the civic musicians were involved in such an event.[88] The poem mentions sounds of trumpets and drums in its descriptions of several of the participants, which suggests that each of them must have employed several musicians as a part of their official party as a way to stir up excitement. As each contestant entered the Piazza Santa Croce he was announced by loud sounds from the instruments, as in the case of Benedetto Salutati:

> *Era un altro caval, con un ragazzo,*
> *di chermisì broccato d'or, col pelo*
> *coperto tutto insino in sullo spazzo;*

> *e tutti I suoi scudier' che vanno a telo*
> *con cioppette di raso paonazzo.*
> *El gran tumulto e 'l suon rimbomba al cielo*
> *di trombe, tamburino e zufoletto*
> *e "Pescia" e "Salutati" e Benedetto."*

[There was another horse with a boy dressed in a shirt of gold brocade with leather covered all around him and down to the ground, and all of his squires came in cloth with coats of purple satin. The great tumult and sound of trumpets, tambourines, and woodwinds resounded to the sky along with [cries of] "Pescia," "Salutati," and "Benedetto."]

The musicians in Lorenzo's entourage were probably the Florentine pifferi:

> *Veniva un palafren poi dopo al fianco,*
> *e di broccato paonazzo questo*
> *d'argento coperto era; e nondimanco*
> *non creder che questo anco sia per resto,*
> *ch'un altro covertato era di bianco,*
> *broccato come quello, e sarà il sesto*
> *per denotar tutti i concepti suoi;*
> *e pifferi e trombon' seguivan poi.*

[A palfrey arrived after that at the side, and this one was covered with purple brocade and with silver; and nevertheless, I do not believe that this [horse] stopped before another [arrived] covered in white, brocaded as the other, and it will be the [colors of the] sesto in order to denote all of its subjects. And then the pifferi and trombones followed.]

Then, on the entrance of Lorenzo into the piazza, the poem describes a parade of citizens who accompanied him, followed by the musicians—this time adding trumpets and a drum. (Because of the large number and the presence of a drum, it is probable that the "trombetti" mentioned in the poem actually included both the trombetti and the trombadori.)[89]

> *E pifferi e trombetti e 'l tamburino,*
> *ch'eran quindici in numer: son vestiti*
> *di seta, chi giornea, chi gonnellino,*
> *colle divise sue tutti puliti;*
> *non vi rimase solo un ragazzino*
> *che non sièno a proposito guerniti'*
> *e chi dinanzi e chi drieto alle spalle,*
> *giunti in sul campo, gridan: "palle, palle!"*[90]

[The pifferi and trumpeters and the tambourine player, fifteen in number, were dressed in silk, some with surcoats, others with short skirts, all wearing very proper uniforms; not a single boy remained who was not decorated for the occasion; and they entered the grounds, some in front, others in the back or at the side, yelling "Palle, palle!"][91]

Only a partial picture has emerged concerning the way in which music was a part of the Medici household during Lorenzo's lifetime, although as in all elite households in northern Italy and elsewhere in Europe, there is no doubt that it had a strong presence. The account of Lorenzo's wedding to Clarice Orsini in June of 1469 reminds us of the lavishness of such festivities and the degree to which music was an important part. The celebration began with the procession of the bride's family, led by trumpets and pifferi, from the home of Benedetto degli Alessandri to the Medici palace. The festa itself, inside the walls of the palace, went on for three days and included banquets for hundreds of guests at each mealtime, with trumpets ushering in each food course and with music and dancing both during and following each meal.[92] There is little doubt that much of the music for all of these events was performed by the members of the civic ensembles.

It is probable that Lorenzo's household staff included some musicians, similar to those of Cosimo and Piero, and as was the custom with a number of other prominent Florentine families such as the Strozzi and Rucellai who are known to have had composers, singers, and instrumentalists on staff.[93] There are no clear records of who Lorenzo's musicians were, but anecdotal records mention that he had "his" lutenists and harp players with him on various occasions.[94] We can assume that these were the musicians who taught instruments, singing, composing, and repertory to Lorenzo's children and to other members of the household, as well as taking part in the frequent after-dinner performances—chamber music. The inventory, taken at the time of Lorenzo's death in 1492, lists a large number of musical instruments that were available in the Palazzo Medici (table 5.3), some of which may be identical to those listed on Piero's inventory of thirty-six years earlier (see table 5.2). Together with the anecdotal reports, the list helps us to form a clear indication of a serious and growing interest in instrumental music as well as in the vocal music that would have accompanied it.

There were no physical changes in the civic pifferi during the time of Lorenzo; their number and official instrumentation remained unchanged since 1443. Instead, Lorenzo's interest was directed toward the quality of the performers and the music they performed, maintaining the highest possible level both for public consumption and for his own enjoyment and display at the Medici Palace. The list of musical instruments in his possession (table 5.3) includes a set of five woodwinds [zufoli], probably recorders, that were for the use of the

## Table 5.3. Lorenzo de' Medici Household Inventory, 1492

An organ of cardboard . . . by maestro Chastellano . . . with three bellows[1]

An organ of cardboard made in the shape of a snail . . . with two bellows

An organ of wood and tin . . . with two bellows

A reed organ

An organetto

A keyboard instrument [*gravicembolo*; probably a harpsichord] that also
    serves as an organ

A simple harpsichord [*gravicembolo*] with stops

A double harpsichord [*gravicembolo*] with stops

Two small simple spinets [or clavichords; *gravicembali*]

Three harpsichords [*gravichordi*], one in the German style

A viola with keys used as a *monachordo* [probably a hurdy-gurdy]

A harp with four strings

A large lute with eleven strings

A small broken lute

Three large viole in different styles [*lire da braccio?*]

A set of large woodwind instruments [*zufoli*][2]

A set of five woodwind instruments [*zufoli*] for the use of the pifferi[3]

Three wind instruments [*zufoli*] with silver rings[4]

*Notes:*

1. On cardboard organs, see Donati, "1470–1490: Organi di cartone."
2. About *zufoli*, see table 5.2, n. 2.
3. Castellani, "I flauti," p. 189, suggests that this set of *zufoli* are the same as the "Quattro zufoli fiaminghi" listed in the 1456 inventory of Lorenzo's father, Piero di Cosimo de' Medici. He also points out that the 1456 inventory lists "Tre zufoli forniti d'ariento," which are probably the same as the last instruments on the 1492 inventory.

4.

Un orghano di carta impastata, lavorato bene con istrafori, di mano di maestro
    Chastellano . . . 3 mantici cho' piombi

Un organo di carta fatto a chiocciola, . . . in una chassa di legno . . . dua mantaci

Un orghano di legname e di stagno e chon grave chordo, lavorato di fogliami e
    straforato . . . chon due mantici in una chasetta

Un orghano di channa, a una channa per tasto semplice, in chassa

Un orghanetto a una mano

Uno gravicembolo ch'à servire anche a orghano, manchavi le channe, sonvi
    tutti gl'altri ingegni e mantaci

Un gravicembolo scempio, cholle tire, in una chassa d'abeto

Uno gravicembolo doppio, cholle tire, buono, in una chassa di nocie e cholle
    taste d'osso

Dua gravicembali scempi, picholi, che n'à uno Alexandro degli Alexandri, in
    una chassa di legno dipinta

Tre gravichordi che ve n'è uno alla tedescha

Una vivuola cho' tasti, a uso di monachordo

Una arpe a quatro filari
Uno liuto grande, a undici chorde
Uno liuto rotto, picholo, in chassa
Tre vivuole grandi di più ragioni
Uno giuocho di zufoli grossi in un guaina
Uno giuocho di zufoli a uso di pifferi, cholle ghiere nere e bianche, sono
    zufali cinque
Tre zufoli ghiere d'argento in una guaina guernita d'argento

ASF: MAP CLXV, fol.10v–11r.

pifferi. This is a clear indication that the civic musicians took part in the chamber music during his private entertainments, where they would have joined with singers from the various church choirs, the Medici household musicians, and the talented guests. For Lorenzo's household to have a set of recorders designated for the pifferi presents another clue to the extent of his detailed interest in the musical sounds at his festas. Since we know from other sources that these musicians played many other instruments in addition to their official shawms, recorders would be obvious choices for the pifferi, both because of the usefulness of the instruments in indoor situations and because of their close technical similarity to the shawms. But Lorenzo obviously was not willing to settle for the uneven quality that might result from instruments individually owned by the pifferi. The five instruments at his palace were undoubtedly purchased as a set so that they would match in terms of intonation and tone color; one more indication of the level of his involvement in the quality of music at his palace, as well as in the city.

A number of the artists and humanists who frequented Lorenzo's residences were amateur musicians who performed on the *lira da braccio*, the favorite instrument for *cantare all'improvviso* performances of their poetry. These included the poet Angelo Poliziano, humanists Marsilio Ficino and Cristoforo Landino, and artists Leonardo da Vinci and Filippino Lippi (who also played lute and recorder).[95] A special evening of entertainment at the Palazzo Medici, therefore, would have included participation by amateurs such as those just mentioned, along with Lorenzo, his sisters, his sons Piero, who played *lira da braccio*, and Giovanni, who played lute,[96] as well as professional musicians such as the Squarcialupis, various *canterini* such as Antonio di Guido and the civic herald, Francesco Filarete. The list of performers would also include composers and singers chosen from the church choirs, along with trombetti and pifferi hired (or borrowed) from the civic ensembles. As a standard feature of all banquets, large or small, there would have been the trombetti to call the guests to table and to announce the arrival of each new course, and the pifferi to play music for dancing, singing, and listening.

To maintain the highest quality among the professional ranks of musicians in the city, Lorenzo continued the practice begun by Cosimo of recruiting musicians from other courts and cities to take up positions in the church choirs (the Baptistry, the Duomo, Santissima Annunciata, and San Lorenzo) and as members of the civic instrumental ensembles.[97] None of this was completely altruistic: in addition to maintaining his interest in the quality of the music heard in Florence, Lorenzo was also making sure that there was an ample supply of fine musicians to grace the private ceremonies and festas held in the Palazzo Medici and at the suburban villa in Careggi. On the surface the Medici household included only the same small number of keyboard and lute players that would have been found in many households of the wealthy and cultured citizens in Florence and elsewhere. But once the musicians were placed on the payrolls of the churches and employed by the government, Lorenzo would have access to them for his own purposes, a tradition that went back to Cosimo and his private employment of the Singers of San Giovanni. This was more than just a clever economic move that ensured the ready availability of competent musicians without the expense of a large domestic payroll such as burdened the Sforza and Este courts. Lorenzo's practice also avoided the appearance of equating the Medici household with those of the ostentatious rulers of Milan, Ferrara, and elsewhere, perpetuating the notion set by Cosimo that the Medici were just one of the many elite families of Florence—an image that fooled no one.

The musical activities at the Medici palace throughout the fifteenth century were undoubtedly the most consistently extravagant of the private entertainments in Florence, but they were not unique. Other prominent families such as the Strozzi and Rucellai maintained household musicians, including composers, singers, and instrumentalists, who undoubtedly formed the core of private entertainments by amateurs and professionals, similar to those recorded for the Medici.[98] We have fewer and less-detailed records of the entertainments held by other Florentine families, but what has survived suggests that there was a general pattern of private entertaining that was typical not only of Florence but throughout northern Italy. Although the civic statutes required that only the civic musical ensembles could be hired for any official entertainment, there was no restriction on who might be employed on an informal basis as an independent musician on private occasions, and a number of singers and instrumentalists, including members of the civic ensembles, found regular employment in this manner. Undoubtedly, however, it was the members of the civic ensembles, so carefully recruited and selected by the Medici, who would have been found performing regularly at the private banquets and entertainments at the Medici palace.

Building on the technique instituted by his grandfather, Lorenzo used his personal and business contacts to help identify potential musicians. He made it clear that he was interested in finding exceptionally talented musicians, as attested by numerous existing letters to Lorenzo as well as the registers of letters sent by him. The *Mediceo avanti il Principato* (MAP) files of the Florentine Archives contain a considerable number of letters from or about musicians hoping to find a place in Florence; many of the nominations coming from friends, business contacts, and agents whom Lorenzo had asked to scout other cities and courts and to make recommendations.[99] The letters help to document Lorenzo's continuing interest in the instrumental musicians who performed in the civic ensembles and demonstrate the detailed way in which he was involved with the musicians.

· In 1469 Mario de' Nobili wrote to Lorenzo about Antonio, a piffero in Siena and a fine musician, stating that he knew Lorenzo was very interested in exceptional performers. Antonio is recommended as being able to play the contratenor part, the tenor, or the soprano, or with the trombone.[100]

· That same year Lorenzo asked Giovanni Bentivoglio to send two trumpets and a trombone, presumably for performance by the civic musicians. The instruments were sent in January of 1470.[101]

· In 1473 Santi trombettiere, a trumpet player working in Ferrara who aspired to become one of the Florence trombetti, asked the civic herald, Francesco Filarete, to intercede for him by writing to Lorenzo with a recommendation.[102]

· In 1478 Leonardo piffaro wrote to Lorenzo from Mantua, recommending himself as a master of the soprano line.[103]

· In 1489, in order to fill the trombone vacancy in the civic pifferi caused by the unexpected death of Johannes di Johannes d'Alamania, another member of that ensemble, Jacopo di Giovanni, was sent to the courts of Mantua, Ferrara, and Modena in search of a replacement. One of the musicians he approached was the composer and trombone player Bartolomeo Tromboncino, who wrote to Lorenzo excusing himself for not being able to leave the Mantuan court. Jacopo also approached Michel Schubinger, a member of a large musical family from Augsburg and one of the pifferi of the Duke of Ferrara, who in turn wrote to Lorenzo recommending his younger brother Augustein, who at that time was in

Innsbruck in the employ of Emperor Maximilian.[104] Augustein accepted the offer and spent the next five years in Florence, returning to Innsbruck in 1494 following the Medici banishment.[105] That the musicians approached by Jacopo responded directly to Lorenzo suggests that although the search was undoubtedly authorized by the Signori, it was closely supervised by Lorenzo, and it probably was Lorenzo who would make the final decisions as to which musicians were to be employed.

· In 1490, Giorgio d'Arrigo, one of the Florentine pifferi, wrote to Lorenzo from Casale (near Venice), where he was pursuing his wife and the belongings that she had taken from their home in Florence. He thanks Lorenzo and the Signoria for loaning him some money to make the trip and vows to pay it back. Until he returns, he requests that his salary be paid to his companion, Jacopo, another of the pifferi.[106] Here we see Lorenzo becoming involved in the minor detail of the redirection of a musician's salary.

· One of the more curious involvements of the Medici in the civic instrumental ensemble concerned Giovanni Cellini, a member of the Florentine pifferi between 1480 and 1514 and father of the famous artist Benvenuto Cellini. According to Benvenuto's autobiography, Giovanni's dismissal from the ensemble in 1491 was the result of direct intervention by Lorenzo and his son Piero, who believed that Giovanni was squandering his talents as a member of the pifferi and therefore arranged for his dismissal so that he would be able to spend more time developing his other artistic talents.[107] Giovanni was reinstated in 1495.[108]

· The best example of Lorenzo's relationship with the members of the civic ensemble dates back to at least as early as 1465, when he was sixteen years old. A series of letters tell the tale of Giovanni Domenico da Firenze, one of the pifferi, who in February 1465 was found guilty of attacking one of the *precettori*, knifing him in the hand, neck, and right ear, then becoming more and more insane and attempting to wound him in many other places. Giovanni was fined a total of 3,150 lire and sentenced to jail in the Stinche. (The fine would have been impossible to pay, amounting to approximately ten years of a piffero's monthly gross salary of twenty-two lire.) A few days after his confinement the prisoner writes to Giovanni Gismondo da Angnullo, asking him to intercede and requesting help from Lorenzo, whom he claims is informed about his case and has always thought well of him.[109] A month later (April 3) Giovanni Domenico writes directly to Lorenzo, asking him to use his influence to free him from jail.[110] Lorenzo must have made some inquiries, because a letter to

Lorenzo from Luca Pitti dated April 11 acknowledges Lorenzo's concern but states that nothing can be done at this time to free Giovanni.[111] Two months later, in mid-June, Giovanni again writes to Lorenzo, requesting that he be released to attend a festa in Naples, which he believes would restore his health that has been deteriorating in the Stinche.[112] Nearly a year later, in May 1466, he writes again to Lorenzo, hoping that Lorenzo will empathize with his pain at being separated from his family and confined to the dark and gloomy jail ("tenebrose e schure charcere"), and notes that he has made arrangements for someone to take his place in the pifferi.[113] The final step in this matter comes in August of that year, when the *Provvisioni registri* state that on compassionate grounds, namely the plight of Giovanni's wife, two sons, and two daughters who are starving, Giovanni will be released from jail on Christmas day, at which time, candle in hand, he will be taken to the Baptistry, preceded by trumpets (probably the trombadori), to ask forgiveness.[114] The pay documents indicate that beginning in January 1467, Giovanni had resumed his position in the civic pifferi. The correspondence reported above shows that even in his teen years, Lorenzo was known to be a source of assistance in serious matters, and that a member of the civic pifferi spoke of him as a friend.[115]

One of Lorenzo's many civic programs was to increase the lavishness of Florentine public ceremonies. Early in his life he was interested in public festivities and promoted and encouraged the citizens to take part, providing the example of his own participation (such as his position as "Signore" for the *armeggeria* during Calendimaggio of 1459, and his participation in the joust during Carnevale in 1469, when he won first honors and received the traditional prize of a helmet decorated in silver with a crest of Mars).[116] He has long been credited with being the instigator of numerous new spectacular ceremonial events, especially those associated with Carnevale and the feast of San Giovanni, as well as being the inventor of the carnival song. According to Francesco Guicciardini,

> Lorenzo showed the same favor to poetry in the vernacular, to music, architecture, painting, sculpture, and to all the arts of mind and hand, so that the city overflowed with all these exquisite things. And these arts flourished all the more because Lorenzo, a universal man, could pass judgement and distinguish among men, so that they competed with one another to please him.[117]

Machiavelli, Vasari, and Grazzini also give Lorenzo great credit for the spectacular celebratory events that took place during the year and noted his participation as an author of many carnival song texts that were presented during carnival season.[118]

Although these claims have recently been proven to be greatly exaggerated,[119] Lorenzo's early involvement with these celebrations is well documented and he undoubtedly had something to do with the renewal of the celebrations during the last few years of his life following a ten-year period of austerity. Elaborate celebrations, especially for San Giovanni and Carnevale, had been a tradition in Florence from very early in the Republic, but during 1478–88 the extravagance was toned down. Florence was engaged in a series of expensive military actions and also suffered several serious epidemics which reduced both the city's financial resources and the willingness of its citizens to mix freely in public, all of which resulted in less spectacular civic ceremonial events. Piero da Bibbiena notes in a 1488 letter to Giovanni Lanfredini that there had not been *edifici* or *trionfi* during the feast of San Giovanni for more than ten years.[120] By 1488, however, the major festivals had been returned to their earlier splendor. By that date peace had been restored on most fronts, which was at least partially the result of Lorenzo's negotiation of a marriage between his daughter Maddalena and Franceschetto Cibo, son of Pope Innocent VIII (a negotiation that also resulted in a cardinal's hat for Lorenzo's fourteen-year-old son, Giovanni).[121] From this point to Lorenzo's death three years later, the grand ceremonial spectacles returned and Lorenzo resumed writing *canti carnascialeschi* texts, a practice he had abandoned in the mid-1470s.[122] But whereas the subject matter of most *canti carnascialeschi* is usually very lighthearted (or obscene), the later texts by Lorenzo are far more introspective and moralistic, as for example his "Canzona di bacco," probably written for Carnevale of 1490, with the following refrain that in retrospect looks like a premonition of Lorenzo's own impending death:

*Quant'è bella giovinezza*
*che si fugge tuttavia:*
*chi vuol esser lieto, sia,*
*di doman non c'è certezza.*[123]

[How beautiful is youth which quickly flies away; if you want to be happy, do it, because tomorrow is uncertain.]

One of the elaborate performances that marked the beginning of the restoration of traditional splendor to Carnevale was a Medici-sponsored *trionfo* in 1488 having to do with the recent victory against the Genovese and the recapture of the castle of Sarzanello, one of the military matters that had occupied Florence during the preceding several years. As narrated in chapter 1, there had been a public ceremony in 1485 in conjunction with the appointment of Niccolò Orsini as captain-general of the Florentine army, during which the poem "Alla battaglia" was presented in his honor. The subject of the poem was encouragement for the army to return to Sarzana and capture the castle, an objective that was finally achieved in the summer of 1487. As an extension of the celebration of that event, Heinrich Isaac, a composer Lorenzo had recruited for Florence in 1485 to work as singer and composer in the choir of San Giovanni, was asked to set the "Alla battaglia" poem as a four-part canzona, to be presented at Carnevale in 1488 as a part of an elaborate *trionfo*. The financial backing for the *trionfo* as well as the music commission came from young Piero de' Medici, although one might assume that at age seventeen he was acting for his father, Lorenzo.[124] The Medici sponsorship of Carnevale continued through to the end of Lorenzo's life, and in 1489 his "Canzona dei sette pianeti," was presented as a part of one of the most elaborate of the allegorical carts.[125]

## After Lorenzo the Magnificent

On Lorenzo's death in 1492, leadership of the family as well as the city moved to the oldest Medici son, Piero, who carried on his father's interest in music as well as the other arts. In addition to his interest in Carnevale, we have noted above that Piero performed the traditional Italian repertory with the *lira da braccio*. From Poliziano we know that he also sang to the accompaniment of the lute and could read music, undoubtedly the result of his tutoring by Heinrich Isaac. His own household staff included three singers and a player of the *lira da braccio*, who apparently performed every evening.[126] Unfortunately, in the area of politics the young man did not inherit the full extent of his father's talents. He proved to be far less capable than his predecessors in leading the city or in engaging in the kinds of foreign negotiations that had kept Florence prosperous and safe over the previous six decades. Rather than imitating the family's traditional diplomatic position of mediator, Piero alienated Milan by siding with Naples in the long-standing feud between the two cities, which encouraged Lodovico il Moro to invite Charles VIII of France to move into Italy, the result of which was the expulsion of the Medici from Florence in 1494. As Nicolai Rubinstein points out, Piero's actions were considered egregious enough that he even lost the confidence of people who had been traditional supporters of his family; the members of the Signoria who turned against him were all members of long-established Medicean families.[127]

At the same time, inside the walls of Florence, another powerful personality, Girolamo Savonarola, had made considerable political headway. During his lifetime, Lorenzo had been a friend and protector of Savonarola, encouraging him to return to Florence in 1490 to oversee reforms at the convent of San Marco. Savonarola, in turn, while preaching against the conspicuous wealth and profane life style of Florentine citizens, refrained from directly criticizing Lorenzo or the government.[128] On the death of Lorenzo, however, Savonarola's long-standing campaign against secularism, which included many of the aspects of public celebrations, gained momentum and support.[129] Following the banishment of the Medici and up until his own death four years later, Savonarola succeeded in changing the contents of the large traditional ceremonies associated with religious observations, eliminating many of the purely secular events, forbidding the wearing of costumes and masks, even eliminating all public gatherings during carnival time,[130] and removing the *palio* from the celebration of San Giovanni and of Carnevale. Little escaped Savanarola's reforms: he eliminated the choirs that sang polyphonic music at the Baptistry, Santa Maria del Fiore, and Santissima Annunciata,[131] and censured secular music, musical instruments, books, games, paintings, modes of dress, and public behavior. These "vanities"—secular books, musical instruments, paintings, and so on—were burned in two famous public bonfires in the Piazza della Signoria in 1497 and '98,[132] to the accompaniment of the civic trumpets and pifferi, who played "to the glory of such a great *trionfo* offered to God."[133] The citizens were urged to turn their attention toward religious thoughts and prayers, as well as to spiritual songs and readings.

A first-person description by Piero di Marco Parenti of the 1495 carnival celebration is a good indication of what changed and what remained the same under Savonarola:

> And because in the past the youths were used to the "ransom of the sticks" [*stili*],[134] Savonarola had them giving alms. Instead, on nearly every street corner altars were seen with crucifixes and other figures, where the youths begged in order to distribute [the proceeds] to the shamefaced poor, and to others according to what Friar Girolamo had directed. The last day of carnival, which the people usually devoted to pleasure, was spent watching the deeds of the youths. Noticeable in such ceremony was the grand obedience which they showed in all the works, but the greatest wonder was to abandon the old custom of stone throwing,[135] *stili*, and *capanucci*,[136] and to turn to beg for [the sake of] God. At the same time, by order of the Friar, two of the oldest customs were eliminated, the first was the running of the *palii*, the second was that to celebrate carnival they stopped having parties in order to attend Mass and processions.[137]

Savonarola's reforms were all-encompassing; even the *martidì grasso* tradition of groups of youths roaming the streets singing carnival songs was replaced by attendance at Mass in the cathedral, followed by a procession of a newly formed youth group numbering 1,700 children between the ages of six and seventeen who marched through the city singing devotional laude, ending with the singing of *Te Deum laudamus* in the Piazza della Signoria along with sounds of the civic pifferi.[138]

By the end of 1497, the citizens of Florence had finally tired of Savonarola's extreme social reforms and began to resist, a reaction that had spread on a much wider scale to his preaching on other matters as well. There was growing opposition in Rome to Savonarola's ideas concerning ecclesiastical reform, and fuelled by the lobbying of various Florentine factions, Pope Alexander VI ended the friar's influence by excommunicating him. Shortly thereafter Savonarola's spectacular rise to power came to an equally spectacular halt when in April of 1498 he was arrested and tried. On May 23 he was executed and his body burned in the Piazza della Signoria on the spot where he had held his "burning of the vanities."[139] The Florentines lost no time in returning to many of their traditional observations of festive occasions.[140]

The social and political instability following the 1494 exit of the Medici lasted through the next eight years until the installation of Piero Soderini as "Gonfaloniere for life" in 1502. This provided a more stable leadership for the commune until Soderini's resignation and exile in 1512, when he was replaced by the return of Medici control of the city in the person of Lorenzo the Younger, Il Magnifico's grandson. At that point events moved very quickly to restore as much as possible of the celebration traditions of Il Magnifico's Florence.[141]

On 14 September 1512, Cardinal Giovanni de' Medici, Il Magnifico's son and now the papal legate to Tuscany, entered Florence with a large number of armed men from Romagna and Bologna. Two days later a *parlamento* was held in the Piazza della Signoria that resulted in the establishment of a *balìa* whose members, selected by the Cardinal, rejected all recent political reforms, dismissed Niccolò Machiavelli from his position as Chancellor, and effectively abolished the idea of the Republic by returning the city to the Medici family while it was under the control of the papacy. (The dependence on Rome was so great during this period that historian Ferdinand Schevill adopted the chapter title "Florence an Annex of the Papacy [1512–27]" in his *History of Florence*.) In November the Cardinal's brother Giuliano (Il Magnifico's youngest son) convened a banquet at the family palazzo, where the Compagnia del Diamante was formed and plans were made to restore the 1513 Carnevale to its former magnificence.[142] For that occasion the Diamante mounted a *trionfo* on the ages of man that consisted of three *carri* symbolizing boyhood, manhood, and old age, in a procession that included over five hundred torchbearers. Another of the companies, the Compagnia del Broncone (founded by Lorenzo the Younger), competing with that of the Diamante, mounted a procession of four hundred torchbearers and a *trionfo* with seven *carri* having an allegorical program representing the effects of good government: religion, virtue and prosperity, victory, poetry and law.[143] In spite of serious political unrest, the good old times had returned to the city, at least in terms of Carnevale!

Throughout these years of reviving the earlier ceremonial traditions after the downfall of Savanarola, the civic musical groups continued to function, and with the Medici restoration in 1512 they once again enjoyed the kind of attention they had experienced in the past. Lorenzo the Younger took a personal interest in the civic music ensembles, although at one point he was unfairly accused of lacking such interest. In 1514, when he was attempting to recruit a piffero and a trombone player away from the city of Cesena, he wrote to request assistance from his relatives in Rome. In reply, Cardinal Giulio de' Medici (later Pope Clement VII), accused Lorenzo of lacking the same enthusiasm for music or the civic ensembles as did he (Cardinal Giulio) and Pope Leo X. Lorenzo immediately replied, strongly defending his interest in music and stating that he was well aware of his duty as a Medici to provide the city with musicians of quality.[144] Pope Leo X acceded to Lorenzo's recruitment request on this occasion, and in addition to lending his support to the transfer of the two musicians from Cesena to Florence, he granted one of them, piffero player Gianjacomo di Stephani da Cesena, rental land in Cervia in order to enhance the financial offer.[145]

There are additional records of attempts by Lorenzo the Younger to staff the Florentine ensembles by recruiting musicians from elsewhere—at one point in direct competition with the Pope, when they were both attempting to attract the household pifferi of the recently deceased Cardinal Luigi d'Aragona.[146] Following the tradition begun in the 1440s by Cosimo, Lorenzo the Younger also privately employed the singers from the choir of the Baptistry to supplement the six musicians on his household staff, which consisted of three singers and three instrumentalists.[147] In 1517, in another move toward increasing the quality and modernizing the entertainment aspect of the civic celebrations, Lorenzo appointed a co-herald to assist Angelo Manfidi: Giovan Battista dell' Ottonaio, who was a noted author of *canti carnascialischi* as well as *sacre rappresentazioni*.

During Lorenzo's short time in Florence (1512 until his death in 1519), he continued along a number of the same musical paths as Il Magnifico. He celebrated his personal triumphs and occasions in the time-honored manner of public display: on the feast of San Giovanni following his appointment as Duke of Urbino in 1516, there were ten *trionfi* in his honor;[148] and for the Florentine celebration of his wedding to Madeleine de la Tour d'Auvergne in 1518 there was an *armeggieria*, as well as "all those things that were ordinarily done for the Feast of San Giovanni,"[149] including grand banquets, dances, and dramatic performance that involved music by the trombetti and pifferi as well as other instrumentalists and singers.[150] In 1515 the Sacra Academia, a Platonic literary group, was founded under the sponsorship of Lorenzo, with a charter and annual financial subsidy from Pope Leo X. The Academia was especially interested in the tradition of *cantare all'improvviso* and numbered among its membership Michelangelo Buonarroti, Bernardo Accolti, Jacopo Corso, and Baccio Ugolini, all known as performers of the *lira da braccio*, as well as the most celebrated player of that instrument, Atalante Migliorotti, who was elected "kithara player in perpetuity" (*perpetuo cytharedo*).[151]

From the beginning of his reign, Lorenzo the Younger received support for his musical interests (as well as some interference and competition) from Rome in the person of Il Magnifico's son (and Lorenzo's uncle) Giovanni, first when he was Cardinal and papal legate to Tuscany, and especially following his 1513 election as Pope Leo X (figure 18). Giovanni, who in his youth had been tutored in music by Heinrich Isaac—his father's favorite composer—had a great fondness for music, especially instrumental music.[152] He himself was a lutenist, and although there are no documents that record Giovanni's earlier interest in the civic musicians, once he resided in Rome he constantly reached back to Florence to support his own musical establishment. This practice included the recruitment of members of the Florentine pifferi, something continued by the next Medici pope, Clement VII (Giulio de' Medici, pope 1523–34).[153]

The earliest record of Leo X's dealings with the Florentine pifferi is Benvenuto Cellini's claim that the reason for his father's final dismissal from the civic pifferi in 1514 was his refusal to move to Rome to join the papal instrumental ensemble.[154] This story is made somewhat questionable by official Florentine documents that state that Giovanni Cellini was replaced because he did not play very well any more and was considered to be too old to be able to tend to the daily obligations. Citing his thirty-six years of faithful service to the commune and the fact that he was a pauper, the civic government awarded him the usual pension for retiring civic musicians, eight lire per month.[155] There is no way to ascertain how much truth to assign to Benvenuto's version, but it is certainly possible that Giovanni's refusal to move could have been one of several factors that led to the decision to place him in retirement: shortly after the date of Giovanni's dismissal (September of 1514), all four of the remaining Florentine pifferi were sent to Rome for a short period at the request of Cardinal Giulio.[156]

Five years later—in 1519—the Florentine instrumentalists were once again borrowed by Leo X; this time to assist in a performance of Ariosto's comedy *I Suppositi*,[157] illustrating a pattern that continued throughout the papacies of Leo X and Clement VII, and including the recruitment of the most accomplished of the pifferi, Gianjacomo di Stephan da Cesena, one of the two musicians Lorenzo the Younger had recruited from Cesena in 1514 with the help of the papacy.[158] Gianjacomo was highly valued in Florence, but after the death of Lorenzo in 1519, he moved from Florence to Rome to join the private musical ensemble of Leo X. On Leo's death in 1521 Gianjacomo returned to Florence at the unprecedented monthly salary of forty-two lire per month (as compared to twenty-nine lire, ten soldi for each of the other pifferi) and remained there for the next four years, although he was frequently on loan to Rome during that time. In early 1526 he transferred back to Rome in the service of Clement VII on a series of two-month leaves, but when he had not returned by November he was dismissed from the Florentine ensemble and Johannes Danieli (probably the son of piffero Danieli Johannes), who had been substituting for Gianjacomo during his absence, was appointed.[159] A final interesting twist in this story is that Gianjacomo, who was initially hired by Florence in 1514 to replace Giovanni Cellini, eventually invited Benvenuto Cellini to come to Rome to perform for Clement VII (sometime after 1526), and later hired him as a member of the papal ensemble of pifferi.[160]

# *The Entrance of Pope Leo X*

A wry inscription on a building in Florence during the papacy of Leo X said the city was protected by two lions—*Marzocco* (the lion on the Florentine crest) and Papa Leone—and two Johns—San Giovanni Battista and Giovanni de' Medici.[161] The extent to which the city believed this is exemplified by Leo X's entrance into Florence in 1515, surely the most splendid of all welcoming ceremonies held during the period under discussion here. There had been many welcoming celebrations for popes in the previous two centuries, but this one was intended from the outset to be extraordinary. The occasion was viewed by the Florentines as not just the usual reception of the shepherd by his flock, but the triumphal entrance of a conqueror, replete with symbolism that tied it directly to the classic Roman *triumphus*.[162] Throughout the fifteenth century it had been the practice of the Medici family to remain as much as possible in the background, avoiding any overt display of power. With one of their members now on

Saint Peter's throne in Rome—the first Florentine to achieve that honor—all this changed. A Medici had ascended to the highest possible position, and the extended family intended to revel in the honor and bask in the glow of the triumph. After decades of working behind the scenes followed by eighteen years of ignoble exile, the Medici—and by extension, all of Florence—had succeeded in fulfilling one of their most cherished dreams. The city was prepared to go to the most extreme lengths to honor the man whom they recognized as the earthly vicar of Christ, the pinnacle of Medici family achievement, and the symbol of Florentine superiority.

The occasion that led to the visit was a stopover on Leo X's trip to Bologna to meet with Francis I of France following the French military triumph at Marignano that had threatened the stability of Italy. The papal party began its journey on November 10, departing from Viterbo with stops at several cities along the way, and arriving at the gates of Florence twenty days later. Pope Leo was greeted by the Florentines, who, with advice from the papal master of ceremonies, had prepared a reception that was a mixture of both Roman and Florentine traditions for the entrance of a pope.

For three days preceding the arrival of Leo X all the church bells of the city rang as a way of putting the citizens in the proper festive mood. On the arrival of the papal party there was the usual meeting of the honored guest at the city gate, although as an exception to tradition, this greeting party included the Priors, who attended in person rather than following their usual custom of awaiting guests on the *ringhiera* in front of the Palazzo della Signoria.[163] Amidst a great noise of trumpets, pifferi, drums, church bells, and soldiers' rifle fire, the Gonfaloniere presented Pope Leo with the key to the city gate and then all the Signori knelt to received the Pope's benediction. The Priors then raised a specially made and beautifully decorated *baldacchino* over the head of the Pope, who was seated on a throne on top of an ornately decorated litter, and accompanied him throughout the procession, walking half on one side of his litter and half on the other, through the city streets behind another *baldacchino* carried by the captains of the Parte Guelfa that covered the Sacred Host enclosed in a highly ornamented tabernacle (figure 19).

The city had been decorated with a lavishness far exceeding anything previously seen. In addition to the usual banners and flags, nine large triumphal arches had been constructed along the route of the procession (figure 2): at the city gate at the Porta Romana; the church of San Felice; the bridge of Santa Trinita; the church of Santa Trinita; in the Piazza della Signoria; at the palace of the Podestà; at the corner of the Canto de' Bischeri; the corner of the Canto de' Carnesecchi; and the ninth at Santa Maria Novella. The theme of the first seven arches, illustrated by paintings on the structures, was a celebration of the seven cardinal and theological virtues (prudence, justice, temperance, fortitude, faith, hope, and charity). The eighth arch directly associated those virtues with Leo X, and the ninth and final arch, which was erected in the street outside the convent of Santa Maria Novella, where the Pope was to stay in the Sala del Papa, depicted human and divine happiness, a glorification of the holiness of Leo X. In addition, a number of copies of Roman structures were built along the procession route: an obelisk resembling one at the Vatican was erected next to the Santa Trinita bridge; a copy of Trajan's column was placed in the Mercato Nuovo; a facade resembling the Castel Sant'Angelo was constructed at the intersection of Via Tornabuoni and Via Porta Rossa; a statue of Hercules stood in the Piazza della Signoria; and in the Piazza Santa Maria Novella, there was a statue of an armed warrior on a horse.[164]

The entrance procession, which lasted seven hours, included hundreds of horsemen, soldiers, carriages, staff, musicians and *famiglia* of the Pope, numerous cardinals, bishops, ambassadors, barons, and other nobles, in addition to hundreds of important Florentines, clergy, confraternities, statesmen, guildsmen, musicians, and citizens, all of whom processed slowly through the streets to the ringing of church bells and sounds of the musicians—the trumpets and pifferi of the Pope as well as all the Florentine civic ensembles. All along the route the pontifical treasurer passed out money to the bystanders, and the cortege stopped at each of the structures for an enactment of the depicted program, some of which included singers who sang verses related to the visual program on the arches.[165] A number of altars had been placed along the route where clerics chanted, and the Florentine pifferi and trombetti performed from the windows of the Palazzo della Signoria (figure 19).[166] With this event coming just ten weeks after the ceremony to bestow the baton of captain-generalship of the city's militia on Lorenzo the Younger in a ceremony similar to that described for Niccolò Orsini (chapter 1),[167] Florence had clearly outdone itself to celebrate the triumphal return of the Medici family as the controlling rulers of the city and leaders of the Christian church.

# The Last Republic

The 1512 revival of Florentine ceremonial splendor under Medici rule, however, could not disguise the actual change in the city's political position. It was a republic in name only. Ruled from the Vatican, its alliances and thus its destiny were closely aligned with those of Rome. And even though Florence had regained its political independence by 1527, it was not possible for the city to avoid the siege of 1529–30 by the Imperial troops. The succession of Francis I to the French throne in 1515 had marked the beginning of a contest for the conquest of Italy. Even with the peace treaty signed by Leo X following the defeat of the Swiss troops at Marignano in 1515, there were only a few years of relative peace until in 1524, enraged by his expulsion from Milan by Charles V of Spain, Francis I renewed his attack on Italy. Pope Clement VII (Giulio de' Medici) aligned both Rome and Florence with the French, who proved to be no match for the Spanish troops that were reinforced by Germans. In 1527 the Imperial Spanish and German troops sacked Rome, giving the anti-Medicean faction in Florence the opportunity to overthrow the government and re-establish the Republic for the last time. The Imperial forces then turned their attention to Florence, and after enduring the year-long siege, the city surrendered to the Imperial officials.[168]

In April of 1532 the Priorate was dissolved and a new constitution was declared which replaced the Republic with a Principate under Alessandro de' Medici, who was proclaimed Duke of the Florentine Republic.[169] The struggles of the previous years had exhausted the treasury, and as part of an effort at economic belt-tightening there was a serious reduction of the staff of the Palazzo della Signoria, resulting in some branches of the *famiglia* being eliminated or reduced in number. Although the number of musicians in the civic ensembles was kept intact, their pay was reduced by half.[170] There is continuous record of payments to the civic music ensembles until early 1533,[171] but after that point, due to incomplete and missing records, there is only sporadic trace of them until mid-century. A list of the *famiglia* of Alessandro de' Medici in 1535 indicates that the civic pifferi as well as a set of trumpet players have been absorbed into the household: three trumpets are listed as a separate group and two trombone players are listed under the heading *musici*, along with five other names whose performance medium is not mentioned (meaning, probably, that they were singers), and two young singers (*dua putti cantori*).[172] The next record is not until 1543, where the list of the *famiglia* includes four trombones along with a lutenist and another musician whose instrument is not named.[173] In 1559, a list of the household staff of Duke Cosimo I indicates that the trumpets were still considered in terms of their traditional ensemble: similar to the 1535 record, three trumpeters are listed separately in one section of the *famiglia*, and three trombone players are named in another section along with singers and other instrumentalists (as well as a dancing master). It would appear, therefore, that as early as 1535, these musicians, the last survivors of the traditional pifferi, were no longer thought of as "pifferi," nor were they separated from the other household musicians. The 1559 list reads as follows:

> Lorenzo da Lucca, trombone
> Giovanne Porro, musico[174]
> Alessandro Striggio, musico[175]
> Bartolomeo di Luigi, trombone
> Mathio di Giovanni, trombone
> Cornelio da Udine, musico[176]
> Bernardino da Milano, musico
> Niccolao Malvezi, organista
> Giovanbattista Rampollini, musico
> Bastiano di Michele, sonatore d'arpe
> Giovane di Guasparre detto papa, ballatore[177]

The remainder of the musicians—another set of trumpet players, the trombadori, and the bannitori—had been transferred to the jurisdiction of the *camarlingo delle Graticole del Monte Comune*.[178] The obvious reason for this division with the establishment of the Principate is that the trombadori and bannitori, whose function was entirely civic, were left as employees of the city, while the Duke absorbed three of the trumpets into his *famiglia* to function in the traditional manner as a sign of his authority. And he had incorporated the pifferi into his household musical establishment, where they were included with other instrumentalists and singers. (The ducal household included the herald as well; in 1539 Domenico Barlacchi succeeded Jacopo di Niccolò del Polta to become the first of the ducal heralds.)[179]

In fact, all of the traditional musical groups—except the pifferi—continued as in the past, with little change other than administrative revisions to accommodate the change from a Republic to a Principate. The trombadori, bannitori, and one set of trombetti continued on in their traditional positions as representatives of the city of Florence, whereas the other set of trombetti, along with the pifferi—now evolved into mostly trombone players—continued in their traditional capacity as the special musical ensembles of the executive branch of government—which now was the person of the Duke. In their new appointment to the ducal household, this set of trombetti would continue in their traditional role, while the former pifferi ensemble would also continue its traditional principal duty of entertaining the civic leaders at mealtime along with singers and other entertainers.[180] Only the exterior administration of the musical ensembles had changed.

# 6

## The Civic Musicians & Their Repertories

The civic musicians of Florence, as we have seen, were highly competent performers, and throughout the time of the Republic the government took pains to recruit the best available talent, both inside and outside the city. The herald was selected from a large field of skilled artists who were involved in drama, poetry, and music; a very popular tradition that was populated by some of the most gifted men in Florentine history. Except for the earliest known appointment to the office of herald, Percival in 1333, all were natives of Florence. The instrumental musicians as well were mostly Italians, although not necessarily from Florence. The trombadori, trombetti, and bannitori are not always identified according to place of origin, which usually means that they were local, but when they were not from Florence the place names most often found are those of nearby cities such as Volterra, Siena, and Fiesole.[1] The biggest exception to this generalization is the pifferi, who from very early on included northerners who were usually identified as "Alemanni," or Germans, a name loosely applied to anyone from the north. In 1443 the government turned that practice into a law which at times caused problems: in 1477, after a year without a permanent trombone player following the death of Jacopo di Johannes, the *Provvisioni* record that the Signori were quite concerned about the incomplete civic ensemble and wished to appoint someone immediately, but noted that by law he must be from outside of Florence, which apparently was causing the delay. The document records the fact that several performers had been approached but were not available, while those who were interested in taking the position were judged to be not sufficiently capable.[2] Not all governments were as fastidious in following the provision concerning foreigners: there was no discussion or hesitation when in 1458 Giovanni di Benedetto, a Florentine from the area of San Frediano, was appointed to the pifferi, nor when Giovanni Cellini, also a Florentine, joined the ensemble in 1480, although these seem to be exceptions; in both of these cases the other three members were all "Alemanni."

There is ample evidence that much of the home-grown talent was taught locally. The members of the Florentine civic instrumental ensembles trained apprentices, including relatives, some of whom subsequently found employment in the ensembles. There is a notable record of positions being handed down from father to son or nephew, sometimes over several generations; a practice true of both the native Florentines and those from elsewhere. This kind of nepotism was not limited to musicians, but was rather broadly in place among civic employees, especially members of the *famiglia*.[3] We have already encountered it in the appointments of the civic herald:

- Geronimo di Meglio was herald briefly from 1376–77; forty years later his nephew Antonio di Matteo di Meglio served in that position (1417–42); after a four-years hiatus Antonio was succeeded by his son Gregorio di Antonio di Matteo di Meglio (1446–48).
- Although not a blood relationship, Francesco Filarete (1456–1505) was succeeded by his son-in-law Angelo Manfidi (1500–27).

These same practices can be found in all of the musical ensembles throughout the period:

- Luca di Silvestro, the first musician appointed to play *cornamusa* in the trombadori in 1357, held that position for forty-four years and was replaced in 1401 by Silvestro di Luca, who was probably his son.
- On the death of Giusto trombetto in 1389, his son Tommaso di Giusto was appointed to the trombetti.[4]
- In 1437 the pifferi ensemble was augmented from three to four with the appointment of Bastiano di Marco, son of Marco d'Andrea, who had been appointed to the pifferi in 1415.[5]

Similarly, musical talent can be seen running through several generations of a family even though the individuals do not necessarily play the same instrument:

· Nicolaio di Giovanni was the *naccherino* in the trombadori, beginning
in 1399[6] and ending in 1434. In 1421 Alberto di Niccolo, probably his son,
was appointed to the trombadori,[7] and in 1446, Nicholaio di Alberto,
probably Alberto's son, became a member of the trombetti,[8] a post he
held until 1461.

Since there are only a few direct records of this kind of succession, the
relationships in some of the above cases are speculative on my part, noting the
similarity of names and the dates of appointment (the exceptions are Tommaso
di Giusto and Bastiano di Marco, whose relationships are stated in the records
of appointment).

The above conjectures are also based on later documentation of the practice:

· We learn from one of the letters sent to Lorenzo in 1466 by the incarcerated Giovanni Dominici, piffero (see chapter 5), that he has made
arrangements for his absence from the pifferi by sending money to one
of the other pifferi, Cornelio di Piero, to be distributed among the other
members of the ensemble for them to assume some of his duties, and
to hire Cornelio's son (and probable apprentice), Giusto di Cornelio, to
fill in.[9] This, of course, was a clever way of keeping the position open
rather than having the Signori hire a permanent replacement. When
released from jail, Giovanni returned to his position, which displaced
Giusto, but two years later Cornelio retired and Giusto, with a record of
two years of prior service in the ensemble, was hired to take his father's
place.[10]

A short while later in the century there are more frequent statements in the
civic documents recording such transactions and affirming the relationship of
the musicians to one another:

· In 1483, Antonio di Nanno, a member of the trombetti for thirty-eight
years, was given permission to turn over his position to his son Michele.[11]
· In 1484, on the death of his father Bartolomeo di Giovanni, Giovanni di
Bartolomeo was appointed to the trombadori.[12]
· When Giovanni di Domenico d'Antonio Fagiuolini retired from the
trombadori in 1508 after forty-six years of service, he asked that the Signoria award his position to his son Raphaello.[13]
· When Pierino di Nicolaio was appointed to the pifferi in 1509, it was
noted that his father, Nicolaio da Volterra, had been a member of the
trombetti for twenty-three years;[14] and when Pierino died in 1521, his
place was taken by his brother, Girolamo di Niccolaio.[15]

- In 1497 Johannes Justi d'Alamania was hired as the second trombone in the pifferi. Thirty years later, while Johannes was still a member of the ensemble, Mathis Johannis Justi, no doubt his son (and probable apprentice), became the third trombone player.[16]

These examples are a sampling of dozens of such records in which a position is passed on to a relative who in most cases probably was an apprentice, although there are no statements to that effect. (For circumstantial evidence for the existence of apprentices, see below.)

There are also some interesting examples of a position in the civic ensembles being used by the incumbent as a bargaining chip or dowry substitute in order to marry off an unwed female relative:

- In 1497, when Anselmo di Bartolomeo retired after twenty-two years in the trombetti, he nominated Pierantonio di Bartolo da Volterra to take his place. This nomination was not one of familial succession, but instead an attempt by Anselmo to find a husband for one of his daughters. The civic documents record Anselmo's statement that he did not have anything to offer as a dowry, and therefore he would award his position in the trombetti to this prospective son-in-law.[17]

- In 1489, when Giovanni di Giorgio, a member of the trombetti, accepted a similar position in Mantua, he attempted to use his Florentine position to achieve two different ends. First, he recommended Bastiano di Simone, his sister's son (and probably his apprentice) for the position of trombetto in the Florentine ensemble. But he also requested that the appointment be dependent upon Bastiano agreeing to marry the daughter of Johannes de Johannes d'Alamania, the trombone player in the pifferi who had recently died. The Signoria agreed to both requests.[18]

- Jacopo di Giorgio da Milano, a member of the pifferi, invented a way to use his position to find a husband for his daughter without having to give up the post immediately. In 1502 he petitioned to have his apprentice, Bastiano di Michele Tornaio, named as his substitute and eventual successor on the condition that Bastiano would promise to marry Jacopo's daughter Geronima.[19] The agreement was that both men would share Jacopo's salary and benefits, including Jacopo's share of the civic musicians' tips. The Signoria agreed, but with the stipulation that Bastiano would be given a two-year trial period before being confirmed as Jacopo's successor. Apparently he passed the trial period because according to a 1509 document, he was still sharing the position with Jacopo but had not yet married Geronima. At that point a new agreement was drawn up that included a dowry made up of clothing, cash, and a rent-free arrangement in Jacopo's house. For this Bastiano had to agree to a marriage within eighteen months and to take on two students without receiving pay.[20] The marriage took place immediately, but later documents record that the relationship between Jacopo and Bastiano soured over the following years. The two men continued to share the single piffero position until finally in 1519, seventeen years after the initial agreement, Jacopo retired and Bastiano received the full salary.[21]

Looking back now at the succession of civic herald Angelo Manfidi to the position vacated by his father-in-law, we may wonder if on that occasion as well, the position of herald might also have been used as a dowry substitute.

## *Perquisites*

Being a member of the *famiglia* of the Signoria had a number of advantages in addition to the steady salary. From the earliest formation of the Priorate certain members of the *famiglia*, including the herald, were expected to sleep in the Palazzo della Signoria; a regulation that was still in force in 1464 when Francesco Filarete was threatened with dismissal for keeping a woman in his room (see chapter 3). Although the instrumental musicians were not a part of that housing arrangement, they did benefit from the dining arrangements: the trombetti, the pifferi, the herald, and (after 1400) the singers of moral songs, all of whom performed at the Priors' Mensa, were privileged to eat at the Mensa. (A similar privilege also extended to the other members of the *famiglia* who lived at the Palazzo, although they did not dine in the same room as the Priors; see chapter 3). Following the deliberations of 1475, however, some limitations were put in place: from that point on, only four of the seven or eight trombetti were permitted to eat at the Mensa, and then only if they had performed on that day.[22] The same deliberations also permitted the herald to live elsewhere, and he no longer was obliged to attend the Mensa. The motive behind the change in the residence requirement probably was the shortage of space in the building. As Nicolai Rubinstein points out, although the Palazzo della Signoria was more than adequate when it was first constructed around 1300, by the mid-fifteenth century it was fully occupied.[23] It is also probable that the duties of the herald had evolved to the point where his presence in the building was no longer necessary since by that point, the daily singing of moral songs at the Mensa had been passed off to other singers.

The most generous benefit of being a civic employee was the pension that was granted to members of the *famiglia,* including the herald and all of the instrument players, if they had been in the employ of the commune for a specified number of years. The earliest records of civic employees receiving this benefit are from 1391, when retiring *famiglii* were granted pensions of half their previous monthly salaries after ten years of service. After 1452 this was amended to allow all members of the *famiglia* over sixty years of age with at least fifteen years of continuous service to retire on a pension of between six and eight lire per month.[24]

In addition to all of these benefits, the civic musicians were not tied to full-time employment by the city. Their freedom to gain money by performing for other cities and for private ceremonies has been discussed above (chapter 5), but in addition, they apparently were free to accept other kinds of employment outside the field of music. Benvenuto Cellini states that his father and all civic musicians were members of the guilds; as he notes, some were even members of the greater guilds of silk and wool.[25] On first thought one might imagine that this meant that they functioned as musicians for events sponsored by the guilds,[26] but as we know from official documents, the civic musicians were permitted to be hired for such functions, meaning that they would have been considered merely hired entertainers, and therefore there would have been no reason to offer them membership.[27] Since there was no musicians' guild in Florence, it is likely that membership in a guild is a sign that they carried on the trade that was a part of the jurisdiction of the particular guild. Benvenuto Cellini states that during the period from 1502 to 1511, his father, who at that time was a full-time member of the pifferi, served the civic government as an engineer.[28] This assertion is supported by Luca Landucci, who records that in 1509, after the death of the architect Simone del Pollaiuolo, whom he had employed to build a temple to San Giovanni Evangelista near the church of San Lorenzo, he involved Giovanni Cellini to pursue the project.[29] Gianjacomo di Stephano da Cesena, the piffero who replaced Giovanni Cellini in the Florentine ensemble, was also an artist. While Gianjacomo was working as a musician in Rome in 1524, a document records payment to him for an *intarsia.*[30]

The implication, therefore, is that membership in the civic musical ensembles did not require full-time attendance, nor did it preclude the practice of other trades. Other details cited above support the conclusion that not all of the civic musicians were required for every regular ceremony, which would help to reconcile this conclusion with the rigorous schedule of public ceremonies and twice-daily service at the Mensa. Certainly the presence of all of the civic musicians would have been required on the grandest ceremonial occasions—

the elaborate welcoming processions and the principal civic celebrations such as the feast of San Giovanni. But we know that attendance at the daily Mensa ceremonies was required of only four of the eight trombetti, and from what we know of Giovanni Cellini's extra activities, it seems possible that not all of the pifferi were required to attend every meal. This also may have been true of the other major civic ensemble, the trombadori: one Francesco di Bartholomeo di Giuliano, a barber, was appointed to play the *cennamella* (shawm) with the trombadori in 1511, which suggests that he may have been practicing both professions at the same time.[31] (Given the low salary for members of the trombadori, a second career would seem to have been necessary.) This freedom to practice more than a single trade included the civic herald as well, since we know that Francesco Filarete worked as an architect during his term (see chapter 3). This custom was not limited to Florence: Benvenuto Cellini, although himself not ever a member of the Florentine ensemble, states that he accepted a position in the papal pifferi during the time of Pope Clement VII (1523–34) while continuing to work as a goldsmith.[32]

The part-time nature of the job of civic musician would also help to explain the curious situation of Giovanni Cellini's reinstatement in the pifferi in 1495 after his four-year absence. His reappointment was as a substitute without pay during the temporary absence of piffero Daniele de Johannis, a position traditionally given to an apprentice who was being considered for membership.[33] Shortly afterward Giovanni made an official request for a change in his appointment to include benefits although still without salary; terms to which the government agreed.[34] He served in that capacity for the next two years until June of 1497, when Adamo d'Adamo, the foreign piffero who had taken Giovanni's place, resigned. At that point Giovanni was elected to a full appointment with salary, a position that was confirmed three months later.[35] The reason the position in the pifferi was only available to Giovanni without pay in 1495 was because that salary had been legally confirmed by the government for only a specific number of official positions, and all of them were filled. Even though Daniele de Johannis was on leave, the position was his until he resigned or was fired, and apparently he continued to receive the salary even while on leave.[36] Giovanni Cellini would have to wait until there was an opening before he could be taken into the ensemble with salary, but by serving as an unsalaried substitute in the meantime, he placed himself in a strong position when an opening did occur. But more importantly, since the Priors had agreed to grant him full benefits during his unpaid membership, he was accruing time toward pension, could eat at the Mensa, and would share in the tips gained by all the civic musicians. Since the position was part-time for all members, he could continue to work at his other professions as engineer, music teacher, and instrument maker, which together with his share of the pifferi tips, would provide sufficient money to support his family. The stability of this kind of a position had always been very important to Giovanni. Benvenuto reports that prior to joining the civic pifferi in 1480, his father had been a independent craftsman working with ivory as well as an engineer who made machines for lowering bridges; occupations that he set aside in order to take up the steady employment in the civic music ensemble.[37] The extent to which Giovanni Cellini valued a position in the pifferi and a steady salary can be seen in his 1497 payment to Adamo d'Adamo of a bribe of fifty florins, approximately a full year's salary, to resign from the pifferi so that Giovanni could be appointed in his place.[38]

A variation on the "work without salary" theme was played by trombone player Johannes Justi, of German parentage but born and raised in Florence.[39] In 1497, while Johannes Johannes was the appointed trombone player, Johannes Justi petitioned to be appointed to the ensemble without pay but to receive only the other benefits of the pifferi (Mensa privileges, share of the tips, rent), to serve whenever Johannes Johannes was unable. The reason given for the petition was "in order to allow him to remain in the city."[40] Justi apparently had substituted with the pifferi on a number of occasions and was considered to be a good musician, and the city accepted his proposal, probably knowing the Johannes Johannes was not well. Within the year Johannes Justi was appointed to the full-time position and Johannes Johannes was given a pension. Justi is still listed as a member of the pifferi thirty-four years later in the final pay records of the Republic in 1531, where he is joined by trombone player Mathias Johannes Justi, probably his son.[41]

## Training

Apparently, the way in which the musical trade was learned was by apprenticeship. We know that by the end of the fifteenth century the official members of the pifferi often allowed their apprentices to perform with the ensemble or even in their stead; a practice that probably comes from much earlier. There is a statement in the statutes of 1415 admonishing the musicians to behave honorably that is worded in such a way as to suggest that the musicians allowed others to perform in their place:

> Considering that many things are committed by the musicians of the Commune of Florence as well as by those who were not appointed by the said Com-

mune . . . And to avoid all occasion of scandal, which can happen among the musicians of the Commune of Florence, and to remove presumptions of shameful monetary greed, we decree that none of the musicians of any ensemble, either of the above-said Commune of Florence or those chosen by the same commune or likewise deputed, dare or presume to go outside the city of Florence to perform when visiting, or otherwise render musical services of any sort.[42]

Benvenuto Cellini records having played with the Florentine pifferi at the Palazzo della Signoria when he was still so young that he performed while seated on the shoulders of a servant. He identifies these performances as taking place during the time when Piero Soderini was Gonfaloniere (1502–12), thus establishing the event as prior to Benvenuto's twelfth birthday.[43] We know that Benvenuto studied several instruments, including the shawm, with his father, and thus it is probable that he served in the pifferi as his father's apprentice from a rather young age.

Giovanni Cellini taught not only his son but also the piffero Pierino da Volterra, who must have been his apprentice before being appointed to the civic pifferi in 1509.[44] There was at the time a network of master teachers in northern Italy and a tradition of sending talented musicians to study and apprentice with them. In the second half of the fifteenth century the pifferi in Ferrara, both shawm and trombone players, served as teachers for Mantuan apprentices, and a member of the Mantuan pifferi taught a school at the Mantuan court for young players of wind instruments.[45] Although Giovanni Cellini was listed as "master" in the Florentine pay records, at some point he chose to send Benvenuto to Bologna to study shawm with Antonio Capistraro, a member of the Bologna civic ensemble.[46] While studying daily with Antonio, Benvenuto also associated himself with Ercole del Piffero, another of the Bolognese pifferi, and reports that he was able to earn some money from performances through this connection; in other words, Ercole passed on jobs to his apprentices.[47] Sample records cited above concerning musicians replacing their fathers or other relatives in the trombadori, trombetti, and pifferi also probably indicate an apprentice relationship.

## Individual Excellence

That the civic musicians were of a very high caliber as well as versatile is evident in the numerous records reported above. Unfortunately, very little detailed information has come down to us about the lives of people at that level of society. A few details can be ferreted out from incidental reports about three of the musicians, however, that can provide the basis for some tentative conclusion about the standards of the trade. The details that have surfaced suggest that members of the pifferi ensemble were very highly trained musicians.

· Augustein Schubinger was hired as the trombone player in the pifferi in 1489. He came from a very musical family in Augsburg, where the first record exists of his father, Ulrich the elder, who performed as a *bombarda* player from as early as 1457. Michel, the eldest of Ulrich's four sons, was also a *bombarda* player who served in Augsburg, Innsbruck, Naples, and Ferrara (where he was known as Michel Tedesco). Son Anton was a piffero who played briefly in Augsburg and specialized in the soprano line, and Ulrich the younger was a trombone player in Augsburg, Mantua, and Salzburg. As with all of his brothers, Augustein's career began in Augsburg (1477), but in 1487 he moved to Innsbruck where Lorenzo de' Medici's agent recruited him two years later. In 1494 he returned to the Hapsburg service under Emperors Friederick III and Maximilian I, remaining there until his death in 1532. Most of the Schubinger sons were versatile musicians: both Michel and Ulrich the younger also performed on viol and lute, and in addition to playing the trombone, Augustein was noted as a performer on the *cornetto* and the lute as well as the composer of at least one *bassadanza*.[48]

· Giovanni Cellini may have come from a family with a long background in the civic musical ensembles of Florence. Benvenuto Cellini's autobiography suggests that Christofano Andree, a member of the trombadori in 1394 and the trombetti in 1399, may have been Giovanni's grandfather.[49] In any case, we do know that Giovanni was a Florentine and one of the few locals appointed to the pifferi after the 1443 legislation that restricted appointment to foreigners only. He was a skilled engineer and instrument builder, as well as a well-educated and versatile musician. Although we do not know where or from whom Giovanni received his training, at various points in his narrative Benvenuto describes his father as playing bowed strings (*violi*) and woodwinds (*flauto* and *pifaro*). On another occasion he mentions that Giovanni constructed organs with wooden pipes (*organi con canne di legno*), harpsichords (*gravicemboli*), lutes and harps (*liuti, arpe*), and that he taught Benvenuto to play recorder, *cornetto*, and shawm, to sing, and to compose. From this we can reasonably assume that Giovanni played all of those instruments as well as sang, and that he must have had considerable theoretical and compositional training.

· Gianjacomo di Stephano da Cesena must have been one of the most capable musicians in Italy in the first few decades of the sixteenth century. He was first hired to take Giovanni Cellini's place in the Florentine pifferi in 1514—one of two pifferi working in Cesena who were recruited that year by Lorenzo de' Medici the Younger with intervention by the papacy (see chapter 5). Over the next twelve years Gianjacomo remained on the payroll of the Florentine pifferi but was constantly on loan to the papal ensemble. In 1519, following the death of Lorenzo the Younger, he transferred temporarily to the private musical ensemble of Pope Leo X, returning to Florence in 1522, although he continued to return to Rome as a visitor, usually for two months at a time.[50] In a Roman document of 1524, while still officially a member of the Florentine ensemble, Gianjacomo is referred to as head of the musicians of Castel Sant'Angelo.[51] In 1526, when he continued to overstay his two-month leave permissions, the Florentine officials ordered him to return and finally replaced him.[52] There are no further references to him in Florence and it is apparent that he remained in Rome for the remainder of his career, in the service of the pope.

The three musicians discussed above were all members of the Florentine pifferi at some point, but similar stories have also survived concerning instrumental musicians in other north Italian cities, supporting the impression that the profession attracted highly talented musicians:

· Corrado piffaro (Corrado de Alemania) worked at the court of Ferrara from 1441 to 1481. He was initially recruited for the Este court from Monferrato, and his employers were sufficiently satisfied with his work that in 1449 he was dispatched back to "Alemania" to recruit additional pifferi. In 1476 he was the highest-paid musician on the Ferrara payroll, earning more than double the amount of most of the others. His reputation as teacher attracted a number of pupils from Mantua to study with him.[53]

· Bernardino piffaro served as a shawm player for the Gonzagas in Mantua from 1477 to 1527. His reputation as a fine performer led to a year in the service of King Ferrante of Naples, and a request for his services from King Louis XII of France. He taught woodwind instruments (*zufoli*) at the court in Mantua to boys selected by the marchese.[54] (The use of the word *zuffoli* rather than *pifferi* or any other specific instrument name strongly suggests that Bernardino taught several different woodwind instruments.)

· Zorzi trombetta (Zorzi di Nicol from Modon, a Venetian colony in the southern Peloponnesus) was a trombone and shawm player in the piffero ensemble of the Doge of Venice, beginning with its establishment in

1458 and remaining there until approximately 1502. Zorzi, leader of the ensemble, was a skilled teacher and arranger of polyphonic music who, with three of his sons, dominated the wind instrument scene in Venice until the early decades of the sixteenth century.[55] (Beginning in 1522,[56] the Florentine piffero ensemble included the trombone player Bartholomeo Aloysii de Venetiis, who probably was Zorzi's grandson.)[57]

· Bartolomeo Tromboncino, the trombone player in Mantua who in 1489 wrote to Lorenzo de' Medici to decline the invitation to join the Florentine pifferi, also taught lute and voice and was the most prolific composer of Italian secular music at the turn of the sixteenth century.[58]

What we see in the meager number of available biographical accounts is that these musicians, who were usually registered in the payroll accounts as pifferi, were talented and versatile musicians, most of whom composed and performed on instruments other than the traditional shawm and trombone. Although it is not probable that all pifferi were as versatile as Giovanni Cellini, there is ample evidence from other Italian sources that members of such ensembles routinely performed on other instruments:

· A small group of musicians petitioning the city council of Verona in 1484 stated that they could play *piffari, trombetti, fiauti, arpe, lauti, organo,* and sing.[59]

· In 1488 the Sforza court in Milan received a request from Naples to borrow the ensemble of pifferi, along with the "shawms, dolzaine [?], small drums, pipes [?], horns, and all those other instruments they play" ("pifari, sordine, tamborini, dopijni, corni et tutti quilli altri instrumenti, con li quali se accordano").[60]

· In 1499 Michele Tedesco (Michel Schubinger), a member of the Ferrara pifferi, was requested by Mantua for a performance at carnival where he would play bowed string instruments (*le viole*); and at a later date he complained that his lute had been stolen.[61]

· The Venetian legates to Rome in 1523 reported banquets at which the pifferi of the pope played before, during, and after the meal in groups that included lutes, keyboards, violins, and voices.[62]

Similar variety in the kinds of instruments played by pifferi are recorded for Mantua, Ferrara, and Siena,[63] and Benvenuto Cellini confirms this in terms of the Florentine ensemble by naming all of the instruments played by his father. But he also reports performing himself on both recorder and *cornetto* with other members of the Florentine pifferi. Since neither of those soft-sounding instruments are normally found in the company of the much louder shawms, it is probable that the other members of the civic pifferi who performed with him were also playing soft instruments.

Since the major assignment for the pifferi from the inception of the ensemble in 1386 was to perform for entertainments at the Mensa of the Signoria, I have concluded throughout the preceding chapters that in addition to their traditional shawms, the musicians also played soft-sounding instruments more suitable for indoor performance. Pagolo di Ser Ambruogio was mentioned in chapter 4 in conjunction with his skill as a performer of viola, rebec, lute, and "other instruments," in addition to his having been a member of the pifferi in 1404. Lorenzo the Magnificent's inventory of 1492 that includes five recorders intended for use by the pifferi lends factual supporting evidence to this conjecture (see table 5.3). As speculated earlier, it is highly likely that from very early on the shawm players in the pifferi, and also the bagpipe player, could play recorder, since the fingering system is quite similar on both instruments. For the same reason it is probable that Augustein Schubinger, who is known to have played the cornetto, also played recorder, since the fingering systems for those instruments also are quite similar.

In this respect it is surprising that some members of the pifferi performed on instruments other than winds and where there is no technical performance relationship. In modern terminology a combination of clarinet and saxophone, for example, would be known as a "natural double," because there is quite a bit of similarity in the ways in which the two instruments are blown and fingered. For the same reason no one is surprised if an organist plays piano (or vice versa). But there is no technical transfer at all when moving from a wind instrument to any of the strings, either bowed or plucked, or from any of those instruments to a keyboard. That Pagolo di Ser Ambruogio and Giovanni Cellini played both bowed and plucked strings as well as woodwinds suggests that the instruments selected for "doubling" were chosen not because of the ease in transferring technique from one instrument to another, but because those were the instruments that would bring their performers the most employment. It is this avenue of exploration that will bring us closest to an understanding of the function as well as the repertory played by the civic musicians during the fifteenth century: the instruments they played were those demanded by the position. Unfortunately, the number of Florentine musicians who are documented as having played a wide array of instruments is quite small, although other information presented above supports the general conclusion that the professionals who were hired principally as wind players were usually quite versatile. In addition to the statements quoted above about versatility in the pifferi from Verona, Milan, Rome, and Siena, we note that the members of the Schubinger family, who were recorded as pifferi, were also skilled at bowed and plucked strings, and that Giovanni Cellini took this a step further by adding keyboard instruments to his list. We will return to the implications of this after looking at the known wind repertory and its techniques.

# *Pifferi Repertory*

In discussing the initial instrumentation, duties, and probable repertory of the pifferi following the creation of the ensemble in 1386, I suggested it was likely that they were expected to perform music polyphonically, although the exact nature of the repertory is very much in question. As with the discussion in chapter 4, clues to what music was probably performed by the ensemble are provided by the instruments themselves as well as by the traditional roles of those instruments in the performance of polyphonic music. The usual assignment of parts in the improvised polyphony of the fifteenth century involved three performing instruments. The basic configuration was derived from the long-standing practice of two-part polyphony: a foundation part, the tenor, which was played by the *bombarda* (alto shawm), and a fast-moving upper part played by the treble shawm. The added third part occupied a middle range between the tenor and treble.[64] It is difficult to imagine that the earliest set of pifferi performed three-part music, since the added middle line would have to have been performed by a bagpipe, which would have added an unwanted drone sound. (In addition, the range and availability of chromatics on a bagpipe are severely limited.) This is undoubtedly why the bagpipe was soon replaced by a third shawm, although even then the music may well have been mostly in two parts, the two treble shawm players spelling one another off. The earliest Italian evidence that establishes the performance of three-part music by pifferi is from Perugia, where in 1432 one Rinaldo da Cesena was appointed as the third piffero, "seeing that a perfect musical sound results from the three."[65] When the slide trumpet was added to the Florentine ensemble in 1443, its role would have been the middle voice in three-part polyphony.[66] And although the presence of four instrumentalists (a fourth shawm) in that ensemble beginning in 1437 might suggest the performance of four-part music, this probably was not the purpose of adding the fourth musician. Until the last decades of the century, the vast majority of polyphonic music was in two or three parts; the exceptions were motets and Masses, which at this time were not the repertory commonly performed by single-line instrumentalists.[67] The more usual practice was that two treble shawm players shared the highest part, taking turns so that one of them was usually resting (as suggested above in my discussion of the earlier ensemble of three performers). The scene in the so-called *Adimari Wedding Cassone* from around 1445–65, in which the slide trumpet player and two shawmists are playing while a third shawm player is resting, is a good depiction of that practice (see figure 14).[68]

Although in chapter 4 I speculated about the nature of the repertory performed by the civic musicians in the early part of the fifteenth century, the only document that actually mentions specific compositions performed by the Florentine pifferi is the *terza rima* celebrating the 1459 visit to Florence of Galeazzo Maria Sforza and Pope Pius II, already discussed in chapters 1 and 5. In the course of the description of a ball that took place in the Mercato Nuovo (see chapter 1), the anonymous poet actually mentions the names of ten dances.

> The worthy youths splendidly dressed, who were agile and light as a bird, danced with the accompanying ladies. And after dancing the saltarello for a long time, they danced a variety of dances as [first] this one and [then] that one was requested. They danced "La chiarintana" very ornately and they did both of the *arrosti* dances with "Laura," "Mummia," and "Charbonata," "Lionciel," "Bel riguardo," and "La speranza," "L'Angiola bella" and "La danza del re," and many others that I omit to mention.[69]

The passage is significant because in addition to the generic *saltarello* dance, specific *balli* and *bassadanze* are named, several of which are known from other sources, and for at least three of them (and possibly as many as six), we have both music and dance steps (see table 6.1, where the named dances are discussed in detail).

Several of the named dances can be identified as a part of a large repertory of choreographed dances that circulated throughout Italy. The tradition they represent is one in which a dancing master (*maestro di ballo*) was hired on festive occasions to plan and supervise activities such as jousts, plays, and tournaments, as well as dances, and to create new choreographies and teach them to the noble patrons. The earliest name associated with this practice is Domenico da Piacenza, whose treatise dates from around 1440 and contains a number of choreographies that are repeated in the treatises of two of his students: Guglieomo Ebreo/Giovanni Ambrosio,[70] and Antonio Cornazano.[71] Giovanni Ambrosio's autobiographical statement, found in one of the copies of his treatise, names a number of such celebrations presided over by him, beginning with the 1444 second marriage of Leonello d'Este in Ferrara, and ending in 1474 at the court of King Ferrante in Naples.[72] Giovanni was one of a number of

**Table 6.1. The Named Dances**

1. "La chiarintana" is known from as early as 1400, appearing in one of the poems in "Il Saporetto," by Simone Prodenzani,[1] and later (ca. 1475) in Luigi Pulci's "La Giostra di Lorenzo."[2] It is probably the *ballo* "Chirintana," ascribed to dancing master Domenico da Piacenza, that appears in the Siena copy of Giovanni Ambrosio's dance manual.[3]

2. "Mummia" (lit., "a mumming") is otherwise unknown, but may be related to "ma mieulx ammée" found in the Brussels *basse danse* manuscript.[4]

3. "Laura" is unknown.[5]

4. "Leonciel," a *ballo* by Domenico da Piacenza, known from the dance treatises of Giovanni Ambrosio. The title probably is a reference to Lionello d'Este.

5. "Bel riguardo," a *ballo* by Domenico da Piacenza, known from the dance treatises of Giovanni Ambrosio. The title probably is a reference to the Este villa near Ferrara named Belriguardo. The residence was begun in 1435, at the time Lionello married Margherita Gonzaga, and it is possible that the dancing master composed these two dances for that occasion.[6] They are also mentioned in a 1454 sonnet for the patron saint of the town of Pergola.[7]

6. "La speranza" may be related to Giovanni Ambrosio's *ballo* "Spero."[8]

7. Although the poem mentions two *arrosti*, only one likely candidate survives in the Italian dance treatises: the *ballo* "Rostibuli gioioso" (also called "gioioso"), which is also found in the Brussels *basse danse* treatise with the name "Roti boully joyeulx."[9]

8. A *ballo* "Charbonata" is named in the choreography of the *ballo* "Principessa."[10] Another possibility mentioned by Daniel Heartz is that in the context of the poetic lines this is not a separate dance but a reference to grilled meat and therefore is another reference to the *ballo* "Rostibuli" ("roasted and boiled").[11]

9. "L'Angiola bella" could be the *ballo* "Angiola" in Giovanni Ambrosio's Siena manuscript.

10. "La danza del Re," a *bassadanza*, is also mentioned in the Siena dance treatise (as "La danza di Re").[12]

*Notes:*
1.
*Con lo liuto fe' "ballo amoroso"*
*Ell' "altadanza," el "trotto" e la "striana":*
*Ciò che lui fa stampita par sorana,*
*Se fatto avesse "Chi ama" 'l delettoso.*
*Volete udir se lui fo virtuoso?*
*Che venir fe' una pignatta sana:*
*Con essa lui vi fe' la "chiarintana,"*
*Puoi fece "Matre mia, questo gilloso."*
*Con la chitarra fe' suoni a tenore*
*Con tanta melodia che a ciascuno*
*Per la dolc eza gli alegrava 'l core.*
*Con la cetera ancor ne face alcuno.*
*Puoi venner pifar sordi con tenore,*
*Solazo incontenente ne prese uno.*

[With the lute he played "ballo amoroso," and the "altadanza," the "trotto" and the "striana," which he plays as an *estampie* as if it were a "sorana." I wish the charming one could have played "chi ama." Do you wish to hear if he was a virtuoso? He requested an unbroken *pignatta* [pot], and with it he play the "chiarintana." And then he played "Matre mia, questo gilloso."

With the guitar small lute [lit., *chitarra*] he sounded the tenor with such melody that he delighted everyone's heart. With the lute again he played some more. Then muted pipes came with a tenor [player] and Solazzo immediately took one of them.]

Published in Debenedetti, *Simone Prodenzani, Il "Sollazzo,"* p. 174; Nádas, "A cautious reading of Simone Prodenzani's *Il Saporetto*," pp. 33–34.

2. "E oltr' a questo, il suo caval fellone, già cominciava a far la chirintana." Pulci, *Opere minori*, "La Giostra," stanza 123.

3. Siena, Biblioteca Comunale, Ms L.V. 29.

4. Brussels, Bibliothèque Royale de Belgique, Ms. 9085, fol. 14v. Sparti, *Guglielmo Ebreo*, p. 49 n. 6, reads the text as *cummunia*, rather than *con mummia*,

5. It probably is not related to the *bassadanza* "Lauro" attributed to Lorenzo de' Medici in two of Giovanni Ambrosio's late-fifteenth century treatises. Lorenzo would only have been eleven years old at the time.

6. See Gallo, "Il 'Ballare Lombardo,'" p. 80. Music and choreography published in Sparti, *Guglielmo Ebreo*, 184–87.

7. Quoted in Heartz, "A 15th-Century Ballo," p. 373.

8. See Sparti, *Guglielmo Ebreo*, 49, n. 6. The choreography and music are printed on pp. 200–201.

9. See the discussion of this dance in Heartz, "A 15th-Century Ballo."

10. See Sparti, *Guglielmo Ebreo*, p. 49 n. 6.

11. Heartz, "A 15th-Century Ballo," p. 360.

12. Siena, Biblioteca Comunale, Ms L.V. 29, fol. 76r.

---

dancing masters who worked at the various Italian courts and noble households, and they would often name their new choreographies in honor of the patron or the event. Several of these men were attached to specific courts for a period of time, while others were itinerants, contracted for specific festas. Dancing was such an important part of every celebration that in 1469 a friend of Lorenzo de' Medici reported to him that his fiancée, Clarice Orsini, was taking dancing instructions in preparation for their wedding.[73] For the same occasion Lorenzo himself was contacted by dancing masters Giovanni Ambrosio and Filippus Bussus, both offering to attend the wedding and to teach "elegant, beautiful and dignified *balli* and *bassadanze*" to Lorenzo, his brother, and sisters.[74] As evidence that Lorenzo's sisters were practiced dancers, we have the description of their performance in 1460 for Rodrigo Borgia, part of which took place after the entire party had danced *balletti* and *saltarelli*, that is, choreographed and unchoreographed dances (see chapter 5). Lorenzo's own interest in dancing can be seen in his composition of two *bassadanza* choreographies, "Lauro," and

"Venus," that are found in three of the redactions of the dance treatise by Giovanni Ambrosio.[75] It is known that Lorenzo danced with the very accomplished dancer Ippolita Sforza when she visited Florence in 1465 on her way from Milan to Naples for her marriage to Alfonso, Duke of Calabria. Her wedding party included dancing master Antonio Cornazano and possibly several other dance teachers.[76]

On the occasion celebrating the presence of Count Galeazzo Maria Sforza and Pope Pius II in 1459, the choreographies named in the *terza rima* must have been well known to all of the participants: the Florentines as well as those from Milan in the company of the count. The complex steps of the *bassadanze* and *balli* would have required the participants to have learned them prior to the occasion; it would not have been possible to participate in the named dances otherwise. As well, the dance music must have been known to the Florentine pifferi, who no doubt had performed them on numerous occasions, both public and private, over the years; the repertory would have circulated throughout Italy as the various dancing masters moved from court to court.

There is considerable difference between the music played for generic dances and that for the named dances, the *bassadanze* and *balli*. Although music performed for the generic dances (*saltarello, istanpitta, piva*, etc.) could have been any number of possible tunes, the music for *bassadanza* and *ballo* was specific to each dance (thus the need to identify each one by name) and was carefully tailored to the choreography, requiring both dancers and musicians to accurately memorize the sequence. The *bassadanza*, probably adapted from the Burgundian *basse danse*, was a stately dance limited mostly to the seven "natural" dance steps that were arranged in a particular sequence, all at a single meter and a steady tempo.[77] *Balli*, which were far more lively and varied, combined both the "natural" and "accidental" steps, as well as their ornamental variations, and comprised a number of changes of meter and tempo. They usually were choreographed as mini-dramas with a particular theme.[78] The musical difference between the two types of choreographed dances is that the notes of the *bassadanza* are of all the same pace, with their number exactly matching the number of steps in the choreography (see example 6.1a),[79] whereas the music for the *ballo* varies in rhythm and meter to match those kinds of changes in the dance steps (example 6.1b).

In contrast to both of these dance types, the generic dances were not specifically choreographed. They consisted of a single step or sequence of steps repeated over and over until the music ended, meaning that the *saltarello* step, for example, could be applied to any *saltarello* dance without the dancers needing to know which *saltarello* was being performed or how long it would last.[80]

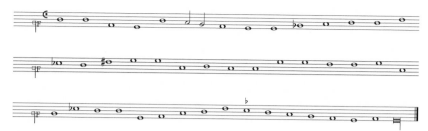

**Example 6.1a.** *Bassadanza* tenor "Re di Spagna." From the dance treatise of Antonio Cornazano, Rome, Bibl. Apostolica Vaticana Capponiano 203, fol. 32r–33v.

**Example 6.1b.** *Ballo* "Mercantia." From the dance treatises of Guglielmo Ebreo/Giovanni Ambrosio. Transcription from Sparti, *Guglielmo Ebreo*, p. 196. By permission of Oxford University Press, Inc.

The music for a *saltarello* needs only to be in a light, bouncing, duple meter (either $\frac{2}{4}$ or $\frac{6}{8}$) that simply continues without change from beginning to end, and the length of the dance can also be variable. (Although all examples of generic dances that have survived consist of double versicles, each with an open and close ending, the dances themselves did not seem to require that formal organization; double versicles may have been the musicians' method of organizing the phrases and providing a convenient method of continuing on or stopping.)[81]

As can be seen in examples 6.1a and 6.1b, the dance music for both the *bassadanza* and *ballo* consists of only a single line, although that would not have been what the listeners heard. The musicians were expected to improvise additional accompanying lines, converting the single line into a polyphonic composition. The way in which this was done was through a set of rules and conventions derived from compositional practices as well as from practical considerations,

**Example 6.2.** Two-part setting of "La Spagna." From Perugia, Bibl. comunale, Ms 431, fol. 105v–106. Transcription from Bukofzer, *Studies in Medieval and Renaissance Music*, pp. 99–200. © 1950 by W. W. Norton & Company, Inc. Used by permission of W. W. Norton & Company, Inc.

allowing the musicians to create a polyphonic sound that resembled the more simple composed polyphony of the era. Essential to good improvisation was that all participating musicians had to be familiar with the monophonic line, the tenor, which would have been played, more or less unadorned, by the alto shawm (the *bombarda*). To this, the player of the treble shawm would add running passages above the tenor line, taking care to arrive at consonant intervals at the initial sounding of each new note in the tenor. This would have been the probable sound of a typical *bassadanza* or *ballo* at the end of the fourteenth century.[82] Example 6.2 demonstrates how an elaborate treble line would be improvised over the "La Spagna" tenor (example 6.1a).

In the early decades of the fifteenth century, however, two-part harmony had given way to three parts, and a slide trumpet or second treble shawm would typically add another line, a contratenor, to an improvised composition. Before circa 1450, the third part would be placed between the tenor and treble; after that date it would be added below the tenor. By knowing the tenor line, the third player would find it easy to avoid dissonant clashes with that part, but problems would arise if both improvising performers (treble and contratenor) chose notes that were consonant with the tenor but dissonant with one another (e.g., if one chose a fourth and the other a fifth above the tenor). A set of rules for both players of added parts kept these clashes to a minimum (e.g., the fourth was allowed only in special cases, and the fifth could be used below but not above the tenor line).[83] This was the technique that would have been applied by the pifferi to all of the choreographed dances, a repertory that at the time must have consisted of several hundred dances, of which fewer than fifty have come down to us as either choreography or music.[84]

As noted above, there was also an Italian repertory of generic dances, although only a few have been found in written sources. There is no doubt that this tradition stems from much earlier and would have included the kinds of dances referred to in the thirteenth- and fourteenth-century accounts quoted in chapter 1. A vivid picture of this kind of dancing is presented by Simone Prodenzani's poems in his *Il Solazzo*. In one scene, the hero, Solazzo, performs dances on a shawm, and in another on a bagpipe.

> On the third evening they danced two by two, beginning with "Ranfo" and then "L' achinea." Here we find Cagnetto and Monna Mea, who did not leave one another during that dance. And the parish vicar also danced; he took Monna Tomea by the hand. And no woman, either good or bad, remained who did not dance with a man of her [social] level. Then came the *ballo* "Pertusata," and after a while came "Palandra." This one danced to [the music of] "Donna innamorata." A lark had never been heard to sing as well as Solazzo on this wind instrument, who was the equal of a piper from Flanders.
>
> In the evening with the bagpipe Solazzo played "La pastorella" and "La picchina," "La forosetta" and then "La campagnina," "A la fonte io l'amai," and "La Marinella." He played "La Palazina" so well you would have said it was the voice of a woman. And [also he played] "La guiduccia," "La montanina," "La casa

bassa," and "La patrona bella." To these sounds they danced in the Roman style in an open style dance holding their breasts high, which for the women is more beautiful than the Tuscan way. Then they made a circle to dance the *rigoletto* arm and arm as if they were peasants; everyone there took great delight in it.[85]

Unfortunately, no music for any of these dances has survived, and it is entirely possible that none was ever written down—that they circulated only by rote imitation, as did most of the repertory performed by instrumentalists. Prodenzani mentions only a single generic dance type by name, a *rigoletto*, which is danced in a circle. The other dances apparently were couple dances; all have titles but are not identified by dance step. Because of the names it is possible to suggest that they may be *istanpitte*, since all of the known *istanpitta* examples from that time have fanciful names similar to those in Prodenzani's poems, such as "Principio di virtu," and "Tre fontane."[86] The performance method of this much older generic repertory would have been quite different from that applied to the new choreographed dances, since these earlier dances were known as melodies rather than as tenors. Instead of the improvised polyphonic practices described above, the dances would have remained basically monophonic, and when played by more than a single instrument the musicians would have added drones and simultaneous heterophonic ornamentation. As the fourteenth-century literary sources imply, there must have been an extensive repertory of such dances in circulation throughout Italy. The number of Italian generic instrumental dances prior to 1450 that has come down to us in notation, however, is quite small; the monophonic dances consist of four *saltarelli*, eight *istanpitte*, one *trotto* and three dance pairs (an opening dance plus after-dance), to which can be added two polyphonic *istanpitte*, making a grand total of only twenty-one dances.[87]

By the end of the fifteenth century the quantity of written dance music had increased, and a substantial number of tunes began to appear among the vocal transcriptions in the keyboard and lute sources such as the Buxheimer keyboard manuscript and the Spinacino, Dalza, and Capirola lute books.[88] All of this repertory is polyphonic—melody supported by accompaniment lines—and much of it is in three parts. The pifferi would have been able to transfer to this repertory the techniques developed for harmonizing the *bassadanza* and *ballo* repertory in three parts, meaning that they could easily have spontaneously harmonized any of the melodies rather than having to rely on composed settings. After circa 1475 the trend in composed polyphony was moving in the direction of a four-part texture: the basic tenor and treble parts, with added harmonic lines both above (altus) and below (bassus) the tenor. It is probable that the pifferi adopted the practice of four-part improvisation around this

**Example 6.3.** Anonymous chanson "Dit le burguygnon," opening phrase. From Petrucci, *Harmonice musices Odhecaton* A, p. 260.

time; the distribution of parts would have been shawms on treble, alto, and bass lines, and the trombone (replacing the slide trumpet at approximately that date) on the tenor line.[89] Example 6.3, "Dit le burguygnon," is a simple four-part dance composition of the type that could have been improvised by the pifferi around the year 1500. To this simple and straightforward tune, the pifferi would have added decorations similar to those seen in examples 6.2, 6.4b, 6.5b, and 6.6b.[90]

Works of art from fifteenth-century northern Italy provide numerous scenes of dances, both public and private, in which the musicians are playing traditional pifferi instruments, which supports the impression that it was customary for that ensemble to accompany dancing. The instruments in the paintings change over the decades: three shawms prior to 1440,[91] two shawms and a slide trumpet after 1440,[92] and the full ensemble of three shawms and slide trumpet after 1450, more or less following the chronological changes in the membership of the pifferi to the end of the century.[93] The performances mentioned in *Il Solazzo* attest to the fact that dances also were often played by solo wind instruments. Iconographical representations of dance scenes also include instruments other than winds; one of the Italian dance instruction manuals includes a painting of a solo harp player with three dancers.[94] Dance ensembles such as two lutes or harp and lute are also found, but a very large number of the scenes include pifferi, which reinforces the association of that ensemble with music for dancing.

At the same time, although the 1459 poem is the only known document that names specific compositions performed by the civic pifferi—and all of that is dance music—there is good reason to doubt that dance music was the total repertory of the ensemble. Dances would certainly have been a very important part of their repertory on the many occasions when they performed for public celebrations such as those described above, or when they were employed for private festas and weddings. But the major daily assignment of the pifferi was to perform at the Mensa of the Signoria, where dance music would have been suitable on only the rarest occasions. In addition, we know that they often performed for private dinners and banquets, which again would suggest a large non-dance repertory, meaning instrumental performance of vocal music, of which there was an extensive written French and Italian repertory. It is certain that beginning early in the fifteenth century, the French chanson was the most favored musical form of the cultured class in Florence, as it was elsewhere in Italy. As noted above, when Bianca de' Medici performed in 1460 for Rodrigo Borgia, three of the four named pieces were French chansons (see chapter 5). The Franco-Netherlandish secular repertory constitutes the vast majority of the music found in seven large anthology manuscripts associated with Florence and originating in the last three decades of the century, continuing the trend from the beginning of the century that was discussed in chapter 4.[95] Given the popularity of this type of music, there is little doubt that the instrumental musicians also would have adopted it for their own. And in fact, in the absence of clear statements of exactly what would have been the non-dance repertory of the Florentine civic musicians, we can learn in general terms the types of music they would have performed and even what it might have sounded like by looking at the general practices for Italian instrumentalists from the time when the pifferi originated in the late fourteenth century.

One of the earliest pieces of musical evidence is the Faenza Codex, a manuscript containing instrumental ornamentation of both Italian and French secular vocal music as well as a few sacred pieces, probably intended for performance by two lutes.[96] Although the manuscript dates from around 1440, its repertory is from the end of the previous century, and because a number of the original vocal pieces still exist we are able to compare the two versions and obtain a clear idea of the kinds of elaboration instrumentalists would have applied to vocal music. As can be seen in music examples 6.4a and 6.4b, the original treble melody of Jacopo da Bologna's "Aquil' altera" is used as the basis for a large quantity of ornamentation. The elaboration is restricted almost entirely to the

**Example 6.4a, b.** Jacopo da Bologna, "Aquil' altera," internal phrase. From Plamenac, *Keyboard Music of the Late Middle Ages in Codex Faenza 117.*

treble voice and consists of running scalar passages that decorate the notes of the original melody.[97] An examination of the compositions in this source shows that there is a great deal of variety in terms of the quantity of ornamentation applied to any particular melodic phrase, the choice of rhythmic gestures, and the extent to which the decorations obscure the original melodic line.[98] Similar treatment of the vocal line can be seen in the circa 1517 lute intabulation by Vincenzo Capirola, example 6.5b, based on the chanson "De tous biens plaine" by Hayne van Ghizeghem (example 6.5a), although in this example the ornamental elaboration is extended to include all parts rather than just the treble as in example 6.4b. The same basic ornamental principles are also evident in the late-fifteenth-century keyboard intabulation of Guillaume Dufay's "Se la face

**Example 6.5a.** Hayne van Ghizeghem, chanson "De tous biens plaine." From Hudson, *Hayne van Ghizeghem: Opera Omnia*, p. 14.

**Example 6.5b.** Lute transcription of "De tous biens plaine." From Gombosi, *Compositione di Meser Vincenzo Capirola*, p. 31.

ay pale" (example 6.6a) in the Buxheimer manuscript (example 6.6b), a German source that includes an international repertory.[99] As in example 6.4b from the Faenza manuscript, the more elaborate ornamentation in the Buxheimer intabulation (example 6.6b) is kept in the upper voice.

It should be noticed that in order to provide examples of instrumental treatment of vocal music above, I have had to resort to music for lute and key-

**Example 6.6a.** Guillaume Dufay, chanson "Se la face ay pale." From Besseler, *Guillelmi Dufay: Opera Omnia*, vol. 6, p. 36.

board because other than the dance repertory discussed earlier, there is no other proven extant Italian repertory for instruments from before the third decade of the sixteenth century. Prior to Pierre Attaingnant's 1533 publication of chansons, which was specifically stated as being intended for flutes and recorders, there are no written sources that are confirmed to have been originally intended for single-line instruments. A number of scholars have claimed that the large quantity of fifteenth-century vocal repertory that is presented in Italian manuscripts without text was intended for instrumental performance.[100] I have argued elsewhere that the absence of text, rather than being evidence of instrumental performance, is proof that Italians often enjoyed singing without texts. Blake Wilson has pointed to the widespread practice of substituting devotional texts in place of secular texts as the reason for so many Florentine manuscripts with missing, incomplete, or garbled texts.[101] It is true that mixed in with the untexted vocal repertory there are also a number of compositions that seem to have been composed with no text in mind and which may have been written intentionally for instrumental performance. These are the compositions that appear in a number of fifteenth-century sources, including the Florentine manuscripts, with titles rather than text incipits as their identifiers, as for example "La Morra," and "La Martinella," and are often referred to in musicological studies as "instrumental *carmina*."[102] These compositions are similar to a set of approximately twenty similar pieces grouped in one section

**Example 6.6b.** Keyboard transcription of "Se le fatze ay pale." Buxheimer Orgelbuch. From Wallner, *Das Buxheimer Orgelbuch*, vol. 37, p. 113.

of the Augsberger Liederbuch (from ca. 1512) that have been connected with the Augsburg civic musicians, and by extension to members of the Schubinger family who were employed in Italian cities, including Florence (see above).[103] The compositional style of the *carmina* is not different from that employed for setting texts, with the exception that they lack a poetic repeat scheme. The evidence for the existence of a specific instrumental repertory in the fifteenth century, therefore, is ambiguous.

Whether or not these pieces actually constitute an early written polyphonic repertory directed at instrumental performance, it is still true that during the period preceding the sixteenth century, the vast majority of written music was intended for vocal performance. This is not to say that the instrumentalists did not perform written music other than dance and possibly the *carmina* discussed above; they undoubtedly performed from the vocal scores. As Keith Polk notes, by 1475, "professional instrumentalists had three basic approaches in their performances: they would play a piece as written, they could add embellishments, or they could improvise."[104] The earliest documentary accounts we have of instrumentalists performing vocal music come from the north, where from 1484 on, the civic wind bands in cities in the Netherlands were directed to perform motets.[105] And in 1494, one of the members of the Venetian pifferi was making five- and six-part instrumental arrangements of motets for performance on trombones.[106] These examples are quite late, however, and there is little doubt that civic pifferi ensembles all over Europe, including Florence, were performing composed polyphonic vocal music from as early as the beginning of the fifteenth century. There is also little doubt that when they performed the vocal repertory they treated it in the elaborate ornamental fashion demonstrated in examples 6.4b, 6.5b, and 6.6b above, taken from the lute and keyboard repertory. The question remains, therefore, as to why there is no extant written polyphonic repertory intended for the wind players similar to that for lute and keyboard.[107]

The reason would seem to be that until around 1500, the single-line instruments were played almost exclusively by professionals whose qualifications included the ability to improvise and ornament music spontaneously. Much of what they performed, therefore, would have been improvised. But even when they were performing from written score, there would not have been any need for music specially arranged for instruments. It is likely that the members of the pifferi could read music from the early years of the ensemble's existence, and with their training in ornamentation and elaboration of the vocal lines *all'improvviso*, they could work with the vocal originals or even improvise harmonic lines for single-line melodies. Written-out harmonizations and ornamental elaborations were needed only by amateurs, and it would seem that prior to the sixteenth century, amateurs did not play the single-line instruments. All of the anecdotal reports we have seen above and in earlier chapters that mention musical performance by amateurs indicate that they could sing, play lute, keyboards, and the *lira da braccio*, but there is no mention of them playing trumpet, trombone, *cornetto*, shawm, recorder, flute, viol, or any other single-line instrument that is mentioned in conjunction with the pifferi or other professional musicians. One of the most gifted amateurs of the time, for example, was Isabella d'Este in Mantua, who played the cittern, lute, *lira da braccio*, and keyboards, but there is no record of her playing a single-line instrument.[108] Even the 1492 inventory of Lorenzo's household instruments indicates that the woodwind instruments in his possession were for the use of the pifferi. It is no surprise, therefore, that the written-out elaborations of vocal music are for lute and keyboard; that is, intended for the instruments that amateurs played. The only exception would seem to be the *lira da braccio*, which we know was played by amateurs as well as professionals, but this is a special case since it never had a written repertory. From its inception the *lira da braccio* was used to improvise accompaniment for an improvised vocal performance of poetry. This is the only area of performance in which it was standard practice for amateurs as well as professionals to improvise.[109]

By the third decade of the sixteenth century this situation would seem to have changed; apparently by that time it had become fashionable for amateurs to play some of the single-line instruments—winds and bowed strings[110]— and from that point on there are manuscripts and printed books intended for amateur single-line instrumentalists.[111] The repertory consists of dances, vocal music, and some new instrumental forms. Typical of all of these works is that the three- or four-part harmony is all included and the parts have written-out ornamentation. The professionals, of course, continued to ornament spontaneously and could improvise accompaniments and counterpoint for the simpler dances and song melodies, and so it is highly improbable that they would have needed this kind of help. It is true that the professionals would have had to read from score or parts in order to reproduce the sophisticated imitative compositions of the period, but even for those works they would have been able to ornament spontaneously and therefore would not need anything but the vocal music. Most amateurs, however, were not so skilled and were dependent on the written score for most of what they performed. Their numbers continued to grow, and beginning in the fourth decade of the sixteenth century, publishing houses found it worth their while to supply printed music for that market. Further evidence of the burgeoning amateur interest in single-line instruments at that time is that in 1535 Sylvestro Ganassi, court musician at the Palace of the Doge in Venice, published the first instruction manual for amateur wind players in which he provides instructions on how to elaborate a simple melodic line.[112] From this point forward, the amateurs could either improvise their own ornaments as per Ganassi's examples, or rely on those supplied in the new printed editions. From the popularity of the printed instrumental editions, it would seem that most amateurs required printed assistance.[113]

The repertory of the civic pifferi in the fifteenth century, therefore, would have consisted of dance repertory and instrumental elaboration of vocal music. For the former, they would have improvised harmonies around the dance tenors (*bassadanze* and *balli*), or elaborated a known monophonic melody (generic dances). For the elaborations of the vocal repertory there were undoubtedly two different approaches: they could have read all parts of a polyphonic vocal score, ornamenting the individual lines as per the examples given above, or they could have improvised harmonies to accompany a given melody. The continuing importance of improvisation for the pifferi can be seen in the 1469 recommendation sent to Lorenzo the Magnificent in which a piffero is praised for his ability to play a treble or contra line. Even as late as the reinstatement of Giovanni Cellini in 1497, the records note that he was hired to play "the contro basso part, or in some cases the soprano line,"[114] meaning that at the end of the century the civic musicians were still specializing in the improvisation of a particular type of part.

# *The Pifferi in the Early Sixteenth Century*

Once the Medici had returned to lead Florence in the second decade of the sixteenth century, the pifferi ensemble seems to have moved more and more in the direction of composed music, and the ensemble membership changed in order to accommodate that repertory. For most of the preceding seventy years the composition of the pifferi ensemble had been three shawms and a single trombone. But in 1514, not long after the arrival of Lorenzo the Younger, the ensemble began a small but significant transformation: a second trombone was added to the ensemble, changing its makeup to three shawms and two trombones, which by 1530 had evolved to two shawms and three trombones.[115] This changed the overall blend of the ensemble in the direction of a dominance of the soft tones of the trombones rather than the more piercing or nasal sound of the double-reed shawms. The change, which had a precedent in Venice as well as in cities of northern Europe, accompanied the expansion of the preferred repertory to include large motets and theater music.

The gradual addition of a second trombone in 1514 and eventually a third during the 1520s suggests that in terms of repertory, the Florentine ensemble was tending in the same direction as the wind band in Venice, which had two trombones and three shawms as early as 1470, and by 1493 was made up of four shawms and two trombones.[116] In 1494 Alvise Trombon, one of the trombone players in the Venetian ensemble (and son of Zorzi Trombetta) was making five- and six-part arrangements for four shawms and one or two trombones that were based on motets, including compositions by the northern composers Jacob Obrecht and Antoine Busnois; in other words, the international repertory. By 1505, encouraged by requests from Ferrara and Mantua, Alvise was making arrangements for an even larger variety of ensembles: five trombones; four trombones and two cornetti; and on one occasion two different arrangements of an eight-part piece, one for four trombones and four shawms, and the other for eight recorders (*flauti*).[117] There is every reason to believe that the six members of the doge's ensemble would have been flexible enough to play all of these arrangements; for the eight-part pieces they probably added two of their apprentices.[118]

There is considerable evidence that there was an increasing demand in all Italian courts for the more sophisticated repertory, in which the pifferi would join with singers and other instrumentalists to play for a variety of musical and music theater presentations:

· A dramatic production in Ferrara at Carnevale in 1509 involved the civic pifferi, who announced the play with drums (*tamburi alla turchesca*) and then played shawms with bagpipe (*piffari cum cornamusa*), all of which was a reference to their more rustic function earlier in the century. During the various *intermedii*, however, they played *sordine* (muted *cornetti*), lutes, and sang.[119]

· A garden party at the Ferrara Belfiore palace in 1529 given by Ippolito d'Este, Archbishop of Milan, for his brother Ercole (later Duke of Ferrara) involved the court instrumental musicians in an elaborate set of musical entertainments during the course of a banquet where they performed along with singers and actors.[120] During the first of three sittings (which included seventeen food courses), the instrumentalists performed in the following ensembles: three trombones with three *cornetti*; *dolziana*, trombone and flute; *dolziana*, viola da gamba, two *cornamuse*, and a *cetra*; three recorders, three *cornamuse*, and viola da gamba; a large ensemble to accompany six voices made up of six viols, lira, lute, citara, trombone, bass recorder, tenor recorder, flute, *sordina*, and two keyboard instruments;[121] and at the end of the banquet, the entire cast danced a *moresca* accompanied by the shawm ensemble.[122]

· In 1519 Pope Leo X borrowed Florentine musicians, including the pifferi, from Lorenzo the Younger in order to assist with a performance of the comedy *I suppositi* by Ariosto.

· Benvenuto Cellini describes his experience playing motets on the *cornetto* along with other members of the pope's instrumental ensemble for a banquet in Rome in the 1520s.[123]

These examples can be taken as indications of very high general expectations of the pifferi in all important Italian courts by the end of the fifteenth century. They were called upon to entertain in a number of different capacities where highly sophisticated music would have been required. And although all of these examples are from quite late and several are from locations outside of Florence, we can use them to better understand what probably took place in Florence beginning early in the fifteenth century. Gregorio Dati's description of the entertainments at the Mensa of the Signoria in the early decades of the century that mentions dancers, actors, singers, and other entertainments would seem to be closely related to the scene at the Ferrara banquet of 1529, described above. The information about the two young singers who performed at the Mensa in 1406 (chapter 4) hints at a broad program of vocal music there at that early date. Involvement of the civic musicians in various *sacre rappresentazioni* throughout the period, as well as in the elaborate *trionfi* during major celebrations such as Carnevale, also associates the civic musicians with dramatic occasions and the broad musical repertory that would have been appropriate to them.

When the above examples are coupled with the information that during the last decades of the Republic the Florentine pifferi were frequently borrowed by the pope for productions of theater music, the strong implication is that in the cultured circles of Florence, as in the other major cities of Italy, the emphasis continued to shift in the direction of performance of a polyphonic repertory that required blended and matching instrumental sounds as well as skill on a number of instruments.[124] Although the pifferi continued to perform as a discrete traditional ensemble on some occasions, especially for dances, by the end of the fifteenth century this was no longer the major focus of their employment. More and more they were involved in the new composed polyphonic repertory, in which they joined with other musicians of the court. It is not surprising, therefore, that when we see the Medici records of payment to musicians in the mid-sixteenth century, the wind players are not singled out as a separate ensemble; they have been incorporated into the general list of household musicians.[125]

# Conclusion

Throughout its early history, the city of Florence had an exalted vision of itself and its place in the world. As early as 1255, inscribed on the wall of the Bargello (at that time the seat of government and called the Palazzo del Popolo) was a bold statement extolling the virtues of the city, its government, and its citizens:

> And may Christ favor and preserve their city in a covenant of peace, because Florence is abounding in riches. She defeated her enemies in war and a great uprising; she enjoys prosperity and distinctions as well as a masterful citizenry. She acquires and affirms and now impulsively she extends her battle camps in safety: she rules the land, she rules the sea, she rules the whole territory. Thus, by her domination all of Tuscany becomes prosperous.[126]

This vision of superiority was never abandoned; it grew over the next four centuries, adding to the military and economic image one of superiority in the arts, humanities, and sciences. Florentines continued to believe that they were the chosen people, and the unending flow of native-born talented artists, thinkers, writers, and statesmen convincingly supports that belief.[127]

Over the 250 years of Republican rule, the civic musicians of Florence played a major role in displaying and celebrating this grandiose self-image, expanding from their medieval model as the needs of the commune evolved. The original instrumental ceremonial ensemble, the trombadori, symbol of the majesty of the city, remained throughout the period virtually unchanged in its composition and function. So too the office and function of the civic herald remained basically unchanged: to celebrate the city, its heroes, and visitors in elegant verse, and to provide continued support for the belief in Florentine supremacy through poetry.[128] But as the city continued to grow and interact with the rest of Europe, its needs for musical representation grew as well. By the end of the fourteenth century the changes in the image of the executives of government to one more closely aligned with royalty was reflected in the creation of the two new musical ensembles, the trombetti and pifferi, both of which were attached directly to the office of the governing executives. Once established, the trombetti ensemble retained its original functions throughout the remainder of the period, although growing in number from two to eight and expanding the quantity and types of events in which it participated. The membership of the pifferi, however, continued to evolve, changing instruments throughout the fifteenth and early sixteenth century as a reflection of the ever-increasing demand for secular entertainment and the growth of interest in polyphonic music. Under the patronage of the Medici family, the pifferi more and more became associated with the private music making of the city's leading family, and upon the establishment of the Principate in the 1530s that association became exclusive.

There is little doubt that throughout the period of the Republic, the Florentine attitude of superiority was well represented by the civic musicians. The constant presence and participation of the trombadori, bannitori, pifferi, trombetti, and herald in an exhausting yearly cycle of celebrations provided daily audible reminders of the exalted self-image of the city.

# Notes

## Preface

1. Zippel, *I suonatori.*
2. The Florentine year began on March 25, thus causing all documents between January 1 and March 24 to bear the date of the previous year in modern terms. For clarity throughout this book, I add the modern dating in square brackets whenever it is different from the old dating.
3. Cellesi, "Documenti."
4. Polk, "Civic Patronage."
5. A singular and exemplary exception is Frank A. D'Accone's study of music in Siena, where all music, including that of the civic employees, is presented in detail; see D'Accone, *The Civic Muse.*
6. It is generally accepted that the word "historian" standing by itself always refers to social and political historians.

## 1. Ceremonial Florence

1. Trexler, *Public Life,* p. 213.
2. Davidsohn, *Storia di Firenze,* vol. 4, p. 377.
3. Trexler, *Public Life,* p. 33, puts the number at "approximately 56." According to Giovanni Villani, in 1336 there were 110 churches in Florence and its suburbs, counting the abbeys and churches of religious friars. Among these were fifty-seven parishes with congregations, five abbeys with two priors and more than eighty monks, twenty-four convents of nuns with more than five hundred women, and ten houses of friars. Villani, *Nuova cronica,* bk. 12, ch. 94; translated in Herlihy, ed., *Medieval Culture and Society,* p. 187.
4. The Parte Guelfa was a political and military organization with traditional links to the papacy.
5. Ciappelli, *Carnevale e Quaresima,* pp. 161–65. See figure 2 for procession routes.
6. See discussion in ibid., pp. 64–66, and in Trexler, *Public Life,* pp. 250–51.

7.

Quando ne viene il tempo della primavera, che tutto il mondo rallegra, ogni fiorentino comincia a pensare di fare bella festa di San Giovanni, che è poi a mezza la state; e di vestimenti e d'adornamenti e di gioie ciascuno si mette in ordine a buon'otta. Chiunque ha a fare conviti di nozze, o altra festa, s'indugia a quel tempo, per fare onore alla festa. Mesi due innanzi si comincia a fare il Palio, e le veste de' servidori, e' pennoni, e le trombe; e i Palii del drappo, che le Terre accomandate dal Comune danno per censo; e cêri e altre cose, che si debbono offerere, e invitare gente, e procacciare cose per li conviti; e venire d'ogni parte cavalli per correre il Pallio: e tutta la città si vede in faccende per lo apparecchiamento della festa, e gli animi de' giovani e delle donne, che stanno in tali apparecchiamenti. Non resta però, che i dì delle feste che sono innanzi, come è Santo Zanobi, e per la Ascensione e per lo Spirito Santo e per la Santa Trinità e per la festa del Corpo di Cristo, di fare tutte quelle cose che allegrezza dimostrino, e gli animi pieni di letizia; et ancora ballare, sonare e cantare, conviti e giostre e altri giuochi leggiadri; che pare, che niuna altra cosa s'abbia a fare in que' tempi infino al dì della vigilia di San Giovanni.

BNF: Pal 560, fol. 29v, quoted in Gori, *Le feste fiorentine*, vol. 2, *Firenze magnifica*, p. 18. Dati's work, which exists in several different manuscript versions, is generally thought to have been written between 1385 and 1405; see Pratesi, *L'"Istoria di Firenze" di Gregorio Dati*, preface.

8. This point is made by Davidsohn, *Storia di Firenze*, vol. 7, p. 562. Much of the following discussion of the feast of San Giovanni is taken from that source, vol. 7, pp. 562–69.

9. Ventrone, "Sulle feste di San Giovanni," p. 89.

10. The Podestà originally was the chief executive of Florence, representing the emperor. Following the establishment of the Priorate in 1282 much of his authority was shared with the Priors; see chapter 2.

11. According to Trexler, *Public Life*, p. 249, by the sixteenth century the festivities had expanded to include additional processions on the three days prior to the saint's day.

12.

Tutti i cherici e preti, monaci e frati, che sono gran numero di regole, con tante reliquie di santi che è una cosa infinita e di grandissima divozione, oltre alla maravigliosa ricchezza di loro adornamenti, con ricchissimi paramenti di vesti d'oro e di seta e di figure ricamate e con molte compagnie d'uomini secolari che vanno innanzi ciascuno alla regola di quella chiesa dove tale compagnia si rauna con abito d'angioli e con suoni e stormenti di ogni ragione e canti maravigliosi, facendo bellissime rappresentazioni di quelli santi e di quella solennità a cui onore fanno, andando a coppia a coppia, cantando divotissime laude. Partonsi da santa Maria del Fiore e vanno per la terra e quivi ritornano.

Quoted in Ventrone, "Sulle feste di San Giovanni," p. 90.

13. Details of the procession are from Davidsohn, *Storia di Firenze*, vol. 7, pp. 562–64, and Trexler, *Public Life*, p. 250. Trexler claims that this was more or less the standard route for religious processions, although some were broader in scope, moving more toward Santa Croce on the east, and toward the Servi and Observant Dominican churches on the north.

14. The dual purpose of the ceremony can be seen in Villani's description of the 1343 presentation ceremony during the short period when Walter Brienne served as Podestà. The gifts of banners (*palii*) and candles were first presented to Brienne and then offered to the saint at the Baptistry:

On the morning of the feast, besides the usual candles from the approximately twenty strongholds of the commune, he received more than twenty-five cloths or banners decorated in gold, and hunting dogs, and hawks, and goshawks as homage from Arezzo, Pistoia, Volterra, San Gimignano, Colle, and from all the counts of Guidi, from Mangona and Cerbaia, from Monte Carelli and Pontormo, and from the Ubaldini, Pazzi, and Ubertini, and from every little baron. Together with the offering of the candles, this was a noble thing and feast. And all the candles and banners and the other tributes were gathered together in the Piazza of Santa Croce, then one after the other went to the Palace where the duke was, and then they offered them at San Giovanni. And to the banner of crimson samite cloth he [Brienne] added to the other side a trim of gray squirrel skin as long as the pole. It was very rich to see. And he made a very rich and noble feast, the first and last he was to hold because of his evil actions.

Villani, *Nuova cronica*, bk. 13, ch. 8; translation after Trexler, *Public Life*, pp. 257–58.

15.
A dì 22 la mattina la processione di tutti gli edifici, e quali detto anno furono e andorono come apresso dirò.

1. El principio mosse la Croce di Santa Maria del Fiore con tutti loro cherici, fancuilli, e drieto a lloro sei cantori.
2. Le compagnie di Jacopo cimatore e Nofri calzaiuolo con circa 30 fanciulli vestiti di bianco e agnoletti.
3. L'edificio di san Michele Agnolo al quale soprastava Iddio padre in una nugola, e in piaza al dirimpetto a' Signori feceno rappresentazione della battaglia angelica, quando Lucifero fu co' sua agnoli maladetti cacciato di cielo.
4. Le compagnie di ser Antonio e Piero di Mariano con circa a 30 fanciulli vestiti di bianco e agnoletti.
5. L'edificio d'Adamo, che in piaza fe' rappresentatione di quando Iddo creò Adamo e poi Eva, fe' loro el comandamento, e la loro disubidenza in fino a cacciargli di paradiso, colla tentazione prima del serpente e altre apartenenze.
6. Un Moisè a cavallo con assa' cavalleria de' principali del popolo d'Isdrael e altri.
7. L'edificio di Moisè, el quale in piaza fe' la rapresentazione di quando Iddio gli diè le legge.
8. Più profeti e sibille con Ermes Trimegisto et altri profetazatori della incarnazione di Cristo.
9. L'edificio della Nunziata, che fe' la sua rappresentazione.
10. Optaviano imperadore con molta cavalleria e colla Sibilla, per fare rappresentazione, quando la Sibilla gli predisse dovea nascere Cristo e monstrògli la Vergine in aria con Cristo in braccio.
11. Templum pacis coll'edificio della natività per fare la sua rapresentazione.
12. Un magnificio e trionfale tempio per edificio de' Magi, nel quale si copria un altro tempio ottangulare, ornato di sette . . . intorno, e da oriente la Vergine con Cristo nato, e Erode intorno a detto tempio fe' sua rapresentazione.
13. Tre Magi con cavalleria di più di 200 cavalli ornati di molte magnificenzie, e vennono a offerere a Cristo nato.
    Intralasciossi la passione et sepultura, perché non parve si convenisse a festa, e seguì:
14. Una cavalleria de' cavaliere di Pilato ordinati a guardia del Sepolcro.
15. L'edificio della sepultura onde risucitò Cristo.
16. L'edificio del Limbo, onde trasse e Padri Santi.
17. L'edificio del Paradiso, dove misse detti Santi Padri.
18. Gli Apostoli e lle Marie che furono presenti all'Asuntione.
19. L'edificio dell'Asuntione di Cristo, cioè quando salì in cielo.
20. Cavalleria di re e reine, e damigelle e ninfe con cani e altre apartenenze al Vivo e Morto.
21. L'edificio del Vivo e Morto.

22. L'edificio del Giudicio, con barella de' Sepolcri e Paradiso e Inferno, e sua rapresentazioni, come per fede si crede sare' in fine de' secoli.

Tutti sopradetti edifici ferono sua rapresentazioni in piaza inanzi a' Signori e durarono infino alle sedici hore.

From "Storia fiorentina di Matteo Palmieri alla processione di San Giovanni," quoted in Bessi, "Lo spettacolo e la scrittura," pp. 103, 105.

16. For more on the details of the *palio*, see Carew-Reid, *Les fêtes florentines*, pp. 72–77.

17. Villani, *Nuova cronica*, bk. 7, ch. 89.

18. Richard Trexler, *Public Life*, p. 217, concludes that rather than an isolated incident, this type of event was a regular diversion of the well-to-do families.

19. A detailed study of carnival and Lent in Florence during the fourteenth and fifteenth centuries can be found in Ciappelli, *Carnevale e Quaresima*. Much of the following description is taken from that source.

20. Ibid., pp. 43–44.

21. Grazzini, *Tutti i trionfi*.

22. Prizer, "Reading Carnival," p. 188.

23. Trexler, "Florentine Theatre," pp. 454–57.

24. According to Gori, *Le feste fiorentine*, vol. 1, *Le feste per San Giovanni*, pp. 40–41, these young men were Andrea Carnesecchi, Jacopo Marzupini, Bartolomeo Bartolini, Lodovico Pucci, Piero Vespucci, Francesco Altoviti, Andrea Boni, and Francesco Girolami.

25. Reported in ibid., pp. 41–44. The account is attributed to a manuscript in the Florentine state archives among the papers of Carlo Strozzi. Gori adds that Benci's efforts to impress Marietta Strozzi were in vain; seven years later she married Teofilo Calcagnini of Ferrara, and the following year Benci married Lisabetta Tornabuoni (p. 44). On the possible political implications of the event, see Trexler, *Public Life*, pp. 230–32. See also Prizer, "Petrucci and the Carnival Song," p. 227, where this event is connected to the text of the *trionfo* "Del'Amore."

26. Ciappelli, *Carnevale e Quaresima*, pp. 142–43.

27. Pulci, *Opere minori*, p. 55.

28. All of this is taken from Ciappelli, *Carnevale e Quaresima*, pp. 123–29.

29. Ibid., p. 137.

30. Ibid., p. 150.

31. "Memoria che addì 10 febbraio 1414 [1415] so fece in Mercato Nuovo una festa di danzare, di donne e di giovani, per una brigata chiamata la brigata della Galea, della quale messer Carlo di Matteo dello Scelto. Fecesi uno steccato intorno a Mercato; furonvi, si disse, circa a secento donne e gran quantità d'uomini: fu ricca e bella festa."

[I remember on the 10th of February in the Mercato Nuovo, a dance festa of women and young men was held by a brigata called the Brigata of Galea by Sir Carlo di Matteo dello Scelto. They placed barriers around the Mercato, and there were, it is said, approximately six hundred women and a great quantity of men. It was a rich and beautiful festa.] del Corazza, "Diario fiorentino," p. 254.

32.

E addì 2 di ferraio [1420] una brigata di giovani cittadini feciono una ricca e bella festa di ballare: in su la piazza de' Signori feciono uno isteccato grandissimo; feciono due doni: una grillanda di cremusi in su 'n un bastone grosso, entrovvi un fermaglietto, e quella si donò a chi meglio danzò de' giovani; e una grilandetta a modo d'una coroncina d'ariento dorata, o vero collare, e quella donorono a che meglio danzava delle giovani e fanciulle. Elessono quatttro donne che avessino a giudicare l'onore delle donne, e stettono a sedere alte come giudicatori; e cosi elessono chi avesse a giudicare quello de' giovani. Quello delle donne dierono alla figliuola di Filippo … d'Amerigo del Bene, e quello de' giovani al figluolo di Bernardo Gherardi. Questa brigata furono 14, e vestirono di cremusi foderati di dosso di vaio, e rimboccato di fuori più di ½ braccio, con un grillo grande di perle in sul braccio manco, con cappucci grandi frappati bianchi e rossi e verdi, e calze divisate con nuove devise bianche e rosse e verdi, ricamate di perle. El signor fu … di Agnolo di Filippo di Ser Giovanni; venne con un vestire di cremusi ispandiante, aconcio a sedere dalla Mercantia, molto signorilmente con molti capoletti e tapeti. E per molto ballare dierono due volte bere con confetti: venivano giovani 22 con 22 confettiere piene di treggiea e pinocchiati, e con nobili vini e poi l'ultima volta, cioè la terza volta, con zuccherini. Poi, dato l'onore, feciono giostrare in sulla detta piazza con lancie lunghe, senza iscudo, con elmetti e armadura da soldati. I pinocchiati furono la prima volta inarientati, e la seconda furono dorati. Il lunedi seguente addi 3 andorono tutti insieme a cavallo per Firenze, in su cavalli grossi. Dicesi che questa fussi delle belle ricche feste che si facessi mai a Firenze, di simile cose, cioè di ballo.

Ibid., p. 276.

33. *Statuta populi et communis Florentiae*, vol. 2, rubric 40.

34. Ciappelli, *Carnevale e Quaresima*, pp. 183–89.

35. For texts of the carnival songs, see Singleton, *Canti carnascialeschi*. For discussions of carnival texts and their purpose and origin, see Prizer, "Petrucci and the Carnival Song"; Prizer, "Reading Carnival"; and Prizer, "The Music Savonarola Burned."

36. Prizer, "Reading Carnival."

37. Ciappelli, *Carnevale e Quaresima*, p. 170, speculates that the Pazzi may have become involved as early as the twelfth century. The present spectacular ceremony, known as the *Scoppio del carro*, is a much later development (pp. 168–72).

38. The change was enacted in May of 1478, following the Pazzi attack that resulted in the wounding of Lorenzo de' Medici and the death of his brother Giuliano. Luciano Artusi and Silvano Gabrielli, *Feste e giochi a Firenze*, p. 101, quoted in Carew-Reid, *Les fêtes florentines*, p. 16.

39. See Ventrone, *Gli araldi*, p. 7.

40. On their possible presence as early as 1417, see Ciappelli, *Carnevale e Quaresima*, p. 174. For other studies of the subject, see Newbigin, "The Word Made Flesh"; Newbigin, *Nuovo corpus di sacre rappresentazioni*; Newbigin, "Plays, Printing and Publishing"; Newbigin, "Piety and Politics"; Ventrone, "La sacra rappresentazione fiorentina"; and Hatfield, "The Compagnia de' Magi."

41. Newbigin, "The Word," p. 368.

42. Barr, "Music and Spectacle," p. 377 and n. 55. The Parte Guelfa permanently employed at least two trumpet players from as early as the fourteenth century, and in the fifteenth century they added one or two pifferi. They were called upon by the city to augment the festive sounds for the more lavish ceremonies.

43. For a list of the earliest manuscripts, see McGee, "The Liturgical Placements."

44. On liturgical drama, see Rankin, "Liturgical Drama."

45. The Fleury Playbook, Ms Orleans, Bibl. Municipale 201, from the twelfth century, for example, contains ten full-length plays on subjects such as the Saint Nicholas legend and Lazarus, in addition to the traditional Easter topic. For discussion and photo reproduction of the manuscript, see Campbell and Davidson, *The Fleury Playbook*.

46. Newbigin, "The Word," p. 368. These were the plays presented during the visit of Galeazzo Maria Sforza in 1471; see below.

47. The appointment of Jacopo Salimbene as herald in 1352 describes him as an author of "comedies," although there is no evidence that at this early date the herald was involved in writing *sacre rappresentazioni*.

48. See discussion of the heralds and these plays in Ventrone, *Gli araldi*.

49. On Feo Belcare, see Ventrone, "La Sacra Rappresentazione," p. 75. On Lorenzo's "Rappresentazione di Giovanni e Paolo," see Ciappelli, *Carnevale e Quaresima*, p. 179.

50. Ventrone, *Gli araldi*, p. 7.

51. On this type of production in Florence, see Barr, "Music and Spectacle"; Newbigin, *Nuovo corpus*; Newbigin, "Plays, Printing and Publishing"; Newbigin, "Piety and Politics"; Newbigin, "The Word Made Flesh"; Ventrone, "Per una morfologia"; Ventrone, "L'eccezione e la regola"; and Ventrone, "La sacra rappresentazione fiorentina."

52. Davidsohn, *Storia di Firenze*, vol. 7, p. 560.

53. Ibid., p. 561.

54. "E per allegrezza e buono stato ogni anno per calen di maggio si faceano le brigate e companie di genti giovani vestiti di nuovo, e faccendo corti coperte di zendadi e di drappi, e chiuse di legname in più parti della città; e simile di donne e di pulcelle, andando per la terra ballando con ordine, e signore accoppiate, cogli stromenti e colle ghirlande di fiori in capo, stando in giuochi e in allegrezze, e in desinari e cene." Villani, *Nuova cronica*, bk. 8, ch. 132.

55. Ibid., bk. 9, ch. 39. For a more colorful account of the incident see Davidsohn, *Storia di Firenze*, vol. 4, pp. 144–45.

56. The numbers are in Pieri, *Cronica*, p. 78, where the date is given as 1303.

57.
Per lo calen di maggio MCCCIIII, come al buono tempo passato del tranquillo e buono sta-to di Firenze, s'usavano le compagnie e brigate di sollazzi per la cittade, per fare allegrezza e festa, si rinnovarono e fecionsene in più parti de la città a gara l'una contrada dell'altra, ci-ascuno chi meglio sapea e potea. Infra l'altre, come per antico aveano per costume quegli di borgo San Friano di fare più nuovi e diversi giuochi, si mandarono un bando che chiunque volesse sapere novelle dell'altro mondo dovesse essere il dì di calen di maggio in su 'l ponte alla Carraia, e d'intorno a l'Arno; e ordinarono in Arno sopra barche e navicelle palchi, e fecionvi la somiglianza e figura dello 'nferno con fuochi e altre pene e martori, e uomini contrafatti a demonia, orribili a vedere, e altri i quali aveano figure d'anime ignude, che pareano persone, e mettevangli in quegli diversi tormenti con grandissime grida, e strida, e tempesta, la quale parea idiosa e spaventevole a udire e a vedere; e per lo nuovo giuoco vi trassono a vedere molti cittadini: e 'l ponte alla Carraia, il quale era allora di legname da pila a pila, si caricò sì di gente che rovinò in più parti, e cadde colla gente che v'era suso; onde molte genti vi morirono e annegarono, e molti se ne guastarono le persone, sì che il giuoco da beffe avenne col vero, e com'era ito il bando, molti n'andarono per morte a sapere novelle dell'altro mondo, con grande pianto e dolore a tutta la cittade, che ciascuno vi credea avere perduto il figliuolo o 'l fratello; e fu questo segno del futuro danno che in corto tempo dovea venirea la nostra cittade per lo soperchio delle peccata de' citadini, sì come appresso faremo menzione.

Villani, *Nuova cronica*, bk. 10, ch. 70.

58. Davidsohn, *Storia di Firenze*, vol. 7, pp. 558–59.

59. Ibid., pp. 553–54.

60. On the compagnia, see Hatfield, "The Compagnia de' Magi."

61.
A dì VI di genaio se fe' in Firenze una solenne e magnia festa alla chiesa de' frati di Sancto Marcho, de' santi Magi e della stella. I Magi andorono per tutta la città, molto orevolemente vestiti e chon chavagli e cho molta conpagnia e co molte novità. I re 'Rode istette a Santo Giovanni e sun uno palcho molto bene adornato, chon sua gente. E passando da Sancto

Giovanni, salirono i su palcho dov'era Erode e quivi disputorono del fanciullo che anda-
vano ad adorare e promettendo di tornare a Erode. E fatta l'oferta i Magi al banbino e non
tornando ad Erode, Erode gli perseghuitò e fe' ucidere molti fanciulli contrafatti in braccio
alle madri e balie, e chon questo finì la sera la festa alle 23 ore.

*Alle bocche della piazza*, p. 89.

62. Hatfield, "The Compagnia de' Magi"; Trexler, "The Magi Enter Florence."

63.

A dì primo di luglio [1387] uscirono e' Signiori Priori di palagio, e' Capitani della Parte
mandorono molti cittadini ghuelfi per Bardo Mancini, il quale era stato Ghonfalonieri di
Giustitia i due mesi passati. E quivi, nel palagio della Parte, molti cittadini ghuelfi raunati
feciono molte belle dicerie, ringraçiando Bardo del magnificare ed esaltare la Parte nel
tenpo del suo priorato, d'avere confinati e privati d'ufici e' cittadini sopra nominati. E quivi,
per rimuneratione di ciò, i Capitani della Parte gli donorono uno chavallo di valuta di fiorini
ottanta d'oro, chovertato de l'arme della Parte, e una lancia chol pinone e una targia cho
l'arme della Parte, e una barbuta fornita tutta d'ariento e una coppa d'ariento dorata co
l'arme della Parte. E con tutte queste cose inançi, fue achonpagniato da grandissima gente
de' cittadini orevoli infino a casa sua.

*Alle bocche della piazza*, pp. 74–75.

64. On this event, see Schevill, *History of Florence*, p. 7.

65. On this see Davidsohn, *Storia di Firenze*, vol. 3, pp. 466–72.

66. Ibid., vol. 7, pp. 569–70.

67.

Domenicha a dì XV di giugno [1387] feciono fare e' Signiori Priori una chaccia nel chortile
del Capitano del Popolo, cioè che ebono uno toro indomito e feciogli lasciare adosso i lioni, e
finalmente, assai avendo conbatuto insiene il toro e' lioni, non fu morto il toro, chome che da
loro avesse di molte trafitte e meso più volte in terra. E 'l toro a' lioni die' di molte percosse
di corna e di calci in abondança. E' lioni che conbatterono furono tre, ma non feciono mai
se non e a solo a solo, per loro gran gentileça.

*Alle bocche della piazza*, p. 74.

68.

Domenicha a dì VIIIIo di giugnio fecino e' Signiori Priori fare una nobilissima e magnia
giostra di nobili giovani cittadini e di gente forestiera, e bandita fu che ogniuno potesse
andare a giostrare con cavagli di meça taglia, e feciono si donasse a chi facesse meglio una
belissima targia cho uno lione d'oro i sun uno prato nel canpo biancho, e una lancia e uno
bacinetto di fine acciaio bene ghuernito. Fu lodato per li giudicatori della giostra che messer
Iacot inghilese avesse fatto meglio e furogli donati le soprascritte donera.

Ibid., p. 73.

69. There were also some instances when the *tavola* would be brought into the city as
part of a grand celebration. When the Florentine army defeated Pisa in 1406, there were
three days of celebration and processions throughout the city, and on the third day the *tavola*
was brought to the city to travel in procession with all of the relics. Anonimo fiorentino,
*Cronica volgare*, pp. 354–55.

70. Trexler, *Public Life*, p. 63. The image is painted on wood and therefore is referred
to as a *tavola*.

71. del Corazza, "Diario fiorentino," p. 254.

72.

[Ottobre 1390] Domenicha a dì XVI si fe' la procisione generale per la città di Firenze,
messer lo veschovo cholla chericeria, cho' pievali e chon cotte indosso e cholla testa di santo
Çanobi e chol braccio di santo Filippo e cho molte altre relique, e tutti religiosi cholle loro
croci e loro relique, e' frati di Certosa cho le loro relique i gran quantità. E venne i questo

dì i Firenze la tavola di Santa Maria in Pianeta, e posesi i su la piaça de' Signiori, e quivi i sulla ringhiera, fatto un grandisimo palcho dove stetono e' cherici, e' Signiori Priori e' loro Cholegi, e uno palcho più alto dove stette messer lo veschovo a cantare la messa, e più palchi più alti, molti adorni, dove stette la moltitudine delle relique, che ogniuno di sulla piaçça le potea vedere, e uno palcho per gli orghani e pe' cantori. E predichò messer lo veschovo fra la messa.

*Alle bocche della piazza*, p. 99.

73. Trexler, *Public Life*, p. 64.

74.

Vene la nona vivanda; e per tramessa, fu udito un cantare di Cherici, ma no veduto, di voci d'ogni maniera, grosse, men grosse, mezzane, picciole et puerili, con una dolciezza soavissima, che renderono cheta tutta la sala, perchè gli atenti orechi di tuti feciono taicere le parlanti lingue, per la soavità de la dolce melodia. Chetato il canto e levato l'ultima vivanda, venono le frutta di diverse maniere, et in su la tavola del Papa furono portati due alberi . . . Stando le frutta dinanzi in su le tavole, vene il mastro cuoco del Cardinale con una brigata di suoi compagni con stormenti inanzi, et furono da trenta, con falcole deficiate, con sonagli, ch'è un giuoco romanesco, et entrarono danzando alegrissimamente per la sala; et così intorniate le tavole tre o quatro volte, si partirono.

Gori, *Le feste fiorentine*, vol. 2, *Firenze magnifica*, p. 4, credited to an unidentified *pergamena* in the Archivio di Stato.

75. Much of following historical account is taken from Lubkin, *A Renaissance Court*, pp. 98–105. Lubkin records that in the year preceding his visit to Florence, Galeazzo had planned a trip to Rome with a company of 1,200, and one to France with 3,600, neither of which was carried out (p. 98). For another description of the visit taken from several contemporary accounts that concentrates on the lavish costumes and festivities, see Gori, *Le feste fiorentine*, vol. 2, *Firenze magnifica*, pp. 94–100.

76. According to Fubini, "In margine," p. 171, the accounts are greatly exaggerated: there were only 623 horses, and although the report states that the Duke's party was met by many women and girls as it processed through the streets, it is far more likely that the women remained inside. The Duke would have met some women at receptions and entertainments within the Medici Palace.

77. Lubkin, *A Renaissance Court*, p. 98.

78. Cesare Paoli, with Luigi Rubini and Pietro Stromboli [Nozze Banchi-Brini], *Della venuta in Firenze di Galeazzo Maria Sforza, Duca di Milano, con la Moglie Bona di Savoia nel 1471: Lettere di due Senesi alla Signoria di Siena*, Florence, 1878; quoted in Lubkin, *A Renaissance Court*, p. 100.

79. Problems with the Duke's own pifferi in Milan had reduced his ensemble from its usual complement of four shawms and two trombones and made it necessary to borrow three of the pifferi from Ludovico I Gonzaga in Mantua; see Prizer, "Music at the Court of the Sforza," pp. 151–52. The actual number of musicians accompanying Galeazzo may have been higher. Motta, "Musici alla corte degli Sforza," p. 48, claims that the number of trumpets and pifferi was forty.

80. "[F]u da grandissimo numero de' nostri preclarissimi cittadini con assai giovani chon ricchi e hornatissimi vestimenti, andatigli sponte incontra, accompagnato più che otto migla, e andarongli e nostri rettori tutti e trombetti e pifferi della nostra città." Trexler, *The Libro*, p. 85. It is difficult to imagine why ordinary citizens would be inspired to "spontaneously" travel eight miles to greet the ruler of Milan. Trexler, *Public Life*, p. 307, states that they were on horseback, but even then, the trip out and back would have taken several hours.

81. The *ringhiera* was first erected in 1323. See Rubinstein, "The Piazza della Signoria," p. 20. On its ceremonial meaning and context, see Trexler, *Public Life*, p. 49.

82. The *Libro cerimoniale* refers to the church by the name of the order that founded it in the thirteenth century, the Servites: "Dipoi andarono a' Servi, chè per voto erano venuti." See Trexler, *The Libro*, p. 85.

83. Another of the honors bestowed on Galeazzo during his visit was a portrait of him by Piero Pollaiuolo commissioned by Lorenzo. See Wright, "A Portrait."

84. Probably performed by the laudesi company of Santa Maria Annunziata e Laudesi della Nostra Donna, described by Vasari in his "Life of Il Cecca," as reported in Henderson, *Piety and Charity*, p. 96.

85. The ascension play was staged regularly by the laudesi company of Sant' Agnese at Santa Maria del Carmine. See Barr, "Music and Spectacle," p. 377.

86. The details of the fire are found in Giusto d'Anghiari, *Memorie*, in BNF: Magl. II.II.127. fol. 96 r and v.

87. Machiavelli, *Legazioni, commissarie, scritti di governo*, vol. 2, p. 206.

88. It had always been the practice for Florence to recruit its army from elsewhere, including the captain-general. See Mallett, *Mercenaries and Their Masters*, pp. 92–93.

89. "Il S[ignor] conte de Pitilgiano [*sic*] è venuto qui incognito. Et questa matina che è il dì de S. Giovanni ad hore 18 et un q[uart]o il comparse in palazo di N[ostri] S[ignori] et essendo tuti la S[igno]ria à tavola per la solemnita del dì il confalonero si leva da tavola et ando com lo canzelero et pochi altri in una camera et le si dete il bastone al dicto conte per puncto de astrologia. Dicessa che sina à qualchi dì se fara poi la ceremonia dicto conte è ritornato a Pisa." G. Aldobrandino to Ercole d'Este, June 24, 1485. Archivio di Stato, Modena, Cancelleria ducale, estro. Ambasciatori, agenti e corrispondenti estensi. Firenze, Busta 4.

90. That is, the investiture of Costanza Sforza, who was made captain-general on October 4, 1481; described in Trexler, *The Libro*, p. 94. Sforza was met by the citizens, the Podestà, the trombetti, and pifferi, and was accompanied by the various dignitaries; he stayed at the home of one of the Florentine elite and was given the usual gifts.

91. The Ten of Balia was a commission with special legislative powers (*balia*), assembled in times of external threat to the city. See Rubinstein, *The Government of Florence*, p. 34.

92. On Bartolomeo Scala, see A. Brown, *Bartolomeo Scala*. The date given for the oration on this occasion (p. 154) is incorrect.

93.

Conte Niccola Orsino conte di Pitiglano prese el bastone a dì 24 di giugno con elettione dello astrolago a hore 18 1/2, anno 1485. Dipoi al tempo degl'altri Signori, se fece la ceremonia publica comme di sotto si nominerà, osservando l'altre ceremonie usate, come sono note nella ceremonia di Gostanzo, ecc. Pure fu la ceremonia. Così vene di verso Pisa. Mandògli incontra el podestà e gli strumenti publici tutti. Venne dal ponte Vecchio in piaza prima per Borgho Santo Iacopo. Smontò a meza la logia, e la Signoria nostra l'aspetta in sulla ringhiera, e fèglisi incontra da sedere perfino a meza la ringhiera. E dipoi andarono a ssedere, e sedero[no] tutti gli oratori con ordine e costume usato. Era piena la ringhiera d'assai numero di cittadini oltre e Diece della balia. Fè l'oratione messer Bartolomeo Scala. Dìglisi prima la bandiera giglata e dippoi la celata giglata e la targha, la quale insegna e celata la fè portare el capitano a suoi capi di squadre. Ultimatamente gli diè, c'àne l'altre cose prime. El gonfaloniere della iustitia fatte le sue parole, el capitano prese ligentia. Accompagnòllo la Signoria el 1/3 della ringhiera, e tornàssi a sedere. La cerca fu da le Prestanze alla Badia, da Fondamenti, girando da' Carnesecchi, su per el ponte a Santa Trinita, per via Maggio a San Felice in Piaza, e giù da Santa Felicità e tra' Bardi e al ponte Rubaconte, da Santa Croce al canto alle Rondine, alla posata, a casa gl'Alessandri.

Trexler, *The Libro*, p. 96.
94. On the tradition of knighthood see Salvemini, *La dignità*.
95. See Schevill, *History of Florence*, pp. 346–47.
96.

Risposi loro, che io era contento d'accettare l'honore, il quale essi m'offerivano; e però immantinente mi partii da Bibbiena; et venni a San Salvi fuori della Porta alla Croce in sabato a' dì 11 d'ottobre 1404 accompagnato d'assai gente d'arme, che erano stati meco nel detto acquisto. Dipoi l'altra mattina, che fu domenica, a' dì 12 di detto mese me vennono incontro i tre Rettori della città, cioè Potestà et Capitano et Esecutore, et tutti i Cavalieri, che allora si ritrovarono nella città, et molti altri cittadini et io mi partii dalla detta Badia di S. Salvi a cavallo, tutto armato, in mezzo di detti Rettori, et accompagnato da tutti e' detti cavalieri, et cittadini et huomini d'arme.

Entrai in Firenze et andai alla Piazza de' Signori, et perchè questo fu uno atto inusitato e nobile, e 'l tempo fu chiaro, fu a vedere gran moltitudine di gente. Giunti alla Piazza, trovammo i nostri Signori sedere a la ringhiera al luogo loro usato e i X della Baliia sedere a' loro piedi. Eravi fatto un gran palchetto d'asse a lato al lione dorato, et in su esso palchetto era a sedere, perchè era gottoso, Messer Lotto di Vanni Castellani, che allora era Gonfaloniere di giustizia, che era stato fatto Sindaco per lo Comune, per li Consigli opportuni sopradetti, quando si deliberò che io potessi esser fatto cavaliere, che esso fusse colui; et ancora in sul detto palchetto Messer Cristofano Spini et Messer Tommaso Sacchetti, et Ser Viviano de' Neri, notaio delle Riformazioni; et io con loro et non altri. Et dette certe parole per lo detto Ser Viviano in honore di me, per parte del Comune et de' Signori che erano presenti, et io resposto con lievi parole, mi trassi di dosso una giacchetta di velluto rosso di grana et messimene un'altra di velluto bianco colla croce vermiglia, cioè l'arma di questo Popolo. Et Messer Cristofano detto mi calzò lo sprone ritto, et Messer Tommaso il manco; et messomi in capo il mio elmetto, Messer Lotto suddetto in nome del Popolo di Firenze mi fece cavaliere, dandomi della spada in sul detto elmetto.

Fatto questo, mi donò il detto Ser Viviano, per parte del Comune un ricco e bello elmetto d'ariento dorato, e su esso elmetto era un grande e bel giglio d'ariento dorato, et un gran pennone con l'arme del popolo, col cavallo covertato di tutto zendado con l'arme del popolo, et simile una targia con la detta arme. Et cosi ricevutosi per me ringratiai i Signori con quelle parole mi parvero honeste, et partiimi accompagnato da tutti i sopradetti che m'avevano fatto compagnia a l'entrare in Firenze, et col detto dono innanzi, il quale dono si fece de' sopradetti fiorini 600 che me furono stanziati.

N'andai alla casa della Parte Guelfa. Quivi trovai i Capitani sedere al luogo usato; et fattomi esssi sedere a lato a loro, per un di loro fu parlato molto laudabilmente inverso di me, et donommi per parte loro et di quella benedetta casa, et tutti i guelfi d'essa, uno ricco et nobile elmetto fornito d'ariento dorato, e su esso un collo d'aquila, al modo che s'usa in simili doni fare la Parte Guelfa, d'argento dorato, et appresso un gran pennone con l'arme della Parte, col cavallo tutto convertato di zendado, con l'arme detta et simile una targia con detta arme. Io accettando detto dono, risposi alle parole loro dette quanto mi parve si convenisse ad esse e simili al dono; et mi partii da loro. Et accompagnato da tutti i suddetti et con i detti doni innanzi, n'andai a S. Giovanni et quivi offersi fiorini due d'oro nuovi; et con la medesima compagnia me ne venni a casa; e quivi ciascuno presse da me comiato. Et i nostri magnifici Signori la medesima mattina m'invitarono a mangiare con loro, et in mia compagnia tutti i cavalieri di questa città et più altri valenti uomini; et fu il convito bello et honorevole.

From the autobiography of Jacopo Salviati, *Delizie degli eruditi Toscani*, vol. 18, p. 224, quoted in Salvemini, *La dignità*, pp. 88–92.
97. For the 1471 investiture of Roberto da Sanseverino as captain-general of the army, for example, the *Libro cerimoniale* states "E dopo le commendabile laude, ricevè el prefato

dono chon molta pompa di trombetti." (And after the commendable praises he received the aforesaid gift [banner and helmet] with much pomp of trumpets.) Trexler, *The Libro*, p. 89.

98. On the orations made on this and other occasions by Chancellor Bartolomeo Scala, see A. Brown, *Bartolomeo Scala*, pp. 153–55.

99. The principal source of the text identifies the author as Gentile Aretino, in Seville, Biblioteca Colombina, 6-3-29, opusc. 25.

100. For the complete text and discussion of the events, see McGee, "'Alla Battaglia': Music and Ceremony." Originally, I had concluded that the composition of "Alla battaglia" by Heinrich Isaac had been for this occasion. Recent research has shown that the polyphonic musical setting was not composed until late in 1487, to be performed during the 1488 carnival season. See Wilson, "Heinrich Isaac among the Florentines." The music is published in McGee, *Heinrich Isaac, Alla Battaglia*.

101. For the full text and translation, see McGee, "'Alla Battaglia'," pp. 299–302.

102. A number of the accounts mention poems recited in honor of a military leader: during the 1472 ceremony in praise of Captain-General Federigo da Montefeltro, Duke of Urbino, a poem by Naldo Naldi was presented and later printed along with the address given by Bartolomeo Scala; see Zannoni, "Il sacco di Volterra."

103.

I Convitati andarono a tavola a suon di trombe e di pifferi in questo modo. . . . Ciascuna vivanda veniva in tavola con buono ordine et a suono di trombe. Et circa a mezzo Convito venne una Mummeria (Mascherata) di otto giovani vestiti a guisa di cacciatori, con corni et cani, et preda, di selvaggiumi i quali erano tutti musichi della Cappella del Signor Re: et giunti in sala davanti alle tavole, cantarono una nuova maniera di canto molto bello, et partironsi.

Quoted in Gori, *Firenze magnifica*, vol. 2, pp. 8–10, citing an eyewitness account in an unidentified Strozzi source at the BNF.

104. Trexler, *Public Life*, p. 308, notes that in 1460 citizens journeyed three miles from the city to greet the marquis of Mantua, and in 1452 they traveled twenty miles north to the village of Scarperia to honor Frederick III, Emperor of Germany. According to Vespasiano da Bisticci, when Pope Eugenius IV traveled to Florence in 1433, he was met in Pisa by some of the dignitaries, and the remainder traveled on horseback to Signa, one of the suburbs to the west, in order to provide an escort; see Vespasiano da Bisticci, *The Vespasiano Memoirs*, p. 19.

105. Trexler, *Public Life*, p. 250.

106. Ibid., pp. 316–17.

107. Ibid., p. 316.

108. Ibid., p. 309.

109. Dei, *La cronica*, p. 66.

110. Trexler *The Libro*, p. 77; Dei, *La cronica*, pp. 66–67; Paolo di Matteo Pietrobuoni, *Diario*, fol. 182r–183v; *Le feste di Firenze del 1459*, BNF: Magl. 1121, excerpts published in Volpi, *Le feste di Firenze del 1459*; Giusto d'Anghiari, "Cronica o memorie," BNF: Magl. II. II. 127, fol. 75r–76r; Cambi, "Istorie"; and *Ricordi di Firenze dell'anno 1459*, BNF: Magl. XXV, excerpts published in Volpi, *Ricordi di Firenze*, vol. 27, no.1. The following description is a combination of these sources.

111. Galeazzo would see the same play at the church of the Carmine twelve years later on his visit in 1471; see above.

112. Dei, *La cronica*, p. 67.

113. The number in the Sforza party is taken from Dei, *La cronica*, who is not too careful about being exact; he reports the visit as happening in 1460 and Galeazzo's age as thirteen. Pietrobuoni, *Diario*, reports 350 horses in the party as does Cambi, "Istoria."

114. Volpi, *Le feste di Firenze*, appendix, p. 45.

115. The numbers are from Cambi, "Istoria," quoted in Ciseri, *L'ingresso trionfale di Leone X*, p. 150.

116. Ciseri, *L'ingresso trionfale di Leone X*, p. 150. Paolo di Matteo Pietrobuoni, *Diario*, fol. 182r, reports that the pope was carried by four noblemen: Sigismondo Malatesta di Rimini, the Signore di Faenza, the Signore di Farli, and the Signore di Carpi.

117. Trexler, *The Libro*, p. 76

118. Ibid., p. 76

119. Volpi, *Le feste di Firenze*, appendix, p. 45.

120. Trexler, *The Libro*, p. 77.

121. Dei, *La cronica*, p. 67.

122. "duo baccini dareiento coll arme del comune di peso di libre cinquantuno; Duo boccali di libre 21; dua confettiere di peso di libre 26; dodici tazze coperte di libre 27. In tutto peserono libre 125. Di valsiute di fiorini dumila." In Paolo di Matteo Pietrobuoni, *Diario*, 182r. The *Libro ceremoniale* records only "[d]ue bacini grandi . . . con due boccali e confettiere e taze." Trexler, *The Libro*, p. 77.

123. "ssonatori d'ogni gientile istrumento." Dei, *La cronica*, p. 66. I assume this was meant to exclude the outdoor instruments such as drums, and those more closely associated with the peasants, e.g., the bagpipe.

124. April 23, 1459; Galeazzo Maria Sforza to his father from Villa Careggi. From Wilson, "Surpassing Orpheus."

125. Piero Rinuccini, Gregorio Marsuppini, Francesco Benci, Antonio Boscoli, Braccio Guicciardini, Piero Vespucci, and Conte Gherardo di Gherardesca. The names are given in BNF: Magl. 1121. BNF: CS, C. IV. 895, fol. 182v, puts the number of participants at eight but does not name them.

126. The judges were Carlo degli Oddi, Alessandro Mirabelli, Manno de' Temperani, Carlo Pandolfini, Tommaso Soderini, and Niccolò Buonanni. BNF: Magl. 1121, fol. 59r.

127. "Uscir di campo que' cavalier fini; con trombe e piffer e più stormenti, tornarsi a casa lor co' lor vicini." BNF: Magl. XXV, 24; Volpi, *Ricordi di Firenze*, vol. 27, no. 1, p. 21.

128. Trexler, *The Libro*, p. 77.

129. BNF: Magl. II. II. 127. Apparently there was an admission charged; Giusto d'Anghiari records having paid five soldi for each of his three sons to see the event. Giusto d'Anghiari, "Cronica o memorie," 1437–82, fol. 76r.

130. From Giusto d'Anghiari and BNF: Magl. 1121, we know that the ball was made of wood.

131.
E lli missono 26 lioni e lionesse vivi, e 'nfra lloro vi missono cinghiali e llupi e ttori e chavagli bravi e salvatichi e altre salvaggine d'animali e fferono fare chaccia in sulla piaza, ed esendo intornno al palazo assai palchetti. E oltre alla chaccia fu messo in su detta piaza de' Signori una palla grossa e tonda alta di braccia 4 vel circha, nella quale v'era inn essa un uomo vivo drento, chongiegniato e ordinato in modo che facea andare la palla là ov'egli volea, e choreva adosso a' lioni e ferivagli per ciertti fori e per ciertti pertugi che aveva detta palla, di modo che non potea a llui esser fatto male dai detti animali, che ffu bella chosa e grandissimo ingiegnio, nè mmai più fatto inn Italia. E venne tal esercizio da un fiorentino lo quale ll'avea visto ne' paesi del soldano e in Soria fare.

Dei, *La cronica*, pp. 67–68.

132. According to the poet of BNF: Magl XXV, 24, although the animals were all afraid of the lions and ran around in fear, the lions lay on the ground as if asleep—this was stated as a metaphor for Florence, which could rest tranquilly and at peace while surrounded by enemies that it was confident it could overcome at will. Volpi, *Ricordi di Firenze*, vol. 27, no. 1, p. 21.

133. Ventrone, "Lorenzo's Politica Festiva," p. 109, describes the *armeggeria* as a "kind of choreographic display."

134. These were the young Lorenzo de' Medici, Andrea Bonsi, Maso Pucci, Lorenzo Neroni, Domenico and Piero della Luna, Giovanni Portinari, Matteo Boni, Jacopo Venturi, Averardo de' Medici, Giovanni and Renato de' Pazzi. The names are given in BNF: Magl. 1121 and Magl. XXV, 24.

135. Additional passages describe the costumes of the citizens in great detail, as well as the food and drink. See the more extended excerpts translated by Giovanni Carsaniga in Nevile, *The Eloquent Body*, appendix 1. My translation follows that by Carsaniga, with a few changes.

136. A *reverance* was the opening gesture of a dance. See Nevile, *The Eloquent Body*, p. 164.

137. Prizer, "Music at the Court of the Sforza," p. 148.

138. Ibid.

139. The herald makes the point that the cost of entertaining the two came to 13,626 florins, a princely sum. Trexler, *The Libro*, p. 78.

140. Quoted above.

## 2. The Trombadori

1. Polk, *German Instrumental Music*, p. 46.

2. On the waits and their function, see Woodfill, *Musicians in English Society*; Rastall, "Secular Musicians in Late Medieval England"; and Conklin, "Medieval English Minstrels."

3. Strohm, *Music in Late Medieval Bruges*, p. 75.

4. For records of trumpeters serving as watchmen in Burgundian castles, see Bowles, "Instruments at the Court of Burgundy," pp. 43–44. A pair of *gaychiatores* served at the papal palace in Avignon during the reign of Pope Gregory XI (1370–78); see Tomasello, *Music and Ritual*, p. 25. On French trumpeters and their role, see Peters, "Urban Minstrels."

5. "Licet enim aliqua instrumenta suo sono magis moveant animos hominum, puta in festis, hastiludiis et torneamentis tympanum et tuba." Rohloff, *Die Quellenhandschriften*, p. 135. English translation from Seay, *Johannes de Grocheo*, p. 19.

6. Evidence that the ceremonial function of trumpets was standard throughout Europe during the late Middle Ages and Renaissance is presented in numerous studies, including Strohm, *Music in Late Medieval Bruges*; D'Accone, *The Civic Muse*; Salmen, "The Social Status of the Musician"; Polk, *German Instrumental Music*; Lockwood, *Music in Renaissance Ferrara*; Nerici, *Storia della musica*; Giazotto, *La musica a Genova*; Prizer, "Bernardino Piffaro"; Merkley and Merkley, *Music and Patronage*; Lubkin, *A Renaissance Court*; and Kurtzman and Koldau, "Trombe, Trombe d'argento." Tarr, *The Trumpet*, p. 36, suggests that the tradition of pairs of trumpets with nakers as symbols of authority comes from Spain under the influence of the Saracens. Sachs, *The History of Musical Instruments*, pp. 280–81, credits contact between the Christian and Arabic military as the European source of the instruments and their tradition. See also Tröster, *Das Alta-Ensemble*, p. 184.

7. Information on the early history of Florence taken from Brucker, "Florence," and Schevill, *History of Florence*, pp. 39–283.

8. D'Accone, *The Civic Muse*, pp. 414–17. D'Accone states that the musicians must have been a part of the civic ceremonies in Siena from well before the records indicate (1230), and that the tradition was similar in most cities of Italy and elsewhere in Europe.

9. Gambassi, *Il Concerto Palatino*, p. 4.

10. Sachs, *History of Musical Instruments*, p. 281.

11. *Soprasberga* refers to a colored garment worn over the chainmail.

12. "& andò con lui molto grande amistà & di Firenze v'andaro per lo comune trecento Cavalieri, che furo cinquanta Cavalieri a Spron d'oro, & cinquanta donzelli, & catuno con due compagni almeno, ed ebbevi di tali che ne menò sei, & chi quattro. Ma catunol avea il soldo pur per due compagni, & pedoni v'andaro da cinquecento, tutti con soprasberghe bianca iv'entro il Giglio vermiglio, li quali fuoro molto bella gente." Pieri, *Cronica*, p. 45.

13. "E 'l detto re Carlo lasciò Carlo prenze suo figliuolo alla guardia del Regno . . . e passò per Firenze a dì XIIII di Marzo, nel detto anno MCCLXXXII, e da' Fiorentini fu ricevuto con grande onore, e fece in Firenze VIII cavalieri tra Fiorentini, e Lucchesi, e Pistolesi." Villani, *Nuova cronica*, bk. 8, ch. 86.

14. This same evidence has led Kurtzman and Koldau, "Trombe, Trombe d'argento," 5.17, to suggest that although the earliest Venetian record of trumpeters functioning as civic heralds is from 1331, they may well have been fulfilling this role for over a century.

15. A document from San Gimignano in 1134 forbids tubatores (trombadori) from joining a wedding procession unless invited by the groom. Reported in Zippel, *I suonatori*, p. 10, n. 1.

16. Pieri, *Cronica*.

17. The guild militia was purely political, intended to defend the guilds against internal enemies and not to be confused with the other militia that defended the city in times of war. See Schevill, *History of Florence*, p. 154. For more on the governmental organization at this time, see Najemy, *A History of Florence*, pp. 66–81; and De Rosa, *Alle origini della Repubblica fiorentina*.

18. The guilds consisted of the following: 1) judges and notaries; 2) Calimala—foreign cloth; 3) Cambio—money changers; 4) Lana—wool; 5) Por Santa Maria—retailers of the shopping street and silk merchants; 6) physicians and apothecaries; and 7) furriers. Schevill, *History of Florence*, p. 153.

19. On the establishment of the Fourteen and their replacement by the Priors, see Najemy, *Corporatism and Consensus*, ch. 1.

20. For a discussion of the changes in the power structure and responsibilities, see Schevill, *History of Florence*, p. 154; and Najemy, *A History of Florence*, ch. 3.

21. On the building of the Signoria, see Rubinstein, "The Piazza," p. 19.

22. ASF: PR No. 3, fol. 50r, for February 8, 1291 [1292].

23. On the transfer of authority at this time, see Brucker, "Florence," pp. 95–96. The office of Standard Bearer of Justice was a part of the Ordinances of Justice, instituted in January of 1293. See Najemy, *Corporatism and Consensus*, pp. 44–45.

24. Six was also the number of trumpeters in Venice. See Muir, *Civic Ritual*, p. 190.

25. D'Accone, *The Civic Muse*, p. 417.

26. See the chart of instrumentalists in ibid., pp. 432–37. D'Accone records the presence of a reed player and trumpet player with the Sienese military in 1251 (p. 415).

27. Marco Antonio Lastri reports that they also performed at a weekly Saturday evening ceremony on the *ringhiera* in honor of the Priors and Gonfaloniere. Lastri, *L'Osservatore*

*fiorentino*, vol. 1, p. 138. He does not give dates for the ceremony, however, and I have not found any other reference to it.

28.

In dei nomine amen. Anno sue salutifere incarnationis millesimo ducessimo LXXXXI Indictione quinta die octavo intrante mense Februarii. Consilium generale trecentorum et speciale LXXXXta virorum, et capitudum xij maiorum Artium cunctorum et communis Florentie. Nobilis Vir dominus Scellius domini Bartholecti de Spoleto, civitatis et commuis Florentie secunda vice potestas, preconata convocatione, campaneque sonitu, in ipsius communis pallio, fecit more solito congregari. In quo quidem consilio, per me. B. notarium subscripto. Exposita et seriatim lecta fuerunt omnia et singula, que die xviij mensis Januarii proxime preterite, in consiliio centum virorum eiusdem corporis. Et sub sequente die xxviij eiusdem mensis Ianuarii proxime pretertite in consiliis speciali, et generali domini defensoris, et Capitanei et Capitudinum xii maiorum Artium civitatis Florentie, successive et debito ordine celebratis et factis, iuxta formam ordinis canonizatis, et statuorum dicti communis, proposita, provisa et firmata fuerunt super provisione, et electione, per dominos priores Artium, in termino, et protermino, et tempore trium Annorum inceptorum in kallendis Ianuarii proxime preteritis facta de infrascriptis sex tubatoribus, et uno cennamellario et uno cemballellario prout et secundum quod in actis consiliorum predictorum, manu mei, B. notarii subscripti publicis scriptis plenius est expressum, Quorum tubatorum cennamellarii, et cembellellarii nomina sunt hec. Guillelmus Niger, Catena deotauiti, Patinus ubertini, Guillelmus Jacobi, Balduccius Buoni, Matheus Niccole, sex tubatores communis Florentie, Gianuccius Niccole, popoli sancti laurenti, cennamellarius, Lore qui vocatur Anghara popoli Sancti Felicis in piaza, cimballellarius.

ASF: PR No. 3, fol. 50r, 8 Feb. 1291 [1292].

29. "et illos pannos portare teneantur et debeant cum lilio Communis, ad hoc ut officium possint honorabilius per Commune Florentie exercere." ASF: Statuti No. 4, 1325, Rubric 14; published in *Statuti della Repubblica*, vol. 2.

30. Davidsohn, *Storia di Firenze*, vol. 2, p. 577, states that there were *cembali, tamburi,* and other instruments accompanying the military from as early as 1229.

31.

Et quando vadunt in exercitum vel cavalchatam pro Communi teneantur eis solvere camerarii solidos quindecim pro quolibet eorum per diem ultra salarium predictum, et ultra vel aliter percipere vel habere non possint donec iverint et steterint et fuerint et rediverint de exercitu vel cavalcata; et habeant et teneant equos in cavalchatis et exercitibus, scilicet quilibet eorum unum, et quando pro aliqua causa iverint extra civitatem Florentie de mandato Potestatis et Defensoris et Capitanei pro ipso exercito faciendo et exercendo et redeundo ea die in civitatem Florentie qua se movebunt, sicut sepe contigit, solvant camerarii eis qualibet dicta die pro vecturis eorum equorum, ultra salarium constitutum pro quolibet eorum, solidos quactuor f.p. tantum, non obstante alio aliquo capitulo costituti Communis.

Published in *Statuti della Repubblica*, vol. 2, Rubric 14.

32. ASF: PR No. 5, fol. 134v, for September 28, 1295. The musicians were paid seventeen lire on this occasion.

33. ASF: CC, CU No. 1, for September 13, 1303, cited in Davidsohn, *Storia di Firenze*, vol. 5, p. 322.

34. "et porrecta et considerato quod ipsi in ipsis offitiis, ministeriis et exertitiis sunt experti, et valde sufficientes. Et quod ipsi offerunt dicto communi pro iure cum tubis argenteis, quas eorum propriis expensis fieri fecerunt pro ipsius communis honore." ASF: PR no. 5, fol. 151v, April 13, 1295. Similar requirements in terms of numbers of trombadori, horses, silver trumpets, etc., can also be found in the records of Milan and Perugia from this period. See Cellesi, "Documenti," 34 (1927): 585, n. 4, and 585–87.

35. Lastri, *L'Osservatore Fiorentino*, vol. 1, p. 124.

36. In the *catasto* of 1427, civic musicians are recorded as living in all four *quartieri* of the city.

37. In some cities, such as Siena, Perugia, and Milan, the duties of the bannitori were carried out by the trombadori. See Cellesi, "Documenti," 34 (1927): 585–86.

38. The uniform material was called *ultramontano* because it came from France, Flanders, or England. ASF: Consulte, II, 445, for November 9, 1294; reported in Davidsohn, *Storia di Firenze*, vol. 3, p. 683.

39.

XXXV—Capitulum pro habendis sex bannitoribus pro communi.

> Item ut commune Florentie honorabiles et sufficientes habeat plus solito bannitores habentes voces altas et claras, statutum et ordinatum est quod bannitores communis Florentie sint sex tantum qui officium banniendi banna dominorum potestatis et capitanei et aliorum officialum communis Florentie sciant facere et sint popullares et decentes de personis ipsorum et sciant legere et scribere quorum quilibet annuaram faciat duas robbas, et trombettam habeat de argento et etiam habeat et teneat unusquisque eorum unum equum qui non scriptus ad cavallatam et sit valoris saltem viginti Florenorum de auro. et pro hiis efficaciter exequendis domini priores artium et vexilliferum Iustitie populi Florentini teneantur et debeant eligere duos bonos viros honorablies populares civitatis Florentie qui hoc possint ducere ad effectum et circa hoc plenam habeant baliam omnia faciendi que fuerint oportuna.

ASF: PR No. 211, fol. 31v, for January 6, 1307.

40. For additional description of the bannitori, see Davidsohn, *Firenze ai tempi di Dante*, p. 467.

41. He also served as one of the four bell-ringers for eighteen years. See Davidsohn, *Storia di Firenze*, vol. 5, pp. 317–18.

42. On Pucci and his career in the bannitori, see Robins, "Antonio Pucci," and Robins, "Poetic Rivalry."

43. ASF: PR No. 157, fol. 84, for August 20, 1466. "Sonitores Palatij teneantur ire cum bannitore et sonent quando bannietur. Quod tabula Sancte Marie in Pruneta ducatur Florentiam." Quoted in Cellesi, "Documenti," 34 (1927): 584, n. 3, and Zippel, *I suonatori*, p. 20. This is the only document I have found that associates the bannitori with the civic musicians, and there is nothing in the wording of the *Provvisioni* to indicate whether this was something new or merely a reminder of traditional practices.

44. According to Polk, *German Instrumental Music*, p. 46, there was also a trumpet that was approximately six feet in length. He identifies this longer instrument as the one made of silver, as opposed to the shorter instrument which was made of brass. This may be true of trumpets in northern courts—his frame of reference—but iconographical evidence suggests that the trumpet of the Italian trombadori was closer to the five-foot length, and that it was definitely made of silver (see discussion below about the brass vs. silver). Downey, "The Renaissance Slide Trumpet," p. 26, reports that the instrument was approximately 150 cm long and pitched in A, based on a surviving instrument made in Siena in 1406, now at Williams College, Williamstown, Massachusetts. Tröster, *Das Alta-Ensemble*, p. 184, states that between the thirteenth and fifteenth centuries the long trumpets were from 150 cm to 300 cm long (approximately 5–10 feet).

45. "Sei Trombadori con le trombe d'argento lunghe di libbre sei, once sei l'una." Gori, *Le feste fiorentine*, vol. 1, *Le feste per San Giovanni*, p. 157. Gori is quoting the document "Modo di andare a Processione, il Gonfaloniere di Giustizia, Priori, Podestà, giudici della Ruota di Firenze, nel Secolo XV–XVI e prima," in BNF.

46. For a good overview of the early history of the trumpet in Europe, see Tröster, *Das Alta-Ensemble*, pp. 181–283.

47. The number of notes possible on the early instruments is a subject of controversy. Polk, *German Instrumental Music*, p. 49, speculates that the larger instruments could play perhaps only one or two notes. Sarkissian and Tarr, "Trumpet," p. 829, claims that the thirteenth-century Parisian theorist Johannes de Grocheio stated that trumpets played the first four partials of the harmonic series. This is repeated in Downey, "The Renaissance Slide Trumpet," p. 26. The passage in the treatise, however, does not say this; it merely discusses the overtone series following a reference to the Psalm 150: "Praise the Lord with the sound of the trumpet." See Rohloff, *Die Quellenhandschriften*, p. 116, and Seay, *Johannes de Grocheo*, p. 6.

48. On the history of trumpet shapes, see Duffin, "Backward Bells and Barrel Bells." According to Downey, "The Renaissance Slide Trumpet," p. 26, the early S-shaped instrument had approximately 175 cm of tubing (approx. 5 1/2 feet), and was pitched in F.

49. The variety of folded instrument shapes are illustrated and discussed in Polk, *German Instrumental Music*, pp. 46–48; Tröster, *Das Alta-Ensemble*, pp. 185–90; Sarkissian and Tarr, "Trumpet," pp. 829–30; and Bowles, *Musikleben im 15. Jahrhundert*.

50. ASF: PR No. 15, for December 4, 1316.

51. "Otto trombetti con le trombe lunghe d'argento di libbre tre, once tre." Gori, *Le feste fiorentine*, vol. 1, *Le feste per San Giovanni*, p. 157.

52. According to Tröster, *Das Alta-Ensemble*, p. 185, the earliest iconographical evidence of the S-shaped trumpet is a tower scene in the Worcester Cathedral from 1397. Sculptures of trombetti and pifferi from the late fifteenth century by Benedetto da Maiano are currently on display in Florence at the Bargello. See Carl, *Benedetto da Maiano*, vol. 1, pp. 423–41, and vol. 2, plates 201–206. Photos also will be published in Carter, *The Early Trombone*.

53. Tröster, *Das Alta-Ensemble*, p. 183.

54. The earliest surviving brass trumpet is the instrument made by Marcian Giutbert in Limoges, dated 1442. See Madeuf, Madeuf, and Nicholson, "The Guitbert." A fourteenth-century English trumpet made of copper also survives; see Lawson and Egan, "Medieval Trumpet"; and Webb, "The Billingsgate Trumpet."

55. Until the development of hammer mills in the fifteenth century, brass could not be made into the thin sheets necessary for processing into musical instruments. See "Correspondence" from metallurgist Karl Hachenberg, pp. 92–93; and Rosenfeld, "Transmuting Silver into Gold," in answer to my article, "Silver or Gold."

56. On Sienese bannatori, their instruments, and duties, see D'Acccone, *The Civic Muse*, p. 417, n. 18; and on the palace trumpeters, pp. 449–52. On the six silver trumpets of Venice, see Muir, *Civic Ritual in Renaissance Venice*, p. 190.

57. Latten is a mixture of copper, zinc, lead, and tin. It is recorded as the material for the trumpets played by one of the minstrels of the Black Prince in the fourteenth century. See Rastall, "Secular Musicians in Late Medieval England," ch. 4. I have not found any evidence of instruments being made of gold, although it was a common practice to gild various objects—even some that were made of silver. This may account for the discrepancy in iconographical evidence where some trumpets appear to be a gold color. Color and material of medieval trumpets is still under discussion; see Myers, "Evidence of the Emerging Trombone," and n. 56, above.

58. On this questions, see my "Silver or Gold."

59. See discussion in Rosenfeld, "Transmuting Silver into Gold."

60. Sachs, *History of Musical Instruments*, p. 281.

61. See D'Accone, *The Civic Muse*, pp. 449–50, 553–54.

62. Local silversmiths are recorded as producing the trumpets for the city of Bruges in the fourteenth century; see Strohm, *Music in Late Medieval Bruges*, p. 91.

63. ASF: MAP, 23, no. 230, for January 24, 1470.

64. See Jahn, "Die Nürnberger Trompeten," p. 34.

65. Sarkissian and Tarr, "Trumpet," p. 830.

66. The image is reproduced in Montagu, *The World*, plate 31.

67. For a discussion of the various names for the instrument, see Marcuse, *A Survey*, pp. 682–88; and Tröster, *Das Alta-Ensemble*, pp. 25–143.

68. For a discussion of the instrument and its repertory, see Baines, "Shawms of the Sardana Coblas."

69. I am grateful to Herbert Myers for the details about shawm sizes, ranges, and construction.

70. Konrad of Megenberg, writing ca. 1350, states that shawms and trumpets "sound well together according to due proportions in 4ths, 5ths and octaves." Cited in Page, "German Musicians and Their Instruments," p. 193. The reference would seem to be to one of each instrument, as illustrated in ibid., p. 198, rather than to a single shawm with a set of trumpets.

71. "L'Intelligenza," stanzas 293 and 294, quoted in Vecchi, *Educazione musicale*, pp. 16–17. The poet may have been the chronicler Dino Compagni; see *Dictionary of the Middle Ages*, vol. 6, col. 651b.

72. I have translated the word *gighe* as "violin," although the violin as we know it was not yet invented. Polk, *German Instrumental Music*, pp. 30–31, speculates that the word *geige* that appears in German sources may have been a rebec. Since the poet refers to a rebec by name (*rebebe*) a few lines later, there must have been some difference between the two instruments. The *organistrum* may be a two-man hurdy-gurdy.

73. I have been unable to identify the *caribi*.

74. ASF: PR No. 12, fol. 140r, for November 6, 1296.

75. ASF: PR No. 10, fol. 219, for April 4, 1300: "et esse debeat cennamellarius dicti communis et in offitio et ad offitium seu ministerium sonandi cennamellam seu sveliam pro communi iamdicto."

76. ASF: PR No. 6 fol 140r, for November 12, 1296; ASF: Statuti No. 6, 1325, Rubric 14, published in *Statuti della Repubblica*, vol. 2. Villani, *Nuova cronica*, bk. 12, ch. 93, also mentions the *sveglia* in his account of the commune's finances during the years 1336–38, but his statement only adds confusion to the question because he lists both a *sveglia* and a *cennamella* as different instruments: "che sono i banditori vi e trombadori, naccheraio e sveglia, cenamelle e trombetta, x, tutti con trombe e trombette d'argento, per loro salaro l'anno libre m di piccioli." The civic pay records attest that at that time the numbers of musicians were six bannitori but only nine trombadori. Villani's error is in counting the performers of *sveglia* and *cennamella* as separate.

77. ASF: CCN No. 1, fol. 40v, for October 11, 1347; ASF: CC, CU No. 223, no folio numbers, for February 22, 1375 [1376].

78. Cited in D'Accone, "Music and Musicians at the Florentine Monastery," p. 141. D'Accone found records indicating that during the mid-fourteenth century the monastery made a regular practice of hiring singers, organists, and instrumentalists, including two civic trumpeters and the nakers player, for the celebration of feasts.

79. "Canto di lanzi sonatori di vari strumenti," lines 23–26. Full text published in McGee with Mittler, "Information on Instruments," pp. 459–60.

80. See Polk, *German Instrumental Music*; and McGee, "The Fall of the Noble Minstrel," pp. 98–120.

81. See Davidsohn, *Storia di Firenze*, vol. 5, pp. 310–11. H. M. Brown, "Fantasia on a Theme," p. 334, concludes that the phrase indicates that the *cennamella* player was the town watchman.

82. A similar confusion of instrument names is found in one of the *canti carnascialeschi* of the early sixteenth century, where reference is made to a *zampognine*. *Zampogna* is another word for bagpipe, and therefore the *zampognine* could mean "a small bagpipe," but context reveals that what is being described is the reed of a shawm. Angelo Poliziano, in his *Feste d'Orfeo*, calls on Mopsus to "take his *zampogna* from his pocket," and later to "tell her, my *zampogna*, how her slender beauty flees with the years." From the context it is clear that the instrument in question is actually a panpipe; the relationship here, as in the *canto carnascialesco*, is the presence of reeds: a panpipe is made of reeds, and the vibrating agent in both a shawm and a bagpipe is a reed. For discussion, see McGee with Mittler, "Information on Instruments," pp. 454, 456.

83. "Uno che suonava le Ciambanelle di bronzo con una nappa lunga, rossa, e bianca, con una coltelliera d'argento a canto." Quoted in Gori, *Le feste fiorentine*, vol. 1, *Le feste per San Giovanni*, p. 157.

84. "Quattro pifferi e due Tromboni d'argento"; ibid.

85. *Folgore da San Gimignano*, poem 5, "D'Aprile."

86. Keith Polk, in private communication, notes that in Bruges during the fourteenth century there were ensembles of trumpets and *riethoorns*. Although the word means "reed horns," he doubts that they were shawms. For a discussion of a similar folk instrument in Catalonia, see Baines, "Shawms of the Sardana Coblas," pp. 9–16.

87. Discussed in chapter 4.

88. See Cocks, Baines, and Cannon, "Bagpipe," p. 480.

89. At various times during the summer months a shawm and bagpipe duo, usually from Sardegna, are still often seen on the streets of Florence.

90. ASF: PR No. 212, fol. 197r, for July 18, 1357; PR No. 45, fol. 105, for December 12, 1357. PR No. 44, fol. 5, from 1356, is the first appointment of a *cornamusa* player but no name is given. The 1357 PR statement incorrectly names Dominico di Baldi as the *cornamusa* player, but numerous pay records over the next several decades continue to list Dominico di Baldi as the player of *nacchere*, while Luca di Silvestro is named as the *cornamusa* player. The document is reproduced in Cellesi, "Documenti," 35 (1928): 563–64.

91. ASF: CC No. 9, fol. 183r, for 1401–1402.

92. The earliest mention of Grullo as a member of the pifferi is in ASF: CCP No. 1, fol. 13v, for March 8, 1390. In PR No. 87, fol. 344, for 1398, it is noted that he has been dismissed.

93. Davidsohn, *Storia di Firenze*, vol. 5, p. 179.

94. Zippel, *I suonatori*, p. 11, states that the instrument was a circle of wood with jingles, i.e., a tambourine. The *Grande dizionario della lingua Italiana*, vol. 2, p. 963, offers "cymbals" player as a translation of *cimballellarus*.

95. "Uno Naccherino, che sonava le Nacchere con un grembiale di drappo con due gigli e una croce nel mezzo, e con esso cuopriva le Nacchere." Gori, *Le feste fiorentine*, vol. 1, *Le feste per San Giovanni*, p. 157.

96. "quod idem Matteus cemballellas valde bene scit ducere et sonare et in offitio et exercitio ducendi et sonandi ipsas cemballellas et etiam alia instrumenta est expertus et mirabiliter exercitatus." ASF: PR No. 9, fol. 12v, for June 19, 1298.

97. ASF: PR No. 12, fol. 128, for January 27, 1304 [1305].

98. ASF: PR No. 59, fol. 96, for April 11, 1371. Francesco Lapi was first appointed to the ensemble in 1357 and retired in 1384.

99. The present state of information on the instruments and their ranges can be found in Polk, *German Instrumental Music*, p. 49; and Baines, *Brass Instruments*, pp. 78–80.

100. The existence of a slide trumpet has been hotly contested over the past several decades, although the opinion now seems to be affirmative. See the discussion in chapter 5.

101. ASF: PR No. 6, fol. 140r, for November 12, 1296.

102. ASF: PR No. 55, fol. 47v, for August 19, 1367.


### 3. The Civic Herald

1. See Pini, "La 'Burocrazia' comunale," p. 235. The description *maestro di ceremonie* was used by the herald Angelo Manfidi when referring to himself in the course of his description of the 1515 ceremony, in which Pope Leo X bestowed the baton of generalship on his nephew, Lorenzo de' Medici the Younger. See Trexler, *The Libro*, p. 118.

2. Flamini, *La lirica toscana*, p. 193, traces the office up to the death of Jacopo di Niccolò del Polta, in 1539; but see Levi, "I cantari leggendari," and Branciforte, "Ars Poetica," p. 119, for a discussion of a much longer history.

3. This was the opening line of a *terzina* by Calderoni as a response to poetry by Il Burchiello, who referred to him as a *buffone*. See Flamini, *La lirica toscana*, pp. 219–20.

4. See Bertolini, *De vera amicitia*, p. 285. The texts recited on that occasion are found in BNF: Pal. 215. Calderoni was not actually appointed to the position of herald until 1442, but he must have been acting in that capacity when writing the cited lines.

5. For a question as to whether or not the herald was a knight in the same sense as others, see Flamini, *La lirica toscana*, p. 194. For a discussion of the link between heralds, knights, and knighthood, see Trexler, *The Libro*, pp. 21–23.

6. The word *istrio* can be translated into Italian as *buffone*, and from there to the English "buffoon," but in the sense of "actor" rather than that of "fool." It is clear that originally the use of this word was quite general, and was applied to people and activities that would fit the category of "entertainer" or "performer" in the broadest sense, including actors of all kinds, jugglers, and minstrels. Unfortunately, the word has evolved to a mostly pejorative meaning in the present day (at least partially due to an eighteenth-century controversy over opera in Paris), leading many modern writers to seriously misjudge the duties and prominence of the position as described here. The discussion of the position in Trexler, *The Libro*, pp. 35–36, falls into this error, perhaps misled by similar remarks in Davidsohn, *Firenze ai tempi di Dante*, p. 522.

7. On this duty, see for example the discussion of Jacopo Salimbene, below. For an example of a *canterino* of Siena acting in this capacity in 1399, see Corso, "Araldi e canterini," pp. 148, 154; and the discussion in D'Accone, *The Civic Muse*, pp. 458–59.

8. On the *sacra rappresentazione* and the involvement of the Florentine heralds, see Ventrone, *Gli araldi*; and Ventrone, "La sacra rappresentazione."

9.

> Item supradicti Priores artium et Vexillifer Justitie attendentes quod in qualibet quasi nobili Civitate tam provincie Lombardie quam Tuscie habentem [*sic*] strenui cantores ad solatium et gaudium Omnium talium huiusmodi Civitatum, quibus per Rettores eorum donantur Vestes In Honorem Civitatum et ipsorum Rettorum, et inter alios solempnes et strenuos cantores esse dicitur dominus Prezzivalle quondam Gianni qui moram trahit in

civitate florentie, sui tantus ministerum in ea cotidie exercendo In Honorem dicte Civitatis et ad solatium et gaudium Civium ipsius et in dicta Civitate dignum sit talibus viris ut in aliis nobilibus civitatibus de vestibus provideri. Habita prius super hiis cum offitio duodecim bonorum virorum diligenti deliberatione, Et demum inter eos secundum formam statutis promisso facto et obtento partito et secreto scruptione ad fabas nigras et albas eorum offitii auctoritate et negotiatione et omni modo et Juris quibus melius potuerunt, Providerunt Ordinaverunt et stantiaverunt Quod domini Potestas Capitaneus et defensor populi et comunis florentie et uterque eorum teneantur et debeant donare et tradere infra tres menses presentes futuros post int[r]oitum sui offitii dicto domino Prezzevalli Unam Honorabilem Robam ad Usum ipsius potestatis, et Capitanei vel pro utroque eorum. Et quod in litetris que transmittentur huiusmodi potestati et Capitaneo et defensori notificat[i]onis Electionis talium potestatis Capitanei et defensoris Inserantur predicta. Et quod si predicti dominus potestas Capitaneus et Defensor predicta non servaverint et cicto domino Prezzevalli robam promissam non tradiderint, vel non donaverint pro utroque eorum ut promittit, Camerarii Camere comunis florentie teneantur et debeant liciter, libere, et impuniter de salariis eisdem Potestati, capitaneo et defensori per ipsum comunem debitis et cuilibet eorum Retinere florenos auri decem, et ipsi domino Prezzevalli libere permissis causis solvere tradere ac donare.

ASF: PR No. 26, f. 40r [24r]. I am indebted to William Robins for this reference. The document is cited in Davidsohn, *Storia di Firenze*, vol. 7, p. 580.

10.

Quod Potestas non roget aliquem donare vestem. Statutum et ordinatum est quod Potestas Florentie vel aliquis de sua familia non possint nec sibi liceat rogare aliquem civem vel comitatinum Florentie ut donet sua vestimenta vel robam alicui ystrioni, et si contra fecerit, perdat de suo salario libras ducentas f.p. Et idem intelligatur de Capitaneo Communis Florentie et quolibet offitiali foretano Communis predicti.

ASF, Statuti No. 4, 1322–25, Liber Quintus, Rubric 18. Published in *Statuti della Repubblica*, vol. 2.

11. In the early fourteenth century the *famiglia* of the Podestà consisted of seven judges, three knights, eighteen notaries, ten horsemen, and twenty *berrovieri*. The *famiglia* of the Capitano consisted of three judges, two knights, four notaries, eight horsemen, and nine *berrovieri*. None of them could be from the city or even from Tuscany. Salvemini, *Magnati e popolani in Firenze*, p. 310.

12. Schevill, *History of Florence*, pp. 198–206.

13. On the early history of heralds, see Wagner, *Heralds and Heraldry*. Trexler, *The Libro*, pp. 13–31, summarizes various traditions of the herald in England, Germany, and France.

14. For a suggestion of how the two traditions may have become united, see Trexler, *The Libro*, pp. 14–17.

15. For discussions of poets and political poetry in the mid-thirteenth century, see Davidsohn, *Storia di Firenze*, vol. 2, p. 42; vol. 3, pp. 42–44; vol. 5, p. 43; vol. 7, pp. 341–44. On the heralds and their duties in Siena, see Corso, "Araldi."

16. Latini, *Il Tesoretto*, no. 15.

17.

Post hec veniamus ad Tuscos, qui, propter amentiam suam infroniti, titulum sibi vulgaris illustris arrogare videntur. Et in hoc non solum plebeia dementat intentio, sed famosos quamplures viros hoc tenuisse comperimus; puta Guittonem Aretinum, qui nunquam se ad curiale vulgare direxit, Bonagiuntam Lucensem, Gallum Pisanum, Minum Mocatum Senensem, Brunettum Florentinum: quorum dicta, si rimari vacaverit, non curialia, sed municipalia tantum invenientur.

Alighieri, *De vulgari eloquentia*, pp. 30–31. Botterill translates *municipalia* as "city council."

18. See Davidsohn, *Storia di Firenze*, vol. 5, pp. 43–44; and Costa, "Latini, Brunetto," vol. 7, p. 382.

19. Other names for the poet-singer were *improvvisatore, dicitore in rima, sonatore, cantore, cantatore, canterino, cantastorie, cantimbanco, cantambanca, cantampanca, ciarlatano,* and *cerretano.* See Haar, *Essays on Italian Poetry*, p. 78.

20.

Nel detto anno MCCLXXXXIIII morì in Firenze uno valente cittadino il quale ebbe nome ser Brunetto Latini il quale fu gran filosafo, e fue sommo maestro in rettorica, tanto in bene sapere dire come in ben dittare. E fu quegli che spuose la Rettorica di Tulio, e fece il buono e utile libro . . . e fu dittatore del nostro Comune. Fu mondano uomo, ma di lui avemo fatta menzione però ch' egli fue cominciatore e maestro in digrossare i Fiorentini, e farli scorti in bene parlare, e in sapere guidare e reggere la nostra repubblica secondo la Politica.

Villani, *Nuova cronica*, bk. 9, ch. 10.

21. See the discussion of Bartolomeo Scala and other chancellors in chapter 5.

22. See entry for "Cavalcanti, Guido," in the *Dictionary of the Middle Ages*, vol. 3, 196. Cavalcanti's poetry is edited in *Poeti del Duecento*, vol. 2.

23. Davidsohn, *Storia di Firenze*, vol. 7, p. 349.

24. According to Villani, *Nuova cronica*, bk. 8, ch. 10.

25. According to Wilson, "Trombetti, Improvvisatori, Laudesi," during the fifteenth century the roster of *canterini* in Perugia was dominated by Florentines. Also see Levi, "I cantari leggendari."

26. I am indebted to Giovanni Ciappelli for assistance with the identification of the name and its tradition.

27. Messer Prezzivale dal Fiesco de' conti dal Lavagna di Genova, vicar of the German emperor in 1286, is mentioned in Villani, *Nuova cronica*, bk. 8, chs. 112 and 114.

28. "Uomeni assai sollazzevoli, mezzi cortigiani, e facevano spesso certi giuochi da dare diletto a' signori." Sacchetti, *Il Trecentonovelle*, p. 440. It is interesting that Boccaccio includes the same two men, Stecchi and Martellino, in his *Decameron*, day 2, novella 1, also referring to them as *uomini di corte.* The *Grande dizionario della lingua Italiana* describes Prezzevale as "Degno di rispetto, do onore o di ammirazione" (vol. 14, p. 324).

29. On medieval minstrels, see Wright, *Music at the Court of Burgundy*, ch. 3, and de Pas, "Ménestrels et écoles de ménestrels."

30. Levi, "I cantari leggendari," pp. 1–4.

31. Raimbaut established residence at the court of Monferrato in 1197, and in 1202 accompanied Bonifacio I, Marquis of Monferrato, when he led the fourth crusade. Among Raimbaut's compositions written specifically for Monferrato is the *estampie* "Kalenda Maya." On the presence of troubadours in northern Italy, see Gallo, *Music in the Castle*, ch. 1.

32. Ibid.

33. Quoted in Baldwin, "The Image of the Jongleur," p. 635; translation from Baldwin.

34. Lines 1745–49. Quoted in ibid., p. 636; translation from Baldwin with changes.

35. "The most striking interconnection . . . appears in the central role of music and its close association with the word in both the lay and the clerical worlds." Ibid., p. 661.

36. Flamini, *La lirica toscana*, p. 48.

37. Davidsohn, *Storia di Firenze*, vol. 7, pp. 590–91.

38. Bonifacio, *Giullari e uomini di corte*, p. 67.

39. See Davidsohn, *Firenze ai tempi di Dante*, p. 552.

40. Davidsohn, *Storia di Firenze*, vol. 1, p. 1142, citing the statutes of Siena from 1262 to 1270.

41. Apparently, in front of the church of San Martino al Vescovo in Florence, the *panca* was a "ledge set in the wall of the church." Kent, *Cosimo de' Medici*, p. 43, n. 27.

42. Ugolini, *I cantari d'argomento classico*, pp. 10, 11; and Levi, "I cantari leggendari," p. 6. Davidsohn, *Storia di Firenze*, vol. 7, pp. 584–98, discusses the presence of *giullari* and other singers on numerous official occasions throughout Europe during the twelfth to the fourteenth centuries. Corso, "Araldi," pp. 148–49, discusses the herald of Siena dating from as early as 1398, but *canterini* serving in the city from much earlier.

43. Davidsohn, *Storia di Firenze*, vol. 7, pp. 587–88.

44. Ibid., vol. 7, p. 589; citing ASF: PR No. 2, fol. 69.

45. For a discussion of Dante's work where music is either mentioned or implied, see Fiori, "Discorsi sulla musica." For discussions of the subject of musical settings of late medieval poetry, see Bent, "Songs without Music," and Beer, "Alcune osservazioni."

46. Sacchetti, *Il Trecentonovelle*. In novella 115 Dante encounters a rustic donkey driver who also is singing his verse, but the narrative is less instructive other than to confirm that Dante's work was often sung.

47. Quoted in Haar, *Essays on Italian Poetry*, p. xvi.

48.

Unde postea apparuerunt comedi idest socij, qui pariter recitabant comedias, idest magnalia que occurebant, unus cantando alter succinendo et respondendo. Et isti comedi adhuc sunt in usu nostro et apparent maxime in partibus Lombardie aliqui cantatores qui magnorum dominorum in rithmis cantant gesta, unus proponendo, alius respondendo.

Quoted in Levi, "I cantari leggendari," p. 10.

49. See also Bonifacio, *Giullari*, p. 18, where the author associates the idea and titles of *joculatores* and *giullari* with Lombard troubadours of the thirteenth century.

50. Ventrone, "La sacra rappresentazione," pp. 81–83, concludes that reference to *recitare* in *sacre rappresentazioni* actually means that the lines were sung, and that in this connection *recitare* and *cantare* are interchangeable, citing as part of her evidence the following statement in one of the manuscripts: "Questo misterio glorioso e santo / vedrete recitar con dolce canto."

51. Branciforte, "*Ars Poetica*"; Trexler, *The Libro*; and Flamini, *La lirica toscana*, simply translate the verbs *recitare* and *cantare* as "spoken" and "sung," implying that the herald presented his verses in both fashions.

52. On the Italian tradition of improvised singing, see Pirrotta, "The Oral and Written Traditions of Music"; and McGee, "*Cantare all'improvviso*."

53. "Cantatore di verse morali ala mensa di signori," and "recitatore di canzoni et di versi morale et d'altre cose simili." ASF: CC No. 14, fol. 251r, v, for 1406–17. See Levi, "I cantari leggendari," for a documentation and discussion of the tradition of singing verse in Italy from the thirteenth to the sixteenth centuries. In a study of similar records in France and the Netherlands, Strohm, *Music in Late Medieval Bruges*, p. 74, concludes that the terms *ménestrel, jongleur, spilman, histrio,* and *mimus* were by and large interchangeable.

54. ASF: PR No. 42, fol. 96, for 1354. Cited in Novati, "Le poesie," p. 67.

55. "Verbis cum delectabili sonoritate proficuis inretiti." ASF: PR No. 63, fol. 102. Quoted in Branciforte, "*Ars Poetica*," p. 13.

56. "Recitando cantilenas morales et sonitios et alea multa moralia et pulcra et laudabilia et etiam delectabilia." Feb. 5, 1376. Novati, "Le poesie," p. 68.

57. For a chronological list of those who held the position of herald, see table 3.1.

58. "Referendarius dicti Comunis et recitator coram Dominis rerum moralium in vulgari et similium . . . in Sindicum et Referendarium dicti Comunis et ad recitandum coram dominis Prioribus et Vexilifero ad mensam et prout est consuetum cantilenas morales et similia." ASF: PR No. 82, fol. 253. Quoted in Branciforte, "Ars Poetica," pp. 17–18.

59. Boccaccio, *Decameron*, pp. 83, 253–54. A related musical example of the use of *dicere* to mean "to sing" can be found in the manuscript Bologna, Civico Museo, Bibliografico Musicale Q 25, in conjunction with the notation of Guillaume Dufay's motet "Inclita stella maris." Instructions for performance of the untexted second contratenor part state, "Secundus contratenor . . . non potest cantarsi nisi pueri dicant fugam" (The second contratenor . . . cannot be sung unless the boys say the canon). Quoted in Fallows, "Specific Information," pp. 128–30. Fallows points out that the scribe was making a distinction between singing with text (*dicere*) and singing without text (*cantare*).

60. For a discussion of the variety of words used to describe musical performance in twelfth- and thirteenth-century French poetry, see Huot, "Voices and Instruments in Medieval French Secular Music," pp. 69–72. She presents (on p. 71) the following excerpt from *Guillaume de Dole* as one of her examples where the verb *dites* clearly refers to singing: "Dame, fet il, une chançon / car nos dites, si ferez bien. / Ele chantoit sor tote rien" ("Lady," he says, "do sing us a song, you will do well." She habitually sang about anything at all).

61. Evidence that poetry was sometimes intended for spoken recitation is presented in Beer, "Alcune osservazioni."

62. On the tradition, see Soldati, "Improvvisatori, canterini e buffoni." The subject is a major theme in the writings of Nino Pirrotta, e.g., "The Oral and Written Traditions of Music."

63. The poetry is studied and discussed extensively by scholars of Italian literature, although they rarely link it with its performance. Serious attention to the activity is found in Branciforte, "Ars Poetica," and Kent, *Cosimo de' Medici*, pp. 46–50.

64. There was a long tradition of singing new text to an older melody, known as the *cantasi come* tradition; see for example Cattin, "I 'cantasi come'."

65. For a discussion of the texts and the practice of improvising melody, see McGee, "Cantare all'improvviso"; and H. M. Brown, "Fantasia on a Theme." Brown points out (pp. 326–27) that Boccaccio, as well as other fourteenth-century writers, considered a *canzona* to be any lyric poem meant to be sung.

66. The reference is to an *istanpitta*, an Italian processional dance. See McGee, *Medieval Instrumental Dances*, pp. 8–11.

67. See Bachmann, *The Origins of Bowing*, plates 69–76. Additional representations can be found in Remnant, "The Diversity of Medieval Fiddles"; and H. M. Brown, "The Trecento Fiddle." Winternitz, "Lira da Braccio," and Jones, *The Lira da Braccio*, discuss the instrument only when it is called a *lira da braccio* in the late fifteenth century.

68. Rohloff, *Die Quellenhandschriften*, pp. 134–36. English translation in Seay, *Johannes de Grocheo*, pp. 19–20.

69. Cserba, *Hieronymus de Moravia*. The section on tunings of the five-string fiddle is reproduced and discussed in Page, "Jerome of Moravia."

70. Jones, *The Lira da Braccio*, chs. 3 and 4, presents tables of the variety of shapes and number of strings found in representations through the later centuries of its popularity. Also see discussion and illustrations in Winternitz, *Musical Instruments*, ch. 5.

71. Scavizzi, "The Myth of Orpheus," includes illustrations of Orfeo with lute, *lira da braccio*, and a seven-string lyre.

72. An early representation of a performer plucking the off-board strings is in a fourteenth-century copy of a Boethius manuscript, Naples Biblioteca Nazionale, Cod. V. A. 14; plate 76 in Bachmann, *The Origins of Bowing.*

73. The issue of construction and repertory for the early viola is somewhat complicated. See discussion in H. M. Brown, "The Trecento Fiddle," pp. 318–23.

74. For a discussion of the heritage and symbolism, see Winternitz, *Leonardo da Vinci,* ch. 4; and Winternitz, *Musical Instruments,* ch. 5. Only two examples of music for the *lira da braccio* survive, and both are from the late sixteenth century. Although they are undoubtedly music to be performed on that instrument, they do not seem to be related to the earlier tradition of *cantare all'improvviso* as described here. See H. M. Brown, *Sixteenth-Century Instrumentation,* pp. 223–25, 412–54.

75. See the discussion of this symbolism in Winternitz, *Musical Instruments,* p. 89. On the representation of Orpheus in Italian art, see Scavizzi, "The Myth of Orpheus."

76. Quoted in Levi, "I cantari leggendari," p. 20.

77. Another practice that appeared in the mid-fifteenth century was that of a *tenorista,* a second musician who performed an accompaniment for the improvisor. See discussion in Prizer, "The Frottola and the Unwritten Tradition," pp. 10–12.

78. Quoted in Pirrotta, "Music and Cultural Tendencies," pp. 93–95. In addition to being praised by Cornazano, Pietrobono was also praised in the writings of Aurelio Brandolino Lippi, Battista Guarino, Filippo Beroaldo, and Raffaello Maffei, and his image was immortalized on medals, an unusual honor for a member of the working class. See Lockwood, "Pietrobono and the Instrumental Tradition," and Lockwood, *Music in Renaissance Ferrara,* ch. 10, "Pietrobono and the Improvisatory Tradition."

79. That Lorenzo played *lira da braccio* is established in a letter to him from Giuliano Catellaccio, December 1, 1466; ASF: MAP, 23, 92 (where it is identified as the *viola*); quoted in D'Accone, "Lorenzo il Magnifico e la musica," p. 234. On Isabella d'Este, see Fenlon, "The Status of Music," p. 61.

80. Reported in Becherini, "Un canta in panca," p. 244. For a discussion of Ficino and *canto improvvisato* see D'Accone, "Lorenzo il Magnifico e la musica," pp. 230–31.

81. Kent, *Cosimo de' Medici,* p. 44, concludes that although the tradition was widespread throughout Italy during the age of the communes, "by the fifteenth century it seems to have survived mainly in Florence."

82. The church, which no longer exists, was located in the area where Dante had lived, near the Torre della Castagna. For a discussion of the church, see Desideri Costa, *La Chiesa di San Martino,* cited in Kent, *Cosimo de' Medici,* p. 47.

83. On Cristoforo, see Renier, *Strombotti e sonetti dell'Altissimo.* On Guido, see Becherini, "Un canta in panca," p. 242, and Flamini, *La lirica toscana,* pp. 155ff. Flamini discusses the work of several who sang in San Martino, pp. 158, 174–75. Becherini relates the repertory of the public minstrel to that sung at the Mensa, and describes such a performer in the early decades of the twentieth century in the mountain town of Piteccio, who improvised *ottave rime* while accompanying himself on the guitar. For an account of a similar position in Siena, see Novati, "Le poesie," p. 57, and D'Accone, *The Civic Muse,* p. 458.

84. An observation made by Kent, *Cosimo de' Medici,* p. 44. For all its popularity in northern Italy during this period, there is little understanding of exactly what the fiddle/*lira da braccio* actually played (or even of the kind of vocal line that would typically be invented by the singer). In addition to the flat bridge, which limited the performer to constant drones, the tuning of the strings would also have been quite limiting in terms of range: the only statement we have prior to the sixteenth century is that by Jerome of Moravia in Paris, ca. 1280,

who provides three tunings: d/G, g, d', d'; d, G, g, d', g'; and G/G, d, c', c'; see Page, "Jerome of Moravia." Sixteenth-century treatises, such as that by Lanfranco in 1533, give the tuning of the seven-string *lira da braccio* as d, d'/g, g', d', a', e''; see H. M. Brown, *Sixteenth-Century Instrumentation*, pp. 223–25. In this tuning the top four strings are identical to the violin, and the bridge was usually slightly curved, both of which suggest more melodic involvement. There is no record of when the instrument converted to this later pattern. During the fourteenth and fifteenth centuries the lute also had doubled strings—usually four or five courses, tuned A, d, g, c' (f'), and therefore was not so severely constricted; see Smith, *A History of the Lute*, pp. 60–61.

85. Flamini, *La lirica toscana*, pp. 3–5; and Gorni, "Storia del Certame Coronario." Flamini describes the performance as declaimed (*declamò*), but his source document uses the word *recitollo*. The texts are reproduced in Bertolini, *De vera amicitia*, and in the appendix of Altamura, *Il Certame Coronario*.

86. Gorni, "Storia del Certame Coronario," pp. 162–63, quotes from Florence, Biblioteca Riccardiana, Ms 1142, fol. 41v that the audience included "l'arcivescovo et molti prelati, ofitiali dello Studio, molti honoratisimi cortigiani et gran popolo, et Secretari di N.S. iudici eletti dalla Signoria prefata et dagl'ofitiali dello Studio." And Bonucci, in his *Opere volgari*, includes a passage from Bibl. Laurenziana Ms XC that there were "i segretarii de prefato Eugenio PP. la Magnifica Signoria di Firenze, Arcivescovo, Ambasciador di Vinegia, infinito numero di Prelati, e poi universalmente tutto il popolo fiorentino." Quoted in Gorni, p. 181.

87. See Ventrone, *Gli araldi*, pp. 144–45, where she suggests a date of 1444–48 and calls it the earliest know datable *rappresentazione*.

88. My suggestion is based on the statement that Jacopo Salimbene, appointed herald in 1352, was noted for his *comediis*. See ibid., p. 126.

89. The date of the performance of Poliziano's work is not secure. See the discussion in Pirrotta and Povoledo, *Li due Orfei*, p. 8; English transl., p. 6, in which a date in the 1480s is proposed; and a more recent discussion of the probable date in Benvenuti, *L'Orfeo del Poliziano*, pp. 89–103, which proposes its origin a decade earlier.

90. On Baccio Ugolini's ability to sing *improvvisatore*, see Del Lungo, *Florentia*, pp. 307–12.

91. Winternitz, *Leonardo da Vinci*, p. 30.

92. Quoted in Rubsamen, "The *Justiniane* or *Viniziane*," p. 174.

93. *Ludovici Carbonis Dialogus de neapolitana profectione*, Vatican City, Biblioteca Apostolica Vaticana, Ms vaticano latino 8618, fols. 32r–79r. Quoted in Gallo, *Music in the Castle*, pp. 69–70.

94. Ibid., p. 70.

95. Pirrotta and Povoledo, *Li due Orfei*, p. 46. I am indebted to Allan Atlas for passing on this reference.

96. Pirrotta, "Music and Cultural Tendencies," p. 105, translates *ad lembum* as "on the lute."

97.

Canendi autem ratio tripertita descriptione secernitur, ex qua una phrygia, altera lydia, tertia dorica nominatur. Phrygia enim est, qua animi audientium acriori vocum contentione abalienari solent: ex quo genere illa numeratur, qua Gallici musici in palatino sacello natalitiis exsuscitatiisque feriis, rituali lege utuntur: lydia autem duplex indicari potest; una quae coagmentata, altera quae simplex nominatur: coagmentata enim est, qua inflexo ad dolorem modo, animi ad fletum misericordiamque deducuntur: qualis ea videri potest,

qua novendilia pontificia, ac senatoria parentalia celebrari solent, quo quidem lugubri
canendi genere semper est natio hispanorum usa, simplex autem est ea, qua languidius
modificata cadit: ut eos P. Maronis versus inflexos fuisse vidimus, qui Ferdinando secundo
auctore soliti sunt a Caritheo poeta cani: at vero dorica ratio multo est aequali mediocritate
temperatior: or quale illud genus videri volunt, quod est, a Divo Gregorio in aberruncato,
rio sacro stataria canendi mensione institutum: quocirca nostri omnem canendi rationem
in litatoria, praecentoria: & carmina comparando seiungunt: litatoria enim sunt ea, in
quibus omnia phtongorum, prosodiarum, analogicarumque mensionum genera versantur,
& in quibus musicorum generi laus cantus praeclare struendi datur. . . . At vero carminum
modi hi numerari solent, qui maxime octasticorum, aut trinariorum ratione constant: quod
quidem genus primus apud nostros Franciscus Petrarca instituisse dicit qui edita carmina
caneret ad lembum nuper autem Seraphinus Aquilanus princeps eius generis renovandi
fuit: a quo ita est verborum & cantum coniunctio modulata nexa: ut nihil fieri posset eius
modorum ratione dulcius: Itaque ex eo tanta imitantium auledorum multitudo manavuit,
ut quicquid in hoc genere Italia tota cani videatur.

Cortesi, *De cardinalatu;* facsimile in Pirrotta, "Music and Cultural Tendencies," pp. 100–
101.

98. Haar, *Essays on Italian Poetry,* p. 85.

99. "Il Lasca" was the pen name of Antonfrancesco Grazzini.

100. For documents and discussion, see Nosow, "The Debate over Song."

101. The two singers were Adriana Basile and Francesca Caccini. Information is included in a letter from Antonio Galli to the Medici court, November 11, 1623, ASF: Mediceo, No. 3645, a portion of which is printed in Rosand, "Barbara Strozzi," p. 254, n. 31. The incident is discussed in McGee, "How one Learned."

102. The use of *citara* (= *kithara*) is a reference to the function as related to ancient Greek practices, similar to the reference cited above with reference to Pietrobono.

103.

Dopo el disinare reductome in una camera con tuttal la compagnia: ò 'ldito cantare con la citara uno Maestro Antonio, che credo che Vostra Exc^tia debba, se non congnoscere, almancho havere oldito nominare . . . narrò ogni cosa con tanta dignità et modo, che 'l magiore poeta né oratore che sia al mundo, se l'havesse havuto a fare tale acto, forse non ne saria uscito con tanta commendatione da ogni canto del dire suo, che in vero fu tale che ognuno fece signare de maraviglia et maxime quilli che più docti sono, vedendo loro, ultra arte comparatione che 'l fece, de quale non so le Lucano né Dante ne facessero mai alcuno di più bella, miscolare tante historie antiche, nome de romani vechi innumerabili, fabule, poeti et il nome de tute quante le muse, or a dire di costui saria grandissima impressa.

April 23, 1459, Galeazzo Maria Sforza to his father from Villa Careggi. From Wilson, "Surpassing Orpheus." On Galeazzo's training and interest in music, see Prizer, "Music at the Court of the Sforza," pp. 150–59.

104. For numerous examples of this repertory, see Lanza, *Lirici toscani.*

105. From ibid., vol. 1, no. 9, p. 179.

106. Published in Saffioti, *I Giullari,* pp. 480–92.

107. *Verzeppe* (or *Verçeppe*) is one of the *balli* credited to Domenico da Piacenza and found in the dance treatises of Antonio Cornazano and Guglielmo Ebreo/Giovanni Ambrosio. Nevile, *The Eloquent Body,* pp. 30–31, 182–88. The meaning of the word is unknown. See the discussion of *balli* in ch. 6.

108.

Octava siquidem et ultima regula haec est quod in omni contrapuncto varietas accuratissime exquirenda est, nam, ut Horatius in sua Poetica dicit, "Cytharedus ridetur corda si semper oberrat eadem." Quemadmodum enim in arte dicendi varietas, secundum Tullii sententiam,

auditorem maxime delectat, ita et in musica concentuum diversitas animos auditorum ve-
hementer in oblectamentum provocat, hinc et Philosophus in Ethicis varietatem iocundis-
simam rem esse naturam que humanam eius indigentem asserere non dubitavit.

Tinctoris, *Liber de arte contrapuncti*, vol. 2, p. 155; trans. Seay, *The Art of Counterpoint*,
p. 139.

109. Vicentino, *L'antica musica*, book 4, ch. 42, p. 245; and Zarlino, *Sopplimenti musicali*, Ottavo & ultimo libro, ch. 11, p. 319. Quoted and discussed in McGee, "Music, Rhetoric,"
pp. 252–57.

110. On the presentation of prose in the *cantare all'improvviso* tradition see Prizer, "The
Frottola and the Unwritten Tradition," pp. 19–20.

111. I do not intend to imply that all of this type of performance consisted of completely
spontaneous material. The amount of spontaneity could have been quite variable on any
given occasion, ranging from a performance that was almost completely rehearsed to one
that had many—or even all—of its parts made up on the spot. Nevertheless, the ability to
put all of these elements together in such a way as to merit praise such as that mentioned
above singles out these poet-singers as major talents. See the discussion of improvisation
below.

112. Cristoforo Fiorentino, canto 1, ottava 13; quoted in Ventrone, *Gli araldi*, p. 111.

113. Cortesi, *De cardinalatu*, book 3, fol. 164; quoted in Pirrotta, "Music and Cultural
Tendencies," p. 112.

114. I follow John Najemy's suggestion in using "elite" rather than a direct translation
of *grandi*: "the greats." See the discussion in Najemy, *A History*, pp. 5–11.

115. Ibid., pp. 11–20.

116.

Qui Andreas, Vexillifer Justitie predictus, incontinenti . . . assumpsit et promovit eundem
dominum Gregorium ad dignitatem militie et eundem militari cingulo decoravit, et in
signum dicte militie accinxit eundem ense et calcaria aurea eidem mitti et apponi fecit
per domicellos dominationis prefate; ac etiam sertum olivarum argentarum super caput
eius imposuit et alapam manu dextra dedit eidem, et omnia alia fecit dixit et observavit in
predictis et inde dependentia, debita et requisita; quibus peractis magnus sonitus tubarum
et pifferorum seu ceramellarum per tubicines et pifferos et sonitores dominationis predicte
factus extitit, secundum ritum et consuetudinem alias in similibus observatam.

ASF: SC, D No. 29, fol. 116, for October 31, 1446; quoted in Salvemini, *La dignità cavalleresca*, p. 94.

117. On the Parte Guelfa, see A. Brown, "The Guelf Party," pp. 41–86.

118. The description is taken from two accounts: one from del Corazza, "Diario fiorentino," p. 244; and the other from the *Cronaca* of Giovanni di Paolo Morelli, 337, as reported
in Salvamini, *La dignità*, pp. 128–29. It is also discussed in Gori, *Le feste fiorentine*, vol. 2,
*Firenze magnifica*, pp. 76–77.

119. See Rubinstein, *The Palazzo Vecchio*, pp. 38, 103.

120. See Brucker, "Bureaucracy and Social Welfare," p. 2.

121. See Rubinstein, *The Palazzo Vecchio*, p. 38.

122. Mazzi, "La mensa dei Priori," p. 363.

123. See Trexler, "Honor Among Thieves," p. 328.

124. Rubinstein, *The Palazzo Vecchio*, p. 21.

125. Ibid., pp. 1–2.

126. Branciaforte, "Ars Poetica," p. 59.

127. ASF: PR No. 39, fol. 133v, for 1351; quoted in ibid., p. 12.

128. Ventrone, *Gli araldi*, p. 127.

129. For examples of all levels of quality, see Flamini, *La lirica toscana*, and Lanza, *Lirici toscani*.

130. Samples of their verse can be found in Branciforte, "*Ars Poetica*," pp. 362–534.

131. ASF: PR No. 82. See note 58 above.

132. ASF: CC, GS No. 48, fol. 84, for 1377. Quoted in Branciforte, "*Ars Poetica*," p. 84.

133. Quoted in Flamini, *La lirica toscana*, p. 55.

134. Branciforte, "*Ars Poetica*," pp. 78–79, charts Antonio's appointment as beginning in 1417, but ASF: CC No. 14, for 1406–1407, records very clearly on fol. 251r, the appointment of "Antonio di Mathio de Fiorenze, cantatore di verse morali ala mensa di signori," for a period of two years, and on 251v, "Antonio ovicio Antonio di Matteo recitatore di canzoni et di versi morale et d'altre cose simili eleto et deputato." ASF: CC No. 17, for 1409–10, includes payments to both Antonio de Meglio and his predecessor, Antonio di Friano, at fol. 235r: "Antonio di Matteo da Firenzaiola cavallaro del comune di firenze"; fol. 251r "Antonio di Piero Friani, cavaliere di corte." See the discussion in Branciforte, pp. 85–87, concerning the confusion of names.

135. Published in Lanza, *Lirici toscani*, vol. 2, pp. 131–32.

136. Biblioteca Riccardiana Ms 2732, f. 47. Published in Lanza, *Lirici toscani*, vol. 2, pp. 95–101. In honor of the same treaty Guillaume Dufay wrote his motet "Supremum est mortalibus bonum," and the ballade "C'est bien raison de devoir essaucier." On Antonio di Meglio's poetry, see Bessi, "Politica e poesia nel Quattrocento fiorentino," and Bessi, "Eugenio IV e Antonio di Matteo di Meglio."

137. A somewhat different view of the position and those who held it is presented in Trexler, *The Libro*, pp. 33–46. Trexler's account is colored by his interpretation of the word *buffone* as referring to a comic actor, whom he refers to variously as "buffoon" (in the modern, derogatory sense of the word), "trickster," and "funster."

138. ASF: PR No. 39, fol. 133; cited in Branciforte, "*Ars Poetica*," pp. 10–11. For the suggestion that Antonio Pucci may have held a position as *canterino* to the Podestà in 1350, see Robins, "Poetic Rivalry," pp. 310–12.

139. See Flamini, *La lirica toscana*, p. 196, and Bonifacio, *Giullari e uomini di corte*, p. 62, n. 4.

140. See D'Ancona, "I canterini dell'antica comune di Perugia," p. 69.

141. The document is dated June 10, 1350. See Branciforte, "*Ars Poetica*," pp. 8–11. According to Trexler, *The Libro*, p. 36, n. 12, the position of *sindicus* existed in 1325, recorded as Statuto 63. The office of *referendarius* seems to have been created on May 17, 1345, with the initial appointment of Giovanni Salvi Affricani, and combined with *sindicus*.

142. It is not clear exactly how the various duties were distributed prior to 1352, although Affricani's title of "Lord" [Ser] indicating that he too was a knight, suggests either that he may have served as herald prior to Gello, or that the office of *Sindaco Proveditore e Referendario* also was held by a knight, as was the custom for that position in the early fifteenth century (see ch. 4).

143. For a discussion of Salimbene's involvement with other poets of the time, as well as a somewhat different interpretation of the position he occupied, see Robins, "Poetic Rivalry," pp. 312–14.

144. On several of Salimbene's ambassadorial missions, see Branciforte, "*Ars Poetica*," pp. 10–13, 81.

145. "verbis cum delectabili sonoritate proficius inretiti." ASF: PR No. 63, fol. 102v, cited in Branciforte, "*Ars Poetica*," p. 13.

146. All of this taken from ibid., pp. 82–83.

147. The unusual and somewhat confusing office swap is discussed in ibid., pp. 14–15.

148. ASF: PR No. 71, fol. 10v–11r. Cited in Branciforte, "*Ars Poetica*," p. 15, n. 13.

149. ASF: PR No. 83, fol. 225r–226r and 238v. Cited in Branciforte, "*Ars Poetica*," p. 20, nn. 23 and 27.

150. In Jacopo Salviati, *Cronache fiorentine, delizie degli eruditi*, 290; quoted in Branciforte, "*Ars Poetica*," p. 85.

151. Found in BNF: Pal. 215.

152. Works by many of these poets are published in Lanza, *Lirici toscani*.

153. Published in Lanza, *Lirici toscani*, vol. 2, pp. 105–21. On di Meglio's friendship with the Medici, see Branciforte, "*Ars Poetica*," pp. 95–98.

154. According to Brincat, *Giovan Matteo*, p. 3, Giovan was eighteen at the time. He was never elected to the post of Florentine herald as was his older brother Gregorio. His poetry is preserved in manuscripts in Florence, Biblioteca Riccardiana 2729, 2734, and 2735; and published in Brincat, *Giovan Matteo*, and in Lanza, *Lirici toscani*, vol. 2, pp. 143–62.

155. Ventrone, *Gli araldi*, pp. 144–45. See also Ventrone, "La sacra rappresentazione," pp. 67–99.

156. Lanza, *Lirici toscani*, vol. 2, pp. 57–58.

157. On the poetry form and this exchange, see Branciforte, "*Ars Poetica*," ch. 4. For additional biography, see *Dizionario biografico*, vol. 16, pp. 616–17.

158. For extended discussion of the lives and poetic works of both men, see Branciforte, "*Ars Poetica*," including appendix 2; and Branciforte, "Antonio di Meglio." Calderoni's election to the Florentine post is recorded in ASF: PR No. 133, fol. 202–203, for October 1443; quoted in Trexler, *The Libro*, p. 41, n. 35.

159. Trexler, *The Libro*, p. 41.

160. Found in BNF: Magl. II.II. 40, fol. 114r, under the heading "fatto di messer Anselmo Chalderoni buffone. Mando a cchosimo de Medici." Published in Lanza, *Lirici toscani*, vol. 1, p. 344.

161. According to Flamini, *La Lirica toscana*, p. 206, poetry by Chianciano is published in *Poeti antichi*, Naples, 1661. About the appointments of all three see Trexler, *The Libro*, pp. 41–43. According to Brincat, *Giovan Matteo*, p. 4, none of Gregorio di Meglio's writings have survived.

162. The first use of the name Filerate is in the *Libro cerimoniale*. A portrait medal in his honor, attributed to Niccolò Spinelli, bears the name Frachiscus Philarithes. See Trexler, *The Libro*, p. 47. For additional biography, see *Dizionario biografico*, vol. 47, pp. 608–609.

163. In a letter of March 22, 1474, Filarete addresses Lorenzo de' Medici as "that most singular and unique comfort of the Florentine republic." See Flamini, *La lirica toscana*, pp. 207–208.

164. The poem is in Florence, Biblioteca Riccardiana Ms 1258, fol. 74.

165. Members of this intellectual circle included Marsilio Ficino, Jacopo Tebaldi, and Benedetto Dei. See *Dizionario biografico*, vol. 47, pp. 608–609.

166. In Rossi, "Memorie di musica civile in Perugia nei secc. XIV e XV," 135; quoted in Zippel, *I suonatori*, p. 22, n. 2.

167. Documents quoted in Branciforte, "*Ars Poetica*," p. 117.

168. Record of a public hearing held on 25 January 1503 [1504], taken from Archivio dell'Opera del Duomo, *Deliberazioni*, 1496–1507, and published in Gaye, *Carteggio inedito*, vol. 2, pp. 455–62, and reprinted in Seymour, *Michelangelo's David*, p. 139.

169. ASF: PR No. 166, fol. 263. Reproduced in Branciforte, "*Ars Poetica,*" pp. 351–53.

170. Edited by Trexler as *The Libro Cerimoniale of the Florentine Republic.*

171. Trexler, *The Libro,* p. 75. For more on this visit, see ch. 6.

172. Trexler, *The Libro,* p. 78.

173. Three poems were presented on this occasion, including one by Naldo Naldi, and an oration by chancellor Bartolomeo Scala, published in Zannoni, "Il sacco di Volterra."

174. From a letter published in Barocchi and Ristori, *Il carteggio di Michelangelo;* quoted in Trexler, *The Libro,* p. 51.

175. Discussion in Trexler, *The Libro,* pp. 55–56. The poems are printed on pp. 131–36.

176. Reported in ibid., p. 51, n. 28.

177. His most famous drama is *L'Ingratitudine,* published in 1559.

178. ASF: SC No. 124, fol. 216v, for February 17, 1522. In order to pay for the additional herald, the sum of 13 lire, 5 soldi, 8 denari per month was removed from Manfidi's salary. Manfidi was quite upset about both the appointment of a co-herald as well as the reduction of his own income. He recorded it in the *Libro,* dated February 24, 1517 [1518], under the heading "Nota d'uno cattivo et adolorato ricordo." Manfidi did not feel that there was any need to add the second herald, and notes that the office had been in the family since the 1450s and that he had served the city faithfully. He also states that he has four sons to support as well as a daughter who could not marry because he was unable to provide a dowery. See Trexler, *The Libro,* pp. 126–27.

179. Branciforte, "*Ars Poetica,*" p. 120, attributing the information to Vasari. I could not find other confirmation that Barlacchi was appointed herald. The entry in the *Dizionario biografico,* vol. 6, pp. 398–99, describes him as an actor, author of comedies, and friend of Giovan Batista dell'Ottonaio, but states that he was a bannitore.

## 4. Revising the Ceremonial Traditions

1. The material in the preceding paragraphs is taken from Brucker, "Florence," pp. 97–99; Brucker, *Renaissance Florence,* pp. 135–36; and Schevill, *History of Florence,* pp. 270–71.

2. On Bruni's opinion, see Najemy, "Civic Humanism," pp. 85–86. For the opinion that it "was something less than a gigantic conspiracy against wealth, tradition and the social order . . . a characteristic Florentine *imbroglio,* neither very bloody nor very destructive," see Brucker, "The Ciompi Revolution," p. 356. Information for the next several paragraphs was taken from Brucker, *The Civic World,* ch. 2; Brucker, *Renaissance Florence,* pp. 46–48, 66–68; and Najemy, *Corporatism and Consensus,* pp. 264–98.

3. Najemy, *Corporatism and Consensus,* p. 229. For a discussion of the *popolo* and guilds, see Najemy, *A History of Florence,* pp. 35–44.

4. The details of the complex legislation from this period are discussed in Najemy, *A History of Florence,* ch. 7.

5. Ibid., p. 264.

6. Baron, *The Crisis,* p. 3.

7. ASF: PR No. 166, for December 29, 1475, and SC No. 93, for November 9, 1475. Quoted in Branciforte, "*Ars Poetica,*" pp. 16, 70–71.

8.

Actendentes magnifici domini domini Priores artium et Vexillifer Justitie populi et co-munis Florentie quantum dominus Johanes Giorgii de Trebbio comitatus Florentie Miles curialis dicti Comunis et hactenus pluries electus et deputatus in Sindicum et Referendarium Comunis predicti, in ipso ministerio seu exercitio se habuit et habet laudabiliter et prudenter; et ex hoc volentes tam pro honore dicti Comunis quam eius exigentibus meritis ipsum prosequi gratia et favore.

ASF: PR No. 72, fol. 136v–137r, for 1383. Quoted in Branciforte, *"Ars Poetica,"* p. 17.

9. This is a reversal of the values expressed in 1338, when the Florentine government passed a statute eliminating a cash award that usually accompanied a knighthood to anyone who was an "ystrio seu buffone sive qui vulgariter appellatur huomo di corte." Quoted in Trexler, *The Libro,* p. 34. The French courtly equivalent was called *valet de chambre* or *faiseur;* see Strohm, *Music in Late Medieval Bruges,* p. 74.

10. Trexler, *The Libro,* p. 23.

11. For a discussion of the early history of the positions, see ch. 3 above, and Branciforte, *"Ars Poetica,"* pp. 8–11.

12.

Et habeant, et habere debeant unum cantorem de cantionibus moralibus ad Mensam praefatorum dominorum, et etiam quamcumque voluerint, cum salario trium florenorum auri mense quolibet, ut supra. Et habeant unum militem curialem, sindicum et referendarium communis Florentiae, qui in eorum conviviis et festis eos honoret, in dicendo et dicerias faciendo, et sociando eum qui ire debeat quocumque missus fuerit per eos, qui habeat pro eius salario libras decem quolibet mense solvendas, ut supra, et ultra habeat a quolibet potestate civitatis Florentiae quolibet semestri unam robbam valoris vigintiquinque florenorum auri.

*Statuti della Repubblica,* vol. 2, 514.

13. Richard Trexler describes this as marking the beginning of an increase of "magnificence in the public sphere," and that this "soon made itself felt in all areas of public, ecclesiastical, familial, and individual behavior." Trexler, *The Libro,* p. 10.

14. Ibid., p. 78.

15. There are a variety of titles or labels found in the archival documents that name Antonio di Piero Friani over the years. This citation is from ASF: CC No. 22, fol. 261, for 1416–17.

16. ASF: PR No. 93, fol. 114, for 1404.

17. ASF: CC No. 17, fol. 246, for 1409–10. It is probable that Bernardo was the son of Cristofano, who was a singer at the Mensa in 1401.

18. ASF: CC No. 22, fols. 265r and 266r, for 1416–17.

19. On pensions in Florence, see Brucker, "Bureaucracy and Social Welfare," pp. 10–12.

20. "Ea que tendunt ad honorem mense dominorum priorum et vexilliferi iustitie populi et Comunis Florentie volentes nedum conservare set etiam augere, Magnifici domini." ASF: PR No. 75, fols. 142v–143r, for October 22, 1386.

21. "Trombettarum electio . . . Pro honore comunis florentie domini Priores Artium et Vexillifer Justitie populi et comunis Florentie." ASF: PR 76, fol. 146, for October 29, 1387; ASF: CC No. 3, fol. 257, for 1393.

22. It is not clear what "ornaments" refers to, since the instruments of the pifferi are made of wood. If it means the metal keys it would only refer to the *bombarda*—the other two instruments had none. It may refer to decorative ornaments that they were to mount on the instruments, but I have not located any pictures of early shawms with decorations on them. D'Accone, *The Civic Muse,* p. 553, cites Siena Palace inventories from the early fifteenth century that list "three silver pifferi," and speculates that "silver" may have referred to casings or sheaths that could have been placed over them for ceremonial purposes.

23. ASF: PR No. 85, fol. 41, for April 26, 1396.

24. ASF: PR No. 75, fol. 142v–143r, for October 22, 1386.

25. On ambiguous references to musical instruments, see McGee with Mittler, "Information on Instruments in Florentine Carnival Songs."

26. See Polk, *German Instrumental Music*, p. 55.

27. ASF: PR No. 45, fol. 105, for December 12, 1356.

28. ASF: CC No. 3, fol. 257.

29. Earliest records of the *cornetto* are from English sources ca. 1400. See Marcuse, *A Survey of Musical Instruments*, p. 772, and Polk, *German Instrumental Music*, pp. 72–73.

30. ASF: PR No. 76, fol. 146, for 1387, and No. 134, fol. 97v, for August 1443.

31. This would seem to be the sense of a similar reference in Bologna from 1352 to players "sonando trombam sive trombettam cornum sive cornettam cenamellam vel nacharas." See Gambassi, *Il Concerto Palatino*, p. 97. I am indebted to Keith Polk for this reference.

32. Until the end of the Republic the three Florentine musical groups maintained their separate identities. Although the statements describing the musical groups in the 1415 statutes are somewhat lacking in specific details, referring instead to "usual" duties, the very fact that the ensembles are described under two different rubrics—one for the trombadori and a separate one for the trombetti and pifferi—reinforces the fact that they were perceived as different.

33. *Statuta populi*, vol. 2, rubric 59. Copious and sometimes detailed records of ceremonies and festas, including the participation of musical groups, can be found in various narrative and poetic accounts; for example Gori, *Le feste fiorentine*; del Corazza, "Diario fiorentino"; Novati, "Le poesie"; and Flamini, *La lirica toscana*.

34. *Statuta populi*, vol. 2, rubrics 40 and 41.

35. See Davidsohn, *Storia di Firenze*, vol. 5, pp. 177–79. The same monastic image is present in the spartan cells in the Palazzo della Signoria where the executive lived during his time in office. On these and other similarities between Florentine and monastic rituals see Trexler, *Public Life*, pp. 49–50.

36.

E la mensa de Signori si dice che è la meglio apparecchiata et riccamente ornata e pulitamente servita, che Mensa de alcuna Signoria del mondo, et per ordine, e come sono diputati ogni due mesi alla loro Mensa fiorini seicento d'oro, tengono piffari et sonatori et buffoni e giocolatori e tutte cose da sollazzo et da magnificenza; ma poco tempo vi mettono, che di presente sono chiamati dal Proposto et posti a sedere per attendere a' bisogni del Comune, che sempre abbonda loro faccenda, e mai non vi manca che fare.

Quoted in the manuscript version of Dati's *Istoria di Firenze* in BNF: Pal 560, fol. 46r. A similar version is quoted in Flamini, *La lirica toscana*, p. 197. Dati was a Prior in 1425 and Standard Bearer of Justice in 1429. Most manuscript copies of his history are thought to have originated before 1405, but there are some that have come from later in the century that include material that postdates his death in 1435. See chapter 5, note 43. This passage is not included in the printed edition of Dati's *Istoria*; perhaps it was thought not to have been an authentic part of Dati's writings. Regardless of who the author was, however, it does represent the observation of a Florentine from the early fifteenth century.

37. ASF: Catasto 79, fol. 594.

38. ASF: SC No. 29, fol. 35v, for October 20, 1404.

39. "viole, ribeche, liuti et aliorum instrumentorum." PR No. R103, fol. 90r, for October 20, 1413; as quoted in Zippel, *I suonatori*, p. 22, n. 5; and Wilson, *Music and Merchants*, p. 250.

40. "E che detto Paolo sia tenuto colla sua viola servire nell' Oratorio di Or San Michele ed inoltre ogni volte che ne fosse richiesto debba colla viola ed altri strumenti servire alla mensa della signoria senza salaria spechiale." ASF: PR No. 102, for October 20, 1413.

41. ASF: CC No. 29, fol. 241r, for 1425–26; CC, UG No. 1, fols. 95v and 99r, for 1426–30; and CC No. 32, fol. 263v, for 1429–30. Because of the similarity of names and the fact that both players were from Germany, it is possible they were father and son.

42. This was not the first appearance of a viola player on the civic payroll: ASF: PR No. 73, for 1384, records an isolated payment to "Chellinus Benini de flor. sonator viole" (fol. 4r). There is no statement about his duties, nor does his name appear again on the pay list. It is interesting to note that the lute and viola were the instruments usually played by *cantastorie*, including the civic herald. It is doubtful that extra instrumentalists would be needed for this duty. It is possible, however, that their purpose was to play instrumental music and accompany singing other than that performed *all'improvviso*.

43. ASF: CC No. 22, 265r, for 1416–17; and CC No. 78, fol. 2r. Cernobi was still receiving a pension more than ten years later; CC No. 32, 267r, for 1429–30.

44. ASF: CC No. 173, for 1422, fol. 1; cited in Branciforte, "*Ars Poetica*," p. 92. I have translated *giocholatore* above as "entertainer," but it could just as well have meant "actor," or even "juggler."

45. ASF: S, C, M No. 26, fol. 139r. Reproduced and discussed in Corti, "Un musicista fiammingo."

46. The absence of any further record of performances at the Mensa by this vocal ensemble has to do with the nature of the documents, which are mostly records of payments and of official appointments to the Signoria. The singers at San Lorenzo were neither appointed nor employed by the government, and thus would not appear in either type of document. The archival records of San Lorenzo do not mention performances of any kind during this period.

47. Francesco da Barberino, *Del reggimento*, appendix 1, pp. 199–200.

48. Bindo Bonichi, quoted in Vecchi, *Educazione musicale*, p. 15, n. 2.

49. As a part of the wedding ceremonies, the personal goods of the bride were transferred to the home of the groom in a procession. The inclusion of musicians to herald the passage was subject to the nobility of the bride. See McGee, "Misleading Iconography," pp. 144–45.

50. Festa, *Un Galateo femminile*, appendix 1, p. 201.

51. See Villani, *Nuova cronica*, bk. 11, ch. 151, for a discussion of details concerning the rules in 1330 for apparel and food at weddings.

52. ASF: GA No. 54, parte 4, fol. 11r–13r, 75r, v, for 1360–61.

53. The earliest record of pifferi in Italy known to me is in the Archivio di Stato, Lucca, Camerlingo Generale for January 1382, which lists payments to three pifferi.

54. The establishment of the shawm duo as a popular ensemble in the northern countries begins ca. 1375, expanding to three players ca. 1380. See Polk, *German Instrumental Music*, pp. 52–53. On the ensemble and its origin see Welker, "Alta Capella."

55. See the discussion of the shawm and its origin in chapter 2.

56. The first recorded instance of a reed ensemble in Florence is from 1384, when three German pipers ("pifferorum et sonatorum cornamusarum et aliorum instrumentorum") were jailed for playing in the streets of the city; ASF: PR No. 73, fol. 74.

57. There were a number of such ensembles in the Low Countries, possibly beginning as early as 1389 in northern cities such as Arnhem, Deventer, and Den Haag, and shortly

after in the German cities of Nuremberg, Augsburg, and Cologne. See Polk, *German Instrumental Music*, pp. 60–64.

58. ASF: PR No. 73, fol. 74, for August 2, 1384. The players may not have actually been from Germany; the designation *Alamanni* (later in the document, *tilimanni*) often was used indiscriminately to refer to all northerners.

59. *Statuta populi*, vol. 2, rubric 40.

60. In this case, it was decided that the players did not know of the law and therefore were pardoned.

61. Playing *mattinate* for processions on Sundays and specific holy days at Orsanmichele was specified in 1388 as part of the duties of the Florentine pifferi and added to the next revision of the civic statutes in 1415. See ASF: PR No. 77, 171r, for October 21, 1388; and *Statuta populi*, vol. 2, rubric 59. For the opinion that *mattinata* referred to loud, ceremonial sounds to attract attention to a morning celebration, see the discussion in Klapisch-Zuber, *Women, Family, and Ritual*, pp. 261–82.

62. On the prominence of German pifferi throughout Europe, see Polk, *German Instrumental Music*, pp. 110–15, and Tröster, *Das Alta-Ensemble*, pp. 150–52.

63. For list of northern cities that employed pifferi ensembles, see Polk, *German Instrumental Music*, pp. 109–10.

64. See Wright, *Music at the Court of Burgundy*, p. 29.

65. On various lavish feasts in Avignon during the mid- to late fourteenth century, see Tomasello, *Music and Ritual*, p. 120.

66. For a discussion of the French influence on the Milan court, see Gallo, *Music in the Castle*, ch. 2. For a discussion of French influence in other Italian compositions of the fourteenth century see Long, "Musical Tastes in 14th-Century Italy," pp. 87–88.

67. The influence in this case would have been more general, along the lines of the reverence for northern values rather than a specific image of the musical ensembles; although trombetti were present in Milan during the fourteenth century, there is no evidence of an ensemble of pifferi until the mid-fifteenth century under the reign of Galeazzo Maria Sforza. Kurtzman and Koldau, "Trombe, Trombe d'argento," 5.15, discusses an ensemble of six trumpets in Milan from the early fourteenth century. Also see Lubkin, *A Renaissance Court*, pp. 104–105.

68. Wright, *Music at the Court of Burgundy*, p. 24. It is interesting that Wright notes that in 1391, John of Aragon also recruited his shawm and bagpipe players from Germany.

69. Trexler, *The Libro*, p. 10.

70. On Philip's lavish events and the attempts of other rulers to imitate him, see ibid., pp. 1–7.

71. Bowles, "Instruments at the Court of Burgundy," p. 43.

72. On the early history of the *basse danse*, see Crane, *Materials*; and Heartz, "The Basse Dance." On the early *bassadanza*, see Sparti, *Guglielmo Ebreo*; and Nevile, *The Eloquent Body*. On the prominence of dance at the Sforza court, see Southern, "A Prima Ballerina."

73. Polk, *German Instrumental Music*, p. 53.

74. This is a point made in Long, "Francesco Landini," p. 86.

75. In Brucker, *Two Memoirs*, p. 49.

76. Wright, *Music at the Court of Burgundy*, pp. 29–32.

77. Ibid., pp. 34–35.

78.

Nota, che a' di 26 di Settembre 1386, in mercoledi, il Comune di Firenze mandò in Francia al Re di Francia ambasceria grande, e bella; e dicesi che son iti per adoperare, che parentado si faccia tra il fiigliuolo del Duca d'Angiò, ed una figliuola del Re Carlo, e per piu altre cose. Gli ambasciadori furono questi: Mes. Gherrdo di Mes. Lorenzo Buondelmonti Cavaliere, Mes. Vanni di Michele di Vanni Castellani Cavaliere, Mes. Filippo di Meser Tommaso Corsini Dottor di Legge. Andarono, e mossonsi in mercoledi mattina, quasi presso valico Terza, detto di 26 di Settembre, molto orrevoli di vestimenta, di compagnia, d'arnesi, e di cavalli.

*Delizie degli eruditi toscani*, vol. 18, pp. 87–88. The event is also recorded in Anonimo fiorentino, *Cronica volgare*.

79. See Najemy, *Corporatism and Consensus*, p. 267.

80. Wright, *Music at the Court of Burgundy*, p. 35.

81. For a description of the ceremonies at the papal court in Avignon, see Tomasello, *Music and Ritual*, p. 120. He reports that during the reign of Gregory XI (1370–78), singers from the papal chapel performed during mealtime.

82. "In queste poesie a me pare sopr'ogni altra cosa notevole la serietà degl'intenti. Non ballatette e madrigali, non canzoni a rigoletto lascive s'intonavano alla Mensa de' Signori." Flamini, *La lirica toscana*, p. 198.

83. Brucker, *The Civic World*, pp. 80–89.

84. Najemy, "Civic Humanism," p. 87.

85. Weinstein, "The Myth of Florence," p. 20.

86. Field, "Leonardo Bruni," p. 1125.

87. I have paraphrased the conclusion of Brucker, "Humanism, Politics," p. 11.

88. Jurdjevic, "Civic Humanism," p. 1005.

89. Ibid.

90. "Quoniam dignitati amplitudini ac decori Florentine civitatis eiusque status et regiminis minime decus esse videtur, titulus dominationis ipsius qui Dominos artium priores appellat, quasi humilibus abiectisque personis atque infimis negotiis presidere eos insinuet." ASF: Balie, 29, fols. 118v–19r, for January 30, 1459; cited in A. Brown, *The Medici*, p. 298. I am indebted to Gene Brucker for bringing this to my attention.

91. See Polk, *German Instrumental Music*, pp. 70–71, where he reports examples of northern pifferi from this period who, in addition to various woodwind instruments, also played string instruments such as lutes.

92. For a discussion of the class distinction concerning which instruments were played, see ch. 6.

93. ASF: PR No. 104, fol. 5r; quoted in Brucker, "Bureaucracy and Social Welfare," p. 8.

94. Atlas, "Pandolfo III Malatesta," p. 53.

95. "Bartolomei Cecchini de Urbino sonatoris cennamelle quamvis sciat etiam sonare alia." ASF: PR No. 94, fol. 39. Bartolomeo is found in the pay records for only this one year.

96. The only instrumentalists known to be musically literate during this period were those closely associated with composition. This included keyboard players and certain lutenists and harpists, but rarely civic musicians or minstrels. See Polk, "Ensemble Performance."

97. Giovanni was sometimes entered in the pay records with the familiar nickname "nanni" or "nannes."

98. Following his dismissal in 1398, Grullo was succeeded for a short time by Bartolomeo Guglielmini, according to ASF: PR No. 87, fol. 344, for 1398. The *Provvisioni* of the following year, however, name Niccolao as his replacement without mentioning Bartolomeo, ASF: PR No. 88, fol. 210, for 1399.

99. ASF: PR No. 94, fol. 39, for 1405.

100. ASF: PR No. 96, fol. 142r, for August 17, 1406; as reported in Zippel, *I suonatori*, pp. 15–16.

101. ASF: CC No. 14, fol. 249, for 1406–1407.

102. ASF: PR No. 105, fol. 228, for 1415. The next year Giorgo Johannis is called "Giorgio di Giovanni della Magna"; ASF: CC No. 22, fol. 257r, for 1416–17.

103. First recorded as a member of the pifferi in ASF: CC No. 20, fol. 266r, for 1414–15.

104. ASF: CC, UG No. 3, fol. 53r, for 1436–39.

105. "Filippo di francesco electo sonatore di ceramella contro tenore cioe piffero del comune." ASF: CC No. 17, fol. 247v, for 1409–10.

106. For a discussion and listing of Italian dances, see Gallo, "Il 'Ballare Lombardo'." For a modern edition of the dances, see McGee, *Medieval Instrumental Dances*.

107. Lute and organ were often played by the same musicians. On the frequency of this occurrence, see Polk, "Vedel and Geige," p. 520.

108. Although there are some records of instruments and voices performing composed polyphony together, the more usual performance practice of the period was for voices to perform without instruments. See Fallows, "Specific Information," and Leech-Wilkinson, *The Modern Invention*.

109. See the discussion of both the monophonic and polyphonic repertory at the Florentine Duomo and at other venues by visiting musicians in D'Accone, "Music and Musicians at Santa Maria del Fiore."

110. On the dissemination of northern repertory through Italy by means of the papal court after 1378, see Di Bacco and Nádas, "Verso uno 'stile internazionale'," and Strohm, *The Rise of European Music*, p. 22.

111. For a discussion of the melodic patterns, see McGee, "Eastern Influences."

112. For a discussion of the differences between Italian and French harmonic practices, see Seay, "Paolo da Firenze," and Long, "Musical Tastes."

113. On Landini's style and influences, see Long, "Francesco Landini."

114. Long, "Musical Tastes," p. 95, makes that point that Florentines accounted for half of the Italians resident in Avignon during the 1360s and 1370s.

115. Strohm, *The Rise of European Music*, p. 22.

116. Ibid. For a list of the singers in the papal chapel between 1376 and 1417, see Di Bacco and Nádas, "Verso uno 'stile internazionale'," pp. 37–62.

117. Ibid., p. 8.

118. Strohm, *The Rise of European Music*, pp. 106–107.

119. Ibid., pp. 117–18.

120. In the Italian manuscript in Paris, Bibliothèque Nationale, fonds Italien 568 (Pit), probably written by Paolo da Firenze ca. 1410, of the 199 compositions, twenty-nine are French: ten ballades, eleven rondeaux, and eight virelais. For a detailed discussion see Reaney, "The Manuscript Paris."

121. The manuscripts showing this influence are listed in Fallows, "French as a Courtly Language," p. 433. According to Fallows, after 1415 the balance changes to approximately 450 French songs vs. fewer than forty Italian ones.

122. The visit is recorded in great detail in del Corazza, "Diario fiorentino," pp. 256–76. See also D'Accone, "Music and Musicians at Santa Maria del Fiore."

123. On the council and its move from Ferrara to Florence, see Najemy, *A History*, pp. 287–88.

124. For detailed descriptions of Eugenius IV's visits, see Vespasiano da Bisticci, *The Vespasiano Memoirs*, pp. 19–23.

125. Anonymous, *Ars cantus mensurabilis*.

126. Johannes de Muris, *Écrits sur la musique*.

127. There is a close relationship between the sentiments expressed in many of these ceremonial motets and those seen in the poetry of the heralds. On the subject of ceremonial motets, see Cumming, "Music for the Doge." On the influence of northern music in Italy, see Strohm, *The Rise of European Music*, ch. 1.

128. See Strohm, *The Rise of European Music*, part 3. Strohm makes the case that by the end of the fourteenth century, leadership in musical matters had gravitated toward Burgundy (pp. 62–64).

129. On the manuscript, its provenance, contents, and the instruments for which it was intended, see Plamenac, "Keyboard Music"; McGee, "Instruments and the Faenza Codex"; Cavicchi, "Sacro e profano"; Memelsdorff, "Motti a Motti"; and Memelsdorff, "New Music."

130. Manuscripts prepared in or for Florence around the turn of the fifteenth century have been identified as Florence, Biblioteca Laurenziana Ms Mediceo Palatino 87; Paris, Bibliothèque Nationale, fonds Italien 568; Florence, Biblioteca Nazionale Centrale Ms Incunab. F.5.5; London, British Library, Ms Additional 29987; Lucca, Archivio di stato, MS 184; Perugia, Biblioteca comunale, "Augusta," Ms 3065; and Florence, Biblioteca Laurenziana, Archivio capitolare di San Lorenzo, Ms 2211. See Nádas, "Song Collections."

131. Pirrotta, "Music and Cultural Tendencies."

132. On sacred music in Florence see D'Accone, "The Singers of San Giovanni."

133. See, for example, the discussion of the importation of chapel singers from France, Burgundy, and the Low Countries by Galeazzo Maria Sforza, in Prizer, "Music at the Court of the Sforza," pp. 156–59. A study of French influence on music in Padua can be found in Hallmark, "Some Evidence."

134. Performance of Franco-Netherlandish polyphonic repertory by the wind ensemble of Philip the Good is described in the opening lines of *Le Champion des dames* by Martin le Franc, written in 1441–42. See Myers, "Slide Trumpet Madness," p. 384.

## 5. Civic Music and the Medici

1. On the background and rise of the Medici family, see Brucker, "The Medici."

2. For details, see Najemy, *A History*, pp. 254–62.

3. For a recent detailed study of Florentine politics and the way in which the Medici manipulated the city and the citizens, see ibid., chs. 9–12. On Cosimo de' Medici, see Kent, *Cosimo de' Medici*.

4. "Canzone di messer Antonio di Matteo, cavaliere araldo della magnifica Signoria di Firenze, fatta nel 1434, finito lo squittinio di questo reggimento, cconfortando i suoi cittadini a conoscere le tante grazie da Dio ricevute." Siena, Biblioteca Comunale, cod. H. XI 54; published in Lanza, *Lirici toscani*, vol. 2, pp. 87–90.

5. In Lanza, *Lirici toscani*, vol. 2, pp. 94–95.

6. "Un chapitolo fatto da giovanni di maffeo volendo ghrazia da cchosimo de medici." BNF: Magl. II. II. 40, fol. 119v; published in Lanza, *Lirici toscani*, vol. 1, pp. 691–92.

7. Quoted in Kent, *Cosimo de' Medici*, p. 118.

8. Ibid., p. 49.

9. The reality was considerably different. See Kent, *Cosimo de' Medici*; and Najemy, *A History*, pp. 278–98.

10. The way in which the Medici faction controlled the government elections is detailed in Rubinstein, *The Government of Florence*.

11. Quoted in ibid., p. 146.

12. Brucker, "The Medici," p. 26. On Medici banking, see Holmes, "How the Medici."

13. Holmes, "How the Medici," p. 358.

14. Kent, *Cosimo de' Medici*; Jurdjevic, "Civic Humanism," p. 1010. On the general atmosphere of art patronage during this period, see Najemy, *A History*, ch. 11.

15. On the Medici Palace, see Hatfield, "Some Unknown Descriptions."

16. Elam, "Cosimo de' Medici," p. 158.

17. The statutes of 1325 are published in *Statuta popoli*, and those of 1415 are published in *Statuti della Repubblica*.

18. In the 1355 statutes the cost of the cloaks had risen to sixteen lire. ASF: Statuti No. 19, 1355, book 1, fol. 38r, v.

19. For speculation on a more musical repertory for fifteenth-century Italian trumpet ensembles, see Downey, "A Renaissance Correspondence."

20. See Polk, "Ensemble Performance."

21. ASF: SC No. 114, fol. 132r, for December 13, 1512.

22. Trexler, *The Libro*, p. 121. This number includes both Jacopo di Giorgi de Mediolano and Bastiano di Michele Tornaio, who were sharing a single shawm appointment; see ch. 6.

23. The records include only Giorgio, Marco, and Filippo as pensioners: ASF: PR No. 134, fol. 147, for October 9, 1443; and fols. 191–93, for January 20, 1444. Bastiano, who by that time had served for only six years, is not mentioned.

24.

Auctoritas in dominos et collegia conducendi tres pifferos et unum sonitorem tube torte cum eis, forenses.

Quinto provvisionem infrascriptam . . . .

Quod domini et collegia, et seu due partes eorum, possint et valea[n]t usque ad per totum mensem octobris proxime futuri eligere et conducere ad servitia dominationis usque in tres pifferos et sonitores pifferorum sive ceramelle, et unum sonitorem tube tortuose cum dictis pifferis, qui sint forenses et alienigene, qui non fuerint neque steterint ad servitium dominationis Florentine, pro tempore et termino unius anni initiandi prout continebitur in sua electione, cum oneribus, salario, emolumentis et aliis ordinatis pro pifferis dominationis eiusdem, solvendis de ea pecunia et per eos et eo modo, de qua et per quos et prout solvi consuevit pifferis et sonitoribus predictis dicte dominationis. . . .

Hoc ad declarationem apposito quod salarium dicti sonitoris tube tortuose sit illud idem quod habent tubicines dominationis eiusdem, pro mense quolibet, singula singulis congrue referendo. . . .

Hoc in predictis proviso et declarato quod huiusmodi conducendi teneantur et debeant et continuo tenere et portare ad pectus smaltum seu formalium argenteum cum signo lilii rubei, et ultra predicta teneantur et debeant habere pifferum et seu ceramellam et seu tubam argenteam prout ordinamenta dicti comunis disponunt

ASF: PR No. 134, fol. 97v, for August 27, 1443.

25. This is not the same person as Giorgio di Giovanni/Giorgius Johannis, who is listed in the same record as on pension.

26. The identifications are found in ASF: CC No. 4, fol. 52, for 1446–48. In a private communication, Keith Polk has suggested that Spuga would most likely be a corruption of Augsburg, a city known at that time for its wind instrumentalists. Another possibility would be Splügen, which would have been a small village at the time.

27. The convoluted and labored descriptions of the *tube tortuose* in the pay records suggest that the scribe was unfamiliar with it and was attempting to relate it to an instrument he knew: a large trumpet, i.e. a trombone, but not exactly. In the pay records it is given several different terms in an attempt to describe it as a large trumpet-like instrument with bends in the tubing: *tube tortuose, trombone grosso cum tromba roto, tube torte*. By this time the civic trombetti had been playing S-shaped instruments for a number of years, and therefore a simple trumpet with bent tubing would not have caused this kind of confusion. By calling this instrument a "large bent tube" and "large trumpet," the scribe must have been attempting to describe an instrument close to the length of a large trumpet, but with unusual bends. It is speculated that at the end of the fourteenth century a slide trumpet was developed: an S-shaped trumpet with a movable mouthpipe, called a *trompette des menestrels*. It is first mentioned at the court of Philip the Bold in 1386, and recorded as a part of the musical entourage of an unnamed German bishop; see Wright, *Music at the Court of Burgundy*, p. 41. (Wright suggests that the bishop may have been Frederick of Saarwerden, archbishop of Cologne.) By the end of the fifteenth century this instrument led to the invention of the double-slide instrument that would now be called a trombone. On the controversy concerning the slide trumpet, see Downey, "The Renaissance Slide Trumpet," and the replies in *Early Music* 17 (1989) by Myers, "Slide Trumpet Madness"; Polk, "The Trombone"; and Duffin, "The *trompette des menestrels*." The date of the invention of the trombone is still in question. On that subject, see Polk, *German Instrumental Music*, pp. 56–68, and McGee, "Misleading Iconography." For a history of the early trombone, see Carter, *The Early Trombone*.

28. D'Aconne, *The Civic Muse*, pp. 515, 521–23.

29. Ibid., p. 522. For more on Garino (Garinus Bornheti) and his time in Avignon, see Peters, "Urban Minstrels," p. 222.

30. "Non fo veduta mai cantar calandra, Comme fece Solazo a questa fiata, Che paria pifer venuto di Fiandra." Debenedetti, *Simone Prodenzani*, appendix B, poem no. 3. Also see Nádas, "A Cautious Reading," p. 31.

31. Context suggests that the *sonate* were a type of plucked instrument, but I cannot identify which one.

32. From the end of Serdini's *capitolo* "Soccorrimi, per Dio," published in *Rimatori del tardo Trecento*, p. 215.

33. Atlas, "Pandolfo III Malatesta," pp. 52–53.

34. Lockwood, *Music in Renaissance Ferrara*, p. 68. A piffero with the same name, Corrado da Alamania, is also recorded in Siena from as early as 1408; see D'Accone, *The Civic Muse*, p. 517.

35. Baroncini, "Zorzi Trombetta and the Band," p. 68.

36. Polk, *German Instrumental Music*, pp. 68–69.

37. D'Accone, "Some Neglected Composers," p. 263.

38. Based on the formula in Goldthwaite, *The Building of Renaissance Florence*, appendix 1. Because the value of the lira and the soldo vs. the florin was constantly changing, these conversions are only approximate.

39.

Sonitorum ceramelle et tube turtuose, augmentum salarii,

Exponitur cum debita reverentia vobis magnificis et potentibus dominis, dominis Prioribus Artium et Vexillifero Justitie Populi et Comunis Florentie pro parte sonitorum
ceramelle et tube turtuose vestre dominationis quod salarium ipsorum est florenorum
quatuor cum dimidio pro quolibet mense et pro quolibet eorum, quod factis defalcationi-
bus que in camera fiunt redit ad minorem summam librarum decem septem cum dimidio
in mense.

Et quod aliqui ipsorum suas uxores et familias conduxerunt et alii conducere vellent
quia dispositi sunt, domino concedente, fermare in hac patria in perpetuum sibi et suis
posteris sedem suam, sed expensa eorum qui suas familias conduxerunt magna fuit et
similiter erit aliorum conducere volentium, et per hoc et quia etiam non sunt naturaliter
assueti vivere cum tam magna parsimonia prout sunt oriundi de istis partibus, non pos-
sent cum tam parvo salario regere et subvenire opportunitatibus eorum familie et ire bene
indutos et decoratos prout convenit honori excellentissime dominationis vestre et iam satis
expenderunt in vestibus et aliis que occurrunt ad exercitium eorum. . . .

Quare Vobis dominis supradictis pro parte predicta divotissime supplicatur et petitur
. . . salarium dictorum sonitorum ceramelle et tube tortuose ad presens conductorum sit
et esse intelligatur auctum et reductum et seu constitutum ad libras viginti duas et soldos
decem flor. parv. pro quolibet ipsorum et quolibet mense temporis futuri.

ASF: PR 136, fol. 209v, for 26 October 26, 1445; published in Cellesi, "Documenti," 35
(1928): 574–75.

40.

Sonitoris tube tortuose presentis augmentum salarii de libris octo

. . . Actento magnifici et potentes domini Priores Artium et Vexillifer Justitie Populi
et comunis florentie quod presens tubicen tube tortuose qui pulsat cum tubicinibus seu
pifferis dominationis et exellens in eo exercitio ut omnibus est notum et intellecto quod
iam secreto extitit requisitus pro parte aliquorum principum et dominorum, ut ad servi-
endum ipsis in huiusmodi exercitio . . . et putantes quod assignando sibi aliquod maius
salarium erit verisimiliter causa obviandi ne pergat alio, sed ad servitia huius dominationis
remaneat. . . .

Et Domini inter ipsos omnes in sufficienti numero congregati in palatio populi Florentie . . . ordinaverunt et deliberaverunt die quarto mensis septembris anno domini millesimo
quadrigentesimo quinquagesimo secundo, indictione quintadecima. Quod dicto presenti
tubatori tube tortuose ultra salarium pro eo ad presens ordinatum dentur et solvantur
nomine augmenti eius salarii libre octo floren. parv. in et pro quolibet mense quo serviet
dominationi . . . sine aliqua retentione vel diminutione.

ASF: PR No. 143, fol. 222, for September 4, 1452; published in Cellesi, "Documenti,"
35 (1928): 577–78.

41. First recorded in ASF: CC No. 15, 1469–73, fol. 22, for 1472.

42. ASF: CC, RD No. 1, 1458, pp. 86–87. The average wage for a skilled worker in
Florence during the fifteenth century was approximately one lira per day (= twenty-four lire
per month), and half that for an unskilled worker. Goldthwaite, *The Building of Renaissance
Florence*, pp. 317–31.

43. According to Trexler, *The Libro*, pp. 42–43, the herald received ten florins per year
from the Capitano del Popolo. According to the version of Gregorio Dati's diary published
in Pratesi, *L'"Istoria di Firenze*," p. 147, the salary of the herald was a total of 120 florins per
year, made up of sixty florins from the office of the Capitano and Podestà, and three florins
per month from the Signoria (an amount confirmed by the pay records). The entry does
not indicate who provided the other twenty-four florins. There is some question as to when
this entry was written and by whom. On the preceding page are found statements about

the numbers and income of the civic musicians that would not have been correct until after 1445, which was ten years after Dati's death and forty years after the reputed writing of his history.

44. By 1515 the ratio of the lira to the florin had deteriorated to approximately 7:1, while the ratio of the lira to the soldo remained fixed at 20:1. See Goldthwaite, *The Building of Renaissance Florence*, appendix 1.

45. Trexler, *The Libro*, p. 121.

46. Brucker, "Bureaucracy and Social Welfare," p. 6, notes that some of the *famiglia* were able to gain tips for assisting certain citizens in gaining access to the Priors.

47.

Tubicines, Pifferi et alii sonitores dominationis non possint ire extra civitatem ad aliquod festum nec intra civitatem ad faciendum aliquam serenatam vel mattinatam.

Magnifici et et potentes domini, domini Priores Artium et Vexillifer Justitie populi et comunis Florentie, considerantes quod multa festa fiunt extra civitatem Florentie ed in variis terris et locis.

Et propterea domini sepe requiruntur a facientibus dicta festa quibus forte opus esset habere tubicines aut pifferos et alios sonitores dominationis pro honorando dicta festa ut eis concedant huiusmodi sonitores. Et quamquam etiam ab ipsismet pifferis et tubicinibus solum requiruntur abque [sic] sepe inconvenientia et scandala oriuntur.

Cum dominationi non debitus resultet honor aut servitium prout decet presertim quia sepe contingit dominos accedentes ad aliquas oblationes aut festa carere suis sonitoribus, aut cum valde paucis accedere, quod non est absque dedecore eiusdem dominationis et consequenter et comunis Florentie. Et propterea volentes huic defectui aliqualiter modum et strictiorem viam prebere ut minus occurrat que sit possibile, habita super his invicem et una cum officiis Gonfaloneriorum societatum populi et Duodecim bonorum virorum dicti comunis deliberatione solemni....

Quod aliquis tubicen seu tubator vel ex pifferis et sonitoribus dominationis seu palatii populi Florentini nullo modo possint ire extra civitatem Florentie ad aliquam civitatem, castrum vel locum, pro seu causa pulsandi, ad festum quodcunque vel solemnitatem que ibi fieret nisi prius concessa fuerit expressa licentia et deliberatio dominorum Priorum Artium et Vexilliferi Justitie et Collegiorum suorum obtento partito et deliberatione inter pre-dictos pro quodlibet vice per xxxiiij fabas nigras eorum ad minus redditas per principales et non substitutos et non aliter. Aliquin incidat in penam librarum centum et amissionis officii seu exercitii eorum a quo ipso facto intelligatur cassus et remotus vigore presentis provisionis.

Itemque nullus predictorum sonitorum palatii possit ire intus in civitate Florentie ad sonandum, seu pulsandum vel faciendum aliquam serenatam aut mattinatam alicui ora-toribus seu ambasciatoribus, dominis, capitaneis, conducteriis [sic] aut conestabilibus vel cuicunque alteri persone cuiuscunque status conditionis fuerit, exceptis quibuscunque offitiis civium ad que accedi consuevit more consueto sub eadem pena et preiudiciis pre-dictis nisi obtenta prius expressa licentia et deliberatione dominorum Priorum Artium et Vexilliferi Justitie per novem fabas nigras eorum redditas per ipsosmet principales et non substitutos.

ASF: PR No. 139, for June 26, 1448. Published in Cellesi, "Documenti," 35 (1928): 575–76. See a similar statement in the 1415 statutes, published in *Statuta populi*, vol. 2, rubric 40, pp. 541–44.

48. ASF: PR No. 158, fol. 13v, for 1467; and PR No. 166, fol. 140v–141v, for 1475.

49. ASF: PR No. 168, fol. 89r–89v, for 10 August 10, 1477; and fol. 159v–160r, for De-cember 7, 1477.

50. Here and elsewhere I refer to the "tips" gained by the musicians when they per-formed in addition to their usual duties, including for private functions. It is probable that

much of this was actually fees charged for services rendered, but I have no documents to substantiate that speculation.

51.

> Et quod omne illud, quod largi fine, & seu pro dono, vel alio modo percipietur per dictos sonatores, seu eis dabitur, vel eis largietur quomodocumque, & sub quacumque spe, vel re, tertia pars intelligatur esse, & sit tubatorum nacharini, & cemmamellarii, & duae reliquae partes sint, & pertineant trombettinis, & pifferis dicti communis, & sic dividi debeat inter eos, & non aliter quoquomodo, nec aliquis ex praedictis aliter, vel alio modo petere possint, vel habere debeant sub poena praedicta, & quoties contrafactum erit.

ASF: Statuti 1415, rubric 40. Published in *Statuta populi*, vol. 2.

52. Ibid.

53. See, for example, ASF: CO, beginning with No. 21, for 1413.

54. As an example of how elaborate these festivities could be, the list of musicians imported from various cities and courts to Urbino for the engagement of Guidobaldo da Montefeltro to Elisabeta Gonzaga on July 1, 1475, was ninety-four trumpets (including four from Florence); twenty-seven pifferi (three from Florence), six trombones, eighteen tamburini (two from Florence), nine lutes, four harps, and two corni (*cornetti?*). Reported in *Nozze, Guidi—Paolucci*, pp. 17–22.

55. The monopoly, of course, would not prevent performances at unofficial public or private celebrations by any capable musician.

56. ASF: SC No. 94, for 1477–78.

57. In this case I have translated *zufolo* as flute rather than as "recorder," as I have in earlier chapters. There is no known association of recorder with drums as a duet.

58.

> Desiderando e magnifici et excellenti Signori pro honore publico et magnificentia della Signoria acrescere il numero de sonatori et havere più varietà di suoni providono et ordinarono che pro virtù della presente provisione Giovanni di Benedetto Fei vocato Feo et Michele de Bastiano vocato Talina, sonatori di zuffolo et tamburino, s'intendino essere et sieno electi et deputati al servigio de magnifico [*sic*] et excellenti Signori ogni volta che la Signoria andrà fuori del palagio et etiam qualunque altra volta per loro parte ne saranno richiesti, con salario di lb 4 il mese per ciascuno di loro sanza altro emolumento.

ASF: PR No. 200, fol. 61v–62r, for 1509–10.

59. This was also the association in Germany at that time; see Polk, *German Instrumental Music*, p. 118.

60. The iconographical evidence is almost exclusively in the context of Swiss military; ibid.

61. Ibid., p. 41.

62. On the songs and the tradition, see McGee with Mittler, "Information on Instruments."

63. Published with original Italian in ibid., pp. 458–60.

64. The existence of this ensemble as a part of the musical ensemble of Maximilian I is mentioned in Polk, "Vedel and Geige," p. 515.

65. The payrolls list five *tibiatores* (i.e., shawm players), but they include both Jacopo di Giorgio de Mediolano and Bastiano di Michele Tornaio, who shared a single position between 1502 and 1519; see below.

66. They are present in the lists of *famiglia* in ASF: SC No. 112, 147r–v, for December 12, 1510; No. 113, fol. 143v, for December 11, 1511.

67. This is clearly explained in D'Accone, "The Singers of San Giovanni," pp. 308–16.

68. ASF: MAP 7, No. 301, for July 8, 1455.

69. See Schevill, *History of Florence*, pp. 371–74. For a different interpretation, see Najemy, *A History*, pp. 98–306.

70. Strozzi, *Lettere*, p. 423. The visit is also recorded in Trexler, *The Libro*, p. 82, although with only three hundred horsemen.

71. Strozzi, *Lettere*, p. 431.

72. Southern, "A Prima Ballerina," pp. 191–93.

73. Ibid., pp. 190–91.

74. D'Accone, "Lorenzo the Magnificent and Music," pp. 269–70; and D'Accone, "Lorenzo il Magnifico," p. 234.

75. See D'Accone, "Lorenzo il Magnifico," p. 226. On the exaggerated myth of Antonio Squarcialupi, see Haar and Nádas, "Antonio Squarcialupi."

76. Letter from Teodoro da Montefeltro to the Marchesa Barbara of Brandenburg, wife of Marchese Ludovico Gonzaga of Mantua, February 6, 1460. Archivio di Stato di Mantova, Archivio Gonzaga, busta 1099, fol. 603–604. Translation from Prizer, "Games of Venus," pp. 3–4.

77. Of the songs in Bianca's repertory mentioned in the above description, "Fortuna" is possibly Johannes Bedyngham's "Fortune, helas," and "Duogl'angoseus" is probably the chanson "Dueil angoisseux" by Gilles Binchois; ibid., pp. 5–6. Prizer notes that keyboard intabulations of both these works are found in the Buxheimer manuscript, Munich, Staatsbibliothek, Ms Cim. 352b.

78. Identification of the named repertory is from Prizer, "Games of Venus," pp. 5–6.

79. It is possible that the accompanying musicians were instrumentalists, although the mixture of instruments with voices in performances of polyphonic repertory is now thought to have begun much later in the century. See Leech-Wilkinson, *The Modern Invention*, ch. 1.

80. There would have been no mention of the musicians because they were hired and therefore, in the eyes of the letter writer, were not guests of the Monsignor, thus not meriting mention any more than the other servants.

81. Kent, *Lorenzo de' Medici*, p. 2.

82. Ibid., p. 28.

83. As pointed out by F. W. Kent in "The Young Lorenzo," pp. 3–4, "He had already, aged sixteen, begun adding to his family's collection of *anticaglie* 'anything precious and rare,' [he] was a book collector when fourteen or so, and was the preternaturally mature acquaintance . . . of leading intellectuals such as Leon Batista Alberti and Marsilio Ficinio."

84. On Lorenzo's involvement in *sacre rappresentazioni*, see Ventrone, "Per una morfologia," and Newbigin, "Politics in the *Sacre rappresentazioni*." On his dance choreographies, see Nevile, *The Eloquent Body*, pp. 29–34.

85. Guicciardini, *The History of Florence*, pp. 70–71. On Guicciardini's views about Lorenzo, see A. Brown, "Lorenzo and Guicciardini." For another assessment of Lorenzo's character and accomplishments see Najemy, *A History*, ch. 12.

86. Trexler, *Public Life*, p. 409, makes the case that after 1471 Lorenzo actually diminished some of the public celebrations as a way of convincing foreign rulers that he was a serious person.

87. The other contestants were Braccio di Niccola de' Medici, Dionigi di Puccio Pucci, Piero di Giovanni Vespucci, Salvestro di Jacopo Benci, Jacopo di Poggio Bracciolini, Carlo di Antonio Borromei, Giovanni del Forte da Vico, Benedetto d'Antonio Salutati, a soldier representing Roberto Sansoverino known only as Boniforte, and three teams: Piero di Luca

Pitti and Piero Piero Antonio di Luigi Pitti, Piero da Trani and Marco da Vicenza, and Francesco and Guglielmo di Andrea de Pazzi. Gori, *Le feste fiorentine*, vol. 1, *Le feste per San Giovanni*, p. 89.

88. Pulci, "La Giostra di Lorenzo," in *Opere minori*, pp. 55–120.

89. A narrative account of the event states that there were many musicians: "più sonatori di tamburi, pifferi, trombe." Quoted in Gori, *Le feste fiorentine*, vol. 1, *Le feste per San Giovanni*, p. 91.

90. Pulci, *Opere minori*, "La Giostra," stanzas 63, 73, and 86.

91. "Palle, palle," which was a rallying call for the Medici, is a reference to the balls on the family crest. A few decades later Heinrich Isaac wrote a composition around the call. See Atlas, "Heinrich Isaac's Palle palle."

92. BNF: Magl. II. IV. 324, 108r; published in Parenti Fiorentino, *Delle Nozze*; and Parenti, *Lettere*, appendix.

93. D'Accone, "Lorenzo the Magnificent and Music," p. 260.

94. D'Accone, "Lorenzo il Magnifico e la musica," pp. 221, 224.

95. The inventory of Lippi's possessions at the time of his death in 1504 includes a lute and five recorders. See McGee "Filippino Lippi and Music," p. 16.

96. On Piero's performance ability, see the letter to Lorenzo from Angelo Poliziano, June 5, 1490, reproduced in Martelli, *Studi laurenziani*, p. 146. On Giovanni's lute performance see Cummings, *The Politicized Muse*, p. 13.

97. Active recruiting of musicians from the north was apparently widespread in northern Italy. It is recorded in references to the vocal and instrumental musical ensembles in Milan, Ferrara, Mantua, and Siena, to name only a few cities that indulged in the practice.

98. D'Accone, "Lorenzo the Magnificent and Music," p. 260.

99. The registers and many of the letters are found in the MAP files of the ASF. Letters to and from Lorenzo are in the process of being published in transcription in Medici, *Lettere*.

100. The letter is translated in D'Accone, *The Civic Muse*, p. 537. Unfortunately for Antonio, the pifferi at that time, Cornelio di Piero of Flanders, Giorgio d'Arigo d'Alamannia, and Giovanni di Benedetto, had been members for over fifteen years, and the ensemble would remain unchanged until 1472, when Cornelio was replaced by his son, Giusto di Cornelio.

101. ASF: MAP 23, 230, for January 24, 1470.

102. ASF: MAP 30, 193, for March 22, 1473 [1474]. It is not clear whether Santi was hired. Two members of the Florentine trombetti were named Santi at this point but both seem to have been members for several years before this date.

103. "Bon maestro di sonare il soprano." ASF: MAP 35, fol. 104. Quoted in Becherini, "Relazione di musici fiamminghi," p. 105. There is no record of a Leonardo as a civic musician in Florence at that time.

104. The letters are from Tromboncino, ASF: MAP 41, 67; and from Michel Schubinger, ASF: MAP 41, 158. Both are published in Becherini, "Relazione di musici fiamminghi," pp. 107–109. Additional dealings of Lorenzo with instrumentalists are discussed in D'Accone, "Lorenzo the Magnificent," pp. 280–82.

105. For details of the performance careers of members of the Schubinger family see Polk, *German Instrumental Music*, pp. 76–77.

106. ASF: MAP 20, 582. Printed in Zippel, *I suonatori*, pp. 34–35.

107. Cordié, *Opere di Baldassare Castiglione*, p. 508, and Symonds, *The Autobiography*, p. 9.

108. On the dismissal and reinstatement see McGee, "Giovanni Cellini, Piffero of Florence," pp. 210–25.

109. ASF: MAP 68, 626; Giovanni piffero to Giovanni Gismondo da Angnullo, March 3, [1465].

110. ASF: MAP 137, 139; Giovanni piffaro to Lorenzo de' Medici, April 3, 1465.

111. ASF: MAP 23, 22; Luca Pitti to Lorenzo di Piero di Cosimo.

112. ASF: MAP 23, 28; Giovanni pifero to Lorenzo de' Medici, June 16, 1465.

113. ASF: MAP 23, 57; Giovanni di Dominico to Lorenzo de' Medici, May 12, 1466.

114. ASF: PR No. 157, fol. 127v, August 20, 1466; and SC, SA No. 32, fol. 133r.

115. Lorenzo's eagerness to be involved in artistic and scholarly as well as political matters at a very early age is the subject of F. W. Kent, "The Young Lorenzo."

116. On the joust and its prize, see the poem "La Giostra," in Pulci, *Opere minori*, pp. 55–120. For a closer look at Lorenzo's irregular participation in public celebrations, see Ventrone, "Lorenzo's Politica festiva." On the Medici and Carnevale, see Plaisance, *Florence*, ch. 1.

117. Guicciardini, *The History of Florence*, p. 72.

118. Machiavelli, *Tutte le opere*, vol. 1, p. 843; Vasari, *Le vite*, vol. 4, p. 602; Grazzini, *Tutti i tronfi*, introduction.

119. See Ciappelli, *Carnevale e Quaresima*, pp. 95–98; Ventrone, "Note sul carnevale fiorentino"; and Prizer, "Petrucci and the Carnival Song."

120. See Ciappelli, *Carnevale e Quaresima*, p. 205. Much of the preceding two paragraphs has been taken from this source. See also Prizer, "Petrucci and the Carnival Song," pp. 219–23; and Newbigin, "Piety and Politics." Trexler, *Public Life*, p. 410, asserts that another reason for the diminished celebration during the ten years was Lorenzo's reluctance to appear in public following the Pazzi conspiracy of 1478.

121. On the long negotiations concerning Giovanni's elevation, especially those concerning the Florentine Chancellor Bartolomeo Scala, see A. Brown, *Bartolomeo Scala*, pp. 102–14.

122. Lorenzo's texts are published in Orvieto, *Lorenzo de' Medici*. See also Orvieto, "Carnevale e feste."

123. For a discussion of several other of Lorenzo's texts that dwell on themes of impending death, see Carew-Reid, *Les fêtes florentines*, pp. 109–14.

124. See Wilson, "Heinrich Isaac." For speculation as to who were the four singers, see McGee, "Florentine Instrumentalists," pp. 152–53.

125. For the text of the "Canzona dei sette pianeti," see Orvieto, *Lorenzo de' Medici*, pp. 83–84. See also Martelli, *Studi laurenziani*, ch. 2. For a recent discussion of the 1489 Carnevale and the "Canzona dei sette pianete," see Ventrone, "Note sul carnevale." For an enlightening and detailed discussion of the entire procedure of producing carnival songs and *carri*, see Prizer, "Reading Carnival."

126. D'Accone, "Lorenzo the Magnificent," pp. 278–79.

127. Rubinstein, *The Government of Florence*, pp. 268–69.

128. See Najemy, *A History*, p. 391.

129. Savonarola's charges are included in his *Trattato circa el reggimento e governo della città di Firenze*, 1498. See Savonarola, *Prediche sopra Aggeo*.

130. Under Savonarola's influence, in 1496 the Otto della Guardia banned *maschere* and public gatherings during carnival. See Ciappelli, *Carnevale e Quaresima*, p. 217.

131. D'Accone, "Some Neglected Composers," p. 263.

132. For a discussion of Savonarola's impact on secular music, see Prizer, "The Music Savonarola Burned."

133. Ibid., p. 13.

134. On *stili*, see ch. 1.

135. A tradition of rival youth groups throwing stones at one another at the Ponte Santa Trinita.

136. *Capanucci* were piles of wood intended for burning—a carnival tradition. See Ciappelli, *Carnevale e Quaresima*, p. 129.

137.

> Et perché prima consueti erano [I fanciulli] 'achattare per li stili, tale acto [Savonarola] fece loro fare per elimosine. Onde quasi in su ogni canto delle strade si vedeano altaruzzi con crocifissi et altre figure, dove 'fanciulli achattavano per distribuirsi poi a' poveri vergognosi et ad altri, secondo che a frate Jeronimo paressi. El dì finalmente di carnesciale, in cui ciascuno dedito essere suole a voluptà, a vedere l'opera di fanciulli si consumò. Notossi in tale cerimonie la ubidientia grande quale ebbono in tutte l'opere, ma molto fu da maravigliarsi del lasciare la inveterata consuetudine del fare a' sassi et fare li stili et capannucci, et ad achattare per dare per Dio volgersi. Così per ordine del frate si levorono due antichissime consuetudini, la prima fu del corrersi e palii, la seconda che per carnasciale il festeggiare si lasciassi et s'attemdessso a messe et processioni.

Piero di Marcho Parenti, Storia fiorentino, fol. 113–14, quoted in Ventrone, "Note sul carnevale fiorentino," p. 339.

138. Prizer, "The Music Savonarola Burned," pp. 9–10.

139. For a discussion of Savonarola's continuing influence in Europe, see Polizzotto, *The Elect Nation*; Dall'Aglio, *Savonarola in Francia*; and Dall'Aglio, *Savonarola e il savonarolismo*.

140. Information for this paragraph is taken from Ciappelli, *Carnevale e Quaresima*, pp. 213–33. A measure of Savonarola's declining power and popularity is recorded in Cerretani, *Storia fiorentina*, p. 242, that during Carnevale of 1498, prior to Savonarola's official fall from grace, a group of youths held a private banquet that included *maschere*, farces, and music; quoted in Prizer, "The Music Savonarola Burned," pp. 7–8. Trexler, "Florentine Theatre," pp. 471–72, records the following sequence in 1498: a "burning of the vanities" on February 28 (Ash Wednesday); after Savonarola's death in May, a festival that included songs mocking Savonarolans; and during the following Christmas season a particularly wild event that included the desecration of the churches of Santissima Annunziata, Santo Spirito, Santa Maria Novella, and the cathedral.

141. This was by no means a period of political stability; the regime of Lorenzo the Younger was perhaps the least popular of all the Medici regimes. See Najemy, *A History*, pp. 428–34.

142. Letter from Jacopo Guicciardini, quoted in Cummings, *The Politicized Muse*, pp. 15–16.

143. The account of the *trionfi* are taken from ibid., pp. 16–21. See also Ventrone, "Note sul carnevale fiorentino," pp. 330–31.

144. The letters are published in Sherr, "Lorenzo de' Medici," n. 12. To these can be added ASF: AD 2, (vol. 185), filza 353, fol. 90, a letter dated March 13, 1514, from the Captains of the Parte Guelfa to Francesco Vettori, urging him to speak with Pope Leo X on this matter. I am indebted to Patrick Macey for this source.

145. Sherr, "Lorenzo de' Medici," p. 628.

146. See discussion in ibid., p. 629.

147. Ibid., pp. 629–31.

148. Corazzini, *Ricordanze*, p. 205, quoted in Cummings, *The Politicized Muse*, pp. 94–95.

149. BNF: Magl. II. IV. 19, fols. 49v–50v, quoted in Cummings, *The Politicized Muse*, p. 99.

150. See discussion of the many events that transpired over several months in ibid., pp. 99–108.

151. Kristeller, "Francesco da Diacceto," pp. 330, 335; and Cummings, "The Sacred Academy."

152. On Giovanni de' Medici and music see Pirro, "Leo X and Music"; and Cummings, *The Politicized Muse*. On Giovanni's participation in vocal music while in Rome, see Brandolini, *On Music and Poetry*, p. 21.

153. On Florentine musicians in Rome, see Slim, "Musicians on Parnassus"; Pirro, "Leo X and Music"; Cummings, "Gian Maria Giudeo"; and Sherr, "Lorenzo de' Medici."

154. Benvenuto's story in this case is somewhat confused. He blames the dismissal on the Gonfaloniere Jacopo Salviati, but he is mistaken insofar as Salviati never held that office.

155. ASF: SC No. 116, fol. 29v, for March 30, 1514. There would seem to be a slight miscalculation in the years of service credited to Giovanni: only thirty-four years had elapsed since his first appointment in 1480, not subtracting the four years between 1491–95 when he was dismissed, and the two during which he was appointed without salary.

156. ASF: SC No. 116, fol. 102r, for September 19, 1514.

157. See Sherr, "Lorenzo de' Medici," pp. 629–30.

158. ASF: SC No. 116, fol. 29v, for March 30, 1514. The other musician was the trombone player Johannes Justi d'Alamania, alias Giovanni Como.

159. The series of permissions and then demands for his return are recorded in ASF: SC No. 128, fol. 12r, for February 15, 1525 [1526]; fol. 30r, for April 18; 53v, for June 30; fol. 84r, for September 6; fol. 97r, for October 28; and fol. 106r, for November 7. According to the salary records in the above document, he continued to be payed a full salary during his absence (fols. 216–25). On the varied employment career of Giangiacomo, see Sherr, "Lorenzo de' Medici"; Cummings, "Gian Maria Giudeo," pp. 312–13; and Frey, "Regesten zur Päpstlichen Kapelle," pp. 57, 140.

160. Cordié, *Opere di Baldassare Castiglione*, p. 539, and Symonds, *The Autobiography*, p. 36.

161. Cummings, *The Politicized Muse*, p. 67. Much of the next two paragraphs is taken from this source.

162. On the symbolism of the entrance, see Ciseri, *L'ingresso trionfale*.

163. This would seem to be the practice only for the visit of a pope. See the description of the 1459 entrance party on the visit of Pope Pius II above, ch. 1.

164. Description of the procession is taken from Cummings, *The Politicized Muse*, ch. 5, and Matteini, "La decorazione festiva," pp. 331–40.

165. For a discussion of the music for the arches, see Cummings, *The Politicized Muse*, ch. 5.

166. Vasari, *Le opere*, cited in Cummings, ibid., p. 72. Material for the preceding paragraphs taken from Trexler, *The Libro*; Ciseri, *L'ingresso*; and Cummings, *The Politicized Muse*.

167. The ceremony for Lorenzo the Younger is described in Trexler, *The Libro*, p. 117, and in Sanuto, *I diarii*, vol. 20, cols. 530–31, cited and translated in Cummings, *The Politicized*

*Muse*, pp. 93–94. The appointment of a local resident to the position of captain-general was in violation of the Florentine custom of appointing only foreign mercenaries.

168. For a detailed account of the end of the republic see Najemy, *A History*, ch. 15. For an account of these events from the point of the military, see Arfaioli, *The Black Bands*, chapter 2.

169. Najemy, *A History*, p. 464.

170. See Cantini, *Legislazione toscana*, vol. 1, pp. 5–17; and Rastrelli, *Storia d'Alessandro de'Medici*, pp. 304–26.

171. The last of the continuous records of the pifferi, trombetti, and trombadori that I could find is in ASF: MC No. 2036, fol. 93v, for January 29, 1532 [1533], which records payments to six trombadori, one naccharino, one cabamallario [*sic*], eight trombetti, three pifferi, and two tromboni.

172. ASF: Strozz., Serie 1, No. 13, fol. 12.

173. ASF: Mediceo No. 631, on a list pasted in the back of the book.

174. The designation *musico* could mean an instrumentalist, a composer, or a singer. These musicians are all listed in Kirkendale, *The Court Musicians*, appendix, along with the year they are first found on the salary rolls. In some cases Kirkendale was able to identify their voice or instrument from later records, but some are unknown.

175. Listed as a composer, ibid.

176. Identified as a basso, ibid.

177. ASF: Mediceo No. 631, 3.

178. D'Addario, "Burocrazia, economia e finanze," p. 377. The record is from 1561.

179. See ch. 3, n. 179.

180. ASF: Mediceo No. 631, 4, for 1559. The list also includes two *buffone*.

## 6. The Civic Musicians and Their Repertories

1. In the earliest records the members of the trombadori are often identified by their *sesto* in Florence, e.g., San Frediano.

2. ASF: PR No.168, fol. 112v–113r, for Sept 10, 1477.

3. For an example not involving musicians, in 1511 one Jacopo di Sandro Campanaio, a bell-ringer for the commune who had succeeded his father to that position in 1499, petitioned to have Bernardino di Bartolomeo di Nofri, his nephew, the son of his sister, appointed in his place since he could no longer serve because he had contracted the illness known commonly ("infermo del male chiamato volgarmente") as the *mal franchese*. ASF: PR No. 201, fol. 26r, for April 30, 1511.

4. ASF: PR No. 77, fol. 322r–323r, for February 12, 1388 [1389].

5. According to Zippel, *I suonatori*, p. 18, n. 1, the outstanding career of Bastiano's father is cited in the appointment, ASF: PR No. 129, fol. 111.

6. ASF: CC, CU No. 320.

7. ASF: CC No. 26.

8. ASF: CC, UG No. 4.

9. ASF: MAP 23, 57. Giovanni di Domenico to Lorenzo de' Medici, May 12, 1466, see ch. 5.

10. ASF: PR No. 159, fol. 208, for December 19, 1468.

11. ASF: PR No. 173, fol. 180r, for March 1, 1482 [1483].

12. ASF: PR No. 175, fol. 89r, for June 22, 1484.

13. ASF: PR No. 199, fol. 44v, for December 5, 1508.

14. ASF: PR No. 200, fol. 4v, for April 23, 1509.

15. ASF: CCN No. 131, f. 58, for June 17, 1521. On Giovanni Cellini's interesting story concerning the death of Pierino, as told by Benvenuto Cellini, see McGee, "Giovanni Cellini," pp. 217–88.

16. ASF: SC No. 134, fol. 29v–30r, for 1531–32. I have not been able to ascertain if Johannes Justi was the son of Justi Corneli, which would extend this succession to four generations of Florentine pifferi covering a period of eighty years: 1452, Cornelio Pieri di Fiandre (Flanders); 1468, Justus Corneli; 1497, Johannes Justi; 1452, Mathias Johannis Justi.

17. ASF: PR No. 188, fol. 46v, for December 31, 1497.

18. Ibid., fol. 76v, for September 16, 1489.

19. ASF: PR No. 193, fol. 56v, for October 13, 1502.

20. ASF: SC No. 111, fol. 49v–50r, for May 30, 1509.

21. ASF: SC No. 121, fol. 127, for December 14, 1519. For more details on the relationship and negotiations, see McGee, "In the Service of the Commune," pp. 734–35.

22. ASF: SC, D No. 163, 1475, reproduced in Zippel, *I suonatori*, p. 33.

23. Rubinstein, *Palazzo Vecchio*, pp. 1–2.

24. Brucker, "Bureaucracy and Social Welfare," pp. 10–11.

25. Cordié, *Opere di Baldassare Castiglione*, p. 508, and Symonds, *The Autobiography*, p. 9.

26. During the same period in England the various guilds sponsored theatrical and social events and regularly hired musicians, including members of the civic ensembles, for these occasions. See Dutka, *Music in the English Mystery Plays*; and the numerous publications of *Records of Early English Drama*.

27. There is also evidence that some of the larger guilds had their own musicians, usually trumpet players; see the various *catasto* records for 1427. The Parte Guelfa had its own trumpets and pifferi, such as Andrea da Panzano, piffero; ASF: Catasto 17, Quartieri Santo Spirito, gonfalone del nicchio, for 1427.

28. Cordié, *Opere di Baldassare Castiglione*, pp. 508–509, and Symonds, *The Autobiography*, p. 10.

29. Landucci, *Diario fiorentino*, pp. 272, 296–97; and Jervis, *Luca Landucci*, pp. 217, 236.

30. See Cummings, "Gian Maria Giudeo," p. 313, n. 3.

31. ASF: PR No. 201, fol. 26r, for April 30, 1511.

32. Cordié, *Opere di Baldassare Castiglione*, pp. 534–36; Symonds, *The Autobiography*, pp. 36–38.

33. The appointment first appears in ASF: SC No. 97, fol. 21r, for February 20, 1494 [1495], which states that Giovanni is appointed to play *contro alto* and *basso*, and then again on fol. 29v, for March 8, which states that he will replace Daniele de Johannis: "ad sonand in locum Danelis." Daniele must have been on a temporary leave, because his name appears on the list of the *famiglia* in that year and for several years afterwards.

34. ASF: PR No. 186, fol. 62v–63r, for June 20, 1495. Florence was not alone in adding members without pay to the musical ensembles. For discussions of this practice slightly later in Bologna and Bruges, see Gambassi, *Il Concerto Palatino*, document 285, and Polk, "Ensemble Instrumental Music," pp. 13–14.

35. ASF: SC No. 99, for 1497, fol. 58r, for June 30, 1497; and PR No. 188, fol. 27v, for October 26, 1497.

36. Note similar instances of a continued salary for an absent musician vis-à-vis Giovanni Domenico while incarcerated in 1466 (see ch. 5), and Gianjacomo da Cesena while on loan to the Vatican in 1526 (see ch 5.).

37. Cordié, *Opere di Baldassare Castiglione*, p. 508, and Symonds, *The Autobiography*, pp. 8–9.

38. ASF: SC No. 100, fol. 86r, for July 28, 1498. For details of this incident see McGee, "Giovanni Cellini," p. 213.

39. In spite of the fact that he was born and raised in Florence, the records always refer to him as "teotonico" or "d'alamania."

40. ASF: PR No. 188, fol. 28v, for October 26, 1497.

41. ASF: SC No. 134, fol. 30r, for October 14, 1531.

42.

Et considerantes, quod per sonatores tam communis Florentiae, quam etiam illos, qui non sunt deputati per dictum commune Florentiae committuntur quamplurima . . . Et ad tollendum omnem materiam scandali, quae posset evenire inter sonatores dicti communis Florentiae, & ad removendum praesumptiones, & etiam verecundas cupiditates lucrandi, decernimus, quod nullus ex sonatoribus cuiuscumque soni, seu infrascripti dicti communis Florentiae, & seu pro ipso communi electus, vel deputatus, quomodocumque possit, audeat, vel praesumat quoquomodo, nec quavis de causa ire extra civitatem Florentiae ad sonandum visitandum, seu aliter quomodocumque ioculandum.

Statutes of 1415, Rubric 40; publ. in *Statuta populi*, vol. 2, pp. 541–44.

43. Soderini was elected Gonfaloniere for life on September 22, 1502, but on August 31, 1512, he was dismissed from office. For description of his election, dismissal from office, and banishment, see Landucci, *Diario fiorentino*, p. 250.

44. ASF: PR No. 200, fol. 4v, for April 23, 1509.

45. See Lockwood, *Music in Renaissance Ferrara*, p. 142, and Prizer, "Bernardino Piffero," pp. 157, 159–60. Also see Polk, "Innovation in Instrumental Music," p. 206.

46. Antonio Capistraro, a Bolognese, is mentioned in a letter by Giovanni Spataro; see Weiss, "Bologna Q 18," p. 88. Susan Weiss has kindly informed me by private correspondence that Antonio was a member of the Concerto Palatino from at least 1513 to 1529 (records from 1506–12 are lost); see Gambassi, *Il Concerto Palatino*, pp. 612–17.

47. Ercole was probably Ercole Albergato, who worked in Ferrara, Mantua, and Bologna as actor, string musician, stage designer, and composer. I am grateful to Susan Weiss for this information.

48. Information about the Schubingers is taken from Polk, *German Instrumental Music*, pp. 76–78, 141–43, and Polk, "Vedel und Geige," p. 527.

49. First listed in ASF: CC No. 4, fol. 264r, for 1394–95, with trombadori; changed to the list of trombetti in ASF: CC, CU No. 320, for December 7, 1399 (no fol. numbers); last listed in ASF: CC, RD No. 1, fol. 83v, for 1458. See my speculation on Giovanni's background in McGee, "Giovanni Cellini," pp. 212–13.

50. See for example ASF: SC No. 128, fol. 12r, for February 15, 1525 [1526].

51. See Cummings, "Gian Maria Giudeo," p. 313, n. 3.

52. ASF: SC No. 128, fol. 106r, for November 7, 1526.

53. Information on Corrado is taken from Lockwood, *Music in Renaissance Ferrara*, pp. 68–69, 142, 180. Lockwood notes that "Alemania" could refer to any of the German-speaking areas of the north, including parts of Switzerland.

54. Prizer, "Bernardino Piffaro."

55. On Zorzi, see Baroncini, "Zorzi Trombetta"; Baroncini, "Zorzi Trombetta da Modon"; and Leech-Wilkinson, "Il libro di appunti."

56. ASF: SC No. 124 (1521–22), fol. 131v, for December 11, 1522.

57. The 1494–95 list of members of the doge's ensemble includes Zorzi de Nichole as well as his three sons: Alvixe de Zorzi, Jeronimo di Zorzi, and Bortholamio de Zorzi. See Baroncini, "Zorzi Trombetta," p. 70.

58. On Tromboncino, see Prizer, "Isabella d'Este and Lucrezia Borgia," and Prizer, "Lutenists at the Court of Mantua."

59. Kurtzman and Koldau, "Trombe, Trombe d'argento," quoting Paganuzzi et al., *La musica a Verona*, pp. 80–82.

60. Prizer, "Music at the Court of the Sforza," p. 181. Neither Prizer nor I can translate the names of some of these instruments with confidence.

61. Prizer, "Bernardino Piffaro," p. 163.

62. Ibid., p.171.

63. For Mantua and Ferrara, see ibid., pp.151–84. For Siena, see D'Accone, *The Civic Muse*, p. 589.

64. See discussion of the technique in Polk, *German Instrumental Music*, ch. 7.

65. "cum musicalis sonus perfectus constet ex tribus." Quoted in Zippel, *I suonatori*, p. 16.

66. According to Johannes Tinctoris the tradition was for the *bombarda* (alto shawm) to play the tenor part, and the trombone played the contratenor. Tinctoris, *Liber de arte contrapuncti*, p. 80.

67. The earliest records of pifferi ensembles performing motets are from the last two decades of the century. See Prizer, "Instrumental Music/Instrumentally Performed," p. 185.

68. Although the *cassone* painting accurately depicts one shawm player resting while the other two play, the painting is quite inaccurate in several other matters. See McGee, "Misleading Iconography." Another depiction of a four-member ensemble with one musician resting can be found in *The Hunt of Philip the Good* (ca. 1430) in the Musée National, Versailles. Examples do exist showing all three shawm players performing together, as in the *Coronation of the Virgin* (ca. 1465) by the Master of the Life of Mary, in the Munich Alte Pinakothek.

69.

I gharzoni mangni dengni et tanto ornati
ch'eran destri et leggier chom'uno ucciello
danzavan cholle dame acchonpangniati.
Et ballato gran pezza al salterello
ballaron poi a danza variata
chome desiderava questo et quello.
Feron la chirintana molto ornata
et missero amendue gli arrosti in danza
chon laura, chon mummia et charbonata
Lionciel bel riguardo et la speranza
l'angiola bella et la danza del re
et altre assai che nominar m'avanza.

BNF: Magl. 1121, fol. 69r; translation based on that by Giovanni Carsaniga in Nevile, *The Eloquent Body*, appendix 1.

70. On the question of the identity of Gugielmo Ebreo as Giovanni Ambrosio, see McGee, "Dancing Masters."

71. On the history of dance in Italy during the fifteenth century, see Sparti, *Guglielmo Ebreo*; and Nevile, *The Eloquent Body*.

72. Italian version published in Gallo, "L'autobiografia"; English trans. in Sparti, *Guglielmo Ebreo*, pp. 248–54.

73. ASF: MAP 23, 153. Reproduced and trans. in McGee, "Dancing Masters," pp. 202, 219.

74. Ibid., pp. 204–205, 220–21.

75. The treatises are "De pratica seu arte tripudii," in New York, Public Library, Dance Collection *MGZMB-Res. 72–254; Florence, Biblioteca Medicea Laurenziana, Antinori 13; and BNF: Magl. XIX. 88. For speculation about the relationship of the *bassadanza* "Venus" to Botticelli's painting *The Birth of Venus*, see Baxandall, *Painting and Experience*, pp. 78–79.

76. See Southern, "A Prima Ballerina," pp. 190–91, and McGee, "Dancing Masters," p. 207.

77. The "natural" steps are *sempio, doppio, ripresa, continenza, meza volta, volta tonda,* and *riverenza*. Occasionally variations of these steps and a few others were admitted, but these were the principal steps for the *bassadanza*. See Nevile, *The Eloquent Body*, pp. 74, 161.

78. For a description of these dances, see ibid., appendix 3, and Sparti, *Guglielmo Ebreo*, ch. 3.

79. To be more precise, I should note that since the *sempio* and *continenza* take only a half-measure to perform, I am counting two of each of them as a full step.

80. For a modern transcription of all known Italian instrumental dances prior to 1450, see McGee, *Medieval Instrumental Dances*.

81. On the forms of late medieval dances, see McGee, *Medieval Instrumental Dances*, pp. 8–19. Long, "Musical Tastes," p. 131, speculates that adoption of the "open" and "close" endings in Italian secular polyphonic songs was also in imitation of French practices.

82. I am grateful to dance historian Jennifer Nevile for confirming that the *balli* tunes are also tenors and would have been treated the same as the *bassadanza* tenors. Two examples have been found that show *bassadanze* with an added upper part: "La Spagna" (example 6.2), found in Perugia Biblioteca Comunale, Ms 431, modern ed. in Bukofzer, *Studies in Medieval*, pp. 199–200; and "Bel fiore dança," in Faenza, Biblioteca Comunale, Ms 117 (Faenza Codex), modern ed. in McGee, *Medieval Instrumental Dances*, no. 47.

83. For a more extensive discussion of the rules and practices of polyphonic improvisation, see McGee, *Medieval and Renaissance Music*, ch. 8; Polk, *German Instrumental Music*, pp. 163–69; and Ferand, *Die Improvisation*.

84. An inventory of Italian dance manuscripts is included in Gallo, "Il 'Ballare Lombardo'." *Bassadanze* and *balli* music is transcribed in Kinkeldey, "Dance Tunes," pp. 89–152, and Marrocco, *Inventory*.

85.
La sera terza a doi a doi ballaro,
Imprima a "ranfo" e puoi a "l'achinea."
Qui se trovò Cagnetto e monna Mea
Che in quel ballo mai non se lasciaro.
E de la terra ancor ballò 'l Vicaro:
Questo pigliò a man monna Tomea;
'N ce remase donna buona nè rea,
Che non balasse con uno uom di paro.
Puoi venne 'l ballo de la "pertusata"
E stando um poco venne la "palandra":

Questa se fe' per "Donna 'nnamorata."
Non fo veduta mai cantar calandra
Comme fece Solazo a questa fiata,
Che paria pifer venuto di Fiandra.

Con la sampogna fe' "La pastorella"
Solazo puoi la sera e "La picchina"
"La forosetta" e puoi "La campagnina,"
"a la fonte io l'amai," "La Marinella."
Tu averesti detto: ella favella!
Tanto ce fece ben "La Palazina."
E "La guiduccia" ancor, "La montanina,"
"La casa bassa" e "la patrona bella."
A questo suon ballaro a la romana,
a ballo steso ed atteza di petto,
Ch'a le donne è più bel che la toscana.
Puoi l'atondaro e fecer rigoletto
Ed a le braccia, ben che sia villana.
Quantunche v'eran n'ebbar gran diletto.

Debenedetti, *Simone Prodenzani, Il "Sollazzo,"* nos. 3, 6. Also see Nádas, "A Cautious Reading," pp. 32, 33.

86. These are found in Lond, British Library, Additional 29987. For a modern edition, see McGee, *Medieval Instrumental Dances.*

87. See ibid., numbers 14–29 and 45–46. For a discussion of performance details, see pp. 23–38.

88. Buxheimer Ms, Munich, Bayerische Staatsbibliothek, Cim 352b, from ca. 1470, modern edition in Wallner, *Das Buxheimer Orgelbuch;* Francesco Spinacino, *Intabolatura de Lauto* 1 and 2 (Venice: Petrucci, 1507); Joan Ambrosio Dalza, *Intabolatura de Lauto* (Venice: Petrucci, 1507); Vicenzo Capirola Lute Book (Venice, ca. 1517), modern edition in Gombosi, *Compositione di Meser Vincenzo Capirola.* For discussion of additional lute sources see Fallows, "15th-Century Tablatures."

89. See the discussion of the technique in Polk, *German Instrumental Music,* ch. 7.

90. See the discussion of instrumental improvisation in Polk, "Instrumentalists and Performance Practices."

91. Appolonio di Giovanni, *Generosity of Scipio,* in Harewood House, Leeds; reproduced in Callmann, *Appolonio di Giovanni,* plate 198.

92. Taddeo Crivelli, *La corte di Salamone,* Modena, Bibl. Estense; reproduced in McGee, "Misleading Iconography," p. 150.

93. Appolonio di Giovanni, *Generosity of Scipio,* London, Victoria and Albert Museum; and the *Adimari Wedding Cassone,* Florence, Accademia, reproduced in McGee, "Misleading Iconography," 147, 150, 141, and as figure 14 in this volume.

94. Guglieomo Ebreo; reproduced in Sparti, *Guglielmo Ebreo,* p. 8.

95. See Brown, "The Diversity of Music," pp. 180–81. The manuscripts, as identified in Atlas, *The Cappella Giulia Chansonnier,* vol. 1, p. 258, are BNF: Magl. XIX. 176; Florence, Biblioteca Riccardiana, Ms 2356; Paris, Bibl. Nat., Ms fr. 15123 (Pixérécourt Chansonnier); BNF: Banco Rari 229; Vatican, Capella Giulia, Ms XIII. 27; BNF: Magl. XIX. 178; Bologna, Civico Museo Bibliografico Musicale, Ms Q17.

96. Faenza, Biblioteca Comunale, Ms 117; facsimile ed. *Faenza, Biblioteca Comunale.* Transcriptions published in Plamenac, *Keyboard Music.* The other possibility is that the manuscript was intended for solo keyboard, or for both keyboard and lute. On that subject

see McGee, "Instruments and the Faenza Codex"; H. M. Brown, *Performance Practice*, pp. 170–71; Eberlein, "The Faenza Codex"; and McGee, "Once Again, The Faenza Codex." For recent work on the manuscript and its contents, see Memelsdorff, "Motti a motti," and Memelsdorff, "New Music."

97. As can be seen in the example, the Faenza ornamentor has concentrated on the superius and tenor voices, almost completely ignoring the notes of the contratenor.

98. For a discussion of the ornamentation, see McGee, "Ornamentation, National Styles."

99. Munich, Staatsbibliothek, Ms Cim. 352b; modern edition in Wallner, *Das Buxheimer Orgelbuch*.

100. On that subject, see H. M. Brown, "Instruments and Voices"; Litterick, "Performing Franco-Netherlandish Secular Music"; Litterick, "Vocal or Instrumental"; and Prizer, "Instrumental Music/Instrumentally Performed."

101. See McGee, "Singing without Text"; McGee, "Florentine Instrumentalists"; and Wilson, *Singing Poetry*.

102. See the discussion of textless compositions in H. M. Brown, *A Florentine Chansonnier*, text vol., pp. 140–42.

103. Although its contents are mostly textless transcriptions of vocal music, the manuscript does include some polyphonic dances (e.g., "Mantuaner dantz"). Augsburg, Staats- und Staadtbibliothek, CIM 43 (2′ Cod 142a); facsimile edition, *Augsberger Liederbuch*. For a study and transcription, see Jonas, *Das Augsburger Liederbuch*. On the manuscript's connection to the Schubingers, see Polk, *German Instrumental Music*, p. 141.

104. Polk, "Instrumentalists and Performance Practices," p. 98.

105. Strohm, *Music in Late Medieval Bruges*, and Polk, "Ensemble Instrumental Music," p. 20.

106. The arranger was Alvise, son of Zorzi trombetta; see above. See Prizer, "Instrumental Music/Instrumentally Performed," p. 185.

107. On the question of whether single-line instruments normally mixed with voices in the performance of the polyphonic repertory see Leech-Wilkinson, *The Modern Invention*.

108. Fenlon, "The Status of Music," p. 61.

109. Beginning shortly after the turn of the sixteenth century, Ottaviano Petrucci published model polyphonic settings that could be used for several types of poetry, thus relieving the amateurs of the need to improvise. See Prizer, "The Frottola," and McGee, "*Cantare all'improvviso*," 35–38.

110. I do not know of any account of performances on trumpets or large percussion (excluding tambourin) by anyone other than professional musicians.

111. The publications are listed in H. M. Brown, *Instrumental Music Printed before 1600*, beginning with Attaingnant's 1533 collection of chansons intended for flute and recorder.

112. Ganassi, *Opera intitulata Fontegara*.

113. This situation persisted well into the seventeenth century; see McGee, "How one Learned."

114. ASF: SC No. 99, 1497, fol. 58r, for June 30, 1497.

115. As recorded in ASF: SC No. 116, fol. 133r, for December 14, 1514; and No. 134, fol. 29v–30r, for October 14, 1531.

116. Baroncini, "Zorzi Trombetta and the Band," pp. 68–70.

117. Prizer, "Instrumental Music/Instrumentally Performed," p. 185. Strohm, *Music in Late Medieval Bruges*, p. 86, reports that as early as 1484, motets were composed in Bruges expressly for performance by the city pipers.

118. Baroncini, "Zorzi Trombetta and the Band," makes it clear that Zorzi, the leader of the ensemble from 1458 to ca. 1502, played trumpet, slide trumpet, trombone, and shawm. Given the other evidence provided here about the versatility of the *pifferi*, we can probably assume that Zorzi's sons as well as the other members of the ensemble were equally versatile.

119. Prizer, "Bernardino Piffaro," pp. 167–68.

120. The account is included in the cookbook of Cristoforo da Messisbugo, steward for the Este family. See description in H. M. Brown, "A Cook's Tour."

121. It is not clear exactly what some of these instruments were. *Dolziana* and *cornamusa* probably were windcap instruments. Usually I have translated *cornamusa* as "bagpipe," but in this case the *cornamusa* was playing with soft instruments, which suggests that the instrument was the much softer French *cornamuse*, an instrument similar in sound to a *krumhorn*. The *sordina* may have been a mute *cornetto*, and the *cetra/citara* is probably a plucked string instrument—perhaps similar to a guitar.

122. Earlier in the banquet dancers entertained the guests with several *bassadanze* and a *branle*.

123. Cordié, *Opere di Baldassare Castiglione*, p. 512.

124. It is curious that during these early decades of the sixteenth century there is little mention of bowed string instruments (viols and violins) in Florence. Polk, "Civic Patronage," pp. 62–64, notes that in Mantua, Ferrara, and a number of other north Italian cities there was a considerable presence of string instruments, although neither he nor I have encountered much evidence of that trend in Florence.

125. For a continuation of the story of the household musicians throughout the era of the grand dukes of Tuscany see Kirkendale, *The Court Musicians*.

126. Quoted in MacCracken, *The Dedication Inscription*, pp. 6–8. MacCracken believes the author may have been Brunetto Latini.

127. Weinstein, "The Myth of Florence," p. 21. Writers continued to sing the praises of the city throughout this period. See, for example, Dei, *La cronica*, where the first several pages are devoted to praise of the city and its riches.

128. On this, see Weinstein, "The Myth of Florence," pp. 30–37; and Becker, "The Florentine Territorial State," p. 110.

# Bibliography

## Archival Documents

ASF = Archivio di Stato, Florence
AD = Acquisti e Doni
Balie
Catasto
CC = Camera del Comune
CCN = Camera del Comune Notaio di Camera
CCP = Camere del Comune Proveditori
CC, CU = Camera del Comune, Camarlinghi, Uscita
CC, GS = Camera del Comune, Grande Serie
CC, RD = Camere del Comune, Riformati Debitori et Creditori
CC, UG = Camera del Comune, Uscita Generale
CO = Capitani di Orsanmichele
GA = Giudice degli appelli e nullità
MAP = Mediceo avanti il Principato
MC = Monte Comune
Mediceo = Mediceo del Principato
PR = Provvisioni Registri
S, C, M = Signori, Carteggi, Missive, Ia Cancelleria
SC = Signori e Collegi, deliberazioni in ordinaria autorità
SC, D = Signori e Collegi, deliberazioni in ordinaria autorità, dupplicati
SC, SA = Signori e Collegi, deliberazioni in speciale autorità
Statuti = Statuti del Comune
Strozz. = Carte Strozziane

Archivio di Stato, Lucca, Camerlingo Generale

Archivio di Stato di Mantova, Archivio Gonzaga, busta 1099

Archivio di Stato, Modena, Cancelleria ducale, estro. Ambasciatori, agenti e corrispondenti estensi, Firenze, Busta 4

## Manuscripts in Libraries

BNF = Biblioteca Nazionale Centrale, Florence
CS = Conventi sopressi
Magl. = Magliabecchiana
Pal. = Palatino
BNF: CS, C. IV. 895
BNF: Magl. 1121
BNF: Magl. II. II. 40
BNF: Magl. II. II. 127
BNF: Magl. II. IV
BNF: Magl. XXV. 24
BNF: Pal. 215
BNF: Pal. 560

Faenza, Biblioteca Comunale Ms 117
Florence, Biblioteca Riccardiana Ms 1258
London, British Library, Additional 29987
Munich, Bayerische Staatsbibliothek, Cim. 352b
Perugia, Biblioteca Comunale, Ms 431
Rome, Biblioteca Apostolica Vaticana Capponiano 203
Seville, Biblioteca Colombina, 6-3-29, opusc. 25
Siena, Biblioteca Comunale, cod. H. XI. 54
Siena, Biblioteca Comunale, Ms L.V. 29

## Printed Sources

Alighieri, Dante. *De vulgari eloquentia.* Ed. and trans. Steven Botterill. Cambridge Medieval Classics 5. Cambridge: Cambridge University Press, 1996.
———. *Opere.* Ed. Fredi Chiappelli. Milan: Mursia, 1978.
*Alle bocche della piazza: Diario di anonimo fiorentino (1382–1401).* Ed. Anthony Molho and Frank Sznura. Florence: Olschki, 1986.
Altamura, Antonio. *Il Certame coronario.* Naples: Società editrice napoletana, 1974.
Anonimo Fiorentino. *Cronica volgare.* Ed. Elina Bellondi. Rerum Italicarum Scriptores 27, 2. Rome: Istituto storico italiano per il Medio Evo, 1907.
Anonymous. *Ars cantus mensurabilis mensurata per modo iuris.* Ed. and trans. C. Matthew Balensuela. Greek and Latin Music Theory 10. Lincoln and London: University of Nebraska Press, 1994.
Arfaioli, Maurizio. *The Black Bands of Giovanni.* Pisa: University Press, 2005.
Atlas, Allan W. *The Cappella Giulia Chansonnier (Rome, Biblioteca Apostolica Vaticana, C. G. XIII. 27),* 2 vols. Brooklyn, NY: Institute of Mediaeval Music, 1976–76.
———. "Heinrich Isaac's 'Palle palle': A New Interpretation." *Analecta Musicologica,* 14 (1974): 17–25.
———. "Pandolfo III Malatesta mecenate musicale: Musica e musicisti presso una signoria del primo Quatrocento." *Rivista musicale italiana* 23 (1988): 38–92.
*Augsberger Liederbuch. Staats- und Stadtbibliothek Augsburg, CIM 43 (2' Cod 142a).* Stuttgart: Cornetto-Verlag, 1997.
Bachmann, Werner. *The Origins of Bowing.* Trans. Norma Deane. Oxford: Oxford University Press, 1969.

Baines, Anthony. *Brass Instruments: Their History and Development*. London: Faber, 1956.
———. "Shawms of the Sardana Coblas." *Galpin Society Journal* 5 (1952): 9–16.
Baldwin, John W. "The Image of the Jongleur in Northern France around 1200." *Speculum* 72 (1997): 635–63.
Barocchi, Paola, and Renzo Ristori, eds. *Il carteggio di Michelangelo*. Florence: Sansoni, 1965.
Baron, Hans. *The Crisis of the Early Italian Renaissance*. 2nd ed. Princeton, N.J.: Princeton University Press, 1966.
Baroncini, Rodolfo. "Zorzi Trombetta and the Band of the Piffari and Trombones of the Serenissima: New Documentary Evidence." *Historic Brass Society Journal* 14 (2002): 59–82.
———. "Zorzi Trombetta da Modon and the Founding of the Band of Piffari and Tromboni of the Serenissima." *Historic Brass Society Journal* 16 (2004): 1–17.
Barr, Cyrilla. "Music and Spectacle in Confraternity Drama of 15th-Century Florence." In *Christianity and the Renaissance*, ed. T. Verdon and John Henderson, pp. 376–404. Syracuse, N.Y.: Syracuse University Press, 1990.
Baxandall, Michael. *Painting and Experience in Fifteenth-Century Italy: A Primer in Social History of Pictorial Style*. Oxford: Oxford University Press, 1972.
Becherini, Bianca. "Un canta in panca Fiorentino, Antonio di Guido." *Rivista musicale italiana* 50 (1948): 241–47.
———. "Relazione di musici fiamminghi con la corte dei Medici: Nuovi documenti." *La Rinascita* 4 (1941): 84–112.
Becker, Marvin B. "The Florentine Territorial State and Civic Humanism in the Early Renaissance." In *Florentine Studies: Politics and Society in Renaissance Florence*, ed. Nicolai Rubinstein, pp. 109–39. London: Faber and Faber, 1968.
Beer, Marina. "Alcune osservazioni su oralità e novella italiana in versi (XIV–XV secolo) e sul 'Sollazzo' di Simone de' Prodenzani." *Schifanoia* 13–14 (1994): 217–33.
Bent, Margaret. "Songs without Music in Dante's *De Vulgari Eloquentia*: *Cantio* and Related Terms." In *"Et facciam dolçi canti." Studi in onore di Agostino Ziino in occasione del suo 65 compleanno*, ed. Bianca Maria Antolini, Teresa M. Gialdroni, and Annunziato Pugliese, vol. 1, pp. 161–82. Lucca: LIM, 2003.
Benvenuti, Antonia Tissoni. *L'Orfeo del Poliziano, con il testo critico dell'originale e delle successive forme teatrali*. Padua: Antenore, 1986.
Bertolini, Lucia, ed. *De vera amicitia: I testi del primo Certame coronario*. Ferrara: Franco Cosimo Panini, 1993.
Besseler, Heinrich, ed. *Guillelmi Dufay: Opera Omnia*. Vol. 6. CMM 1, Rome: American Institute of Musicology, 1964.
Bessi, Rosella. "Eugenio IV e Antonio di Matteo di Meglio." In *Firenze e il Consilio del 1439*, ed. Paolo Viti, vol. 2, pp. 737–50. Florence: Olschki, 1994.
———. "Lo spettacolo e la scrittura." In *"Le tems revient"—"L tempo si rinuova": Feste e spettacoli nella Firenze di Lorenzo il Magnifico*, ed. Paola Ventrone, pp. 103–17. Milan: Silvana, 1992.
———. "Politica e poesia nel Quattrocento fiorentino: Antonio Araldo e Papa Eugenio IV." *Interpres* 10 (1990): 7–36.
Boccaccio, Giovanni. *Decameron*. Ed. Cesare Segre. Milan: Mursia, 1977.
Bonifacio, Gaetano. *Giullari e uomini di corte nell '200*. Naples: Cav. A. Tocco, 1907.
Bowles, Edmund A. "Instruments at the Court of Burgundy (1363–1467)." *Galpin Society Journal* 6 (1953): 41–51.

——. *Musikleben im 15. Jahrhundert.* Leipzig: VEB Deutscher Verlag für Musik, 1977.

Branciforte, Suzanne. "Antonio di Meglio, Dante, and Cosimo de' Medici." *Italian Studies* 50 (1995): 9–23.

——. *"Ars Poetica Rei Publicae:* The Herald of the Florentine Signoria." Ph.D. diss., University of California at Los Angeles, 1990.

Brandolini, Raffaele. *On Music and Poetry (De musica et poetica, 1513).* Trans. Ann E. Moyer, with Marc Laureys. Medieval and Renaissance Texts and Studies 232. Tempe: Arizona Center for Medieval and Renaissance Studies, 2001.

Brincat, Giuseppe, ed. *Giovan Matteo di Meglio, Rime.* Florence: Olschki, 1977.

Brown, Alison. *Bartolomeo Scala, 1430–1497: The Humanist as Bureaucrat.* Princeton, N.J.: Princeton University Press, 1979.

——. "The Guelf Party in 15th-Century Florence." *Rinascimento* 20 (1980): 41–86.

——. "Lorenzo and Guicciardini." In *Lorenzo the Magnificent: Culture and Politics,* ed. Michael Mallett and Nicholas Mann, pp. 281–312. London: Warburg Institute, 1996.

——. *The Medici in Florence: The Exercise and Language of Power.* Florence: Olschki, 1992.

Brown, Howard M. "A Cook's Tour of Ferrara in 1529." *Rivista italiana di musicologia* 10 (1975): 216–41.

——. "The Diversity of Music in Laurentian Florence." In *Lorenzo de' Medici New Perspectives,* ed. Bernard Toscani, pp. 179–201. New York: Peter Lang, 1993.

——. "Fantasia on a Theme by Boccaccio." *Early Music* 5 (1977): 324–39.

——. *A Florentine Chansonnier from the Time of Lorenzo the Magnificent.* 2 vols. Monuments of Renaissance Music 7. Chicago: University of Chicago Press, 1983.

——. *Instrumental Music Printed before 1600: A Bibliography.* Cambridge, Mass.: Harvard University Press, 1965.

——. "Instruments and Voices in the Fifteenth-Century Chanson." In *Current Thought in Musicology,* ed. John W. Grubbs, pp. 89–137. Austin: University of Texas Press, 1976.

——. *Sixteenth-Century Instrumentation: The Music for the Florentine Intermedii.* Rome: American Institute of Musicology, 1973.

——. "The Trecento Fiddle and Its Bridges." *Early Music* 17 (1989): 309–29.

——, and Stanley Sadie, eds. *Performance Practice: Music before 1600.* New York: W. W. Norton, 1989.

Brucker, Gene A. "Bureaucracy and Social Welfare in the Renaissance: A Florentine Case Study." *Journal of Modern History* 55 (1983): 1–21.

——. "The Ciompi Revolution." In *Florentine Studies: Politics and Society in Renaissance Florence,* ed. Nicolai Rubinstein, pp. 314–56. London: Faber and Faber, 1968.

——. *The Civic World of Early Renaissance Florence.* Princeton, N.J.: Princeton University Press, 1977.

——. "Florence." In *Dictionary of the Middle Ages,* ed. Joseph R. Strayer, vol. 5, pp. 91–104. New York: Charles Scribner's Sons, 1989.

——. "Florence and Its University, 1348–1434." In *Action and Conviction in Early Modern Europe: Essays in Memory of E. H. Harbison,* ed. Theodore K. Rabb and Jerrold E. Siegel, pp. 220–36. Princeton, N. J.: Princeton University Press, 1969.

——. *Florentine Politics and Society 1343–1378.* Princeton, N.J.: Princeton University Press, 1962.

——. "Humanism, Politics and the Social Order in Early Renaissance Florence." In *Florence and Venice: Comparisons and Relations,* vol. 1, pp. 3–11. Florence: La Nuova Italia Editirice, 1979.

——. "The Medici in the Fourteenth Century." *Speculum* 32 (1957): 1–26.

———. *Renaissance Florence*. New York: John Wiley & Sons, 1969.

———. *Renaissance Florence: Society, Culture, and Religion*. Goldbach: Keip, 1994.

———, ed. *Two Memoirs of Renaissance Florence: The Diaries of Buonaccorso Pitti and Gregorio Dati*. New York: Harper & Row, 1967.

Bukofzer, Manfred. *Studies in Medieval and Renaissance Music*. New York: W. W. Norton, 1950.

Bullock-Davies, Constance. *Menestrellorum Multitudo: Minstrels at a Royal Feast*. Cardiff: University of Wales Press, 1978.

Callmann, Ellen. *Appolonio di Giovanni*. Oxford: Clarendon Press, 1974.

Cambi, Giovanni. "Istorie." In *Delizie degli eruditi toscani*, ed. P. Ildefonso di San Luigi. Florence, 1785–86.

Campbell, Thomas P., and Clifford Davidson, eds. *The Fleury Playbook: Essays and Studies*. Early Drama, Art and Music Monograph Series 7. Kalamazoo, Mich.: Medieval Institute, 1985.

Cantimori, Delio. "Rhetoric and Politics in Italian Humanism." *Journal of the Warburg and Courtauld Institutes* 1 (1937): 83–102.

Cantini, L. *Legislazione toscana raccolta ed illustrata*. Florence, 1800–08.

Carew-Reid, Nicole. "Feste e politica a Firenze sotto Lorenzo il Magnifico." *Quaderni medievali* 24 (1987): 25–55.

———. *Les fêtes florentines au temp de Lorenzo il Magnifico*. Florence: Olschki, 1995.

Carl, Doris. *Benedetto da Maiano, ein florentiner Bildhauer an der Schwelle zur Hochrenaissance*. 2 vols. Regensburg: Schnell & Steiner, 2006.

Carrai, Stefano. "Il leggere, il cantare e il tovare." *Lingua nostra* 46 (1985): 97–99.

Carter, Stewart. *The Early Trombone: A History in Pictures and Documents*. Forthcoming.

Castellani, Marcello. "I flauti nell'inventario di Lorenzo il Magnifico (1492)." In *Sinne musica nulla Vita: Festschrift Hermann Moeck*, ed. Nikolaus Delius, pp. 185–91. Celle: Moeck Verlag, 1997.

Cattin, Giulio. "I 'cantasi come' in una stampa di laude della Biblioteca riccardiana (Ed. r. 196)." *Quadrivium* 19 (1978): 5–52.

Cavicchi, Andrea. "Sacro e profano. Documenti e note su Bartolomeo da Bologna e gli organisti della cattedrale di Ferrara nel primo Quattrocento." *Rivista italiana di musicologia* 10 (1975): 46–71.

Cellesi, Luigia. "Documenti per la storia musicale di Firenze." *Rivista musicale italiana* 34 (1927): 579–602; 35 (1928): 553–582.

Cerretani, Bartolomeo. *Storia fiorentina*, ed. Giuliana Berti. Florence: Olschki, 1994.

Ciappelli, Giovanni. *Carnevale e Quaresima*. Temi e Testi, n. s. 37. Rome: Edizioni di storia e letteratura, 1997.

Ciseri, Ilaria. *L'ingresso trionfale di Leone X in Firenze nel 1515*. Biblioteca Storica Toscana 26. Florence: Olschki, 1990.

Conklin, Rosalind. "Medieval English Minstrels, 1216–1485." Ph.D. diss., University of Chicago, 1964.

Cocks, William A., Anthony C. Baines, and Roderick D. Cannon. "Bagpipe." In *The New Grove Dictionary of Music and Musicians*, 2nd ed., ed. Stanley Sadie, vol. 2, pp. 471–84. New York: Grove's Dictionaries, 2001.

Corazzini, Giuseppe Odoardo, ed. *Ricordanze di Bartolomeo Masi, calderaio fiorentino, dal 1478 al 1526*. Florence: Sansoni, 1906.

Cordié, Carlo, ed. *Opere di Baldassare Castiglione, Giovanni Della Casa, Benvenuto Cellini*. Milan: Ricardo Ricciardi editore, 1960.

Corsi, Giuseppe. *Poesie musicali del trecento*. Bologna: Commissione per i testi di lingua, 1970.

Corso, Cosimo. "Araldi e canterini nella repubblica senese del Quattrocento." *Bullettino senese di storia patria* 62 (1955): 140–60.

Cortesi, Paulo. *De cardinalatu libri tres*. Castel Cortesiano, 1510.

Corti, Gino. "Un musicista fiammingo a Firenze agli inizi del Quattrocento." *L'Ars nova italiana del Trecento* 4 (1975): 177–81.

Costa, Elio. "Latini, Brunetto." In *Dictionary of the Middle Ages*, ed. Joseph R. Strayer, vol. 7, p. 382. New York: Charles Scribner's Sons, 1986.

Crane, Frederick. *Materials for the Study of the Fifteenth Century Basse Danse*. Brooklyn: Institute of Mediaeval Music, 1968.

Cristoforo Fiorentino detto L'Altissimo. *Il primo libro de'Reali de M. Cristoforo fiorentino detto Altissimo poeta laureato cantato da lui all'improvviso*. Venice: Giovanni Antonio de Nicolini da Sabio, 1533.

Cserba, Simon M. *Hieronymus de Moravia Tractatus de musica*. Regensburg: Friedrich Pustet, 1935.

Cumming, Julie E. "Music for the Doge in Early Renaissance Venice." *Speculum* 67 (1992): 324–64.

Cummings, Anthony M. "Gian Maria Giudeo, sonatore del Liuto, and the Medici." *Fontes Artis Musicae* 38 (1991): 312–18.

———. *The Politicized Muse: Music for Medici Festivals, 1512–1537*. Princeton, N. J.: Princeton University Press, 1992.

———. "The Sacred Academy of the Medici and Florentine Musical Life of the Early Cinquecento." In *Musica Franca: Essays in Honor of Frank A. D'Accone*, ed. Irene Alm, Alyson McLamore, and Coleen Reardon, pp. 45–77. Stuyvesant, N. Y.: Pendragon, 1996.

D'Accone, Frank A. *The Civic Muse*. Chicago: University of Chicago Press, 1997.

———. "Lorenzo il Magnifico e la musica." In *La Musica a Firenze al tempo di Lorenzo il Magnifico*, ed. Piero Gargiulo, pp. 219–48. Florence: Olschki, 1993.

———. "Lorenzo the Magnificent and Music." In *Lorenzo il Magnifico e il suo mondo*, ed. Gian Carlo Garfagnini, pp. 259–90. Florence: Olschki, 1994.

———. "Music and Musicians at the Florentine Monastery of Santa Trinita." *Quadrivium* 12 (1971): 131–52.

———. "Music and Musicians at Santa Maria del Fiore in the Early Quattrocento." In *Scritti in onore di Luigi Ronga*, pp. 99–126. Milan and Naples: Ricciardi, 1973.

———. "The Singers of San Giovanni in Florence during the 15th Century." *Journal of the American Musicological Society* 14 (1961): 307–58.

———. "Some Neglected Composers in the Florentine Chapels, ca. 1475–1525." *Viator: Medieval and Renaissance Studies* 1 (1970): 263–88.

D'Addario, Arnaldo. "Burocrazia, economia e finanze dello stato fiorentino alla metà del Cinquecento." *Archivio storico italiano* 121 (1963): 362–456.

Dall'Aglio, Stefano. *Savonarola e il savonarolismo*. Bari: Cacucci editore, 2005.

———. *Savonarola in Francia. Circolazione di un'eredità politico-religiosa nell'Europa del Cinquecento*. Turin: Nino Aragno-Istituto Nazionale di Studi sul Rinascimento, 2006.

D'Ancona, Alessandro. "I canterini dell'antica comune di Perugia." In *Varietà storice e letterarie*, vol. 1, pp. 39–73. Milan, 1883.

Dati, Gregorio. *Il libro segreto*, ed. Carlo Gargiolli. Bologna, 1869.

———. *Istoria di Firenze*, ed. Luigi Pratesi. Norcia: Tonti, 1904.

Davidsohn, Robert. *Firenze ai tempi di Dante*. Florence: Bemporad, 1929.

———. *Storia di Firenze*. 8 vols. Florence: Sansoni, 1956–68.

Debenedetti, Santorre. *Simone Prodenzani, Il "Sollazzo": contributi alla storia della novella, della poesia musicale e del costume nel Trecento*. Turin: Bocca, 1922.

Dei, Benedetto. *La cronica: dall'anno 1400 all'anno 1500*. Ed. Roberto Barducci. Florence: Francesco Papafava, 1984.

del Corazza, Bartolommeo di Michele. "Diario fiorentino di Bartolommeo di Michele del Corazza, anni 1405–1438," ed. Giuseppe Odoardo Corazzini. *Archivio Storico Italiano*, ser. 5, vol. 14 (1894): 233–98.

Del Lungo, Isidoro. *Florentia. Uomini e cose del Quattrocento*. Florence: G. Barbèra, 1897.

*Delizie degli eruditi toscani*. Florence, 1784.

de Pas, Justin. "Ménestrels et écoles de ménestrels à Saint-Omer, XVe et XVI siècles." *Bulletin de la Société des antiquaires de la Morine* 14 (1929): 68–80.

De Rosa, Daniela. *Alle origini della Repubblica fiorentina: Dai consoli al "primo popolo" (1172–1260)*. Florence: Arnaud, 1995.

Desideri Costa, Leona. *La Chiesa di San Martino del Vescovo, L'Ortorio dei Buonomini e gli affreschi sulle opere di misericordia in Firenze presso le case degli Alighieri*. Florence, 1942.

Di Bacco, Giuliano, and John Nádas. "Verso uno 'stile internazionale' della musica nelle cappelle papali e cardinalizie durante il Grande Scisma (1378–1417): Il caso di Johannes Ciconia da Liege." In *Collectanea* I, ed. Adalbert Roth, pp. 7–74. Capellae Apostolicae Sixtinaeque Collectanea Acta Monumenta 3.Vatican City, 1994.

*Dictionary of the Middle Ages*, ed. Joseph R. Strayer. 13 vols. New York: Charles Scribner's Sons, 1982–89.

*Dizionario biografico degli Italiani*. Rome: Istituto della Enciclopedia Italiana, 1960–.

Donati, Pier Paolo. "1470–1490: Organi di cartone degli studioli dei principi." In *La musica a Firenze al tempo di Lorenzo il Magnifico*, ed. Piero Gargiulo, pp. 275–80. Florence: Olschki, 1993.

Downey, Peter. "A Renaissance Correspondence Concerning Trumpet Music." *Early Music* 9 (1981): 325–29.

———. "The Renaissance Slide Trumpet: Fact or Fiction?" *Early Music* 12 (1984): 26–33.

Duffin, Ross. "Backward Bells and Barrel Bells: Some Notes on the Early History of Loud Instruments." *Historic Brass Society Journal* 9 (1997): 113–29.

———. "The *Trompette des Menestrels* in the 15th-century *Alta Capella*." *Early Music* 17 (1989): 397–402.

Dutka, Joanna. *Music in the English Mystery Plays*. Early Drama, Art, and Music 2. Kalamazoo, Mich.: Medieval Institute, 1980.

Eberlein, Roland. "The Faenza Codex: Music for Organ or for Lute Duet?" *Early Music* 20 (1992): 460–66.

Elam, Caroline. "Cosimo de' Medici and San Lorenzo." In *Cosimo "il Vecchio" Medici, 1389–1464. Essays in Commemoration of the 600th Anniversary of Cosimo De' Medici's Birth*, ed. Francis Ames-Lewis with intro. by E. H. Gombrich, pp. 157–80. Oxford: Clarendon, 1992.

*Faenza, Biblioteca Comunale, Ms 117*. Facsimile edition. Musicological Studies and Documents 10. American Institute of Musicology, 1961.

Fallows, David. "15th-Century Tablatures for Plucked Instruments: A Summary, a Revision and a Suggestion." *Lute Society Journal* 19 (1977): 7–33.

———. "French as a Courtly Language in Fifteenth-Century Italy: The Musical Evidence." *Renaissance Studies* 3 (1989): 429–41.

———. "Specific Information on the Ensembles for Composed Polyphony, 1400–1474." In *Studies in the Performance of Late Medieval Music,* ed. Stanley Boorman, pp. 109–59. Cambridge: Cambridge University Press, 1983.

Fenlon, Iain. "The Status of Music and Musicians in the Early Italian Renaissance." In *Le concert des voix et des instruments à la Renaissance,* ed. Jean-Michel Vaccaro, pp. 57–70. Paris: CNRS, 1995.

Ferand, Ernest. *Die Improvisation in der Musik.* Zurich, 1938.

Festa, Giovanni Battista. *Un Galateo femminile italiano del Trecento.* Bari: Gius. Laterza & Figli, 1910.

Field, Arthur. "Leonardo Bruni, Florentine Traitor? Bruni, the Medici, and an Aretine Conspiracy of 1437." *Renaissance Quarterly* 51 (1998): 1009–1150.

Fiori, Alessandra. "Discorsi sulla musica nei commenti medievali alla commedia dantesca." *Studi e problemi di critica testuale* 59 (1999): 67–102.

Flamini, Francesco. *La lirica toscana del Rinascimento anteriore ai tempi del Magnifico.* Pisa, 1891; repr. Florence: Le Lettere, 1977.

Folgore da San Gimignano. *I Sonetti dei mesi ed i componenti la brigata in una cronaca perugina del Trecento.* Ed. Ubaldo Morandi. Siena: Edizioni Cantagalli, 1991.

Francesco da Barberino. *Del reggimento e de' Costumi delle donne.* Published as *Un Galateo femminile italiano del Trecento,* ed. Giovanni Battista Festa. Bari: Gius. Laterza & Figli, 1910.

———. *Documenti d'amore* (ca. 1300–10). Rome: Vitale Mascardi, 1640.

Frey, Herman-Walther. "Regesten zur Päpstlichen Kapelle unter Leo X. un zu seiner Privatkapelle." *Die Musikforschung* 8 (1955): 58–73, 178–99, 412–37; and 9 (1956): 46–57, 139–56, 411–19.

Fubini, Riccardo. "In margine all'edizione delle 'lettere' di Lorenzo de' Medici, 1: La vista a Firenze del duca di Milano nel 1471; 2: L'ambasciata a Roma di Alamanno Rinuccini nel 1476." In Garfagni, *Lorenzo de' Medici: Studi,* pp. 167–232.

Gallo, F. Alberto. "L'autobiografia artistica di Giovanni Ambrosio (Guglielmo Ebreo) da Pesaro." *Studi musicali* 12 (1982): 189–202.

———. "Il 'Ballare Lombardo' (circa 1435–1475)." *Studi Musicali* 8 (1979): 61–84.

———. *Music in the Castle.* Chicago: University of Chicago Press, 1995.

———. "La tradizione orale della teoria musicale nel medioevo." In *L'etnomusicologia in Italia,* ed. Diego Carpitella, pp. 161–66. Palermo: S. F. Flaccovio, 1975.

Gambassi, Osvaldo. *Il Concerto Palatino della signoria di Bologna.* Florence: Olschki, 1989.

Ganassi, Sylvestro. *Opera intitulata Fontegara.* Venice, 1535. Modern ed. Hildemarie Peter. Berlin: R. Lienau, 1956.

Garfagnini, Gian Carlo, ed. *Lorenzo de' Medici studi.* Florence: Olschki, 1992.

———, ed. *Lorenzo il Magnifico e il suo mondo: Convegno internazionale di studi (Firenze, 9–13 giugno).* Florence: Olschki, 1994.

———, ed. *Lorenzo il Magnifico e il suo tempo.* Florence: Olschki, 1992.

Gaye, Giovanni. *Carteggio inedito d'artisti dei secoli XIV, XV, XVI.* Florence: 1840; photo repr. Turin: Bottega d'Erasmo, 1961.

Giazotto, Remo. *La musica a Genova nella vita pubblica e privata dal XIII al XVIII secolo.* Genoa: Società industrie grafiche e lavorazioni affini, 1951.

Giusto d'Anghiari. "Cronica o memorie." BNF: II. II. 127, fol. 75r–76r.

Goldthwaite, Richard. *The Building of Renaissance Florence.* Baltimore, Md.: Johns Hopkins University Press, 1980.

———. *Private Wealth in Renaissance Florence.* Princeton, N. J.: Princeton University Press, 1968.

————. *Wealth and the Demand for Art in Italy 1300–1600*. Baltimore, Md.: Johns Hopkins University Press, 1993.

Gombosi, Otto. *Compositione di Meser Vincenzo Capirola: Lute Book (circa 1517)*. Neuilly-sur-Seine: Société de musique d'autrefois, 1955.

Gori, Pietro. *Le feste fiorentine attraverso i secoli*. Vol. 1, *Le feste per San Giovanni*. Vol. 2, *Firenze magnifica*. Florence: Bemporad, 1926, 1930.

Gorni, Guglielmo. "Storia del Certame Coronario." *Rinascimento* ser. 2, 12 (1972): 135–81.

*Grande dizionario della lingua Italiana*. Ed. Salvatore Battaglia. Turin: Unione Tipografico-Editrice Torinese, 1961–.

Grazzini, Antonio Francesco (Il Lasca). *Tutti i trionfi, carri, mascherate o canti carnascialeschi andati per Firenze dal tempo del Magnifico Lorenzo Vecchio de Medici*. 2 vols. Florence, 1559.

Guicciardini, Francesco. *The History of Florence*. Trans. Mario Domandi. New York: Harper & Row, 1970.

————. *Storie fiorentine dal 1378 al 1509*. Ed. R. Palmarocchi. Bari, 1931.

Haar, James. *Essays on Italian Poetry and Music 1350–1600*. Berkeley: University of California Press, 1986.

Haar, James, and John Nádas. "Antonio Squarcialupi: Man and Myth." *Early Music History* 25 (2006): 105–68.

Hachenberg, Karl. "Correspondence." *Historic Brass Society Journal* 18 (2006): 92–93.

Hallmark, Anne. "Some Evidence for French Influence in Northern Italy ca. 1400." In *Studies in the Performance of Late Medieval Music*, ed. Stanley Boorman, 193–225. Cambridge: Cambridge University Press, 1983.

Haraszti, Emile. "La Technique des improvisateurs de langue vulgaire et de latin au Quattrocento." *Revue belge de musicologie* 9 (1955): 12–31.

Hatfield, Rab. "The Compagnia de' Magi." *Journal of the Warburg and Courtauld Institutes* 33 (1970): 107–61.

————. "Some Unknown Descriptions of the Medici Palace in 1459." *Art Bulletin* 52 (1970): 232–49.

Heartz, Daniel. "The Basse Dance, Its Evolution circa 1450–1550." *Annales Musicologiques, Moyen Age et Renaissance* 6 (1958–63): 287–340.

————. "A 15th-Century Ballo: Rôti Bouilli Joyeux." In *Aspects of Medieval and Renaissance Music: A Birthday Offering to Gustave Reese*, ed. Jan La Rue et al., pp. 359–75. New York: Norton, 1966.

Henderson, John. *Piety and Charity in Late Medieval Florence*. Oxford: Clarendon Press, 1994.

Herlihy, David, ed. *Medieval Culture and Society*. New York: Harper, 1968.

Holmes, George. "How the Medici Became the Pope's Bankers." In *Florentine Studies: Politics and Society in Renaissance Florence*, ed. Nicolai Rubinstein, pp. 357–80. London: Faber & Faber, 1968.

Hudson, Barton, ed. *Hayne van Ghizeghem: Opera Omnia*. CMM 74. American Institute of Musicology, 1977.

Huot, Sylvia. "Voices and Instruments in Medieval French Secular Music: On the Use of Literary Texts as Evidence for Performance Practice." *Musica Disciplina* 43 (1989): 63–113.

Jahn, Fritz. "Die Nürnberger Trompeten- und Posaunenmacher im 16. Jahrhundert." *Archiv für Musikwissenschaft* 7 (1925): 23–52.

Jervis, Alice de Rosen, trans. *Luca Landucci, A Florentine Diary from 1450 to 1516*. Freeport: Books for Libraries, 1927; repr. 1971.

Johannes de Muris. *Écrits sur la musique Jean de Murs*. Trans. Christian Meyer. Paris: CNRS, 2000.

Jonas, Luisa, ed. *Das Augsburger Liederbuch*. 2 vols. Berliner musikwissenschaftliche Arbeit 21. Munich: E. Katzbichler, 1983.

Jones, Sterling. *The Lira da Braccio*. Bloomington: Indiana University Press, 1995.

Jurdjevic, Mark. "Civic Humanism and the Rise of the Medici." *Renaissance Quarterly* 51 (1999): 994–1020.

Kent, Dale. *Cosimo de' Medici and the Florentine Renaissance*. New Haven, Conn.: Yale University Press, 2000.

Kent, Francis William. *Lorenzo de' Medici and the Art of Magnificence*. Baltimore: Johns Hopkins University Press, 2004.

———. "The Young Lorenzo, 1449–69." In *Lorenzo the Magnificent: Culture and Politics*, ed. Michael Mallett and Nicholas Mann, pp. 1–22. London: Warburg Institute, 1996.

Kinkeldey, Otto. "Dance Tunes of the Fifteenth Century." In *Instrumental Music: A Conference at Isham Memorial Library*, ed. David G. Hughes, pp. 3–30, 89–152. Cambridge, Mass.: Harvard University Press, 1959.

Kirkendale, Warren. *The Court Musicians in Florence During the Principate of the Medici*. Florence: Olschki, 1993.

Klapisch-Zuber, Christiane. *Women, Family, and Ritual in Renaissance Italy*. Trans. Lydia Cochrane. Chicago: University of Chicago Press, 1985.

Kristeller, Paul Oskar. "Francesco da Diacceto and Florentine Platonism in the Sixteenth Century." In *Studies in Renaissance Thought and Letters*, 287–336. Rome: Edizioni di storia e letteratura, 1956.

Kurtzman, Jeffrey, and Linda Maria Koldau. "Trombe, Trombe d'Argento, Trombe Squarciate, Tromboni and Pifferi in Venetian Processions and Ceremonies of the Sixteenth and Seventh Centuries." *Journal of Seventeenth-Century Music* 8 (2002). http://www.sscm-jscm.org/jscm/v8/no1/Kurtzman.html (accessed June 2005).

Landucci, Luca. *Diario fiorentino*. Ed. Jodoco del Badia. Florence: Sansoni, 1883.

Lanza, Antonio. *Lirici toscani del Quattrocento*. 2 vols. Rome: Bulzoni, 1973, 1975.

Lastri, Marco Antonio. *L'Osservatore fiorentino sugli edifizi della sua patria. Terza edizione eseguita sopra quella del 1797 riordinata e compiuta dall'autore, coll'aggiunta di varie annotazioni del professore Giuseppe del Rosso* . . . 8 vols. Florence: Ricci, 1821; repr. Bologna: Forni, 1977.

Latini, Brunettto. *Il tesoretto*. Milan: Biblioteca universale Rizzoli, 1985.

Lawson, Graeme, and Geoff Egan. "A Medieval Trumpet from the City of London." *Galpin Society Journal* 41 (1988): 63–66; 44 (1991): 151–56.

Leech-Wilkinson, Daniel. "Un libro di appunti di un suonatore di tromba del quindicesimo secolo." *Rivista italiana di musicologia* 16 (1981): 16–39.

———. *The Modern Invention of Medieval Music*. Cambridge: Cambridge University Press, 2002.

Levi, Ezio. "I cantari leggendari." *Giornale storico della letteratura italiana*, Suppl. 16 (1914).

Litterick, Louise. "Performing Franco-Netherlandish Secular Music of the Late 15th Century." *Early Music* 8 (1980): 474–85.

———. "Vocal or Instrumental? A Methodology for Ambiguous Cases." In *Le concert des voix et des instruments à la Renaissance*, ed. Jean-Michel Vaccaro, 157–78. Paris: CNRS, 1995.

Lockwood, Lewis. *Music in Renaissance Ferrara, 1400–1500*. Cambridge, Mass.: Harvard University Press, 1984.

————. "Pietrobono and the Instrumental Tradition at Ferrara in the Fifteenth Century." *Rivista italiana di musicologia* 10 (1975): 191–246.

Long, Michael P. "Francesco Landini and the Florentine Cultural Élite." *Early Music History* 3 (1983): 83–99.

————. "Musical Tastes in 14th-Century Italy: Notational Styles, Scholarly Traditions, and Historical Circumstances." Ph.D. diss., Princeton University, 1981.

Lubkin, Gregory. *A Renaissance Court: Milan under Galeazzo Maria Sforza.* Berkeley: University of California Press, 1994.

MacCracken, Richard. *The Dedication Inscription of the Palazzo del Podestà in Florence.* Florence: Olschki, 2001.

Machiavelli, Niccolò. *Legazioni, commissarie, scritti di governo.* Ed. Fredi Chiappelli. 2 vols. Bari: G. Laterza, 1971.

————. *Tutte le opere.* Ed. Mario Martelli. Florence: Sansoni, 1971.

Madeuf, Pierre-Yves, Jean-François Madeuf, and Graham Nicholson. "The Guitbert Trumpet: A Remarkable Discovery." *Historic Brass Society Journal* 11 (1999): 181–86.

Mallett, Michael. *Mercenaries and Their Masters.* London: The Bodley Head, 1974.

Marcuse, Sibyl. *A Survey of Musical Instruments.* London: David & Charles, 1975.

Marrocco, W. Thomas. *Inventory of 15th Century Bassedanze, Balli and Balletti.* New York: Cord, 1981.

Martelli, Mario. *Studi laurenziani.* Florence: Olschki, 1965.

Matteini, Anna Maria Testaverde. "La decorazione festiva e l'itinerario di 'rifondazione' della città negli ingressi trionfali a Firenze tra XV e XVI secoli." *Mitteilungen des Kunsthistorischen Institutes in Florenz* 32 (1988): 323–52.

Mazzi, Curzio. "La Mensa dei Priori di Firenze nel secolo XIV." *Archivio storico italiano* 20 (1897): 336–68.

McGee, Timothy J. "'Alla Battaglia': Music and Ceremony in Fifteenth-Century Florence." *Journal of the American Musicological Society* 36 (1983): 287–302.

————. "*Cantare all'improvviso:* Improvising to Poetry in Late Medieval Italy." In *Improvisation in the Arts of the Middle Ages and Renaissance,* ed. Timothy J. McGee, pp. 31–70. Early Drama, Art and Music 30. Kalamazoo, Mich.: Medieval Institute, 2003.

————. "Dancing Masters and the Medici Court in the 15th Century." *Studi musicali* 17 (1988): 201–24.

————. "Dinner Music for the Florentine Signoria, 1350–1450. *Speculum* 74 (1999): 94–114.

————. "Eastern Influences in Medieval European Dances." In *Cross-Cultural Perspectives on Music,* ed. Robert Falck and Timothy Rice, pp. 79–100. Toronto: University of Toronto Press, 1982.

————. "The Fall of the Noble Minstrel: The Sixteenth-Century Minstrel in a Musical Context." *Medieval and Renaissance Drama in England* 7 (1995): 98–120.

————. "Filippino Lippi and Music." *Renaissance and Reformation/Renaissance et Reforme* 30 (2006/07): 5–28.

————. "Florentine Instrumentalists and Their Repertory circa 1500." *Basler Jahrbuch für Historische Musikpraxis* 29 (2005): 141–55.

————. "Giovanni Cellini, Piffero of Florence." *Historic Brass Society Journal* 12 (2000): 210–25. Originally published in Italian as "Giovanni Cellini, piffero di Firenze." *Rivista italiana di musicologia* 32 (1997): 201–21.

————, ed. *Heinrich Isaac, Alla Battaglia.* Toronto: Elliott Chapin, 1988.

————. "How one Learned to Ornament in Late Sixteenth-Century Italy." *Performance Practice Review* 13 (2008): 1–16.

————, ed. *Improvisation in the Arts of the Middle Ages and Renaissance*. Early Drama, Art and Music 30. Kalamazoo, Mich.: Medieval Institute, 2003.

————. "Instruments and the Faenza Codex." *Early Music* 14 (1986): 480–90.

————. "In the Service of the Commune: The Changing Role of Florentine Civic Musicians, 1450–1532." *Sixteenth Century Journal* 30 (1999): 727–43.

————. "The Liturgical Placements of the *Quem quaeritis* Dialogue." *Journal of the American Musicological Society* 29 (1976): 1–29.

————. *Medieval and Renaissance Music: A Performer's Guide*. University of Toronto Press, 1985.

————. *Medieval Instrumental Dances*. Bloomington: Indiana University Press, 1989.

————. "Misleading Iconography: The Case of the 'Adimari Wedding *Cassone*.'" *Imago Musicae* 9–12 (1992–95): 139–57.

————. "Music, Rhetoric, and the Emperor's New Clothes." In *Music and Medieval Manuscripts: Paleography and Performance: Essays in Honour of Andrew Hughes*, ed. John Haines and Randall Rosenfeld, pp. 207–59. New York: Ashgate, 2004.

————. "Once Again, the Faenza Codex: A Reply to Roland Eberlein." *Early Music* 20 (1992): 466–68.

————. "Ornamentation, National Styles, and the Faenza Codex." *Early Music New Zealand* 3 (1987): 3–14.

————. "Silver or Gold: The Color of Brass Instruments in the Late Middle Ages." *Historic Brass Society Journal* 17 (2005): 1–6.

————. "Singing without Text." *Performance Practice Review* 6 (1993): 1–32.

————, with Sylvia E. Mittler. "Information on Instruments in Florentine Carnival Songs." *Early Music* 10 (1982): 452–61.

Medici, Lorenzo de'. *Lettere*. Florence: Giunti-Barbèra, 1977–.

Memelsdorff, Pedro. "Motti a motti: Reflections on a Motet Intabulation of the Early Quattrocento." *Recercare* 10 (1998): 39–68.

————. "New Music in the Codex Faenza 117." *Plainsong and Medieval Music* 13 (2004): 141–61.

Merkley, Paul A., and Lora L. M. Merkley. *Music and Patronage in the Sforza Court*. Cremona: Brepols, 1999.

Montagu, Jeremy. *The World of Medieval and Renaissance Musical Instruments*. London: David & Charles, 1976.

Motta, E. "Musici alla corte degli Sforza." *Archivio storico lombardo* 14 (1887): 29–64, 278–340, 514–61.

Muir, Edward. *Civic Ritual in Renaissance Venice*. Princeton, N. J.: Princeton University Press, 1981.

Myers, Herbert. "Evidence of the Emerging Trombone in the Late Fifteenth Century: What Iconography May Be Trying to Tell Us." *Historic Brass Society Journal* 17 (2005): 7–35.

————. "Slide Trumpet Madness: Fact or Fiction?" *Early Music* 17 (1989): 383–89.

Nádas, John. "A Cautious Reading of Simone Prodenzani's *Il Saporetto*." *Recercare* 10 (1998): 23–37.

————. "Song Collections in Late Medieval Florence." In *Trasmissione e recezione delle forme di cultura musicale. Atti del XIV Congresso della Società Internazionale di Musicologia*, ed. Angelo Pompilio et al., pp. 126–37. Turin: Edit, 1990.

Najemy, John M. "Civic Humanism and Florentine Politics." In *Renaissance Civic Humanism: Reappraisals and Reflections*, ed. James Hankins, pp. 75–104. Cambridge: Cambridge University Press, 2000.

———. *Corporatism and Consensus in Florentine Electoral Politics, 1280–1400.* Chapel Hill: University of North Carolina Press, 1982.

———. *A History of Florence, 1200–1575.* London: Blackwell, 2006.

Nerici, Luigi. *Storia della musica in Lucca.* Memorie e documenti per servire alla storia di Lucca 12. Lucca: Tipografia Giusti, 1880.

Nevile, Jennifer. *The Eloquent Body.* Bloomington: Indiana University Press, 2004.

Newbigin, Nerida. *Nuovo corpus di sacre rappresentazioni fiorentine del '400.* Bologna: Commissione per i testi di lingua, 1983.

———. "Piety and Politics in the Feste of Lorenzo's Florence." In Gafragnini, *Lorenzo il Magnifico e il suo mondo,* pp. 17–41.

———. "Plays, Printing and Publishing, 1485–1500: Florentine 'sacre rappresentazioni.'" *La Bibliofilia* 90 (1988): 269–96.

———. "Politics in the *Sacre Rappresentazioni* of Lorenzo's Florence." In *Lorenzo the Magnificent: Culture and Politics,* ed. Michael Mallett and Nicholas Mann, pp. 117–30. London: Warburg Institute, 1996.

———. "The Word Made Flesh. The 'Rappresentazioni' of Mysteries and Miracles in Fifteenth-Century Florence." In *Christianity and the Renaissance: Image and Religious Imagination in the Quattrocento,* ed. Timothy Verdon and John Henderson, pp. 361–75. Syracuse, N. Y.: Syracuse University Press, 1990.

Nosow, Robert. "The Debate over Song in the Accademia Fiorentina." *Early Music History* 21 (2002): 175–221.

Novati, Francesco. "Le poesie sulla natura delle frutte e i canterini del Comune di Firenze nel '300." *Giornale storico della letteratura italiana* 19 (1892): 55–79.

*Nozze, Guidi—Paolucci,* Pesaro, 1883.

Orvieto, Paolo. "Carnevale e feste fiorentine del tempo di Lorenzo de' Medici." In Garfagnini, *Lorenzo il Magnifico e il suo tempo,* pp. 103–24.

———, ed. *Lorenzo de' Medici: Canti carnascialeschi.* Rome: Salerno Editrice, 1991.

———. *Pulci medievale: Studio sulla poesia volgare fiorentina del '400.* Rome: Salerno Editrice, 1978.

Paganuzzi, Enrico, Carlo Bologna, Luciano Rognini, Giorgio Maria Cambié, and Marcello Conati. *La musica a Verona.* Verona: Alfio Fiorini, 1976.

Page, Christopher. "German Musicians and Their Instruments." *Early Music* 10 (1982): 192–200.

———. "Jerome of Moravia on the *Rubeba and Viella.*" *Galpin Society Journal* 32 (1979): 77–98.

Paoli, Cesare, with Luigi Rubini and Pietro Stromboli. *Della venuta in Firenze di Galeazzo Maria Sforza, Duca di Milano, con la moglie Bona di Savoia nel 1471: Lettere di due senesi alla Signoria di Siena.* Nozze Banchi-Brini. Florence, 1878.

Paolo di Matteo Pietrobuoni. *Diario.* BNF: CS, C. IV. 895, fol. 182r–183v.

Parenti, Marco. *Lettere.* Ed. Maria Marrese. Istituto nazionale di studi sul Rinascimento, Studi e testi 39. Florence: Olschki, 1996.

Parenti, Piero di Marco. *Storia fiorentina.* Ed. Andrea Matucci. 2 vols. Florence: Olschki, 1994, 2005.

Parenti Fiorentino, Piero. *Delle nozze di Lorenzo de' Medici con Clarice Orsini nel 1469.* Ed. D. Bonamici. Florence: Bencini, 1870.

Parigi, Luigi. *Laurentiana: Lorenzo dei Medici, cultore di musica.* Florence: Olschki, 1954.

Peters, Gretchen. "Urban Minstrels in Late Medieval Southern France: Opportunities, Status and Professional Relationships." *Early Music History* 19 (2000): 201–35.

Petrucci, Ottavio. *Harmonice musices odhecaton A*. Venice, 1502. Modern ed. Helen Hewitt and Isabel Pope. Cambridge, Mass.: Harvard University Press, 1942.

Pieri, Paolino. *Cronica di Paolino Pieri fiorentino delle cose d'Italia dall'anno 1080 fino all'anno 1305*. Ed. A. Adami. Rome: Giovanni Zempel, 1755.

Pini, Antonio Ivan. "La 'Burocrazia' comunale nella Toscana del trecento." In *La Toscana nel secolo XIV: Caratteri di una civiltà regionale*, ed. Sergio Gensini, pp. 215–40. Pisa: Pacini, 1988.

Pirro, André. "Leo X and Music." *The Musical Quarterly* 21 (1935): 1–16.

Pirrotta, Nino. "Music and Cultural Tendencies in Fifteenth-Century Italy." In *Music and Culture in Italy from the Middle Ages to the Baroque*, pp. 80–112. Cambridge, Mass.: Harvard University Press, 1984.

———. *The Music of Fourteenth-Century Italy*. 5 Vols. Rome: American Institute of Musicology, 1954–64.

———. "The Oral and Written Traditions of Music." In *Music and Culture in Italy from the Middle Ages to the Baroque*, pp. 72–79. Cambridge, Mass: Harvard University Press, 1984; originally published as "Tradizione orale e tradizione scritta nella musica." In *L'Ars nova italiana del Trecento*, pp. 431–41. Centro di studi sull'ars nova italiana del trecento 3, Certaldo, 1970.

Pirrotta, Nino, with Elena Povoledo. *Li due Orfei da Poliziano a Monteverdi*. Turin: RAI, 1969; Trans. Karen Eales, *Music and Theater from Poliziano to Monteverdi*. Cambridge: Cambridge University Press, 1982.

Plaisance, Michel. *Florence in the Time of the Medici*. Trans. Nicole Carew-Reid. Toronto: Centre for Reformation and Renaissance Studies, 2008.

Plamenac, Dragan. "Keyboard Music of the 14th Century in Codex Faenza 117." *Journal of the American Musicological Society* 4 (1951): 179–201.

———. *Keyboard Music of the Late Middle Ages*. CMM 52. Rome: American Institute of Musicology, 1972.

*Poeti antichi*. Naples, 1661.

*Poeti del Duecento*. Ed. Gianfranco Contini. 2 vols. Milan: R. Ricciardi, 1957.

Polizzotto, Lorenzo. *The Elect Nation: The Savonarolan Movement in Florence, 1494–1545*. Oxford: Clarendon Press, 1994.

———. *La missione di G. Savonarola in Firenze*. Pistoia: Quaderni di Koinonia, 1996.

Polk, Keith. "Civic Patronage and Instrumental Ensembles in Renaissance Florence." *Augsberger Jahrbuch für Musikwissenschaft* 3 (1986): 51–68.

———. "Ensemble Instrumental Music in Flanders—1450–1550." *Journal of Band Research* 2 (1975): 12–27.

———. "Ensemble Performance in Dufay's Time." In *Dufay Quincentenary Conference*, ed. Allan W. Atlas, pp. 61–75. Brooklyn, N. Y: Department of Music, School of Performing Arts, Brooklyn College of the City University of New York, 1976.

———. *German Instrumental Music of the Late Middle Ages*. Cambridge: Cambridge University Press, 1992.

———. "Innovation in Instrumental Music 1450–1510: The Role of German Performers within European Culture." In *Music in the German Renaissance*, ed. John Kmetz, pp. 202–14. Cambridge: Cambridge University Press, 1994.

———. "Instrumentalists and Performance Practices in Dance Music, c. 1500." In McGee, ed., *Improvisation in the Arts*, pp. 98–114.

———. "The Trombone, the Slide Trumpet and the Ensemble Tradition of the Early Renaissance." *Early Music* 17 (1989): 389–97.

———. "Vedel and Geige—Fiddle and Viol: German String Traditions in the Fifteenth Century." *Journal of the American Musicological Society* 42 (1989): 504–46.

*Polyphonic Music of the Fourteenth Century.* Ed. Leo Schrade. Monaco: Éditions des l'Oiseau-lire, 1956–.

Pratesi, Luigi. *L' "Istoria di Firenze" di Gregorio Dati dal 1380 al 1405.* Noricia: Tonti, 1902.

Prizer, William F. "Bernardino Piffaro e i pifferi e tromboni di Mantova: strumenti a fiato in una corte italiana." *Rivista italiana di musicologia* 16 (1981): 151–84.

———. "The Frottola and the Unwritten Tradition." *Studi musicali* 15 (1986): 3–37.

———. "Games of Venus." *Journal of Musicology* 9 (1991): 3–56.

———. "Instrumental Music/Instrumentally Performed Music ca. 1500: The Genres of Paris, Bibliothèque nationale, Ms. Rés. Vm.7 696." In *Le concert des voix et des instruments à la Renaissance,* ed. Jean-Michel Vaccaro, pp. 179–98. Paris: CNRS, 1995.

———. "Isabella d'Este and Lorenzo da Pavia, 'Master Instrument Maker'." *Early Music History* 2 (1982): 87–127.

———. "Isabella d'Este and Lucrezia Borgia as Patrons of Music: The Frottola at Mantua and Ferrara." *Journal of the American Musicological Society* 38 (1985): 1–33.

———. "Lutenists at the Court of Mantua in the Late Fifteenth and Early Sixteenth Centuries." *Journal of the Lute Society of America* 13 (1980): 4–34.

———. "Music at the Court of the Sforza: The Birth and Death of a Musical Center." *Musica Disciplina* 43 (1989): 141–93.

———. "The Music Savonarola Burned: The Florentine Carnival Song in the Late 15th Century." *Musica e Storia* 9 (2001): 5–33.

———. "Petrucci and the Carnival Song: On the Origins and Dissemination of a Genre." In *Venezia 1501: Petrucci e la stampa musicale,* ed. Giulio Cattin and Patrizia dalla Vecchia, pp. 215–51. Venice: Fondazione Levi, 2005.

———. "Reading Carnival: The Creation of a Florentine Carnival Song." *Early Music History* 23 (2004): 185–252.

Prosdocimo de' Beldomandi. *Contrapunctus.* Ed. Jan Herlinger. Lincoln and London: University of Nebraska Press, 1984.

Pulci, Luigi. *Opere minori.* Ed. Paolo Orvieto. Milan: Mursia, 1986.

Rankin, Susan. "Liturgical Drama." In *New Oxford History of Music,* vol. 2, pp. 310–56. Oxford: Oxford University Press, 1990.

Rastall, George Richard. "Secular Musicians in Late Medieval England." Ph.D. diss., Manchester University, 1968.

Rastrelli, Modesto. *Storia d'Alessandro de' Medic primo duca di Firenze.* 2 vols. Florence: Benucci, 1781.

Reaney, Gilbert. "The Manuscript Paris, Bibliothèque Nationale, fonds italien 568 (Pit)." *Musica Disciplina* 14 (1960): 33–63.

*Records of Early English Drama.* Toronto: University of Toronto Press, 1979–.

Remnant, Mary. "The Diversity of Medieval Fiddles." *Early Music* 3 (1975): 47–51.

Renier, Rodolfo, ed. *Strombotti e sonetti dell'Altissimo.* Turin: Loescher, 1886.

*Rerum italicarum scriptores.* Ed. Lodovico Antonio Muratori. 25 vols. Milan, 1723–51; new edition, ed. Giosue Carducci, Vittorio Fiorini, and Pietro Fedele, Bologna, 1935–.

*Rimatori del tardo Trecento.* Vol. 1. Ed. Natzlino Sapegno. Rome: Edizioni dell'Ateneo, 1967.

*Rimatori del Trecento.* Ed. Giuseppe Corsi. Turin: Unione tipografico-editrice torinese, 1969.

Robins, William. "Antonio Pucci, guardiano degli Atti della Mercanzia." *Studi e problemi di critica testuale* 61 (2000): 29–70.

———. "Poetic Rivalry: Antonio Pucci, Jacopo Salimbeni, and Antonio da Ferrara." In *Antonio Pucci e la cultura fiorentina alla vigilia del Rinascimento*, ed. Maria Predelli, pp. 307–22. Florence: Cadmo, 2006.

Rohloff, Ernst. *Die Quellenhandschriften zum Musiktraktat des Johannes de Grocheio.* Leipzig: VEB Deutscher Verlag für Musik, 1972.

Rosand, Ellen. "Barbara Strozzi, *virtuosissima cantatrice:* The Composer's Voice." *Journal of the American Musicological Society* 31 (1978): 241–81.

Rosenfeld, Randall. "Transmuting Silver into Gold: Cautionary Notes on the Iconography and Symbolism of Silver Trumpets." *Historic Brass Society Journal* 19 (2007): 1–10.

Rossi, Adamo. "Memorie di musica civile in Perugia nei secc. XIV e XV." *Giornale di erudizione artistica* 3 (1874): 129–52, 193–205.

Rubinstein, Nicolai. *The Government of Florence under the Medici (1434–1494).* 2nd. ed. Oxford: Clarendon Press, 1997.

———. *The Palazzo Vecchio, 1298–1532.* Oxford: Clarendon Press, 1995.

———. "The Piazza della Signoria in Florence." In *Festschrift Herbert Siebenhüner*, ed. Erich Hubala and Gunter Schweikhart, pp. 19–30. Wurzburg: Kommissionsverlag Ferdinand Schöningh, 1978.

Rubsamen, Walter. "The *Justiniane* or *Viniziane* of the Fifteenth Century." *Acta musicologica* 29 (1957): 172–84.

Sacchetti, Franco. *Il Trecentonovelle.* Ed. Valerio Marucci. Rome: Salerno Editrice, 1996.

Sachs, Curt. *The History of Musical Instruments.* New York: W. W. Norton, 1940.

Saffioti, Tito. *I Giullari in Italia. Lo spettacolo, il pubblico, i testi.* Milan: Xenia Editione, 1990.

Salmen, Walter. "The Social Status of the Musician in the Middle Ages." In *The Social Status of the Professional Musician from the Middle Ages to the 19th Century,* ed. Walter Salmen, trans. Herbert Kaufman and Barbara Reisner, pp. 1–29. New York: Pendragon, 1983.

Salvemini, Gaetano. *La dignità cavalleresca nel Comune di Firenze.* Florence: Ricci, 1896.

———. *Magnati e popolani in Firenze dal 1280 al 1295.* Florence: Carnesecchi, 1899.

Sanuto, Marino. *I diarii di Marino Sanuto (MCCCXCVI–MDXXXIII).* Ed. R. Fulin et al. 58 vols. Venice, 1879–1903.

Sarkissian, Margaret, and Edward H. Tarr. "Trumpet." *The New Grove Dictionary of Music and Musicians,* 2nd ed., ed. Stanley Sadie, vol. 25, p. 823–41. New York: Grove's Dictionaries, 2001.

Savonarola, Girolamo. *Prediche sopra Aggeo con il Trattato circa il reggimento e governo della città di Firenze.* Ed. Luigi Firpo. Rome: Belardetti, 1965.

Scavizzi, Giuseppe. "The Myth of Orpheus in Italian Renaissance Art, 1400–1600." In *Orpheus: The Metamorphoses of a Myth,* ed. John Warden, pp. 111–62. Toronto: University of Toronto Press, 1982.

Schevill, Ferdinand. *History of Florence from the Founding of the City through the Renaissance.* New York: Frederick Ungar, 1961.

Seay Albert. *Johannes de Grocheo Concerning Music.* Colorado Springs: Colorado College Music Press, 1973.

———. "Paolo da Firenze: A Trecento Theorist." In *L'Ars nova italiana del Trecento,* ed. Bianca Becherini, pp. 118–40. Certaldo, 1959.

Seymour, Charles, Jr. *Michelangelo's David: A Search for Identity.* Pittsburgh: University of Pittsburgh Press, 1967.

Sherr, Richard. "Lorenzo de' Medici, Duke of Urbino, as a Patron of Music." In *Renaissance Studies in Honor of Craig Hugh Smyth,* ed. Edward Morrough et al., vol. I, pp. 628–38. Florence: Giunti Barbera, 1985.

——. *Music and Musicians in Renaissance Rome and Other Courts*. Aldergate: Ashgate, 1999.

Singleton, Charles S. *Canti carnascialeschi del Rinascimento*. Bari: Laterza, 1936.

Slim, H. Colin. "Musicians on Parnassus." *Studies in the Renaissance* 12 (1965): 134–63.

Smith, Douglas Alton. *A History of the Lute from Antiquity to the Renaissance*. Lute Society of America, 2002.

Soldati, Benedetto. "Improvvisatori, canterini e buffoni in un dialogo del Pontano." In *Miscellanea di studi critici pubblicati in onore di Guido Mazzoni dai suoi discipali*, vol. 1, pp. 321–42. Florence: Galileiana, 1907.

Southern, Eileen. "A Prima Ballerina of the Fifteenth Century." In *Music and Context: Essays for John M. Ward*, ed. Anne Dhu Shapiro, pp. 183–97. Cambridge, Mass.: Harvard University Press, 1985.

Sparti, Barbara, ed. *Guglielmo Ebreo of Pesaro: De pratica seu arte tripudii*. Oxford: Clarendon Press, 1993.

*Statuta populi et communis Florentiae*. 3 vols. Freiburg, 1778–83.

*Statuti della Repubblica Fiorentina*. Ed. Romolo Caggese. 2 vols. Florence: Galileiana and Ariani, 1910–1921.

Strohm, Reinhard. *Music in Late Medieval Bruges*. Rev. ed. Oxford: Oxford University Press, 1990.

——. *The Rise of European Music, 1380–1500*. Cambridge: Cambridge University Press, 1993.

Strozzi, Alessandra Macinghi. *Lettere di una Gentildonna Fiorentina*. Ed. Cesare Guasti. Florence: Sansoni, 1877.

Symonds, John Addington, trans. *The Autobiography of Benvenuto Cellini*. 1927; repr. Garden City, N. J.: Doubleday, 1948.

Tarr, Edward. *The Trumpet*. Trans. S. E. Plank and Edward Tarr. London: B. T. Batsford, 1988.

Tinctoris, Johannes. *De Inventione et usu musicae*, 1487.

——. *The Art of Counterpoint (Liber de arte contrapuncti)*. Trans. Albert Seay. American Institute of Musicology, 1961.

Tomasello, Andrew. *Music and Ritual at Papal Avignon, 1309–1403*. Ann Arbor: UMI Research Press, 1983.

Trexler, Richard. "Florentine Theatre, 1280–1500: A Checklist of Performances and Institutions." *Forum Italicum* 14 (1980): 454–75.

——. "Honor Among Thieves: The Trust Function of the Urban Clergy in the Florentine Republic." In *Essays Presented to Myron P. Gilmore*, ed. Sergio Bertelli and Gloria Ramakus, vol. 1, pp. 317–34. Florence: Giunti Barbera, 1978.

——, ed. *The Libro Cerimoniale of the Florentine Republic*. Geneva: Droz, 1978.

——. "The Magi Enter Florence: The Ubriachi of Florence and Venice." *Studies in Medieval and Renaissance History*, n.s. 1 (1978): 127–213.

——. *Public Life in Renaissance Florence*. New York: Academic Press, 1980.

Tröster, Patrick. *Das Alta-Ensemble und seine Instrumente von der Spätgotik bis zur Hochrenaissance (1300–1550), Eine musikikonografische Studie*. Tübingen: MVK, 2001.

Ugolini, Francesco A. *I cantari d'argomento classico*. Florence: Olschki, 1933.

Vasari, Giorgio. *Le Vite dei più eccelenti pittori, scultori e architetti*. Ed. Carlo Ragghianti. 4 vols. Milano, 1942. English trans. Gaston Du C. de Vere, *Lives of the Most Eminent Painters, Sculptors, and Architects*. 3 vols. New York: AMS Press, 1976.

Vecchi, Giuseppe. *Educazione musicale, scuola e società nell'opera didascalica di Francesco da Barberino*. Biblioteca di "Quadrivium" serie musicologica 7. Bologna, 1966.

308 · Bibliography

Ventrone, Paola. *Gli araldi della commedia: teatro a Firenze nel rinascimento.* Ospedaletto: Pacini Editore, 1993.

———."L'eccezione e la regola: le rappresentazioni del 1439 nella tradizione fiorentina delle feste di quartiere." In *Firenze e il Consilio del 1439,* ed. Paola Viti, pp. 409–35. Florence: Olschki, 1994.

———. "Lorenzo's Politica Festiva." In *Lorenzo the Magnificent: Culture and Politics,* ed. Michael Mallett and Nicholas Mann, pp. 105–16. London: Warburg Institute, 1996.

———. "Note sul carnevale fiorentino di età laurenziana." In *Il carnevale: Dalla tradizione arcaica alla tradizione colta del Rinascimento,* ed. Maria Chiabò and Federico Doglio, pp. 321–66. Rome: Centro di studi sul teatro medioevale e rinascimentale, 1990.

———. "Per una morfologia della sacra rappresentazione fiorentina." In *Teatro e culture della rappresentazione; lo spettacolo in Italia nel Quattrocento,* ed. Raimondo Guarino, pp. 195–225. Bologna: Società editrice li Mulino, 1988.

———. "'Philosophia. Involucra fabularum': La fabula di Orpheo di Angelo Poliziano." *Comunicazioni sociale* 19 (1997): 137–80.

———. "La sacra rappresentazione fiorentina: Aspetti e problemi." In *Esperienze dello spettacolo religioso nell'Europa del Quattrocento,* ed. Maria Chiabò and Federico Daglio, pp. 67–99. Rome: Torre di Orfel, 1993.

———. "Sulle feste di San Giovanni: Firenze 1454." *Interpres* 19 (2000): 89–101.

———, ed. *"Le tems revient"—"'L tempo si rinuova": Feste e spettacoli nella Firenze di Lorenzo il Magnifico.* Milan: Silvana, 1992.

Vespasiano da Bisticci. *The Vespasiano Memoirs: Lives of Illustrious Men of the XVth Century.* Trans. William George and Emily Waters. Toronto: University of Toronto Press, 1997.

Vespasiano da Bisticci. *Vite di uomini illustri del secolo XV.* Ed. L. Frati. 3 vols. Bologna, 1892.

Vicentino, Nicola. *L'antica musica ridotta alla moderna prattica.* Rome, 1555.

Villani, Giovanni. *Nuova cronica.* Ed. Giuseppe Porta. 3 vols. Parma: Fondazione Pietro Bembo. 1990.

Volpi, Guglielmo. *Le feste di Firenze del 1459: Notizia di un poemetto del secolo XV.* Pistoia, 1902.

———. ed. *Ricordi di Firenze dell' anno 1459 di autore anonimo.* Rerum italicarum scriptores 27, no. 1. Città di Castello, 1907.

Wagner, Anthony. *Heralds and Heraldry in the Middle Ages: An inquiry into the Growth of the Armorial Function of Heralds.* Oxford: Oxford University Press, 1960.

Wallner, Bertha Antonia, ed. *Das Buxheimer Orgelbuch. Das Erbe deutscher Music,* vols. 37–39. Kassel, New York: Bärenreiter, 1958–59.

Webb, John. "The Billingsgate Trumpet." *Galpin Society Journal* 41 (1988): 59–62.

Weinstein, Donald. "The Myth of Florence." In *Florentine Studies: Politics and Society in Renaissance Florence,* ed. Nicolai Rubinstein, pp. 15–44. London: Faber and Faber, 1968.

Weiss, Susan F. "Bologna Q 18: Some Reflections on Content and Context." *Journal of the American Musicological Society* 41 (1988): 63–101.

Welker, Lorenz. "Alta Capella: Zur Ensemblepraxis der Blasinstrumente im 15. Jahrhundert." *Basler Jahubuch für historische Musikpraxis* 7 (1983): 119–65.

Wilson, Blake. "Heinrich Isaac among the Florentines." *Journal of Musicology* 23 (2006): 97–152.

———. *Music and Merchants: The Laudesi Companies of Republican Florence.* Oxford: Clarendon Press, 1992.

————. *Singing Poetry in Renaissance Florence: The Cantasi Come Tradition ca. 1375–1550.* Florence: Olschki, forthcoming.

————. "'Surpassing Orpheus': Niccolò Cieco, Antonio di Guido, and the Vernacular Improvisatory Tradition in Renaissance Florence." Paper read at the American Musicological Society, Annual Meeting. Columbus, Ohio, October 2002.

————. "Trombetti, Improvvisatori, Laudesi: Public Performance and Republican Culture in 15th-Century Florence." Paper read at the Renaissance Society of America. Florence, March 2000.

Winternitz, Emanuel. *Leonardo da Vinci as a Musician.* New Haven, Conn.: Yale University Press, 1982.

————. "Lira da Braccio." In *Die Musik in Geschichte und Gegenwart,* vol. 8 (1960), col. 935–54.

————. *Musical Instruments and Their Symbolism in Western Art.* New Haven, Conn.: Yale University Press, 1967.

Woodfill, Walter L. *Musicians in English Society from Elizabeth to Charles I.* Princeton, N.J.: Princeton University Press, 1953.

Wright, Alison. "A Portrait for the Visit of Galeazzo Maria Sforza to Florence in 1471." In *Lorenzo the Magnificent: Culture and Politics,* ed. Michael Mallett and Nicholas Mann, pp. 65–92. London: Warburg Institute, 1996.

Wright, Craig. *Music at the Court of Burgundy 1364–1419: A Documentary History.* Henryville: Insitute of Mediaeval Music, 1979.

Zannoni, Giovanni. "Il sacco di Volterra: Un poema di N. Naldi e l'orazione di B. Scala." *Rendiconti della R. Accademia dei Lincei* 5 (1894): 239–44.

————. *Trionfo delle lodi di Federigo da Montefeltro.* Bologna, 1890.

Zarlino, Gioseffo. *Sopplimenti musicali.* Venice, 1588; facsimile ed. New York: Broude Bros., 1979.

Zippel, Giuseppe. *I suonatori della Signoria di Firenze.* Trent: G. Zippel, 1892.

# Index

Timothy J. McGee is a music historian with research interests in the performance of music before 1750, and the music of Canada. He is the author and editor of ten books and more than sixty articles, including *Medieval and Renaissance Music: A Performer's Guide; Medieval Instrumental Dances* (Indiana University Press, 1989); *Singing Early Music: The Pronunciation of European Languages in the Late Middle Ages and Renaissance* (Indiana University Press, 1996); *The Sound of Medieval Song: Vocal Style and Ornamentation According to the Theorists;* and *Improvisation in the Arts of the Middle Ages and Renaissance.* He is currently Honorary Professor at Trent University, where he teaches music courses in the continuing education program.